Storytelling in Motion

Storytelling in Motion

*Cinematic Choreography and
the Film Musical*

JENNY OYALLON-KOLOSKI

OXFORD
UNIVERSITY PRESS

Oxford University Press is a department of the University of Oxford. It furthers
the University's objective of excellence in research, scholarship, and education
by publishing worldwide. Oxford is a registered trade mark of Oxford University
Press in the UK and certain other countries.

Published in the United States of America by Oxford University Press
198 Madison Avenue, New York, NY 10016, United States of America.

© Oxford University Press 2024

All rights reserved. No part of this publication may be reproduced, stored in
a retrieval system, or transmitted, in any form or by any means, without the
prior permission in writing of Oxford University Press, or as expressly permitted
by law, by license, or under terms agreed with the appropriate reproduction
rights organization. Inquiries concerning reproduction outside the scope of the
above should be sent to the Rights Department, Oxford University Press, at the
address above.

You must not circulate this work in any other form
and you must impose this same condition on any acquirer.

CIP data is on file at the Library of Congress

ISBN 978–0–19–760267–6 (pbk.)
ISBN 978–0–19–760266–9 (hbk.)

DOI: 10.1093/oso/9780197602669.001.0001

Paperback printed by Marquis Book Printing, Canada
Hardback printed by Bridgeport National Bindery, Inc., United States of America

For my family

Contents

Acknowledgments	ix
About the Companion Website	xiii
Introduction	1

PART I | MUSICAL FOUNDATIONS

1. Formal Conventions and Musical Practices: *Singin' in the Rain* (1952) — 27

2. Seeing Movement in Cinema: An Introduction to Laban Movement Analysis — 53

3. Agency, Control, and Space: *West Side Story* (1961) — 56

PART II | MUSICAL ECLECTICISM

4. Minimalism and Excess: *Les Demoiselles de Rochefort* (1967) — 91

5. Musical Unease: *Trois places pour le 26* (1988) — 125

6. Endless Conversations: Reflexive Musical Clusters — 155

PART III | MUSICAL REALISM

7. Diegetic Flutters: Views from the Bridge — 159

8. Imperfect Bodies: *Jeanne et le garçon formidable* (1998) — 161

9. Rhythmic Realism: *La La Land* (2016) — 188

Appendix 1: Laban Movement Analysis "Cheat Sheet"	223
Appendix 2: Analytical Data	227
Notes	231
References	261
Index	277

Acknowledgments

Much of this book came together during the Covid-19 pandemic, and I am grateful to all those who assisted me in the organization, research, and completion of this project. Norm Hirschy saw promise in the earliest versions of the book manuscript. My thanks to him, Laura Santo, Zoe Barham, and all the staff at Oxford University Press for seeing this book across the finish line. I extend my thanks to the anonymous reviewers whose extensive feedback helped me to strengthen and clarify this book's methodological and argumentative throughlines. The production histories in this book benefited from the archival holdings at the New York Public Library for the Performing Arts, Ciné-Tamaris, the Cinémathèque française, and the Jérôme Seydoux-Pathé Foundation. Special thanks to archivists Fanny Lautissier, Marie Bergue, Cécile Verguin, Alice Duchesnes, and Shérine El Sayed Taih, for their assistance, as well as to Agnès Varda and Rosalie Varda-Demy for granting me access to the family archives. My profound appreciation goes to Damien Chazelle, Olivier Ducastel, Jacques Martineau, Mandy Moore, Sylvie Giron, and Katy Varda for graciously agreeing to be interviewed and to Gérome Barry for key introductions. Chazelle's assistant Alissa Goldberg was also very generous with her time, and I am grateful for her help in arranging meetings and sharing production documents.

An earlier version of the argument from chapter 8 on *Jeanne et le garçon formidable* was published in 2014 in *Studies in French Cinema*. Parts of that article are reproduced here with permission from the journal.

Many brilliant teachers nurtured my scholarship and my intellectual curiosity. My thanks to the professors at Carleton College who inspired me to pursue the subjects grounding this book: to Nikki Melville for the music tutelage, Mary Easter and Jane Shockley for leading me to dance, Judith Howard for pointing me toward Laban Movement Analysis, Susan Jaret McKinstry and Pierre Hecker for sharpening my analytical eye, and Carol Donelan for her reading lists and wealth of film wisdom. At the Laban/Bartenieff Institute of Movement Studies, Rachelle Tsachor and Cheryl Clark, in particular, expanded my understanding of fundamental movement principles.

X ACKNOWLEDGMENTS

Much of this book grows out of my graduate work in the Department of Communication Arts at the University of Wisconsin, Madison. A 2013 Chancellor's Fellowship allowed me to conduct extensive research in Paris on Jacques Demy's cinema. Many faculty and fellow students helped me to refine early versions of this work, and I remain grateful for their insights. Professors Kate Corby, Chris Walker, Karen McShane Hellenbrand, Collette Stewart, Li Chiao-Ping, and Jin-Wen Yu kindly let me take their modern dance technique classes as I was completing my graduate coursework. Fellow CommArts grads Charlie Michael, Colin Burnett, Maria Belodubrovskaya, Kyra Hunting, Brandon Colvin, Eric Dienstfrey, and Kaitlin Fyfe offered smart suggestions that have clarified key threads of this book. Amanda McQueen deserves particular thanks for suggesting relevant musical numbers to study and for sharing her profound knowledge of the musical genre. Lea Jacobs, J. J. Murphy, Vance Kepley, Jeff Smith, Eric Hoyt, and Kristin Thompson shaped my understanding of film history and offered valuable feedback on early versions of this writing. Special thanks to Andrea Harris for pointing me toward important dance history research and to David Bordwell for his methodological suggestions. My sincerest thanks to my mentor, Kelley Conway, for her keen insights and her unceasing support of this work.

In the Department of Media and Cinema Studies at the University of Illinois, I give my thanks to office administrator Theresa Harris and to my colleagues C. L. Cole, James Hay, Julie Turnock, Anita Chan, Angela Aguayo, Amanda Ciafone, Courtney Cox, Rachel Kuo, Marisa Hicks, Jon Knipp, Josh Heuman, Victor Font Bas, and Carrie Wilson-Brown for their support. Many thanks to my graduate student Tingyu Chen for her assistance in formatting this book's references. This work benefited from a Humanities Teaching Release Time award in the spring of 2021 from the University of Illinois's Campus Research Board. I am also grateful for the feedback I received on an early version of the book prospectus from the 2019–2020 First Book Writing Group at the University of Illinois. My profound thanks to coparticipants Julie Gaillard and Maria Lopez, faculty and press advisors Marc Doussard, Carol Symes, Shelley Weinberg, and Daniel Nasset, and session organizers Maria Gillombardo and Cynthia Oliver, for their suggestions and encouragement.

I entered the world of videographic criticism in the months between finishing my PhD and starting my academic position at the University of Illinois. I will be forever grateful for the career-shifting initiation to this form provided by the 2017 Scholarship in Sound & Image workshop at Middlebury College. My thanks to all my fellow video-campers, now videographic colleagues, for their emotional and intellectual support, and to Katie Bird in particular for helping me to better understand Steadicam practices. To our mentors, instructors, and fearless leaders—Catherine Grant, Cory Creekmur, Liz Greene, Ethan Murphy, August Laska, Christian Keathley, and Jason Mittell—thank you for introducing me to this practice and for welcoming me into this community. I presented an early version of the "Diegetic Flutters" chapter from this book on a videographic panel at the Society for Cinema and Media Studies with Chelsea McCracken and Desirée Garcia; my thanks to them and to our respondent, Jeffrey Romero Middents, for their valuable suggestions.

I am so grateful to my family and friends for supporting this project and my overall well-being over the past decade; thanks to you all for your love and kindness. My mother-in-law, Ursula, and aunt, Janice, whom we lost during these years of writing, were always there with a caring word. My son, Henry, born in 2020, helped me find joy during the hardest moments; merci pour tout, mon petit chou. My deepest thanks and love to my parents, Bernie and Monique, for a lifetime of encouragement, their comments on the manuscript, the extensive childcare assistance, and their company in our "pandemic pod." Finally, all my love to my partner, Derek Long, whose support and companionship during the isolating trifecta of book writing, young parenthood, and a global pandemic was and remains unwavering.

About the Companion Website

www.oup.com/us/storytellinginmotion

Oxford has created a website to accompany *Storytelling in Motion: Cinematic Choreography and the Film Musical,* in order to provide material that cannot be made available in a book, namely the three video essay chapters. The reader is encouraged to consult this resource in conjunction with the chapters' written introductions. Examples available online are indicated in the text with Oxford's symbol ▶

Introduction

In early 2022, director Guillermo del Toro wrote extensively on Twitter about the intricate opening shot of the "Dance at the Gym" sequence from Steven Spielberg's film adaptation of *West Side Story* (2021). We see Anita, Bernardo, María, and Chino enter the gym from the school's hallway, and the camera's long take moves the viewer through the space as the groups of Jets, Sharks, and liminal characters vie for dominance of the space through dance. "Pure, masterly clockwork precision and a lot more complex than 'seamed' shots or steadicam-to-crane 'relay' shots," del Toro effuses, describing such distinctions between camera technologies as "profound and spiritually different choices." Beyond the skilled control of cinematic technology, del Toro highlights this brief excerpt of *West Side Story* as an example of cinema's essence and purpose:

> Cinema is written not in theme, story or character but in painterly, symphonic terms. Discussing a film purely on its dramaturgy is like describing a Van Gogh as "A painting with a bunch of flowers." . . . The dramaturgy is 50% of the point, but another 50% is submerged in the craft. This is not just virtuoso for the craft's sake, its [sic] virtuoso for the art's sake. It's a musical so, [Spielberg] makes the camera dance.[1]

Del Toro's Twitter thread draws attention to the essential role that cinematic form plays as an art and in creating meaning. Notably, while one of his points is that all the cinematic crafts deserve greater recognition, his discussion places most of the agency for this film musical's success in the director's and cinematographer's hands rather than the choreographer's (Justin Peck) and the work of the dancers.

A 2017 awards season *Hollywood Reporter* article ranks Academy Award musicals by how many "unique songs with lyrics" they have (i.e., when people are singing), discounting dance numbers as central to a categorization of the genre.[2] This piece is an important reminder that for many viewers, musicals are predominantly about singing rather than dancing or visual style. I don't

Storytelling in Motion. Jenny Oyallon-Koloski, Oxford University Press. © Oxford University Press 2024.
DOI: 10.1093/oso/9780197602669.003.0001

2 STORYTELLING IN MOTION

count myself among this number. Musicals, to me, are as much if not more about the choreography of dancers—and the way that figure movement shifts the film and its setting in and out of fantastical situations—as they are about characters bursting into song. I still get shivers down my spine every time I watch the opening choreography in Jerome Robbins and Robert Wise's *West Side Story* prologue (1961), as one Jet coolly relevés into a suspension that moves in perfect counterpoint to the direction of the gliding camera and the rest of the group. For a brief instant the pulls—of on-screen motion, diegetic grounding, and the viewer's attention—are all disrupted as the character takes control of the space.

The meaning film viewers take from dancing sequences is oblique. Whereas song lyrics often directly tell you what the characters are feeling, choreographed movements can be more indirect in their methods of narrative communication. Choreographer Mandy Moore emphasizes this, describing how "the same shape can mean something so different to somebody depending on what they experienced five minutes ago. Or what they experienced when they were a kid. . . . But also I think sometimes that is the brilliance of choreography, good choreography . . . it allows people some space to feel something."[3] From the standpoint of the Academy Awards, there is also a clearer binary between singing and nonsinging that allows for a simpler identification of sung numbers and, as a result, what "counts" as a musical. The lines between (still carefully crafted) natural movement, acting, staged postures, and dancing are often ambiguous, making this figure movement difficult to categorize, which is precisely why I find those musical moments so fascinating. Some of this movement preference is personal; as someone who has danced on and off since she was three years old, the performative possibilities of movement on screen catch and hold my attention more than the soundtrack or song lyrics. But the way characters move and how they are filmed is also essential to our understanding of films' aesthetic and narrative patterns and more meaningful, I argue, than songs alone. After all, singing also comes from a body in motion.

This book is about the narrative and stylistic impact of figure movement in cinema. More specifically, it is about the subtle power of cinematic choreography, those moments when filmmakers deliberately combine the strengths of film style, coordinated camera movements especially, and organized figure movement to convey narrative meaning through motion. Throughout this book, I integrate vocabularies and analytical systems from Laban/Bartenieff Movement Studies, film studies, and related fields to parse

INTRODUCTION 3

cinematic figure movement on multiple formal levels. I also use performative research methods from videographic criticism to show the poetic and oblique connections between these films through videographic material in chapters 2, 6, and 7, drawing on the methodological strengths of presenting knowledge in audiovisual, as well as written, form. This book demonstrates how figure movement can serve as a versatile strategy of meaning-making, particularly when filmmakers attend to the relationship between choreographed movement and film style.

Because I want to focus on how choreography contributes to cinematic storytelling, my examples are from the film musical genre—specifically work where dance and choreographed figure movement occurs throughout the plot—chosen from specific moments in American and French film history. Stanley Donen and Gene Kelly portray the wide aesthetic possibilities of stylistic and narrative genre experimentation in *Singin' in the Rain* (1952), while still expanding the possibilities for making meaning with musical form. Cinematic choreography subsequently functions as a storytelling marker of prejudiced conflict in *West Side Story* (Jerome Robbins and Robert Wise, 1961), aesthetic play in *Les Demoiselles de Rochefort* (Jacques Demy, 1967), generic discomfort in *Trois places pour le 26* (Jacques Demy, 1988), the politics of illness in *Jeanne et le garçon formidable* (Olivier Ducastel and Jacques Martineau, 1998), and decision-making in *La La Land* (Damien Chazelle, 2016). I could have chosen entirely different examples to anchor this book, because cinematic choreography extends globally across the musical and beyond the genre. My own cultural upbringing in a Franco-American context allows me to speak with greater expertise to French and American cinema and the transnational flow between these nations.[4] More significantly, the films I discuss tell a clear story of how cinematic choreography was used by French and American filmmakers to innovate storytelling through figure movement, inspired by their predecessors' aesthetics while working within differing industrial conditions.

This book is also about those material conditions needed to make figure movement a significant component of narrative filmmaking: time, money, rehearsal space, institutional support, and performers and crew with the necessary embodied and institutional knowledge. As I illustrate throughout these chapters, the elements needed to convey stories through figure movement are not a guaranteed fixture of film (or other media) industries around the world, and changes to these conditions impact filmmakers' formal choices. There is still much to learn about how filmmakers choose to

4 STORYTELLING IN MOTION

incorporate choreography into their craft, the resources needed to do so, and the functions that figure movement on screen fulfills in narrative cinema.

Cinematic Choreography

How do filmmakers guide viewer attention through the frame using the movement of bodies on screen? What do they seek to communicate through their use of such approaches to cinematic choreography? And how were those choices shaped by the industrial conditions available to them? These questions guide the focus of this book through an attention to the nuances and historical constraints of film form, the unique possibilities available to filmmakers organizing movement in a cinematic context, and a closer examination of the meaningful ways that the musical genre can play with diegetic layers, or plurality. Consider, for example, the final musical number from Jacques Demy's *Trois places pour le 26*. The number occurs toward the end of the film and is a duet performed diegetically by Yves Montand (playing a semifictionalized version of himself) and Marion (Mathilda May), an up-and-coming performer, as part of the premiere performance of Montand's stage show. Montand sings the song "Douce Folie" as the two perform a parsed-down dance. They barely touch each other and execute only a few steps before holding in place as the curtain falls. Marion's performance as her on-stage character is stiff, precise, and emotionally detached. It's easy to view the number as a conventional, uninspired, stage-bound sequence that can slide neatly into a backstage musical formula.

When observed in context, it's much more than that. This version of the "Douce Folie" number is a minimalist repetition of a moment Montand shares earlier with his former lover, Marie-Hélène (Françoise Fabian). The two meet in a bar, twenty-two years after their affair, and get up to dance as the "Douce Folie" song begins to play over the sound system. The choreography, which parallels the moves performed later, is still simple but reveals an important change in Marie-Hélène's movement patterns. She relaxes visibly during the dance, shifting away from the stiffer and more detached demeanor that has dominated her movement earlier in the scene with Montand and which quickly returns once the music ends. Despite this shift in performance, the number can be justified within the norms of the diegesis, or story world. The music has a diegetic source, and the simple moves performed are within the physical capacities of these two characters, as one could plausibly see in a dance hall.

INTRODUCTION 5

But by its very existence, this earlier number calls into question the diegetic plausibility of the later, stage-bound number, or at the very least raises some distracting questions. What is the relationship between these two numbers? How did the movement patterns from a spontaneous encounter make their way into a diegetically motivated stage number? What distinguishes the two women's movement qualities, and what do those differences communicate? And why introduce this kind of diegetic ambiguity at all? These are questions we may avoid asking ourselves while engaging with the suspension of disbelief that accompanies a genuine enjoyment of the musical genre. But investigating these sorts of inferences allows for a better understanding of how filmmakers have experimented with musical conventions and the often-subtle ways that cinematic figure movement and dance cue us to comprehend pivotal storytelling decisions.

Dancing on Film

Dance and an interest in the choreographed body has been part of cinema since its beginnings, when William K. L. Dickson made films of vaudeville dancers Carmen Dauset Moreno (*Carmencita*, 1894) and Annabelle Moore (*Annabelle Butterfly Dance*, 1894), as well as strongman Eugene Sandow (*Sandow*, 1894). American Delsartism was also a significant aspect of Hollywood actors' training in the first decades of the 1900s in part through choreographer Ted Shawn's training of actors working for Biograph.[5] Moving and dancing bodies on screen communicate much about the conditions in which their films were made, encouraging us to understand their affective influence on audiences and the representation of those bodies beyond their cinematic formal functions. Choreographed figure movement also conveys crucial narrative and stylistic information to viewers, serving a central artistic purpose. This book considers choreography of figure movement (danced or otherwise) within the medium-specific aesthetic context of cinema and the ways in which filmmakers mobilized cinematic choreography to accomplish meaning-laden pairings through the complex interplay between camera and figure movement.

The definitions of choreography and figure movement I use in this book are deliberately broad in order to consider the organization of dancing and staged performances in space as well as the relationship between the moving camera and the figure(s) in question. My approach aligns with Susan Foster's

6 STORYTELLING IN MOTION

framing of choreography as "a structuring of movement, not necessarily the movement of human beings . . . both the kinds of actions performed and their sequence or progression."[6] The mise-en-scène in film encompasses the movement of bodies on screen, and that work is frequently categorized as acting or performance. Figure movement as a term connects the aesthetic, material, and expressive functions that human movement can evoke in cinematic contexts. Moreover, cinematic form inherently mediates the materiality of such human movement in deliberate and historically contingent ways. As David Bordwell discusses, mise-en-scène can refer to the product as well as the process of crafting movement on screen;[7] I am interested in the meaningful performances that come from figure movement but also the historical conditions that create them. Who were the people who choreographed, filmed, and performed these movements, what was their training, and what relationship did they have to the filmic firmament?

Much of the figure movement I discuss in this book is more complex dancing, requiring extensive training or technique, and often the result of codified human movement practices.[8] However, I don't want to isolate that form of movement from the rest of these musicals' use of simple, rhythmically motivated, staged figure movement. Like Adrienne McLean, Erin Brannigan, and Usha Iyer, I'm interested in the meaningful ways that figure movement functions in different forms and iterations of performance.[9] Cinematic staging is the central purview of the film's director, and David Bordwell refers to a nimble instance of this craft as "fairly careful choreography," emphasizing the organizational complexity that underlies this aspect of film style.[10] Cinematic choreography requires more extensive coordination across units, and filmmakers often discuss a shared sense of authorship over such work, even if the director still ultimately has the final say. Considering the formal differences between danced and staged movements draws our attention to the film's division of labor and the training of the performers, revealing more about the collaborations that occurred between the films' performers, cinematographers, camera operators, directors, and choreographers.

While many written approaches to analyzing bodily movement focus on individual dance forms with the goal of training the reader in choreographic composition practices,[11] my approach to studying movement form draws principally from my training in the discipline of Laban/Bartenieff Movement Studies (LBMS), which I find translates more clearly to this interdisciplinary context.[12] The inclusion of nonhuman movement is essential to this focus, given the effect that mobile framing has on our perception of figure movement on screen. Yet even that movement is not fully inanimate, as the camera operator's individual body and training also impacts the feel of the moving frame.[13]

Within the context of film musicals, the staging of performers on screen and the choreography of figure movement function as key formal devices that guide crucial elements of film style and viewers' narrative comprehension. Cinema and dance often function as distinctive art forms and medium-specific practices. In these films, however, dance functions as a part of the filmic whole, as music does, or as "one piece of that puzzle," per choreographer Mandy Moore's description of her role in La La Land's production process. She adds, "It was this perfect concoction of all these departments coming together to create a piece of work. . . . Yes, I trained Ryan [Gosling] and Emma [Stone], and ultimately the steps came from my body and my team. And the dynamics and what I felt physically in those shapes are from me. But I think what resonated with people are not necessarily the shapes, it's the shapes within everything else that was happening."[14] As a result, this book differs from the research done in dance studies on theatrical or live dance, in which any filmic media used is secondary to the performance,[15] and screendance research, which assumes a more equal, hybridized relationship between the two artistic practices.[16]

To understand the historical context of cinematic figure movement we cannot completely separate the poetic qualities of performance from their cultural and political ones, as my chapters on West Side Story, Jeanne et le garçon formidable, and La La Land particularly draw attention to. This positioning builds off existing accounts of dance in narrative cinema, most often focused on the classical Hollywood era, that provides historical, critical, and theoretical foundations to understand the ways that cinematic bodies function formally and in broader cultural contexts.[17] I have chosen to focus on the narrative and stylistic aspects of movement on screen not because I find the extrafilmic characteristics unimportant but rather because there is still so much to learn about the internal workings of cinematic figure movement, particularly in a French context, and that understanding lays a foundation for discussions of how these films function in a wider cultural space. As such, I see my argument less as a contribution to performance theory and more as an expansion of film history, with the addition of a few analytical tools that facilitate that investigation. When I use the term "performance" in my analysis, I use it not to refer to the identity formation at play, as Andrew

8 STORYTELLING IN MOTION

Parker and Eve Kosofsky Sedgwick do,[18] but to the material elements shaping the narrative and style of the film. My work here is therefore less centered on questions of identity or theory than is commonly found in the domains of performance or acting studies[19] and is directed toward the form of the body in an aesthetic, qualitative sense more so than the quantitative, social-scientific, or therapeutic approaches developed in nonverbal communication research.[20] I don't intend for this book to weigh in on debates about ideal approaches to dance documentation, a topic already thoroughly historicized in Adrienne McLean's work,[21] or to posit a platonic ideal of dance on screen. Instead, I hope to illuminate the changing ways that filmmakers have crafted cinematic choreography and musical form to tell stories through figure movement and draw attention to the historical conditions that shaped their ability to do so.

Overactive Viewing and Performative Research

Figure movement in film is a powerful tool for guiding viewer attention through the craft of cinematic staging. Choreographed movement can provide denotative information—referential or explicit—that shapes our understanding of narrative details. Most frequently, however, the moving body on screen enriches our experience of the film through implicit information (connotative meaning) that we must interpret from the available low-level (referential) and denotative formal cues.[22] We understand cinematic images and sounds thanks to knowledge structures (schemata) that we learn to apply to films. These schemata come from applying our (referential) knowledge of the world onto film, such as understanding person-like agents, or characters, as having fully fleshed out psychological and emotional qualities and bodies that adhere to anatomical principles and the laws of physics.[23] We also apply our knowledge of films we have seen onto new ones; we are able to recognize a film as a musical from parsing the various cues we come to recognize as endemic in the genre. While viewers may seek a variety of information from the film form at hand, the majority will be parsing the images and sounds they perceive in order to better comprehend narrative meaning.[24] Film viewing, as a result, is an active process. Spectators are active, not passive, viewers, who as Kristin Thompson describes, "can cope with films to the degree that they have learned the norms appropriate to those films, and also to the degree that they have learned to be aware of and question those norms."[25] The meaning we glean from figure movement functions on numerous formal levels, requiring additional investment of viewer activity and, from an analytical perspective, benefiting from the practice-led methods that drive Laban/Bartenieff Movement Analysis and videographic approaches to audiovisual criticism.

Filmmakers have learned intuitively how to emphasize salient narrative details based on where and how viewers are likely to pay attention. One of the fundamental purposes of stylistic denotation is directing the viewer's attention to the important parts of the frame.[26] As cognitive film research demonstrates, filmmakers shape their films into forces for guiding attention that deliberately focus viewer perception on the structures in scenes or shots most rife with narrative meaning and content.[27] Information overload can be an issue, which is why selectivity of stimuli is a powerful tool in the cinematic toolbox.[28] Filmmakers accordingly use these low-level features—the quantitative, physical elements involved in filmmaking—in selective ways to ensure viewer comprehension. Color, motion of any kind, film structure (techniques like shot duration and editing conventions), contrast (such as abrupt movements and a change in brightness), and the center of the frame (what Tim Smith calls "center bias") are central to a viewer's process of narrative identification and construction.[29] Significantly, people's faces and gestures will usually draw our attention, given that we recognize those structures frequently contain significant information.[30] If sound (dialogue, especially) is issuing from that face, all the better. By choosing to isolate key attention-grabbing elements in the frame and soundscape, filmmakers are able to precisely and nimbly guide our attention to the details we need for narrative comprehension and emotional engagement.[31] In contrast, certain cinematic approaches deliberately exploit concepts of inattentional and change blindness through an overabundance of stimuli, challenging viewer perception and encouraging a rewatching and reprocessing of the filmic content.[32]

Musicals can use both of these selective and excessive stylistic options to shape viewer attention. Existing cognitive film research has yet to account for the role that dance would play in this already complex equation for guiding viewer focus through the frame. Yet we know that viewers are likely to fix their attention on bodies and faces and that movement in all its forms is central to our sensory perception mechanisms.[33] Understanding how characters move on screen can help to explain how a viewer understands a story in

10 STORYTELLING IN MOTION

question and the skillful ways that filmmakers have learned to guide our attention to salient narrative details.

Elements of film form also mediate these movements of the human figure in significant ways. In addition to the effects low-level features discussed above have on viewer attention, mobile framing and cinematographic craft closely complement the choreography of figure movement on screen. In musical numbers, mobile framing is predominantly motivated by (dancing and staged) figure movement; a follow shot aesthetic determines many of the cinematographic choices about where and how to place the camera. This does not necessitate a static or singular relationship, however. Patrick Keating demonstrates that Hollywood directors developed follow shot techniques that ranged from more minimalist, or "invisible," to more complex, or "flamboyant"; in the latter, the camera was more likely to deviate from its primary function of keeping the figure centered in the frame.[34] Keating's discussion of follow shots is predicated on a walking character; this aesthetic can vary even more when we consider the dancing body and its multiple focal points or the potential for contradictory pulls of attention from the presence of multiple bodies on screen.

This book takes active viewing as a research practice a step further. To argue for how figure movement patterns drive narrative comprehension and stylistic experimentation, this research engages with practice-led (performative) methods to mobilize ideas from videographic criticism and Laban/Bartenieff Movement Studies (LBMS). Disseminating research through the form of the video essay, as I do with select chapters of this book, allows analytical findings to generate knowledge about audiovisual content while simultaneously using that audiovisual form as an argumentative tool.

Videographic approaches to moving image analysis can communicate ideas about figure movement in motion instead of in stasis, engaging with what Henri Bergson has called an intuitive knowledge of movement. Whereas intellectual knowledge perceives movement as snapshots in time, an intuitive understanding perceives movement as a "flowing continuity fluctuating endlessly."[35] Form is often discussed intuitively as a concept with static (predominantly spatial) rather than mobile (predominantly temporal) qualities, when it is in fact both.[36] Being able to mobilize both static and motion-driven approaches to perceiving an inherently time-based art form has obvious benefits. Creating videographic research generates both new knowledge about the object of study and a new audiovisual object;[37] the research process that I employ as a videographic scholar fundamentally changes the output. As a result, the attentional mechanisms I use to produce this knowledge differ from my writing-based methods and, by extension, individuals' viewing practices in approaching this material will likely be different as well. Jason Mittell points to the transformative value of entering moving images through nonlinear editing, arguing that "even if you don't make something new with the sounds and images imported into the editing platform, you can still discover something new by exploring a film via this new interface."[38] In this practice-led, or performative, approach to research, symbolic data and material forms of practice function as "utterances that accomplish, by their very enunciation, an action that generates effects,"[39] as Brad Haseman argues. The videographic researcher engages with the logic of the medium on its own terms in a way that encourages experimentation and play by applying artistic principles to scholarship.[40]

Numerous guides to researching dance form also encourage a practice-led approach to understanding movement by reproducing the forms in one's own body.[41] For some, education or self-mastery of the movement is the primary goal, rather than a primarily intellectual study of dance for historical or theoretical purposes. But these methods do not negate the need for precise language-based descriptors of figure movement. Much of the dance scholarship that provides extensive vocabularies for movement analysis is focused on three of the major dance types: ballet (classical), modern, and postmodern/contemporary. In contrast, more popular, commercialized dance types like modern jazz, Broadway, or social (ballroom) dance characterize much of the dance observable in my examples. Because of its rigorous vocabulary to describe both danced and ordinary movements of the body, the taxonomic approach to human movement at the center of Laban/Bartenieff Movement Studies (LBMS) and Laban Movement Analysis (LMA)[42] integrates well with cinematic formal analysis. As a result, much of my analysis of figure movement in this book uses the language from this movement analysis system as a foundation for thorough, pattern-based micro and macro analysis of the expressivity of human movement.

LMA branches out from the work of Rudolf Laban (1879–1958).[43] Four themes, or scaffolds, run through its approach: inner/outer, function/expression, mobility/stability, and exertion/recuperation. At its core, the work of an LBMS-trained analyst is to discover movement essences: what makes someone's movement expressive within their unique context. The work encourages the analyst to understand the movement in question in relation to its context, the environment, and the mover's broader movement patterns and preferences. This taxonomy functions by breaking movement down into smaller constituent parts and situating those parts along various spectra, which complements this book's categorization of musical numbers, as I elaborate on in chapter 1. "Teasing phenomena into polar opposites and defining continua along the polarities is at the heart of Laban's work," Karen Bradley argues.[44] In many instances this analytical approach consists of dividing categories into smaller and smaller subsections to isolate limited—and in some cases, bipolar—fluctuations in the body. Laban Movement Analysis also provides a vocabulary for distinguishing between the dynamic qualities of the human body in motion and the shapes it creates when considered in a static context. Carol-Lynne Moore as a result sees similar ties between Bergson's categorizations of intellectual and intuitive perception and the movement analysis system at the core of Laban/Bartenieff Movement Studies.[45]

The human body and its meaning-making capacities are remarkably complex. Any system that claims to comprehensively and unequivocally explain how human movement creates meaning without taking into account historical and cultural context is selling snake oil. LMA provides a rich toolbox for the analyst hoping to describe human movement with precision and consistency but, like all approaches to figure movement analysis, it has limitations. It is designed to isolate the expressive essence of a movement (in words or with symbols) based on analytical determinations and is not a comprehensive notation system.[46] LMA's conception of human movement is strictly constructed around the singularity of the individual in relation to the environment and the balance between an inner emotional life and external (outer) stimuli. For the individual on screen, however, our access to an understanding of their movement is mediated through the relationship between the performer and the film frame, and our attention is guided by the careful construction of elements of cinematic choreography. Because this movement system is not tied to a particular dance or movement tradition, it is effective at comparing different forms.[47] However, LBMS's bases for human movement all come from studies of people in Western cultures, and we therefore cannot assume it would adequately describe the complexities of human expression around the world.[48] While Laban's original work does suggest a certain universality to his principles, his observations were based primarily on white European bodies, and so his research cannot inherently fulfill such a promise of ubiquity with so small a human sample. In this book, I therefore use this movement analysis system as a taxonomic right hand to the historical context of a particular movement practice that allows for a rigorous consistency of movement vocabulary across chapters and figure movement forms.

Describing and analyzing figure movement is an inherently complicated process; Adrienne McLean describes bodies as "complex corporeal sources as well as manifestations of many levels of meaning."[49] Filmic bodies also exist within the pluralistic nature of cinematic movement, what Jordan Schonig calls the "inexhaustibly various *forms* through which cinematic motion manifests itself."[50] Figure movement can expressively change and move through space in a plethora of ways. Sometimes those shifts present contradictory information, and often that divergent rendering occurs simultaneously in different parts of the body, making the meaning we take away dependent on our individual learned frameworks but also dependent on which part of the body we happen to be observing at any particular moment. Experiencing the phrase in one's own body helps to isolate which aspect of the figure is driving the observation. In videographic criticism, movement analysis, and this book, the act of performative (re)creation is integral to the research process.

The Film Musical

Musicals typically require significant resources and are notoriously expensive, given their proclivity for triple-threat star talent, large set pieces, expansive singing and dancing ensembles and musicians, and the personnel, studio lots, equipment, and rehearsal time needed for implementation. Filmmakers' access to these conditions changes over time. Each film has a unique mode of production, and each filmmaker is tasked with the challenge of how to convey the story on the page through the available sonic and visual options. Filmmakers' choices are consistently impacted by key generative mechanisms—technological innovations, social forces, dominant aesthetics, and the economic institution—that affect each film's production process.[51] In particular, the evolution of mobile camera technology and techniques, the relationship between dance and film culture at the time of production, aesthetic norms of practice within the genre, and the industry's capacity and willingness to greenlight musical films most significantly impact creative options in this mode of filmmaking.

We cannot assume that filmmakers working with divergent resources will resort to the same stylistic or narrative choices even when presented with similar problems. Considering these challenges through a problem-solution framework offers a useful model to determine the relationship between historical conditions and the look and sound of the final artwork. It is through stylistic choices that filmmakers are able to achieve the goals they set for themselves.[52] Filmmakers are active agents and we should acknowledge them, David Bordwell argues, as "concrete forces for stability or change (or both)" in the study of stylistic history.[53] Those individuals' choices are also influenced and shaped by the artistic institution in which their art is made, with an eye toward the aesthetic norms and financial goals of those institutions. Filmmaker interviews and archival preservation of production documents and correspondence emphasize how deliberate the filmmakers I discuss here were in shaping the cinematic choreography that anchors their musicals. In many instances, these documents provide material evidence of the ways that the filmmakers adjusted their approaches when the industrial conditions around them changed.

Technological Mobility

Technological availability affects every filmmaker's aesthetic and storytelling decisions. Films would not exist without the machines that create them.[54] Synchronized sound technology is of course crucial to providing the musical and rhythmic sonic anchors of the genre.[55] Most significantly for dance-driven musicals, the camera's range of motion accordingly affects the body's visible range of motion and the whole choreographic process as a result. The musical filmmakers discussed in this book were frequently concerned with how and when to move the camera. Directors, cinematographers, and choreographers design the movement of their musical numbers in relation to the mobile technology available to them. For filmmakers working after the mid-1970s, this means access to Steadicam and other forms of camera stabilization.[56] *Singin' in the Rain*'s cinematographer Harold Rosson, in contrast, dollies and cranes the camera through the street set to follow and reframe Kelly in the space as he dances. The make, weight, and mobility mechanisms of the camera and its operator affect how quickly or nimbly the equipment (and as a result, often the performer) can move through the space. It also impacts the design of the shooting location to accommodate the bulk of the camera equipment and the overall pathways of larger groups of performers through space.[57]

INTRODUCTION   15

Prioritizing editing and the extensive segmentation of the mise-en-scène can be counterproductive to the goals of cinematic choreography when cutting serves as the dominant way of guiding the viewer's eye through the frame. Editing and staging go hand-in-hand, but you can't develop the latter if the former is dominant; you lose the subtleties and nuances of physical performance.[58] Yet segmenting cinematic space with continuity editing techniques is an established method of creating spatiotemporal clarity for viewers, and filmmakers use it in conjunction with cinematic choreography to powerfully guide the viewer's attention, as we see with *West Side Story* in chapter 3.

Changes in audio recording have had a significant impact on the sonically dependent musical genre,[59] as have changes to aspect ratio standards and anamorphic lenses. The aspect ratio profoundly affects the arrangement of bodies on screen.[60] *Singin' in the Rain* was shot in the Academy ratio (1.37:1), soon before MGM began making musicals in CinemaScope. In an interview, Gene Kelly expressed a distaste for the new anamorphic aspect ratio, calling it "an abomination" for dancers during solos, duets, or trios, formats that he favored.[61] Yet the more rectangular frame was less abhorrent to the later filmmakers discussed in this book. Director Damien Chazelle and cinematographer Linus Sandgren explicitly chose to shoot *La La Land* with anamorphic lenses and maintain the wider aspect ratio (and the subtle optical distortion it creates) because of its evocation of Hollywood widescreen aesthetics of the 1950s.[62] Technological availability and access—as well as perceptions about that technology's ideal usage—affects the choreography of bodies on screen. Cinematographic technology is also heavily dependent on the training and expertise of the camera operator; the choreographer and director work with the physicality of their camera crew as well as that of the dancers and actors.

Shifting Dance Cultures

The training of camera operators has had a profound effect on the filming of musical numbers, but the strongest determining social force in dance-heavy musical production is the cultural status of dance and its relationship to the film industry. Gene Kelly's musical stardom in the 1950s was not inevitable; it was the result of decades of training in an industry that grew to embrace the musical genre and the infrastructure it required for implementation. Through an evolution of dance styles and a close symbiotic relationship

16 STORYTELLING IN MOTION

between Broadway and Hollywood, white dancers trained in song, dance, and acting could find steady work as lead performers or below-the-line personnel during the studio era. Much of this evolution of movement came from the labor of Black performers, whose choreographic innovations allowed jazz dance to become a staple of mainstream dance culture without affording its creators the job security and recognition given to their white colleagues.[63]

The aesthetic possibilities of the social relationship between dance and film culture become even more visible through absence. The musical genre was never dominant in France in part because of the divergence between its film and dance cultures.[64] As a result, filmmakers like Jacques Demy, Olivier Ducastel, and Jacques Martineau turned to international corps of dancers, alternate dance styles, and nonprofessional dancers to incorporate choreographed figure movement into their films. Gene Kelly, Stanley Donen, Jerome Robbins, and Robert Wise, in contrast, had access to corps of dancers who were trained to dance on screen during the studio era for their ensemble numbers in the 1950s and 1960s. Hollywood iterations of the genre similarly had to evolve after this period, when the industry and its star system shifted away from prioritizing triple threat talent and companies no longer kept dancers on contract. Filmmakers like Damien Chazelle making musical cinema in the twenty-first century now often have to recreate much of that infrastructure from scratch.

Genre-specificity

These changes in industrial conditions and the changing expectations for cinematic star talent to be trained as singers and dancers impact the shape of musical filmmaking, as virtuosic performances often anchor the genre. Musical films are also built around a unique relationship between numbers and their surrounding narrative. When musical buffs get into heated arguments about whether a film should be included in the generic category, those areas of disagreement usually stem from one of two points: the film's numbers predominantly do or don't relate to the surrounding plot, or the film's numbers predominantly adhere to or deviate from the norms of the diegesis. To some viewers, musical numbers carry an association of halting the film plot—they exist primarily as showstoppers—but our attention to the film we are viewing does not stop. Genre norms and expectations play a significant role in filmmakers' ability to guide that attention. The use of the musical genre's convention of moving away from diegetic grounding is not arbitrary; it profoundly impacts the ways that audiences make meaning of sung and danced moments. Each musical sequence serves a particular function (or series of functions) within the larger narrative. And each number can adhere to or deviate from the spatiotemporal and acting performance norms that govern the diegesis. As a result, the implicit meaning created by cinematic choreography is guided not only by figure movement but also by the pluralistic ways that choreographed content shapes the diegeses of musical numbers.

Shifts in social forces closely interact with producer and audience expectations of genre conventions. Producer expectations of what the musical genre should look and sound like often determine the level of experimentation afforded to a filmmaker or their future career prospects, as my discussions of *West Side Story*, *Les Demoiselles de Rochefort*, and *Jeanne et le garçon formidable* demonstrate. Spectator expectations are similarly crucial to an understanding of how viewers comprehend film genres and the various scholarly and popular responses to such work. Kelly Kessler describes genre cinema as a "mutual contract" between filmmakers, film viewers, and contemporary culture,[65] and Steve Neale, drawing on Tom Ryall and Andrew Tudor, stresses the importance of audience knowledge and expectations in understanding the facets of genre cinema.[66] Taste and evaluation are culturally contingent, as Adrienne McLean emphasizes; critical and popular perceptions of what "good" dancing or "virtuosic" dancing bodies should look like changes, but we can better understand how danced content was received at the time through a study of historical documentation.[67] The relationship between filmmakers' formal choices and audience expectations of the musical genre is therefore a significant one. Aesthetic norms of practice in musical form evolve over time, both impacted by and impacting industrial, technological, and social norms of practice.[68] This profoundly affects the construction of musical numbers and impacts their quantity, form, and function relative to the overall film narrative.

Money Speaks

In the end, the broader infrastructure (or lack thereof) of a film industry most profoundly impacts the choices available to filmmakers, especially those making expensive musical cinema. Social forces, aesthetic norms, and

18 STORYTELLING IN MOTION

technological access are all intrinsically linked to economic forces.[69] Musicals were popular with American audiences in the early 1950s, and the antitrust Paramount Decree that would lead to the Hollywood majors divesting themselves from their exhibition wings would not fully take effect for a few more years, allowing studios to have vast pools of below-the-line personnel on contract.[70] *Singin' in the Rain*—and in many ways *West Side Story*—were made in the ideal industrial conditions for musical filmmaking as a result. The scope of a film's budget affects the execution of the storytelling, and dance-heavy musicals require additional funding to pay for trained corps of dancers and the space and time to rehearse them.

Industrial priorities also propel technological innovation and aesthetic norms of practice. Musical productions were prestigious in Hollywood during the studio period; they appealed to audiences and were an ideal genre to showcase innovative technology like synchronized sound, CinemaScope, and Technicolor thanks to their reputation for showstopping set pieces. However, the key factors that affect the shape of dance-heavy musical production—industrial priorities, genre expectations and aesthetic norms, the cultural relationship between dance and film, and mobile camera technology—are not static. The American and French filmmakers discussed throughout the chapters of this book made their musicals in conditions that differed from the ones that Gene Kelly and Stanley Donen experienced with *Singin' in the Rain*. All, however, found innovative ways to experiment with the construction of musical numbers and the incorporation of choreographed figures to shape their cinematic stories.

"Reading" This Book

I hope this work will be of interest to a variety of audiences, and as such I have designed it with a certain level of extractability in mind. The book as a whole tells the story of the profound effect that poststudio era changes to the filmmaking industry and dance culture had on Franco-American musical form. The written chapters move chronologically, isolating a focused discussion of the book's core film examples, from *Singin' in the Rain* to *La La Land*. Readers who are predominantly interested in these films' historical contexts can focus on the "Production History" sections that anchor the start of chapters 1, 3, 4, 5, 8, and 9. The videographic chapters (chapters 2, 6, and 7), by contrast, function in a more nonlinear, a-chronological fashion to poetically interrogate the aesthetic links between these core examples and other musical films. Throughout the written chapters, movement vocabulary from Laban/Bartenieff Movement Studies supports my analytical findings, but I recognize that, like any other form of training, the descriptive precision of its language carries less value for nonpractitioners. Those readers interested in the LMA structures supporting the book's movement analysis can find that language in the chapter notes. When these precise terms are included in regular sentence flow, I capitalize terms from the LBMS-specific vocabulary to signal that a word carries greater linguistic significance beyond everyday use. This provides the reader with the descriptive data that supports the book's analytical findings with, I hope, minimal semantic clumsiness. Appendices at the end of the book summarize the core vocabulary from the LBMS system and present in table form the quantitative data that provides a basis for economic and stylistic comparisons.

Part I lays the historical, analytical, and theoretical foundations that support the rest of this book. Chapter 1 uses Stanley Donen and Gene Kelly's *Singin' in the Rain* (1952) and its centrality to American musical criticism to illustrate my focus on cinematic choreography and the ways that musical genre conventions create meaning. Through an extensive dissection of musical numbers' form, this chapter categorizes the ways that musical numbers can move through various narrative, aesthetic, and stylistic functions, using instances from *Singin' in the Rain* and other Hollywood musicals to illustrate the genre's norms of practice. *Singin' in the Rain* is a canonical example of the genre because it explores the many ways that musicals can use song, dance, and multiple diegetic layers in their storytelling. Through a focus on the film's titular number, this chapter also emphasizes how much of this film musical's magic comes from its use of movement and the implicit meanings it generates by weaving narrative depth, multi-diegetic complexity, and stylistic richness in between its musical notes. *Singin' in the Rain* was also made in the ideal industrial conditions for musical filmmaking; the support provided a wealth of resources for the film, in addition to the invaluable institutional memory of the Freed production unit at Metro-Goldwyn-Mayer.

Using *Singin' in the Rain* and other musical examples from classical Hollywood cinema, chapter 2 provides a videographic introduction to Laban/Bartenieff Movement Studies and the taxonomic principles that guide Laban Movement Analysis. Through an explanatory approach to videographic form, this chapter uses voiceover, graphic and written annotations, and carefully chosen examples from the figure movement of these films to walk

20 STORYTELLING IN MOTION

the viewer through the fundamentals of this movement system. While this chapter's goal is to make sense of the intersections between elements of the LMA toolkit and provide specific manifestations of its categories—Body, Effort, Space, and Shape—appendix 1 also provides a glossary of LBMS terms for quick reference.

West Side Story (1961) is a pivotal and influential example of film musical form, as chapter 3 emphasizes. Codirectors Jerome Robbins and Robert Wise demonstrated new ways to use cinematic choreography as a powerful storytelling tool by using dance to illustrate the differences as well as the similarities between the gangs of Sharks and Jets that fuel their escalating conflict. Despite a desire for an aesthetic of narrative realism in portraying the tensions between the white and Latinx/o/a teenagers, *West Side Story*'s producers did not prioritize inclusive hiring practices in casting its Puerto Rican characters, and the film remains a multifaceted text in studies of media representation, serving as an emblem of Hollywood's patterns of cultural exclusion and essentialism. Those patterns of exclusion, and a vying for dominance of one's space, are also central to the narrative's cinematic choreography. A close analysis of the film's prologue and "Cool" demonstrates how crucial the danced musical numbers are to our narrative comprehension of the tensions between the Sharks and Jets. Emphasizing both the characters' individuality and the importance of a collective cohesion, *West Side Story* uses cinematic choreography to show the Sharks' and Jets' mutual desire for a space to call their own, while the Jets' entitled dominance of their unwillingly shared environment demonstrates their violent resistance to change.

The prototypical Western musical—with songs, dances, narratively woven numbers, showstopping moments, large set-pieces, large groups of performers, and innovative audiovisual style—may feel inevitable. But this is not the case. Musicals were a significant genre in Hollywood from the early 1930s until the late 1950s, yet they never dominated screens in France, another country known for its commitment to the seventh art. Part II of this book shifts away from Hollywood to investigate why this was the case and explores the links between French and American musical practices, predominantly through an exploration of the transnational musical films of French filmmaker Jacques Demy.

Demy's films often experiment with the musical genre's core conventions. Chapter 4 focuses on his first sung-and-danced musical, *Les Demoiselles de Rochefort* (1967). The film is inspired by choreographed phrases and aesthetic impulses from 1950s and 1960s Hollywood musicals; Demy uses

INTRODUCTION 21

cinematic choreography in eclectic ways to parametrically explore the narrative and expressive functions of musical sequences. Through the repetition of choreographed phrases—citations of Hollywood musicals, choreographer Norman Maen's original creations, and Demy's simple staging of actors as they sing—*Les Demoiselles de Rochefort* withholds the romantic pairings associated with the genre to keep the viewer in suspense about the outcome. French dance culture in the mid-1960s was not prioritizing the same stylistic needs as those of musical cinema, so Demy and Maen's corps of dancers populating the on-location settings of the quiet, southwestern Rochefort-sur-Mer were hired from England. The French musical film also had direct ties to Hollywood through a coproduction arrangement with Seven Arts Productions, which stipulated casting a few American actors as well: Grover Dale, George Chakiris, and Gene Kelly. Demy's rigorous staging of figure and camera movement makes even the simplest gestures during musical numbers part of the film's intricate patterns, allowing the viewer to discover new details and parallels on each subsequent viewing. But his unconventional approach to the musical and refusal to cooperate with the financial priorities of film industries meant that he struggled to produce ambitious musical projects for the remainder of his career.

A notable exception to Demy's career-long financial challenges is his final feature, *Trois places pour le 26* (1988), the focus of chapter 5. French producer Claude Berri provided him with substantial resources to create a musical project, with the stipulation that the film would revive an earlier abandoned collaboration with French singer and actor Yves Montand. With the material conditions secured to carefully design all aspects of production, Demy creates a backstage musical that flips the conventions of the subgenre in complex and discomposing ways. We get to the end of the film unsure of the diegetic realities posited by the narrative and its presentation of the mostly stage-bound numbers. Demy also worked closely with American choreographer Michael Peters and their cast—particularly Mathilda May, Françoise Fabian, and Yves Montand—to make the cinematic choreography crucial to our understanding of character development and central to the subtle ways that the film's use of musical numbers challenges the conventions of the show musical. By the late 1980s, dance culture in France had expanded, thanks to the emigration of jazz dancers from the United States and government initiatives to financially support the art form, leading to more experimental contemporary movement forms (*danse contemporaine*) that would inspire Demy and the French filmmakers his work influenced.

Trois places pour le 26 is deliberately reflexive in relation to the musical genre, and this premise opens the videographic exploration of cinematic citations in chapter 6. While much of this book is about how movement works intrinsically in films to enhance our narrative comprehension, it also gestures to the extrinsic functions of cinematic choreography. This chapter draws attention to the inherent ways that genres create meaning by recycling, repeating, and engaging with figure movement material from their predecessors. Framing the inherent reflexivity of genre cinema and the citational practices of many genre films as a kind of conversation, this chapter draws attention to the stylistic and narrative conventions of musical films' cinematic choreography. More than chapter 2, this videographic work develops in a poetic fashion: playfully using a cyclical approach, multiscreen audiovisual juxtapositions, and the epigraphic video essay genre to convey varied instances of intertextual connections between the films analyzed in this book and those that inspired them, leading us to the more fantastical diegetic departures the genre is known for.

If film as art should aspire toward an asymptotic relationship with reality, as André Bazin would have us believe,[71] then the musical is a radical deviation from that goal. Many spectators' fundamental objection to (or discomfort with) the musical genre is based on what Steven Cohan calls a "commonly held prejudice against the genre that arises . . . out of a naïve or at least unwarranted sense of fidelity to cinematic realism."[72] However, it is precisely through the tensions between realism and fantasy that the musical builds narrative meaning, emotional resonance, and stylistic specificity, as the chapters in part III of this book emphasize. Much of our conceptual understanding of this tension describes the relationship as binary, when it is in fact more complex and less inherently distant; "realism and fantasy are less divided than is sometimes thought," Carl Plantinga argues.[73] That complexity relates to how movement on screen conveys meaning in musical cinema.

The musical genre, stylistically, is all about the tension between the film's diegetic conception of realism and the fantastical departures from it. Choreographer Mandy Moore describes this moment of transition from the diegesis into a musical number as a bridge. Musical numbers usually solidify in their diegetic departures from the narrative, but the numbers from the musicals discussed in this book often resist that permanence, fluttering in and out of the diegetic plurality created by musical sequences. What can we learn by observing those impermanent moments of transition? Chapter 7

INTRODUCTION   23

videographically explores this specific practice to draw attention to the ambiguity, joy, and utopian resistance of such moments.

The threads of musical realism that we see in Hollywood films like *West Side Story* continue through Jacques Demy's musicals before weaving together more tightly in the work of contemporary musical filmmakers. Whereas *West Side Story*'s narrative content and use of dancing to convey conflict is strongly read by critics as problematic in its avoidance of the political potentials of its representation, chapter 8 emphasizes how directors Olivier Ducastel and Jacques Martineau deliberately sought to foreground the political symbolism of their choreographic choices in *Jeanne et le garçon formidable* (1998). Their film, which centers on an HIV positive character, makes the dancing body crucial to the narrative's double emphasis on romance and the cultural erasure of the AIDS epidemic during this period, combining fictional and documentary modes of filmmaking. Choreographer Sylvie Giron uses *danse contemporaine* and its emphasis on pedestrian vocabulary to blend the movements of the professional corps of dancers and the lead actors (Mathieu Demy and Virginie Ledoyen), who were amateur dancers. Dance functions as an essential element in *Jeanne et le garçon formidable*, drawing attention to the resilience of the human body as well as its impermanence.

Damien Chazelle's *La La Land* (2016) continues this tradition of casting nonprofessional dancers (Emma Stone and Ryan Gosling) in an extensively choreographed film about show business that echoes the reflexive aesthetic approaches in *Trois places pour le 26* and *Singin' in the Rain*. As I discuss in chapter 9, Chazelle, like Ducastel and Martineau, is strongly influenced by Demy's musical aesthetic, in particular by the more subtle ways that musical numbers slip away from their diegetic grounding. In *La La Land*, an aesthetic of realism blended with fantasy is linked to duration and rhythm through the professional stagnation of Mia's character (Stone), who jumps through the hoops of the Hollywood film industry to pursue an acting career but gets nowhere. Even more so, these patterns of rhythmic realism manifest through the collaborations between Chazelle, choreographer Mandy Moore, cinematographer Linus Sandgren, and Steadicam operator Ari Robbins. To explore these ideas, I apply the analytical methods from Laban Movement Analysis to the camera's mechanical range of motion, analyzing it both as a character with agency in the cinematic space as well as an extension of Robbins's own craft-specific figure movement. *La La Land*'s stylistic design has the camera dance through the space, guided by Robbins's labor and his embodied knowledge. The film also introduces narrative ambiguity through its dream ballet number, which uses durational aesthetics and a blend of realist and fantastical styles to cast doubt on its diegetic status. Despite *La La Land*'s evocation of classical Hollywood musical conventions, many of the resources central to the studio era musical had changed by 2016, and the filmmakers' choices emphasize what is lost as well as the rich ongoing potential of cinematic choreography.

Musicals demand a lot from their audience. They ask viewers to process singing and dancing for both their aesthetic and narrative significance, to draw on knowledge of generic norms and adapt their expectations accordingly, and to be familiar with the attention-directing schemata used by filmmakers to focus eyes and ears on pertinent audiovisual information. To this we add our own individual background knowledge and predilections, which may guide us to focus more on one aspect (singing, dancing, star presence) or be repulsed by another (music style, casting choices, cultural essentialism or erasure). Each reader of this book will have distinctive meaning-making processes that affect their understanding of the musicals discussed in this book.

The storytelling power of choreographed movement in these musical films and cinema in general has not yet received the full attention it deserves. This book foregrounds the importance of these significant meaning-making mechanisms in musicals, contextualized within an understanding of the resources available to filmmakers seeking to communicate through cinematic choreography. In considering these alternative paths through the organization of dance and staged human movement on screen, it becomes clear how figure movement is crucial to the musical's meaning-making processes and how much more there is still to learn about the role of figure movement in cinema more generally. I hope that this book enriches an understanding of how these films mobilized their use of cinematic choreography and inspires further exploration of such impacts in broader corpi of media.

PART I
MUSICAL FOUNDATIONS

1

Formal Conventions and Musical Practices

Singin' in the Rain (1952)

Imagine you must pick a single iconic moment to epitomize the musical genre. What do you choose? The first image to come to mind might be Gene Kelly posed on a lamp post in the titular number from *Singin' in the Rain* (Gene Kelly and Stanley Donen, 1952), soaking wet and umbrella in hand (figure 1.1). It's a reasonable choice. Most people familiar with musicals have seen the film or could at least identify the source. The film's reputation as "the greatest movie musical of all time" continues to grow,[1] and you're hard-pressed to find a book that discusses the film musical that doesn't include it (including, now, this one).[2] Despite the sonic emphasis of the title, for many it's the film's dancing that contributes to its formal and historical significance, with some considering the titular number as "the most famous," "most memorable ... most instantly recognizable" filmed dance number and the epitome of the musical genre itself.[3]

The "Singin' in the Rain" number is a powerful sequence thanks to its communication of expressive narrative information about Gene Kelly's character. Significantly, it is the number's dancing, not the memorable song lyrics, that drives its narrative and stylistic importance. But how do we, as film viewers, process those meaning structures in the first place, and how did this lead to the film's—and this number's—enduring prominence? What are the formal cues Kelly, his codirector Stanley Donen, and their collaborators used to communicate that information through figure movement, a form that is often more implicit in its meaning-making structures? And how were they able to materialize those choices?

By applying the methodological approaches that guide the analysis of musicals throughout this book, we can better understand how *Singin' in the Rain* and its titular number gained such fame. Simply put, directors Donen and Kelly use their film to revisit, and in some cases expand on, the many ways that classical Hollywood filmmakers had experimented with incorporating musical numbers into cinema since the widespread adoption

Storytelling in Motion. Jenny Oyallon-Koloski, Oxford University Press. © Oxford University Press 2024.
DOI: 10.1093/oso/9780197602669.003.0002

Figure 1.1 Gene Kelly poses on a lamp post in *Singin' in the Rain*'s titular number.
Source: Metro-Goldwyn-Mayer.

of synchronized sound in the late 1920s. From the faster editing and abstraction associated with Busby Berkeley's work for Warner Bros., to Gene Kelly's own emphasis on extended dream ballet sequences for Metro-Goldwyn-Mayer in the late 1940s and early 1950s, to the myriad ways that song and lyrics can guide the narrative or shape character expressivity, the filmmakers explore the history of Hollywood's most lavish genre in comprehensive and playful ways.

Through an examination of *Singin' in the Rain*'s production history and broad incorporation of musical number styles, this chapter lays out the generic categories and industrial contexts that impact the rest of the films discussed in this book. The film's production conditions were ideal for musical cinema, giving Gene Kelly, in particular, the resources needed to create cinematic choreography that draws on the musical parameters he and his colleagues pioneered during the studio era and to create complex, ambiguous meanings through choreographed figure movement. *Singin' in the Rain*'s place in musical cinema history draws attention to key historical mechanisms that impact the creation of dance-and-movement-heavy musicals, and the norms of practice musical filmmakers developed, both narrative and stylistic, for musical number conventions.

Vast Resources for Genre Codification (Production History)

Gene Kelly and Stanley Donen did not direct *Singin' in the Rain* in a fledgling production context. By the early 1950s, Arthur Freed's film unit at Metro-Goldwyn-Mayer had earned its reputation as the most prestigious musical production unit in Hollywood.[4] Freed was a powerful figure, and he wanted to showcase the work he had created early in MGM's foray into synchronized sound and musical productions. Yet *Singin' in the Rain*'s legacy is not only that of a jukebox musical paying tribute to Hollywood's most powerful and successful producer of musical cinema. It also serves as a concise historical record of the conventions filmmakers developed to make meaning through song, dance, and the diegetic ambiguity generated by the juxtaposition of narrative and number.

The Stars Align

The film property of *Singin' in the Rain* was built around the song catalogue Freed developed in collaboration with composer Nacio Herb Brown in the 1920s and 1930s while working as a songwriter for MGM. As a result, the conditions in which *Singin' in the Rain* was made were ideally suited to the musical genre, and Gene Kelly's choices for choreographing and directing the "Singin' in the Rain" number, in particular, were possible thanks to the industrial resources available to him and his cinematic collaborators.

Producers of musicals are more likely to greenlight a project if it adheres to contemporary norms of practice, and *Singin' in the Rain*'s emphasis on dance and Kelly's physical persona aligned with what producers and audiences would have expected from an MGM musical of the early 1950s. "Singin' in the Rain" is one of Freed and Brown's songs repurposed for the film, and the number adheres closely to the movement aesthetic Beth Genné associates with Gene Kelly by including dancing in the street, with a movement vernacular that encapsulates both playful and athletic qualities.[5] The narrative and stylistic importance of dance in the number also aligns with Sean

30 STORYTELLING IN MOTION

Griffin's assessment of 1950s musical conventions. During this period, dance solidified itself as a narrative component of the genre.[6] For Steven Cohan, the choice to reuse Freed and Brown's song and add "and dancin'" to the original lyrics "puts forward dancing as the singular modernizing element characterizing the MGM musical's development."[7] The expectation of significant dancing in the musical genre during this period occurred thanks to Hollywood's consistent investment in the resources needed to film such elaborate productions.

Debbie Reynolds's memories of making *Singin' in the Rain* point to key elements that facilitated the dance training and efficient-but-exploitative working conditions at Metro-Goldwyn-Mayer during this period. Gene Kelly was apparently displeased to have her as his romantic lead, given her lack of professional dance training. To prepare for the role of Kathy, Reynolds had three months of full-day dance training sessions with three teachers: Ernie Flatt, Carol Haney (Kelly's assistant choreographer for *Singin' in the Rain*), and Jeanne Coyne. After a particularly difficult rehearsal with Kelly, Fred Astaire apparently found her crying and invited her to watch his (private) rehearsal session with choreographer Hermes Pan so she could observe their own intense work process. During the film shoot, Reynolds had to go on bed rest after intense, day-long shoots of her dance numbers, which infuriated the studio heads because of the time's impact on the production schedule (and budget). She attributes her ongoing good health to her personal doctor, who insisted on two days of rest instead of allowing MGM's resident doctor to administer the addictive "vitamin" shots given to Judy Garland and others at the time that would have more quickly gotten her back on her feet at a lower financial cost to the studio.[8]

Reynolds's experience points to the infrastructural efficiency, creative moments of happenstance, and labor exploitation of the Hollywood studio system. Working with Reynolds as his romantic lead and duet partner was an aesthetic constraint to Kelly, but she was able to improve her technique rapidly due to the in-house infrastructure at MGM and the on-contract presence of other trained professionals like Fred Astaire, as well as an unrelenting, physically exhausting work pace. The addition of a dream ballet sequence that deviates from the constraints of the film's plot also allowed Kelly to partner with dancer Cyd Charisse for more elaborate dance duets.

Throughout the production, the ability to develop solutions to narrative and stylistic problems was facilitated by the studio's vast resources. Kelly alludes to this in discussing the titular "Singin' in the Rain" number, indicating that moving the number along the street set "cost a little more money, because they had to make more rain pipes down the street." Art director Randall Duell and his crew dished out and repaved portions of the set to create puddles at the precise places Kelly needed them for his number.[9] MGM's infrastructure also allowed the filmmakers to do more with less; MGM had many stock units of set pieces and costumes that could be reused and modified, which ultimately saved the company money.[10] As a result, Griffin argues, "That system created the perfect environment for the musical genre to grow and thrive."[11] Arthur Freed's musical unit at MGM gave its filmmakers access to the best resources available.

Musical Norms

Due to Arthur Freed's influence, the 1950s is often seen as a period of codification of musical conventions. Novelty acts declined in prominence, and the greater influence of choreographers during this period is significant to Sean Griffin, who argues that we see a greater uniformity of "'integrated' dancing that reveals character emotion instead of a straightforward spectacle of technical proficiency. Just as novelty and eccentric dancing or flash acts fell out of favor in the Freed Unit, so too did they gradually disappear from musicals at other studios" during this time.[12] Tino Balio echoes this distinction to emphasize the differences between Freed and fellow MGM producer Joe Pasternak. "Unlike Freed's integrated musicals, which used music to advance the narrative," Balio declares, "Pasternak's musicals were musical extravaganzas" that connected various performance styles through a lose plot structure.[13] This distinction identifies the Freed unit with more complex storytelling in which the characters performing the numbers are also central agents in a larger narrative, as opposed to the Pasternak unit's development of more thematically driven revue films. But Balio's choice to describe Freed's films as "integrated" rather than "narrative" or "narratively driven" musicals implies that all films in this category have numbers that develop a similar relationship to their surrounding plots. This is far from the case even within the corpus of Freed films, *Singin' in the Rain* in particular.[14]

Both these accounts of genre codification focus on the concept of integration: the relationship between the musical numbers and the film's form. Musical integration, and its relative importance, frequently drives theoretical conceptions of what constitutes the ahistorical essence of the genre,[15] and

32 STORYTELLING IN MOTION

invoking that moniker·suggests that the musical numbers in question have a close relationship of some kind to their parent film. Integration in the musical genre means different things to different people; the same term is used to describe several inconsistent ways that musical numbers interact or combine with the rest of the film.[16] These contradictory definitions underscore that the musical genre uses this relationship in playful and dynamic ways for a variety of purposes, while also emphasizing that clearer semantic consensus can help to identify the specific ways this genre experiments with narrative and stylistic tendencies.

Musical integration can describe a whole corpus or subgenre of musical form.[17] The backstage and revue subgenres are more likely to be categorized as nonintegrated or what Steven Cohan calls "aggregate" musicals, in which numbers predominantly occur "without regard for narrative unity or continuity,"[18] whereas subgenres like the folk musical may be more frequently narratively integrated.[19] More often, however, the concept of integration relates to a specific musical number, with the term emphasizing varying ways that the musical content relates to the narrative or style of the surrounding film. Occasionally, integration refers to the need for coherent unity between the setting, costumes, performance, lighting, and camera choices for musical numbers[20] or for a number to be conceived within the aesthetic choices of film style.[21] Narrative integration is the most common usage (and often the assumed meaning when "narrative" is not specified), in which numbers are deemed narratively significant or causally essential to the plot.[22] The term "integrated number" (or, sometimes, "fully" integrated number) also describes sequences that seem to emerge "naturally" from the story, that is, which are not motivated as a stage number nor as a premeditated performance that maintains a clear diegetic plausibility and continuity.[23]

While the latter definition—the idea that characters just burst into song and dance—may assume narrative importance, the two are not intrinsically linked. Sometimes these definitions overlap, as we see in "Singin' in the Rain," which both serves a narrative purpose and is not motivated as a stage-bound or premeditated performance. However, while there is often a relationship between numbers that are narratively essential to the plot and numbers in which characters spontaneously break into song and dance, we should not assume that the presence of one quality automatically ensures the other. The "Moses Supposes" number from *Singin' in the Rain* is not causally essential to the plot, for example, but it does emerge as a mostly spontaneous song-and-dance number. Importantly, one person prioritizing narrative integration might consider this number nonintegrated, while someone else might categorize it as the opposite given that it isn't motivated as a rehearsed performance.

Moreover, numbers can be more or less overt in their relationships to the larger narrative. In many instances, musical sequences are clearly identifiable as such—Gene Kelly singing while dancing in the rain, for example—but other times they are not. Filmmakers often subtly play with these boundaries to toy with our expectations and enrich their application of genre conventions, as the examples discussed throughout this book demonstrate. Especially in stage-bound (diegetically motivated) numbers, it can be challenging to distinguish between numbers that would not appear uncomfortably out-of-the-ordinary in a nonmusical film and those that epitomize the genre, either by advancing the plot or deviating from diegetic plausibility.

Such lack of consensus over the meaning of musical integration points to the rich, complex ways that musical numbers can interact with their surrounding stories. More to the point, the varying definitions of integration in relation to the musical genre emphasize that the relationships between narrative and number are not binary, but plural. Across these accounts the terms integration, integrated musical, and integrated musical number refer to different relationships between a musical sequence and the film's narrative, style, or broader cultural context.[24] Significantly, these variations still don't encompass the full range of relationships that musical numbers can mobilize, as creators of musical cinema further dissect the spatiotemporal possibilities of cinema to experiment with diegetic expansion and ambiguity. Further categorical dissection may seem overly pedantic to some, but how a musical number is integrated narratively or stylistically into cinematic form impacts how viewers make meaning of its content. As such, a more nuanced distinction between these approaches merits our attention.

Narrative and Stylistic Categories for Musical Numbers

Codirectors Stanley Donen and Gene Kelly were aware of the myriad ways that musical numbers can interact with and add meaning to a film's narrative and style. Over the course of *Singin' in the Rain*, Donen's and Kelly's design for the musical numbers covers the whole expanse of norms for connecting narrative to number. *Singin' in the Rain* is in many ways the epitome of the musical precisely because it incorporates the genre's many paradigms into its

34 STORYTELLING IN MOTION

form. The film's titular number includes both singing and dancing and moves from film diegesis (the fictional world) to musical number and back. What do these choices communicate to the viewer?

Many discussions of the musical describe the relationship of narrative to number as binary: narrative or number, integrated or nonintegrated, diegetic or nondiegetic. But the formal patterns of these films change over the course of the narrative as part of the inherent diegetic shifts between musical numbers and the surrounding narrative that the genre is known for, creating diegetic pluralities that challenge audience expectations and give filmmakers a complex cinematic environment for storytelling and experimentation. Sometimes musical moments also flutter toward and away from the stability of the diegesis to ease into the shift or resist the solidification of a full musical number, as I discuss in chapter 7.[25] Categorizing how the musical genre formally incorporates its essential elements of song and dance along spectra instead of firm binaries can show how filmmakers use song, dance, and the device of diegetic plurality to make meaning, revealing a historical plethora of stylistic norms and industrial practices. Categorizing these options also provides a tool for comparing how filmmakers have implemented the unique qualities of the musical genre throughout this book.

Two broad paradigms anchor these practices: function and diegetic plurality. By subdividing musical numbers (or larger sequences) into several formal subcategories, we can better understand the relationship between narrative and number or the existence of a diegetic shift that occurs as a result of a musical number. This allows for the assessment of individual sequences, but I don't intend these categories to serve as a prescriptive structure arguing for a particular inclusive or exclusive corpus of films. Instead, the result is a more refined tool to analyze musical numbers and compare content made in different national, historical, and industrial contexts or one-off numbers in otherwise nonmusical media.

Organizational Paradigms: Musical Functions

Musical numbers—and formal devices more generally—serve a variety of purposes in relation to a film's narrative. They can contribute causal information that becomes crucial to a full comprehension of the plot or the specific sequence of explicitly presented filmic material. They can also contribute more minor details to the full system of events suggested by the narrative,

FORMAL CONVENTIONS AND MUSICAL PRACTICES   35

either implicitly or explicitly, known as the story.[26] Four broad functions of film style—denotative (narrative), expressive, symbolic, and decorative (aesthetic)—allow for a more precise division of a number's function.[27]

Numbers serving a denotative or narrative purpose carry the most story-telling weight. These functions encompass all information that a stylistic device gives us about the fictional story world and characters' actions, motives, and background.[28] However, we can further subdivide this category into causal and informative narrative functions. Musical numbers that serve a causal narrative function are essential to a comprehension of the film's plot.[29] Hollywood film narratives are redundant to ensure viewer comprehension of the story, so numbers whose absence from the film would confuse the audience are rarer in this industry than numbers that serve an informative narrative function. The distinction between numbers that are causally essential to a comprehension of the narrative and numbers that contribute nonessential denotative information is important, however, and stresses the value of considering the number's role within the larger film narrative. Lina's reprise of "Singin' in the Rain" at the end of the film is an example of a number that functions in a causal manner through song. She agrees to "sing" after the film premiere to appease the audience, and R.F., Don, and Cosmo pull open the curtain to reveal Kathy singing for her, simultaneously ruining Lina's career, boosting Kathy's screen prospects, and repairing Kathy and Don's relationship. The "Dancing in the Dark" number from *The Band Wagon* (Vincente Minnelli, 1953) also contributes essential information to the film's plot as Fred Astaire and Cyd Charisse's characters learn to trust and dance with each another.[30] Cutting these examples out of their respective films would leave significant narrative gaps.

Numbers serving an informative narrative function, in contrast, communicate plot or character information but not in a way that would cause confusion if the number were removed from the film. Because of Hollywood's tendency to repeat key plot elements through various stylistic devices, these numbers are more common. "Would You?" from *Singin' in the Rain* shows Kathy recording the songs for Lina's character, Lina struggling to practice her lip syncing, and the successful results of the dubbing in *The Dancing Cavalier* as producer R.F. watches the dailies. In the "Barn Dance" number from *Seven Brides for Seven Brothers* (Stanley Donen, 1954), the escalating danced competition between the Pontipee brothers and their town rivals demonstrates their physical superiority and ends with the six townswomen choosing the former as their preferred partners. These examples function to communicate narrative information, but we understand this context from moments outside of the musical numbers as well.

Musical numbers serving an expressive function emphasize a character's emotion or set a particular tone more than they advance the plot or reveal specific plot and character details. The musical genre is closely associated with such numbers that occur because of an overflow of emotion. These moments redundantly characterize the emotional life of characters or establish a specific mood that relates to the narrative or setting.[31] Don's duet with Kathy in "You Were Meant for Me" on the sound stage provides him with the "proper setting" to express his affection through song. Similarly, Cosmo's "Good Morning" number, primarily through dance and movement, serves to cheer up Don. Expressive numbers can also suggest a more complex blend of emotions if the emotional content of the song and dance contradict one another. We can observe this in Don's recounting of his rise to success through a montage sequence that contrasts a vocal description of his dignified upbringing with the comic number he and Cosmo perform in a music hall. Similarly, in "How Lovely to Be a Woman" from *Bye Bye Birdie* (George Sidney, 1963), Kim expresses in song her joy to be growing into womanhood while changing into an increasingly childish outfit.

Numbers can represent information in more implicit ways through the use of symbolic functions to evoke more associative, general, or conceptual meanings. Often this function arises through more abstract sung and danced content. The danced sequences in musical numbers often referred to as dream ballets are rife with meaning obliquely expressed through movement. Gene Kelly's hoofer character falls for a femme fatale (Cyd Charisse) in *Singin' in the Rain*'s dream ballet and imagines the two of them engaging in a romantic duet in an even more abstracted space, only to have her reject his advances as he approaches. *Oklahoma!*'s (Fred Zinnemann, 1955) well-known dream ballet also symbolizes Laurie's anxieties over Jud and her love for Curly. In "Pick-a-Little, Talk-a-Little" from *The Music Man* (Morton DaCosta, 1962), the women's gossip is interspersed with a chorus that, through music and lyrical design, makes them sound like clucking hens, a meaning that is reinforced through their head movements and feathered hats (the sequence cuts to actual chickens as well to make absolutely sure we haven't missed the point).

Finally, musical numbers and the musical genre more generally are known for their aesthetic functions, emphasizing stylistic patterning and spectacle over narrative efficiency. *Singin' in the Rain*'s "Beautiful Girl Montage" showcases a feeling of excitement about the transition to sound and plays off the decorative flourishes associated with Busby Berkeley's musical numbers choreographed for Warner Bros. and MGM. The film's "Broadway Melody" dream ballet is also a self-contained, showstopping sequence. The "Triplets" number from *The Band Wagon* functions as a comic novelty number—the humor arising from the song's lyrics and the characters' performances—contributing perhaps to viewers' nightmares but not to their narrative comprehension.

For musical analysis, considering narrative (causal and informative) and aesthetic functions are particularly useful in articulating the different ways that musical numbers can serve the surrounding narrative and how filmmakers have historically prioritized certain relationships over others. It can be helpful to consider narrative and aesthetic functions as a sort of spectrum, paralleling Cohan's categories of integrated and aggregated musical form.[32] However, these categorizations merit some additional caveats. I find it important to consider both musical (sung and instrumental) and danced content in this discussion, even though this book's focus is on choreographed figure movement.[33] When both song and dance are present in a number, how they make meaning for the viewer through their juxtaposition becomes as important as their individual function(s), as the earlier example from *Bye Bye Birdie* demonstrates. And significantly, the variety of content in musical numbers can be more explicit or implicit in meaning, and articulating dance's relationship to this split, especially, is essential to a clearer understanding of how filmmakers have used choreographic content as an element of film style.

To illustrate this, we can take as an example the "Dancing in the Dark" number from *The Band Wagon*, which Mueller elevates to the highest level of narrative integration. The number serves an explicit causal function. Before the scene begins, Tony and Gabrielle are unsure if they will be able to match each other's dance styles; the tension has dissipated in subsequent scenes (and, more importantly to the overall plot, they have begun to fall in love). But understanding that the film demonstrates their movement and romantic compatibility through narratively integrated danced content requires processing the implicit meaning of the choreography. The previous scene has cued us to pay attention to their compatibility (or lack thereof) with Gabrielle's line "can you and I really dance together?," but there are no song lyrics to draw additional attention to that idea during the number itself. Take as a point of contrast Fred Astaire's duet with Ginger Rogers in *Shall We Dance* (Mark Sandrich, 1937) to "Let's Call the Whole Thing Off," in which

38 STORYTELLING IN MOTION

Ira Gershwin's lyrics explicitly lay out the stakes: "But oh! If we call the whole thing off / Then we must part / And oh! If we ever part / Then that might break my heart!" Whatever choreographic compatibility we observe in the danced duet is reinforced by the explicit meaning of the lyrics. We lack that explicit anchor in "Dancing in the Dark," or, at the very least, the line between explicit and implicit meaning recognition from the choreography becomes blurred. Viewers need to tap into a range of existing schemata, or learned frameworks, to correctly parse the central function of the number. Those trained in dance technique (or dance appreciation) will observe how the number deviates from the dance styles each character has previously embodied (ballet and tap-inflected hoofing) to a partner-based choreography that draws on both characters' (and actors') physical strengths. Mueller argues that the shift in the characters' relationship is "accomplished entirely in dance terms,"[34] but the fluid camerawork that parallels the performers' pacing as they travel through the space also reinforces this newfound coordination.

Viewers experienced in musical form will also apply those learned frameworks to correctly parse the generic convention of a duet between leads that successfully initiates or progresses their romantic relationship. To these viewers, the causal narrative function of dance in "Dancing in the Dark" will be explicit and obvious, but this is the result of learned schemata and a trained eye. An uninitiated viewer could just as easily miss the narrative significance of the content while still appreciating the aesthetically pleasing patterns of the choreography. As the examples above demonstrate, numbers can communicate these functions through song and music or through dance and staging, or both. Identifying and isolating when and how these various aspects of the numbers take the lead in driving the denotative or aesthetic role of a number allows for even greater analytical and historical specificity.

Numbers and the formal elements within them frequently serve multiple functions. While most will lean more heavily toward a denotative or aesthetic focus, the two are not mutually exclusive. Jacques Demy's *Les Demoiselles de Rochefort* (1967) takes the incorporation of musical numbers serving a decorative function to a new extreme, yet to categorize this use exclusively in relation to aesthetic excess misses the way those numbers also force the viewer to engage in a playful game of romantic compatibility between characters. Part of the pleasure of musical form is observing how numbers change and develop their relationships to the surrounding narrative. Notably, in examining how classical American musicals use musical numbers for narrative purposes, we can see that it is rare for these sequences to provide the only source of crucial narrative information, given Hollywood cinema's reliance on narrative redundancy. Considering the spectrum of functions numbers can serve is therefore beneficial in determining historical norms, auteur tendencies, and subgenres. The way musical numbers challenge the stylistic stability of the surrounding film form is equally consequential.

Pluralistic Paradigms: Musical Style

Most musical numbers go through a range of shifts in their relationship to intrinsic narrative and stylistic norms. These narrative and stylistic tensions are related, but separate, structures that shape the musical's form and how its musical numbers add filmic meaning. In addition to serving a variety of narrative or structural functions, these sequences shift their relationship to the diegesis by establishing new stylistic rules for their numbers, in essence creating diegetic plurality. Rick Altman describes this change as a move to a supradiegetic space,[35] whereas Martin Rubin evaluates numbers based on the relative "impossibility" of their content.[36] This creates what Steven Cohan describes as a "dual register, thereby breaking with the cinema's dominant codes of realism as a means of securing the unity of time and space for a film's fictive world or 'diegesis.' " The creation of multiple diegeses that build tensions between spectacle and story is a crucial aspect of this relationship,[37] one that creates as a result a "shifting and volatile dialectic between integrative and nonintegrative elements."[38] As I argue, however, analyzing diegetic plurality and the various forms that musical spaces can take is a stylistic concern even more than it is a narrative one.

What we observe when a musical number shifts, to the "supradiegetic" or a sense of "impossibility," is the film introducing a new range of stylistic norms that are in conflict with those previously established by the diegesis. The result is a plurality of diegetic space, in which the various stylistic rules of the diegesis may no longer accord with those of the space created by musical numbers. Moments of diegetic plurality are also usually visually or audibly noticeable, serving as ways to draw attention to the shifting registers and impacting how audiences make meaning from these sequences. Musical numbers can modify the spatiotemporal and acting performance norms that govern the film's diegesis in a variety of ways, and different aspects of the sequence can stay grounded in or move away from the diegesis simultaneously, creating concurrent, contradictory diegetic layers within the frame. In

40   STORYTELLING IN MOTION

categorizing musical numbers' stylistic relationships to the filmic diegesis, it is useful to subdivide the ways that a number can shift to a new set of aesthetic parameters. Such analysis could be divided ad infinitum, but for the purpose of discussing musical numbers, two large categories—spatiotemporal shifts and performative shifts—more clearly draw attention to subtle distinctions between musical content.[39] These elements—embodied primarily in the mise-en-scène, songs, and dances of musical numbers—provide musical filmmakers with many layers for diegetic experimentation.

Spatiotemporal Distinctions

The rules governing space and time of a musical film's environments can serve as a number's diegetic grounding, or these elements can expand the diegetic distance from previous stylistic norms. These changes can encompass adjustments or expansions to the setting in more or less overt ways and impact elements of both audio and visual style. Moreover, these spatiotemporal elements do not always shift together, allowing the environment to subtly react to the move to a musical number, or the mise-en-scène can change entirely, creating an entirely new diegetic space that severs ties to the original stylistic rules governing the narrative's story world.

Spatial shifts can be sonic or visual. Changes in sound quality during and leading into musical numbers—volume adjustments, the introduction of seemingly nondiegetic orchestral accompaniments, or a perceivable shift in "aural fidelity"[40] or texture—are common and more pervasive than visual spatial shifts. Such shifts occur in almost every musical sequence. In "You Were Meant for Me" from *Singin' in the Rain*, Don's visual enhancement of the setting he needs to express his love for Kathy is diegetically motivated, but the orchestral accompaniment to his song is not. Strictly speaking, the sonic additions we associate with musical numbers are the result of introducing extradiegetic music to existing diegetic norms, so it is worth articulating whether that change is also accompanied by additional, more subtle changes to existing diegetic elements.

Visually, elements of the mise-en-scène, cinematography, lighting, special effects, and editing techniques can contribute to this category to signal shifts between stylistic conventions. Whereas the visual shifts in "You Were Meant for Me" are playfully grounded in the diegesis as Don turns on the sound stage's equipment, Gene Kelly's character dances a duet with a superimposed, translucent version of himself in the "Alter Ego" dance sequence from *Cover Girl* (Charles Vidor, 1944). Smaller stylistic changes can occur, like a change

FORMAL CONVENTIONS AND MUSICAL PRACTICES   41

in lighting, added or subtracted set elements, or a moment of temporal elision through editing to create improbable set, costume, or staging changes. The latter is used on a larger scale in the musical montage "New York, New York" from *On the Town* (Stanley Donen and Gene Kelly, 1949); the editing technique reinforces the passage of time, but the sheer amount of sightseeing the sailors do is realistically implausible in the story time that passes. Similarly, halfway through the Nicholas Brothers' spectacular dance number in *Stormy Weather* (Andrew L. Stone, 1943), the mise-en-scène changes. The duo exits off-screen right and enters into another seemingly stage-bound but diegetically tenuous space that features the large staircase set they will jump down for their finale. After their bows the film cuts back to Cab Calloway cueing up the final number in the original club venue as if the secondary space never existed.

Numbers can also expand the diegetic space of a musical sequence by cutting to parallel, "impossible" spaces that pull the viewer as far as possible away from the conventions of the surrounding narrative. *Singin' in the Rain*'s "Broadway Melody" number moves through a number of spaces that exist in parallel to the diegesis, including one that exists within the hoofer's (Gene Kelly's) imagination, which creates an additional diegetic shift within the diegetic shift. This complete change in setting is closely associated with American dream ballet sequences but occurs in other musical forms as well, particularly in musical sequences from popular Indian cinema. Rubin refers to this kind of impossibility that frequently occurs in Busby Berkeley numbers as existing "on the level of effects," moments when "the numbers create configurations that are feasible only with a movie camera, on an editing table, or in a special effects lab, and that would be either impossible or incomprehensible on a theatrical stage."[41] However, because this sense of impossibility can exist elsewhere in the diegesis thanks to cinematic norms of editing and eliding moments of the plot that can be inferred by spectators, it is beneficial to notice if these moments differ in musical numbers from the surrounding narrative.

Temporal shifts primarily lead to a different rhythmic or durational organization of style and as such are frequently guided by auditory changes. Auditory and rhythmic shifts are more likely to occur at a higher frequency than spatial shifts over the course of a musical number. A shift of this category is also dependent on the motivations of the other two (spatial and performative); a change to rhythmic speech patterns or singing as part of a performance may be considered motivated by the surrounding plot, in which

42 STORYTELLING IN MOTION

case no diegetic plurality would occur. Often during musical numbers the sonic space is enhanced with the inclusion of a nondiegetic orchestra, but a number can also be grounded in the diegetic space by on-screen (diegetically motivated) singing or instruments. "Make 'Em Laugh" from *Singin' in the Rain* begins with Cosmo playing the piano, after which the nondiegetic orchestra takes over. This aspect of stylistic shifting in musical numbers is one of the most common—it occurs in all the examples listed above—and aligns with Altman's discussion of the audio dissolve.[42] The presence or disappearance in the soundtrack of sound effects is also important to note, since those auditory cues ground or distance the performers from their surrounding physical environment. Visual changes in time—like the slowing down or speeding up of the image—are rarer in musical numbers during the Hollywood studio era, but we can observe this use of temporal shifting in the dream sequence from *Yolanda and the Thief* (Vincente Minnelli, 1945), where Lucille Bremer's character moves in reverse to emphasize an unusual movement of the fabric that billows around her as she walks. *Singin' in the Rain* uses slow motion as the disastrous screening of *The Dueling Cavalier* moves out of synchronization, later inspiring Cosmo to suggest Kathy dub Lina's songs.

Performance Distinctions

The "body" portion of the space-time-body division is separated from spatiotemporal examinations because of the genre's emphasis on performance, especially star performance.[43] Many of the shifts in musical numbers take place at the level of individual characters. I base this category's subdivisions on generally observed musical trends, but additional significant groupings or schemata will certainly emerge over time as the genre evolves. Shifts of performance encompass both singing (or music-based performances more generally) and dancing, as both are tied to a specific character/actor. These shifts can also happen at an individual or collective (ensemble) level. When such a performative shift occurs, it is usually not a question of "impossibility" in the way that Rubin uses the term to describe a musical number's space. The actor is usually performing the movement or song without the help of special effects or other cinematic techniques,[44] so it is more beneficial to consider the improbability of whether the performance can be motivated within the diegetic context. Films can create hybrid bodies through vocal or body doubles, but the intent is generally to create a unified character, rather than emphasize the blend.[45] *Singin' in the Rain* mirrors its own fictional

FORMAL CONVENTIONS AND MUSICAL PRACTICES 43

dubbing process, with Jean Hagen using her own voice for the moments when Kathy is supposed to be dubbing Lina's speech, while ghost singer Betty Noyes rather than Debbie Reynolds provides the sung voice for Lina's character.[46] Similarly, dancing stars like Cyd Charisse and Vera-Ellen were routinely dubbed for the singing parts of their studio-era roles without the film's credits reflecting that performative hybridization. Hollywood performers or the production's choreographic assistants recording each other's taps in post-production was common practice as well. Since part of the appeal of the musical is to draw attention to the virtuosity of performances, the act of dubbing has been frowned on at various points in the genre's history, but one could argue that substituting different voices and bodies in the musical numbers—as we see with Hagen, Reynolds, and Noyes's vocal performances in *Singin' in the Rain*—is the ultimate diegetic shift.[47]

Even more so than an evaluation of spatiotemporal shifts, decisions of whether there is a performative shift must be based on narrative cues and compositional motivations. Could the performer(s) in question sing or dance in this way as part of the narrative diegesis? If not, we should consider their performance as motivating a diegetic shift, and this determination may differ in part from the schemata individuals draw upon. Part of this inferential process comes from the referential knowledge of the viewer. In the backstage musical, there is a compositional motivation for people to burst into song and dance on stage; it is their profession. When Kathy and the other hired performers sing and dance "All I Do Is Dream of You" at R.F.'s party, there is not a performative shift within the context of the film because we know they have rehearsed and practiced the number (the source of their musical accompaniment remains less clear). While there is still a change in vocal and physical qualities, such performances remain grounded in the stylistic norms of the diegesis because that is what we expect performers to do. Once such a performance moves into improbable territory, however, diegetic plurality can occur. The gangsters' performance of "Brush Up Your Shakespeare" from *Kiss Me Kate* (George Sidney, 1953) creates a performative shift as it occurs off-stage, and their increasingly polished number is implausible given their profession and earlier ineptitude on stage. Professional performers suddenly singing and dancing to a number they have never heard before or performed long ago—"Wunderbar" from *Kiss Me Kate*, for example—is somewhat motivated by their background but still provides a subtle shift in the norms of the diegesis.

We can consider the performers and musicians (or "extras" in the space) as well. The boundary between the distinction of performative and

44   STORYTELLING IN MOTION

nonperformative space can be permeable, depending on whether or not the musicians' performance is foregrounded in the number. In the former instance, the musicians add to the spatial atmosphere without standing out individually, and therefore it makes sense to discuss them as part of the space. In the latter, the musicians stand out or contain shifts separate from the space that contains them, making it appropriate, in that case, to analyze them as engaging in a collective performative shift. We see Cosmo and the orchestra underscoring Don's singing of "You Are My Lucky Star" to Kathy in the final moments of the film, Cosmo's directing of the musicians supplying some diegetic motivation while the ambiguity of how they know the tune muddies any clear diegetic grounding.

Four additional subcategories help to organize the shifts that can occur in musical numbers. Performance shifts occur at the individual or group level and can be split according to singing (vocal shifts) and dancing (corporeal shifts). Individual performative shifts frequently occur because a character is alone in a space. But occasionally characters' performances will shift an aspect of the diegesis while observers' actions remain diegetically motivated, as we see in *Singin' in the Rain*'s "Moses Supposes," when Don's vocal coach watches Don and Cosmo's performance and is used by the duo as a reluctant prop for their big finale. In contrast, by the end of "Ya Got Trouble" from *The Music Man*, Harold Hill has drawn the whole crowd into a diegetic shift and collective panic by convincing them of the disreputable potentials of a pool table. Group performance shifts can similarly occur with or without a change in the main characters. The former is more common in Hollywood musicals, as the example from *The Music Man* demonstrates. Instances do exist of a collective shift occurring with the exclusion of a character; we can observe this in "You Did It" from *My Fair Lady* (George Cukor, 1964), where Eliza's exclusion from the collective group shift emphasizes her separation from Henry Higgins's aristocratic environment.

A performative shift can occur through singing (an auditory shift) or choreographed figure movement (a corporeal shift), though the two frequently occur with some level of overlap. Auditory and corporeal shifts can also be immediate or progressive. Speaking can become rhythmic before it becomes song, but that change is relatively immediate. By contrast, figure movement can flow almost seamlessly from organized pedestrian movements, which provides additional grounding to the diegesis, to simple staged choreography into more complex danced content, which solidifies a shift to diegetic plurality. Cosmo moves in and out of increasingly complex

FORMAL CONVENTIONS AND MUSICAL PRACTICES   45

choreography in "Make 'Em Laugh," and such distinctions draw attention to the subtle and embellished uses of shifting diegetic movement in films like *Les Demoiselles de Rochefort, Jeanne et le garçon formidable,* and *La La Land.*

Diegetic Complements and Contradictions

Musical numbers can also blend stylistic changes in ways that add additional layers of complexity or ambiguity. Reflexive musical content, in which characters openly acknowledge their participation in a musical number, throws the whole diegetic system off-kilter, assuming we commit ourselves to determining numbers' diegetic plurality based on the intrinsic stylistic and narrative norms set by the surrounding narrative. Even if a number exhibits signs of diegetic shifts—the introduction of nondiegetic music, the shift from talking and walking to singing and dancing—when the number also acknowledges itself as such, should we not then posit the diegesis of the narrative as one in which explicitly established forms of musical content can be diegetically motivated? *Singin' in the Rain* dips a toe into such territory with its titular number, in which the lyrics Gene Kelly sings point to the heightened diegetic activity he engages in during the number. The film does not go so far as to explicitly acknowledge the number as such, however, and Don's actions are ultimately motivated as the manic manifestations of being madly in love. More recent musicals, in particular those made as television series, exaggerate this approach. *Galavant* (ABC, 2015–2016) plays extensively with the narrative premise that its characters are sometimes aware of their participation in musical numbers and the televised medium more generally. In the first episode of the second season, aptly named "A New Season aka Suck It Cancellation Bear," the opening showstopper has the characters openly acknowledge, among other things, the need for a new theme song— "it's a new season so we won't be reprisin' that tune"— and their amazement at the show's renewal for a second season—"give in to the miracle that no one thought we'd get." While this number takes such reflexivity to a new extreme, it is but one of many examples from the series in which musical numbers are acknowledged as such.

A musical number's function can affect the diegetic status of a number as well. These two categories—the multiple functions of a number and the varied ways a number can create diegetic plurality through shifting stylistic norms—should not be seen simply as independent entities but rather as mutually influencing one another. Jeff Smith sees the "liminal space" between nondiegetic and diegetic music as a point to fruitfully analyze music's role in

46   STORYTELLING IN MOTION

cinematic storytelling.[48] He discusses these moments in relation to Robynn Stilwell's theory of the "fantastical gap," but argues that such moments of sonic ambiguity take on "more saliency in ... connection with what [Claudia] Gorbman calls *metadiegetic* music—music that is narrated or imagined by a particular character within a film."[49] Similarly, subtle stylistic shifts in musical numbers can lead to inferences about the denotative or expressive function of a number in relation to the surrounding story and its characters.

Numbers can create diegetic plurality by circumstance (the setting is unusual for bursting into song or dance, for example) but also can be pluralistic by content. They can lack a clearly defined performative or spatiotemporal shift but still evoke a sense of implausibility through the number's content or effect on the plot. Sometimes diegetically motivated numbers—stage-bound performances, for example—contain content (lyrics, dancing, movement, or interactions) that would otherwise appear unmotivated or implausible. A number that is diegetically motivated by a character's subjectivity—often cued by editing (dis)continuity conventions like cross-fades or ambiguous point-of-view shots—could be considered as creating a more subtle diegetic shift than one that cannot be as easily justified as existing within a character's mind. Considering each larger category in relation to the other is especially useful when analyzing the status of stage-bound numbers that do not seem to include any spatiotemporal shifts but whose content strongly parallels the larger concerns of the story. When Kathy sings "Singin' in the Rain" on stage after the film premiere, her performance is seemingly diegetically motivated; she/Lina tells the band the name of the number and the key to perform it in and Lina also seems to know the words that she pretends to sing along to. But there is a hint of implausibility here, given that Don has previously performed the number at a diegetically heightened level. Identifying moments of diegetic shifts that result from plot-related implausibilities in addition to performative or spatiotemporal shifts allows for an additional level of analytical nuance.

As this final example demonstrates, musical numbers create meaning through their relationship to the plot but also through their relationship to one another, often in ways that can contradict their earlier diegetic status or add narrative ambiguity. What they communicate through lyrics or figure movement contributes to our understanding of their function, but how they move through song and dance is just as significant. The implicit levels with which numbers use this kind of diegetic nuance to make meaning also emphasizes that viewers' knowledge structures and expectations will significantly impact where they focus their attention. A hypothetical audience member who daydreams during a number because they perceive it to be a "showstopper," and therefore insignificant to the plot, will come away with a different interpretation of the film than their neighbor who is focused on how the dancing styles of the duet partners are revealing their artistic incompatibility, cueing them to anticipate the later conflict that their neighbor views as unmotivated. Subdividing the form of these shifts emphasizes that numbers can be more or less motivated by the diegesis and the film's narrative; studying diegetic plurality allows us to catalog changing norms and audience expectations.

Dancing with the Frame: The Meaningful Plurality of "Singin' in the Rain"

These categorizations provide us with precise ways to consider the formal relationships musical numbers—or other cinematic sequences—can build with the film that houses them. Gene Kelly and Stanley Donen were aware of the range of ways to stage musical numbers to fulfill various functions and effects, and they had the infrastructural means to do so with few material limitations. So where does "Singin' in the Rain" fit within these categorizations, and how does the number create meaning through its cinematic choreography?

Stylistically, the number creates clear performative shifts on the individual level, as Don's singing and dancing moves his performance to an implausible diegetic space in relation to the rhythmic temporal shifts of the extradiegetic orchestral music. This is countered with aspects of spatial and performative diegetic grounding. The number includes no spatial shifts; we continue to hear Don's feet and the sounds of his body interacting in the space,[50] and the policeman whose presence ends the number remains obstinately opposed to a performative shift, refusing to engage in the fantastical nature of Don's physical release.

Functionally speaking, the number's relationship to the narrative is more complex. "Singin' in the Rain" epitomizes the genre by serving an expressive function and giving us access to a diegetically heightened, emotional expression of Don's joy. However, it is the dancing that communicates this information to us, not the singing. Freed and Brown's lyrics are loosely connected to the situation—"singin' and dancin'[51] in the rain," "I'm happy again"—and

48 STORYTELLING IN MOTION

broadly point to the emotional resonance of the number, as do Kelly's sung performance and the slower tempo. But they do not cue us to recognize the emotional nuances of Don's character in this moment. If the choreography were different, the number would function more as a decorative number than an expressive one. And it does just that in both *The Hollywood Revue* (Charles Reisner, 1929) and *Little Nellie Kelly* (Norman Taurog, 1940), two earlier MGM films in which the Freed/Brown song appears. Both versions are motivated as stage performances, with simple staging, that serve a predominantly aesthetic function. The musical arrangement emphasizes the difference of tone in the 1952 version, but it is Kelly's movement that drives the shift in function. The filmmakers' changes to the "Singin' in the Rain" musical number from earlier filmic iterations determined the sequence's stylistic and narrative relationship to the film plot and shows the ways that song and dance can fulfill complementary functions.

"Singin' in the Rain" provides redundant cues to pay attention to Kelly's dancing so not to miss the expressive salience of the choreography, but we can see how ignoring the movement in favor of the singing could lead some viewers to process the number differently. The meaning gleaned from the dancing in "Singin' in the Rain" is also more implicit, so what knowledge structures are leading us to understand Kelly's figure movement as a tool for formal comprehension?

Kelly's solo number shows Don shifting farther away from the diegesis as he and the camera move down the street, into dance and a deeper understanding of his emotions. The spatial environment around him remains diegetically grounded, though meticulously crafted by MGM's set designers to appear that way. Discussions of "Singin' in the Rain" emphasize the camera's expressive contributions to our understanding of Don's emotional journey and the stylistic parallels between the mobile camera and figure. Most focus on the latter half of the number, when a crane shot captures Kelly dancing in the street set. In this moment the camera "sweeps exhilaratingly back up" during the "emotional and musical climax of the dance";[52] "when the camera [does] a sudden leap into the air . . . it [matches] the joyous energy of Kelly's character."[53] The flamboyance of this shot makes it stand out, but earlier moments of cinematic choreography set up the meaningfulness of this ostentatious moment.

Throughout the first half of the number, Harold Rosson's cinematography employs a follow shot aesthetic that sets up a predictable pattern. The camera primarily keeps Kelly centered in the frame and matches his tempo,

FORMAL CONVENTIONS AND MUSICAL PRACTICES 49

paralleling his increasing quickness, for example, as he jumps onto the lamp post or begins to dance in circles in front of the drug store's cigarette girl ad.[54] It's worth noting, however, that the camera is not in constant parallel with the performer. The mobile frame also adjusts the shot scale distance from Kelly's figure, notably craning up and back as Don turns the corner to anticipate his aforementioned upward leap. The camera also does not match every lateral movement in the dance; when Kelly repeats side-to-side weight shifts as he extends a leg and swings his umbrella in front of the drug store, the camera does not also make slight lateral adjustments. It is not the norm for *Singin' in the Rain*'s cinematography to match these kinds of little choreographic moments; instead, we can observe follow shots that holistically parallel the figure movement. A more invisible aesthetic focuses viewer attention on the choreography and allows the more flamboyant moments to stand out as stylistically or narratively significant. Each shot before that famous crane shot also follows the same reframing pattern, beginning with Kelly in a long shot and roughly keeping him in frame center as he dances before pushing in to a closer framing as his choreography decreases in range of motion or he pauses in a pose (on the lamp, to remove his hat, to soak his head under the rain spout).

These stylistic choices are doing a lot of work. Using follow shots reinforces center bias[55] to remind viewers what is most narratively significant (Kelly's character). There are relatively few other elements of stimulus in the frame, but Kelly's grey costume and dark umbrella do not contrast much with the dark street he dances on. Pushing in frequently to medium and medium-close up framings minimizes the potential visual distractions presented by the bright and more colorful shop windows of the set. This also draws attention to Kelly's smiling face, which reinforces Don's emotional state as well as Kelly's star status. Many of these subtle camera movements are also more minutely matching Kelly's movement than the bigger crane shot; in that moment the camera does not surge vertically in parallel to Kelly's jump into the street, and as he circles back to the sidewalk the more extreme long shot framing means that the camera needs to reframe left only slightly to keep him centered in frame. The camera's height from the crane shot is more dynamic, but the intensity comes more from the shift in orchestration and Kelly's locomotion through the space.

The camera's movement doesn't encapsulate the expressive range Don moves through that demonstrates how caught up he is in his love for Kathy; that meaning comes from the figure movement itself. Accounts of

50 STORYTELLING IN MOTION

this moment agree that the number expresses "an unabashed declaration of joy"[56] and "the hero's euphoric responses to falling in love."[57] Kelly himself also emphasized the "thesis" of the number as becoming "happier and happier as you dance."[58] However, this number does not just show us a man in love, which it does redundantly throughout the sequence. It serves to indicate a key shift in Don's character as well. Kelly points to this moment in his discussion of the number: "Finally you revert to childish humor where you're stamping in the puddles and getting yourself soaked and wet, and *you just don't give a hoot about anything* [emphasis mine]."[59] As Don stomps in the puddles, his movements shift to an inner focus that dynamically intensifies.[60] Throughout the number Kelly moves with a feeling of increasing strength and a nimble control over timing,[61] which are common to his movement baseline and choreographic aesthetic. A strong awareness of the environment around him is also key to his character in *Singin' in the Rain*;[62] Don cares about what people think of him. We see him striking clear shapes throughout his "Singin' in the Rain" dance, like his pose on the lamp post, but he also engages with the various pedestrians who cross his path as he dances, changing his facing and waving to acknowledge them.

This outer awareness diminishes as Don plays in the puddles. His movement dynamics[63] favor a greater control and restraint throughout the film,[64] but as his movements intensify and he jumps in the street, we see a greater engagement with a fluid, ongoing quality instead.[65] When he dances in circles through the street in the previous shot, his movements are large but bound; his extended arms hold the umbrella with control, creating smooth pathways through the space. As he splashes in the puddles, we can observe more little reverberations through his arms and torso that cause the umbrella to bob and shake. Most significantly, gone are the clean shapes and outer focus of the earlier choreography;[66] here a deliberate messiness takes over as Don attempts to splash the water as far as he can.[67] His reengagement with those qualities comes as he recognizes the policeman's presence and regains his composure.[68] That Don relinquishes this control at all is significant, given the importance of "dignity" and sophistication in the construction of his diegetic star persona but also in their impact on his relationships with other characters throughout the film. While the cumulative aesthetic highpoint of the number may occur in the previous shot as the camera cranes up on Don's spinning body, the narrative payoff comes as the number concludes, emphasizing to the viewer not that he is in love but rather the profound effect falling in love has had on his personal and professional priorities.

Conclusions

Gene Kelly and Stanley Donen were aware of the advantages of these varied methods and incorporated all these norms of practice in shaping the musical numbers for *Singin' in the Rain*. Considering the context of "Singin' in the Rain" from the methodological prism I propose in this book deepens our understanding of its various functions. The number owes its existence to the Freed/Brown song that appeared in earlier MGM musicals and to producer Arthur Freed's desire to showcase his earlier song work in a new musical product. Director-choreographers Kelly and Donen were able to achieve their stylistic choices thanks to their privileged standing in MGM's Freed unit, which afforded access to elevated budgets, studio equipment and lots, and a trained team of always-working below-the-line personnel and performers. This gave Kelly extraordinary control in directing and choreographing the film's titular number, down to the placement and size of the rain puddles he jumps in as the number ends.

As a result, broadly considering the narrative and stylistic choices in presenting music, song, and dance within a film's structure—ranges of narrative and stylistic integration—allows for more subtle distinctions and draws attention to the parameters and norms of musical practice encompassed by the classical studio period and thoroughly represented in *Singin' in the Rain*. Numbers can shift away from the conventions of the diegesis for the sake of both narrative and spectacle, to fulfill both denotative and decorative functions. Many also include a shift from the rules of the diegesis to a new set of stylistic norms, creating a coexistence of diegeses or diegetic plurality. These concepts lay the foundation for a broader approach to the diegetic status of musical numbers, in which these sequences embody stylistic rules that depend less on realistic motivation than the surrounding narrative's norms.

This problem-solution approach to studying stylistic history sheds light on the factors that filmmakers prioritized based on the resources available to them. Using genre theory frameworks to subtly dissect "Singin' in the Rain" according to its relationship to the film's form reveals that the dancing, not the singing, is the more significant player in communicating the narrative relevance of the number. Despite the historical legacy of the song's melody and lyrics, in addition to the iconic image of a rain-soaked, umbrella-wielding Kelly suspended on a lamp post, it is the choreography of Kelly's movement that conveys the layers of narrative meaning and character development.

52 STORYTELLING IN MOTION

The dancing, more than the singing, is what allows the viewer to link this number to the film's narrative threads as Don leaves Kathy's home on a rainy morning. Connecting and mobilizing these approaches enriches our understanding of why *Singin' in the Rain* and its titular number continue to serve as case studies for musical scholars. But while *Singin' in the Rain* was made in ideal conditions for the musical genre, this was not the case for most of the musicals discussed in this book. The film production drew on standards of practice that subsequent films struggled to match as industrial conditions, cultural practices, and audience expectations shifted.

2

Seeing Movement in Cinema

An Introduction to Laban Movement Analysis

Figure 2.1 Title screen and analytical sample from the "Seeing Movement in Cinema" videographic chapter. Video duration: 15 minutes. Images courtesy of the author.

The videographic essay accompanying this written statement can be found on this book's companion website: www.oup.com/us/storytellinginmotion.

This chapter draws on examples from classical Hollywood musicals to introduce viewers to the movement taxonomy from Laban/Bartenieff Movement Studies (LMBS).[1] Laban Movement Analysis (LMA) provides this book's foundation for thorough, pattern-based micro and macro analysis of the expressivity of human movement.[2] As a result, it articulates how LMA provides a descriptive-analytical language toolkit to systematically tackle the complexity of human movement, allowing viewers to better understand how this taxonomic framework supports the research findings throughout the book. This explanatory videographic chapter gives the viewer an overview of the four core categories from LMA: Body, Effort, Space, and Shape.[3] It isolates elements for those unfamiliar with the movement system and

Storytelling in Motion. Jenny Oyallon-Koloski, Oxford University Press. © Oxford University Press 2024.
DOI: 10.1093/oso/9780197602669.003.0003

54 STORYTELLING IN MOTION

provides examples of how aspects of figure movement manifest in combination to create layers of meaning.

Rudolf Laban, who pioneered this movement system, initially divided his observations of movement into two large categories, one more quantitative (Space) and one more qualitative (Effort). Space considers the changing shape of the Kinesphere, or "the space within the reach of the body."[4] This category describes the directions and dimensions through which the body moves away from and toward the body center, determining where the body is in relation to the environment. Effort, in contrast, considers the abstract, expressive space of the Dynamosphere, providing language to explain the qualities with which we move this way or that, with hints at the psychological motivations for our choices.[5] Much of Laban's work in Effort and what he called Space Harmony—which maps expressive elements of the Dynamosphere onto physical directions in the Kinesphere—aims to explain the (albeit unconscious) psychological motivations behind every movement. The study of these areas together describes what Laban called "the connection between outer movement [Space] and the mover's inner attitude [Effort]."[6] Two more categories complete the current LBMS approach. Body encompasses a wide range of anatomical and neuromuscular considerations, determining what parts of the body are moving and in what sequence.[7] Shape considers in a more qualitative way how the body is relating to its environment, focusing in particular on the shifts between an inner focus on self and an outer focus on the world around us.

Chapter 2 moves through an explanation of the more quantitative categories first (Body and Space) and the more qualitative categories second (Effort and Shape), culminating in examples of how these categories interact in the meaning-making process. Much of the LBMS work can accordingly provide low-level, referential descriptions of the movement in question. The Basic Body Actions from the Body category, for example, can help the analyst articulate the difference between a jump (Leap) and a weight shift (Change of Support) in a dance phrase, whereas the Effort category's various Effort factors can draw attention to one performer's frequent use of more constricted movements, like Bound Flow Effort, versus another's preference for greater fluidity, or Free Flow Effort. Analyzing movement by applying these descriptors at scale can allow for detailed identification of formal movement patterns but does not convey higher-level semantic meaning. However, LMBS also aims to provide the trained analyst with a framework to determine the more implicit meaning behind a person's movement and understand what that outer movement communicates about a person's inner emotional life.

Many of these determinations align with the four broader themes that permeate the system: whether the movement is more Functional or Expressive, if the mover is in a pattern of Exertion or Recuperation, how relatively Mobile or Stable they are, and whether their focus is turned more inward (Inner) or focused on their relationship to the environment (Outer). LBMS's frameworks also offer ways to observe and describe how a camera's movement qualities can operate in parallel with or in opposition to the movements of the bodies it is framing. We cannot simply apply LBMS principles to the moving camera and call it a day; Laban's taxonomy applies to the human body, not a mechanical object, which will have an inherently different range of motion, as chapter 9 discusses.[8] These higher-level frameworks must of course be taken with a grain of salt; no system can comprehensively apply semantic meaning to an isolated movement. Like any analysis of form, context is crucial. However, LBMS's movement taxonomy can be a powerful tool in illuminating the storytelling significance of movement on screen, especially when paired with an understanding of the historical/cultural mechanisms, genre conventions, and cinematic formal structures that affected filmmakers' choreographic choices.

3

Agency, Control, and Space

West Side Story (1961)

West Side Story (1961) redefined the visual language of musical cinema. In telling its adaptation of William Shakespeare's *Romeo and Juliet* through dance, the cinematic choreography provides narrative nuances that build up the tragic tensions between the clashing Sharks and Jets. *West Side Story* marks a few important departures from Hollywood musical norms in its centering of narratively integrated ensemble numbers and increased editing pace. Yet the film also benefited from holdovers of the studio system's fraying infrastructure, most notable in the filmmakers' ability to hire triple-threat talent to play the rival gang members and the choice to hire predominantly white actors to play the Puerto Rican Sharks instead of adopting more inclusive hiring practices. As a result, *West Side Story*'s stylistic significance is in constant tension with its legacy as a pivotal and problematic emblem of Latinx/o/a representation in Hollywood cinema.

The original stage version of *West Side Story* opened on Broadway in 1957, praised in part because of the smooth coordination between the narrative, the musical score, and the choreography. This resulted from a collaborative effort among several artists. Jerome Robbins directed the play and choreographed the dancing, Arthur Laurents wrote the script, Leonard Bernstein composed the score, and Stephen Sondheim wrote the song lyrics. The men developed the elements of the play concurrently and sought to make the components of the story weave together in a natural and coherent way. Film codirectors Robert Wise and Jerome Robbins were clear in their preproduction correspondence that the approach to adapting *West Side Story* from stage to screen would be central to its ultimate success or failure. The issue of how to transpose the story and the choreography caused Robbins great concern during the film's preproduction period. An excerpt from a worried, multiple-page memo to Wise shows that the stylistic portrayal of *West Side Story*— particularly the musical numbers—was a central concern in both media:

Storytelling in Motion. Jenny Oyallon-Koloski, Oxford University Press. © Oxford University Press 2024.
DOI: 10.1093/oso/9780197602669.003.0004

The stage play was special because of its theatrical technique (or style) in telling its story. Its score, book and dances arose from that style rather than made it. Separated from the show, the score, book and dances are great, and we own them. But we haven't yet found a creative film style to justify them . . . a style which will allow them to arise logically out of the web and texture of the total film.[1]

Although Robbins did not have much filmmaking experience before working on *West Side Story*,[2] he was aware that the new medium would require approaching the play's material differently, and his extensive writing on the subject emphasizes that he found the prevalent norms for filming and staging dance in Hollywood unsatisfactory. His insistence on finding a "creative film style" at the expense of a careful management of financial resources also meant that *West Side Story* was his last contribution to a film project.[3] Yet the production's ultimate success in reinventing film musical norms emphasizes the variety of solutions available to filmmakers grappling with the problem of how to use cinematic choreography as a central narrative element.

Musical numbers exist on a spectrum between narrative centrality and decorative excess. Jerome Delamater suggests that narrative and stylistic integration in musicals is of paramount importance,[4] what Rick Altman describes as a "reduction of distance between narrative and number . . . to the point where the song and dance numbers *are* narrative."[5] For Delamater, musical integration is not just about the advancement of narrative through sung and danced content but also "an integration of the entire cinematic process."[6] Despite this assertion, he sees the dancing in *West Side Story* as "relegated almost exclusively to a supporting role;"[7] by this assessment the production failed in its ultimate goal. By contrast, this chapter argues that the cinematic choreography in Robbins's and Wise's film is nothing short of essential to its narrative and stylistic design.

Robbins's choreography communicates to the audience how similar yet different the Sharks and Jets are to each other in the way that they struggle to control their unwillingly shared environments and yearn for a space of their own. We can most clearly see how *West Side Story* uses cinematic choreography to advance its formal goals by closely examining the first and ultimate danced numbers: the film's prologue, which establishes the tensions between the Sharks and Jets, and "Cool," in which in the Jets grapple internally with Riff's death and the consequences of their actions. *West Side*

58   STORYTELLING IN MOTION

Story's plot doesn't show an equivalent scene of community among the Sharks after Bernardo's death; instead, scenes after the fateful rumble follow Anita, Maria, and Chino's individual actions. Their major danced ensemble number, "America," occurs earlier in the plot, emphasizing playful sexual tension between the girls (led by Anita) and the boys (led by Bernardo) to further align the viewer with the characters but with lower stakes for the central tensions of the narrative. The prologue and "Cool," by contrast, are of paramount importance to our narrative comprehension. They are ensemble numbers by design, emphasizing the individual members of the Jets and the Sharks as parts of a greater whole and reinforcing the ways the Jets' social and cultural power in the narrative is reflected in the formal centrality of their dancing.

New Styles, Old Practices (Production History)

From the get-go, *West Side Story*'s filmmakers wanted to do things differently. Director Robert Wise, new to making musicals, was happy to work further away from the major studios' constraints by partnering with the independent Mirisch Corporation and Seven Arts Productions after United Artists acquired the rights to the stage play.[8] Jerome Robbins insisted on codirecting as well as choreographing to better shape the material's translation to a new artistic form. To some, including *West Side Story*'s producers, Jerome Robbins's involvement as a codirector was a liability.[9] From a financial standpoint, this is a fair assessment. With a final production budget of $6.75 million, *West Side Story* set new records for musical budgeting in part because of Robbins's insistence on meticulous shooting schedules, extensive rehearsals, numerous takes, and a regular review of the dailies. These practices led to the production running almost $2 million over budget and the Mirisch brothers dismissing him from the project partway through production.[10] Robbins miscalculated the professional risks of overshooting with what Harold Mirisch described as "*fantastically expensive*" 70mm film (emphasis in the original),[11] effectively ending his Hollywood career before it truly began. Yet his close involvement was crucial to shaping the film's cinematic choreography and the ways that dance drives the film's narrative.

Robbins's and Wise's preproduction correspondence emphasizes how they wanted to reinvent the approach to musical form and move away from the conventional practices of studio-era Hollywood. Stylistically, *West Side*

AGENCY, CONTROL, AND SPACE 59

Story achieves this through a faster editing pace, a greater emphasis on ensemble numbers to drive the narrative, and a rethinking of the narrative functions musical sequences can provide. Yet some studio-era practices, like the casting of white actors to play characters representing more diverse races and ethnicities, remain unchanged and even unquestioned. The film's producers were also able to craft new approaches to cinematic storytelling through innovative applications of anamorphic widescreen and screen performance thanks to the industrial vestiges of the studio system that had for decades committed resources, personnel, and institutional memory to the musical genre.

Stylistic Solutions

Preproduction memos between Robbins and Wise indicate that the two directors—Robbins especially—were concerned about the cinematic treatment of the material. Robbins hoped to find an aesthetic that would deviate from existing norms. This is less, it seems, because of a desire to do something different for the sake of doing something different and more because what Robbins saw of Hollywood musicals did not reflect his vision for the film, its treatment of dance and movement especially.

Part of this discussion dealt with, as Robbins put it, "the basic problem of filming 'West Side Story.'" Robbins stressed repeatedly to Wise in correspondence that they must find a "new set of conventions, *inherently cinematic*" (emphasis in the text) to portray the "organic unity" of the various elements involved. What he stressed to Wise about what he saw as cinematic conventions, however, is that "it is necessary that we all go way past the factual and realistic documentation that is usually associated with film techniques."[12] In his reply to Robbins, Wise agreed with this, quoting himself from a memo he had sent to producer Harold Mirisch:

> [*West Side Story*] uses most effectively music, songs, highly stylized dancing and lyrical and theatrical treatment to tell its story. But against real New York streets, playgrounds and other completely realistic locations, the very unreality of parts of "West Side Story" becomes something that needs very special handling in order that it not be embarrassing to watch. It simply cannot be done in a purely documentary fashion. We have to find a photographic and cinematic treatment that will act as a catalyst between

60   STORYTELLING IN MOTION

the unreal and the real and create the special world in which "West Side Story" takes place.[13]

In the longer memo shared with Robbins, Wise clearly wants to distinguish *West Side Story*'s treatment from contemporaneous theatrical adaptations like *Porgy and Bess* (Otto Preminger, 1959) and *Can-Can* (Walter Lang, 1960), which he refers to as "standard screen numbers."[14] One trend that Wise likely wanted to distance his production from was the norm of long-take sequences in musicals of this period.[15] *Porgy and Bess* has several numbers, like "Summertime" and "It Ain't Necessarily So," in which shots average fifty seconds or longer. The film relies on an even larger ensemble cast than *West Side Story*, and the two numbers mentioned are filmed with wider shots, favoring, for the most part, long or extreme-long shots. *Can-Can*'s numbers, in general, have lower average shot lengths, and the final can-can scene is even more rapidly edited. Two of the large dance set pieces, however—the "Apache Dance" and the "Garden of Eden" numbers—have average shot lengths of thirty-six and fifty-three seconds, respectively, and most numbers show performers in long and extreme-long shots. *West Side Story*, by contrast, has an average shot rate of fourteen seconds for its musical numbers with an average of twenty-three seconds for "Maria," the number with the slowest editing pace.

Both *Porgy and Bess* and *Can-Can* were choreographed by Hermes Pan, who was quite vocal in interviews about his avoidance of quick cutting, insert shots, and numerous camera set-ups, expressing his distaste for "an excessive amount of cutting during a dance routine."[16] The interview was specifically about Pan's experience with the new Todd-AO technology (which he also worked with in *Porgy and Bess*), but Pan's preference was present before the industry transition to widescreen in the 1950s and was one that he shared with his long-time collaborator Fred Astaire. Wise and Robbins's reference to a "documentary" style may refer to a more neutral use of the camera evoked by Astaire's films and Pan's choreography, a style that was the norm for filming prestige musical productions by the late 1950s.

Robbins and Wise also agreed that they also wanted to avoid an "arty" approach to filmmaking, a word that in their correspondence both used with clear distaste. In his memo, Wise writes, "I'm sure you'll agree that our 'approach' wants to be creative and imaginative but not necessarily slow and obviously 'arty,'" adding that screen productions demand a "heightened tempo," or pacing.[17] Robbins vehemently agreed in a reply: "*I don't want anything artsy or slow or phoney*" [emphasis in original].[18] Given that the films Wise references were also Broadway adaptations, it seems likely that he disagreed with the creative decisions made in their translation to film. Both filmmakers' correspondence puts emphasis on narrative clarity and coherence over stylistic experimentation but not at the expense of aesthetic value. Most musical numbers inherently vary the spatiotemporal norms of the filmic diegesis, but this variation also commonly adheres to a set of normative stylistic practices, practices that Robbins and Wise wanted to revise without abandoning completely.

What we see in *West Side Story* is neither an attempt at a transparent filmic rendering of Robbins's choreography nor a completely experimental approach to filmmaking. The film's opening prologue number has an average editing pace of just under six seconds, over seven times faster than some of the numbers in *Porgy and Bess* or *Can-Can*. At times the filmmakers use the aspect ratio of the frame to draw attention to a more abstract sense of composition. A high-angle, high camera-placement shot in the prologue emphasizes the way the Jets walk around a young girl's sidewalk chalk drawing, creating a parallel curved cluster of bodies (figure 3.1). But Wise and Robbins also create a coherent sense of space through staging in depth, clear matches on action, and tight eye-line matches to emphasize that the Jets and Sharks are acutely aware of one another's presence.

Robert Wise was "looking to escape the constraints of the studio system" by partnering with the Mirisch Corporation, Ernesto Acevedo-Muñoz

Figure 3.1 A high-angle shot emphasizes graphic contrast to show Riff and the Jets choosing not to cross a girl's line drawing in *West Side Story*.
Source: The Mirisch Corporation.

62 STORYTELLING IN MOTION

argues,[19] and the memos between Wise and Robbins emphasize the level of creative control they had in shaping a new style for their film. Notably, *West Side Story*'s cinematographer, Daniel L. Fapp, and editor, Thomas Standford, were not known for their previous work on Hollywood musicals. However, the filmmakers' ability to make big-budget musical cinema benefited from the institutional memory and lingering infrastructure of the studio system, despite its predominant dismantlement by the early 1960s.[20] Most significantly to a musical production, the same performers who had trained as triple threats while under contract with one of the major studios were still employable for their singing, dancing, and acting talent. To this, Robbins added an insistence of auditioning performers who had performed for the London or New York *West Side Story* theatrical productions,[21] several of whom, like George Chakiris (Bernardo), had extensive experience in both environments. Several of the lead dancing stars—Rita Moreno (Anita), Russ Tamblyn (Riff), and Chakiris—had prior fixed-term contracts with a Hollywood major or minor studio.[22] Robbins, Wise, and screenwriter Ernest Lehman were able to audition close to five hundred performers for the dancing roles of Jets and Sharks,[23] an opportunity that would be inaccessible to most of the filmmakers discussed in later chapters of this book.

Engrained (White) Infrastructure Norms

Nowhere in their discussion of the narrative challenges involved in mediating a sense of reality and a sense of fantasy in their musical do the two directors discuss the question of representation in relation to casting practices, despite controversies that arose from the play's release and preproduction discussions about the film's social and political consequences.[24] The filmmakers' production research was thorough; they went to great lengths to do field work in New York City to study gang life, Puerto Rican culture, and tensions between the city's gangs, extending the research the stage play's creators had begun a few years before.[25] Yet within all this planning for cultural specificity and investment in creating an environment of authentic gang experiences, the producers made no commitment to casting exclusively Puerto Rican performers to play the Sharks.[26] Instead, as Brian Eugenio Herrera indicates, "*West Side Story*'s casting of Latina/o characters (in both its stage and screen versions) was aligned with the normative casting conventions of the period, wherein Latina/o actors enjoyed no special priority for Latina/o roles."[27]

The production's failure of inclusive casting remains a central part of *West Side Story*'s cultural resonance as a hurtful reminder of industrial and cultural patterns of exclusion. Acevedo-Muñoz describes *West Side Story* as a "polymorphous text" given the Puerto Rican ambivalence over the film; because of its legacy, "most Latino performers have had to think about, deal with, or assimilate *West Side Story* at some point."[28] As such, many discuss the film's complex and problematic relationship to Latinx/o/a representation in relation to both *West Side Story*'s stage and film adaptations. As a Hollywood, mainstream representation of Puerto Rican culture, and the earliest to portray specifically Puerto Rican characters,[29] it remains an influential text for both identification and disidentification through its essentialized construction of Latinx/o/a identity.[30] Herrera describes the film as "one of the most emblematic—and problematic—depictions of Latinas/os in US popular performance," emphasizing that *West Side Story* continues to "generate long-standing cultural debates interrogating the musical's particular contributions to the limiting repertoire of Latina/o depictions in US popular performance."[31] The tension over *West Side Story*'s representation of Latinx/o/a characters and culture also reinforces the film's production within the remnants of the studio system, where white actors performing or voicing characters of other races and ethnicities was commonplace.[32]

West Side Story's musical form also contributes to its polymorphism and its mixed reception. Desirée Garcia argues that the genre's association with both escapism and long-standing popularity often situates musical films in a paradoxical position of simultaneous cultural irrelevance (as escapist media) and centrality to cultural debates (especially in relation to questions of representation).[33] Many of the dance and music styles at the core of the American musical genre are built on the artistry and labor of Black and Latinx/o/a creators,[34] but Hollywood films and institutional memory rarely acknowledge them.[35] The Jets' choreography and musicality reflects this practice as well. The orchestration of their numbers is predominantly jazz-driven,[36] and their ensemble number "Cool" draws extensively on elements from the Lindy Hop, both originally African American music and dance forms, respectively. Yet within the context of the musical genre, cinematic representations of realism become more complicated through displacement.[37] "The musical cannot be measured by 'realism,'" Acevedo-Muñoz argues, given its foregrounding of performance, which leads him to read white actors George Chakiris's and Natalie Wood's performances in *West Side Story* as a form of drag.[38]

64 STORYTELLING IN MOTION

The musical's emphasis on the visibility of the dancing body further adds to the contradictions of meaning associated with representations of race and ethnicity in the genre. This is perhaps the case even more so for the Jets than the Sharks. The latter gang members have a unified ethnic identity unlike the Jets; production notes specify that "the SHARKS are Puerto Ricans, the JETS a potpourri of what is called 'American,'" with a brief mention of Tony's Polish ethnicity in the film.[39] Instead, the Jets' whiteness and behavior define their collective identity through their physicality and the entitlement they feel as they fill up the spaces they occupy. "Being visible as white is a passport to privilege," Richard Dyer writes, but he also argues that whiteness so defined has an inherent paradoxical dynamic: "Whites must be seen to be white, yet whiteness as race resides in invisible properties and whiteness as power is maintained by being unseen. To be seen as white is to have one's corporeality registered, yet true whiteness resides in the noncorporeal."[40] The musical genre's inherent tendencies enhance these tensions by making all bodies not only visible but the focal point of visual attention, challenging hegemonic categorizations of race, sexuality, gender, and identity more broadly.[41] Moreover, this visibility of the body is an active, rather than passive, choice. "A dancing body is not only the object of the gaze," Adrienne McLean argues, "but also a subject who participates and presents chosen aspects of her self to that gaze, willingly and consciously."[42] Despite the genre's further complication of representations of realism, the plethora of reactions to *West Side Story*'s formal choices and grounding in traditional modes of production emphasizes that the performances of ethnicity continue to significantly impact how viewers make meaning of its diegetic and choreographic conventions.

Breathtaking Panavision

The Mirisch Corporation and Seven Arts Productions planned *West Side Story* as a big-budget roadshow picture, shot on prestigious (and expensive) 70mm film with widescreen, anamorphic Panavision lenses.[43] By the early 1960s, Panavision had resolved the technical challenges provided by the introduction of anamorphic CinemaScope lenses in 1953,[44] and Hollywood filmmakers had developed solutions to the stylistic problems of the new technology. Depth of field was extremely limited with the initial CinemaScope lenses especially at close distances, and parallax problems made it difficult for the camera operators to gauge focus properly, leading to recommendations that actors not be shot in closer framings and move as little as possible. The optical distortions of the anamorphic technology also tended to create a bowing of shapes along the horizontal axis and vertical bulging at closer distances, leading to some stars in close-ups being diagnosed with the "Scope mumps."[45]

Certain Hollywood choreographers reviled the widescreen format. Like Hermes Pan, Gene Kelly was vocally resistant to widescreen for dance numbers, calling it an "abomination" and only usable for group numbers. He found the narrower 1.37:1 Academy ratio—the standard before the mid-1950s—more effective for solo or duet forms.[46] New technologies create tangible physical constraints that can profoundly change stylistic norms, David Bordwell argues, yet filmmakers presented with these formal problems rarely resolve them with a consistent solution.[47] Director Rouben Mamoulian and choreographers Eugene Loring and Hermes Pan use humorous staging to mock the challenges of the new CinemaScope aspect ratio in *Silk Stockings* (1957). Director Stanley Donen and choreographer Michael Kidd use longer takes and the width of the Scope frame to show not one couple but seven simultaneously in *Seven Brides for Seven Brothers* (1954). *Seven Brides*' dance sequences usually focus on the performers as a unit, rather than situating a star in the narrative foreground. Like other early anamorphic features, Donen and Kidd's staging in *Seven Brides* emphasizes lateral, or "clothesline," staging to fill the frame with actors and emphasize the aspect ratio's "spacious horizontality."[48]

The centrality of ensemble numbers for narrative purposes and the presence of multiple couples on screen simultaneously are some common solutions to the musical genre's grappling with the wider anamorphic frame, seen in other early CinemaScope musicals like *How to Marry a Millionaire* (Jean Negulesco, 1953) or *Guys and Dolls* (Joseph Mankiewicz, 1955). Earlier "flat" musicals shot in the Academy ratio tend to use ensemble numbers as part of an aggregate approach,[49] as a source of spectacle that has more tenuous narrative connections, particularly exemplified by Busby Berkeley's numbers for Warner Bros. in the 1930s, or as a backdrop to a more prominent performer or duet.

West Side Story's ensemble numbers balance the isolation of key characters with an emphasis on the Sharks and especially the Jets as unified groups. Herrera interprets the Jets as a unified protagonist, "an ensemble comprised of idiosyncratic characters who maintain their individuation, even

66 STORYTELLING IN MOTION

as—through shared movement, motive, and melody—they move as one."[50] The greater horizontal space of the 2.35:1 frame creates "strips of modules," Bordwell argues, "and these can be juxtaposed in breadth or depth, in order to isolate characters or establish relationships."[51] The filmmakers take advantage of the vast aspect ratio of anamorphic space through lateral spacing, recessional staging, and the blocking and revealing of groups of dancers.

The film's narrative focus on conflict between the Jets and Sharks is thematically appropriate to the widescreen technology's stylistic strengths; "Scope's width invited—demanded, some directors felt—a partitioning of the visual field."[52] Robbins and Wise in *West Side Story* employ continuity editing and tighter framings to further dissect the space, allowing the choreography to move both laterally and into depth. In addition, Robbins does not stage the choreography to contain the character's bodies within the film frame. Instead, he uses off-screen space and movements in and out of frame as a key part of his choreographic aesthetic. Although Robbins's choreography frequently uses the horizontal, vertical, and recessional space of the anamorphic frame to show large ensembles of dancers, the characters' unrest, energy, and tensions often push them to splay and extend beyond the frame into off-screen space. Despite the seemingly vast expanse of the wider aspect ratio, the Jets and Sharks still need more room to move.

The Prologue: Formal Parallels and Narrative Exposition

West Side Story's prologue sequence contains iconic dance positions that are isolated from their narrative context through citation and for promotional purposes. The Sharks' first unison développé, with opposite arm raised (figure 3.2), is duplicated in film posters,[53] on book covers,[54] in commercials,[55] and as citations in films and media more broadly.[56] However, Robbins uses such repeated phrases, careful staging, and easily recognizable postures to show how the Jets and the Sharks respond to one another and imitate the others' cues. The dancing is virtuosic, and the meaning of the movement is presented with clear redundancy, aided by editing techniques that enforce a legible spatiotemporal continuity. Significantly, singing is absent and dialogue is minimal in this musical number, allowing figure movement to signal narrative exposition instead. The film's prologue number establishes the social rules of conduct for the film, rules that have been set by the Jets, the film implies, and that are both maintained and challenged by the Sharks.

Figure 3.2 The Sharks' iconic développé in the prologue from *West Side Story*.
Source: The Mirisch Corporation.

West Side Story's filmmakers make clear attempts to define the white Jet and Latino Shark gangs through difference: with racial and ethnic markers, including "brown-face" make-up and the use of accents for the Puerto Rican characters;[57] with color and costume design; and with music and dance selections. Yet the narrative—through the film's choreography especially— also constructs strong similarities between these characters. Through choreographic phrases that carry across the number, the Jets and the Sharks throw movements and gestures back at each other as the Jets vie for dominance over and the Sharks struggle for access to their reluctantly shared spaces.

Intrinsic Norms of Conduct

The cinematic choreography of the prologue establishes the tensions between the Jets, Sharks, and those around them and emphasizes how frequently they come in contact with one another through repeated depth staging, tightly framed follow shots, and off-screen space. The Jets' first encounter with Bernardo illustrates the way the prologue sets up a claustrophobic feeling of physical proximity in the film, emphasizing how the shared environment contributes to the tensions between the Jets and the Sharks. The sequence quickly establishes its intrinsic norms of tight, clustered staging, precise camera reframing, and shifting blocking of on- and off-screen space to introduce the relationships between the Jets, the Sharks, and their shared

68 STORYTELLING IN MOTION

community. The actors' performances, as well as the staging of on- and off-screen space in relation to the reframing camera, do the heavy lifting in establishing this crucial narrative exposition.

West Side Story begins with helicopter top shots drifting over Manhattan before zooming in on a group of Jets sitting in a basketball court where other teenagers are also playing.[58] The first close framing of Riff establishes the prologue's pattern of using tighter framings and off-screen space to conceal and reveal characters. We see Riff in profile in the right of the frame, with excessive negative space to the left, where we see empty concrete and a few children in the far background. The camera pans right to center Riff in the frame as he snaps his fingers, revealing Ice just behind him, now occupying the right third of the frame. Soon after the camera pans right again to reveal Action as well, the three Jets now comfortably filling the anamorphic aspect ratio. The next shot cuts back to a low-angle position, revealing Baby John and A-Rab sitting beside them; this pattern repeats again with two more Jets as the cluster of characters continue to snap as they stare forward, toward the left of the frame. Even though the earlier extreme long shot shows us the whole group, the sequence's sound design also reinforces the reveals, incorporating the sound of each additional Jet snapping only once they appear on screen. The prologue immediately establishes the constant presence of others, using tight framings to evoke the dense populations of urban environments and suggesting an impossibility of privacy or isolation. Riff appears alone, only to have Ice take his place in the frame as the camera moves. The result is a tense feeling of spatial displacement, overlap, and claustrophobia.

As the prologue continues, the sequence establishes the film's social order as the Jets "mark their turf."[59] The pattern of cutting on the axis away from the Jets continues to show the cluster of characters in long shot, once again in the right of the frame with an excess of negative space to the left. A baseball flies into frame from the left, bouncing off the chain-link fence behind the Jets. Action catches the ball as a white teenager runs in after it, pausing in the left of frame as he looks at the Jets. Both remain stationary until Riff looks at Action and jerks his head toward the boy, giving him permission to return the ball. Soon after, Riff stands and repeats the head gesture, signaling to the Jets to follow him. This simple, redundant movement efficiently establishes Riff's leadership and the Jets' power over their non-Jet white peers. The prologue repeats this relationship a few shots later as the Jets walk through a few other teenagers' basketball game. The boy holding the ball drops it at Action's feet as the Jets approach, and Action grabs the ball, passing it to A-Rab as the other Jets leap and extend their arms to block a pass in the background. Riff, who has continued walking forward, claps to get A-Rab's attention and demands the ball, which he passes back to the boys. Though no explicit dialogue or lyrics accompany the movements, the multiple iterations and pantomimic clarity provide the efficient narrative redundancy associated with Hollywood's storytelling techniques.[60]

While the Jets walk through the playground, they also take actions that establish their sense of morality and the boundaries they set for themselves. A young girl sits in the middle of a large chalk circle she is coloring in; the camera cuts to a high-angle shot as we see the Jets' feet approach her. The shot begins with Riff stepping on his left foot mere inches away from the edge of her drawing. As he moves his right foot forward, it passes over her drawing before he swings his leg over the left to step to the outer edge of the circle. He continues to walk around the periphery and through the frame as the rest of the Jets follow suit (figure 3.1 mentioned before). There are some lines that Riff will not deliberately cross, the prologue implies, and the Jets copy his actions. They deviate only as much as they have to, however, walking very close along the perimeter of the chalk circle but respecting the boundary nonetheless.

The palpable tension between the Jets and their white peers dissipates as the gang members continue moving through the city streets, only to return more significantly a few shots later in their first encounter with Bernardo. The Jets' mostly pedestrian and pantomime-based staging shifts into syncopated dance as they développé, kick, slide, leap, jump, and twirl their way across the street. As the choreographed phrase progresses, their movements become larger as they individually and collectively take up more space.[61] They are aware of their surroundings—Riff turns his head to look as children run past them in the foreground—but confident enough in their control of the environment to allow their movements to progress with little constraint,[62] especially as they dance over the large "Jets" tag on the road. As they complete a traveling leap that carries them toward the left frame, however, a cut to a new mobile framing follows their leftward movement to show them moving rapidly toward the opposite sidewalk, where the pan left reveals Bernardo. The physical shift is immediately palpable. Bernardo, who was mid-step, freezes in place, his weight leaning slightly forward to reinforce his previous forward momentum and his whole attention focused on the group of Jets in front of him as he exhibits a "quality of restraint."[63] Similarly, as they see Bernardo, the Jets' focus becomes narrow and they halt their momentum from the spin, coming briefly to stillness

70 STORYTELLING IN MOTION

in a crouch.[64] The Jets once again follow Riff's lead as he laughs at Bernardo and then jerks his head to follow. Herrera argues that the Jets "emerge as a cinematic embodiment of whiteness in peril—at once newly consolidated and newly under siege... guarding an increasingly urbanized color line from those threatening to violate that racialized border: The Sharks."[65] As with the girl's drawing, the Jets walk uncomfortably close to Bernardo as they circle him, avoiding (for the moment) crossing the line of direct physical confrontation while asserting their entitled dominance of the shared space.

"Where are the vile beginners of this fray?"

West Side Story's prologue establishes choreographic cues that draw attention to the gangs' similarities in addition to their differences without offering any real solutions.[66] Garcia argues that *West Side Story* uses the structures of the folk musical "to expose rather than eliminate social difference."[67] It emphasizes the tragic nature of their conflict, making all involved complicit in the escalating violence and, through that approach, emphasizes the film's fictional distance from—or avoidance of—the extrinsic realities of contemporary American systemic inequality and racism.[68] Through this predominantly danced sequence, the film's narrative establishes the viewer in the middle of the Shark–Jet conflict and positions them as rivals with conflicting, but similar, goals.

The film's balancing of our attention toward—and alignment with—both gangs is apparent in the initial shots of the Sharks. As the Jets leave their tense encounter with Bernardo, the camera initially pans left with them. It then stays with Bernardo as two of the gang members deviate from the group and turn back to him while he walks away from the confrontation and into the foreground. Ice and Tiger follow Bernardo while making taunting noises and pass him to block his passage, framing him with their bodies as Tiger puts his elbow on Ice's shoulder and not-too-subtly forms his hand into a fist in the next shot. They leave when Bernardo refuses to escalate the encounter. His composure cracks slightly as we see him brace against a red wall and form a fist himself before slamming his hand into the bricks, a movement punctuated by an accented note in the orchestration. As the shot of him walking parallel to the wall continues, two Sharks join him on screen. Like the framing of the Jets earlier, Pepe and Juano enter the frame one by one, the medium-close up hiding their presence until they begin to walk and snap with the group.

Their choreographed staging moves them across New York City streets and leads them into a brief dance phrase that mirrors that of the Jets.

Like the Jets, the Sharks' first brief dance segment ends in a unison crouch with arms outstretched. Because of the repeated pattern we can anticipate that they are reacting to the Jets, and the next shot shows A-Rab and Baby John stealing from a bodega, only to be stopped in their tracks by the three Sharks who have interrupted them. They mockingly wave the Jets through and then follow them tauntingly. A parked truck mostly blocks the camera's view of the group as it dollies down the road to follow them, eventually revealing a cluster of Jets leaning against the back of the vehicle. Now that the Jets outnumber the Sharks, A-Rab takes the apple back from Bernardo and mockingly imitates his earlier outstretched arm gesture before the Jets chase the Sharks off screen.

The Sharks' and Jets' movement phrases in the prologue imitate and build off each other's as the two groups repeatedly interact in shared spaces. While initially contactless, the simmering tension shifts into a physical brawl by the end of the sequence, intensifying after the altercation between the Sharks and Jets on the basketball court. Notably, the Sharks initially make an effort to de-escalate or avoid conflict. We see this in Bernardo's initial refusal to engage with the Jets' taunts and again later when the Jets chase a group of Sharks away from a game of cards they are playing quietly under some sidewalk construction scaffolding.

Individualism comes through in performative differences. Most noticeably, while repeated stylistic choices like head jerks and a centering in staging clusters emphasizes that Riff and Bernardo are the leaders of their respective groups, actor Russ Tamblyn's bouncy, gymnastic athleticism for Riff contrasts with George Chakiris's smooth gracefulness for Bernardo. Choreographic contrast also signals the ways the Jets and Sharks move differently through their environment. The Jets' dancing is big everywhere—on the sidewalks, in the street, on the basketball court—with a tendency toward ongoing, multifocused attention (figure 3.3).[69] The Sharks' first dance phrase, by contrast, shows constraint and takes up less space (figure 3.4).[70] Bernardo, Pepe, and Juano run and twirl as the Jets do, but they remain slightly crouched with lowered centers of gravity. They extend their arms to the side rather than upward in the vertical plane, returning their folded arms tightly to their chests as they spin.[71] Only once they are in a more isolated area do they take up more space, extending their right arms and left legs, raising up on their toes of the supporting foot (figure 3.2 mentioned before). Even this moment of

Figure 3.3 The Jets take up space in *West Side Story*.
Source: The Mirisch Corporation.

Figure 3.4 The Sharks demonstrate restraint in *West Side Story*.
Source: The Mirisch Corporation.

release is quickly contained, as they follow the movement with a controlled and focused crouch to the opposite side,[72] arms once again in flexion and hands balled into fists. This pattern continues as the violence escalates and the groups chase each other through the streets. The Sharks prioritize speed and shapes that allow them to quickly change direction, whereas the Jets jump and spin more frequently, performing tour jeté leaping turns with an arm raised overhead as they chase the Sharks (figure 3.5).

The Sharks and Jets engage with oppositional movement qualities when performing similar movement phrases. The Sharks emphasize a control

Figure 3.5 The Jets expand as the Sharks contract in *West Side Story*.
Source: The Mirisch Corporation.

of their ongoing motion, and their attention is often focused on a specific element (usually a Jet). As a result, they tend to move into the ground—lowering their center of gravity—and keep their limbs closer to the center midline of the body. The Jets also control their forward momentum when they encounter the Sharks, but more often their flow is ongoing and expansive and their attention to space is multifocused. Their resulting held body shapes[73] are big as they extend their limbs into space and embrace the ability to take up as much space as possible. While the groups' Effort qualities are in opposition—the Jets' Free Flow and Indirect Space versus the Sharks' Bound Flow and Direct Space—they are all often engaging both Flow and Space Effort Factors as they deliberately navigate their environments.[74] They pursue their goals differently, but nonetheless both want something similar: a space all to themselves.

Contiguous Découpage

The prologue emphasizes this importance of space by making the characters' navigation of the environment highly legible. Thomas Standford's editing of the sequence adheres to classical guidelines of continuity editing. He maintains clear spatial legibility within individual environments and links discontiguous spaces with graphic matches that continue the Sharks' and Jets' movements across cuts. *West Side Story*'s filmmakers shoot most of the number in more distant framings—medium-long shots, long shots, and

74 STORYTELLING IN MOTION

extreme long shots—to show the dancers' full figures and contextualize them spatially within the exterior urban setting of New York City. While much of the choreography is visible in full frame, the camera also shifts to tighter framings to emphasize facial expressions, physically separate characters, or create moments of surprise through a careful use of on- and off-screen space, as the first few shots of the Jets demonstrate. The prologue also relies heavily on editing and shorter takes. With an average shot length of 6.6 seconds, the prologue number is one of the most quickly edited numbers in *West Side Story*, along with the "Dance at the Gym" (6.1 seconds) and the rumble (3.6 seconds), all of which emphasize direct physical conflict between the Sharks and the Jets.

This pattern features prominently in the moments that initiate the violent escalation of fighting and deliberate attacks between the two gangs. A high-angle shot tilts down to follow the Jets as they dance down a street, forcing two women pedestrians to turn sideways to avoid collision. Once the Jets are directly below the camera, three Sharks run into frame from the left only to be chased back off-screen by the former. The Jets then leap up with their arms extended vertically, and the scene cuts to a low-angle shot of their arms still extended. The graphic match efficiently shifts us back to the basketball court where the Jets are playing. The Jets relevé and extend their arms as they spin, repeating earlier dance phrases as they dribble and move across the concrete. The final shot of the game begins with the group near the building wall where the hoop is attached as they dance their way across the court and toward the camera. Once in medium-long shot, Riff avoids various Jets' attempts to steal the ball from him and eventually passes it to the left as (Bernardo's) hands reach into frame to catch it. The red shirt sleeves and black leather cuff make Bernardo easily identifiable even before we see his face, amplified by the look of concern on the Jets' faces as they come to a halt before the ball (figure 3.6). The establishing framing that began the shot makes it clear that Bernardo and the Sharks were not in the space seconds before. Yet Riff passes the ball deliberately to someone, his prejudice perhaps softened by the heightened diegetic euphoria of the number. As before, the opposite party freezes in place and the countering group follows suit, all coming to stillness and once again blocking any possibility of achieving the number's utopian potential.[75]

The following shots establish a clear axis of action for the rest of the scene in the basketball court, during which tensions escalate. Increasingly tight framings cut back and forth between the Jets and the Sharks as Riff demands the ball back and tells them to "beat it." When Bernardo jerks his head for the

Figure 3.6 Riff passes the ball to an unseen player (Bernardo), whose hands appear in frame to catch it in *West Side Story*.
Source: The Mirisch Corporation.

Sharks to follow, they proceed past the Jets rightward in the frame as the Jets pass through their group and exit toward the background left. Rather than returning to their game, they leave the court through the left-most gate as the Sharks do on the opposite side of the space. We watch Loco observe this as he turns back to look off-screen left at the Jets who are leaving, just as we see the last of his fellow Sharks leaving the court in the right background. Loco knows that he is alone with Action, who is watching the final Sharks leave, before he slides out a leg to trip him. The reverse shots between them as Action appears to make peace before hitting Loco make it clear that their friends are still moving away, yet unaware of the conflict. Matches on action make the progression clear, as we see Loco's spit leaving his mouth as Action walks off-screen, only for the (simulated) spit to hit the back of Action's head after the axial cut back to a more distant framing of the two. Graphic matches on the choreography similarly connect discontiguous spaces, as we see several times in subsequent shots that use matches on the Jets' leaps to show them leaving the ground by the chain-link fence of the basketball court and landing on a sidewalk in a different part of the neighborhood.

The prologue makes it clear for the viewer where the characters are in space and emphasizes how frequently the groups in conflict often literally run into each other. The frequency with which the Jets and Sharks appear in-frame together reflects this. The beginning of the number uses multiple shots to show the Jets and Sharks separate from one another, interspersed with moments of conflict as they interact. As the number continues and the conflict escalates, however, most shots contain members of both groups; the axial cut-ins of Baby John defacing the Sharks' tag are the final shots that isolate a member of the different gangs.

The ten-minute prologue establishes the intrinsic norms of conduct between the Sharks, the Jets, and their surrounding community and does so almost entirely through dance and pantomime. Through choreography, editing, and cinematographic choices, the number creates a feeling of claustrophobic physical proximity, communicates the gang hierarchies and the individual members' personalities, and suggests strong similarities between the Jets and Sharks in addition to their differences. The diegesis shifts throughout the number, moving from plausibly grounded pedestrian movement to pantomimed gestures accented in accordance with the music (in a mickey-moused style) to stylized fighting to virtuosic dance phrases. These levels of diegetic plurality maintain a clear spatiotemporal logic through eyeline matches, shot-reverse shot framings on an established axis of action, and matches on action for both spatial contiguity and graphic match purposes. We are constantly aware of the environment beyond the shot as the dancers frequently exceed the frame's constraints, extending limbs out of sight, and appearing suddenly as camera movement and staging reveal characters in the space just off screen. The number flutters in and out of diegetic plurality rather than building toward a continuous number that deviates from diegetic norms, emphasizing how both groups cannot fully give in to the unifying nature of the musical's utopic potentials, given their deeply engrained conflict.

"Cool" and Kinesthetic Narrative Integration

Multiple musical numbers in *West Side Story* like the prologue, "Dance at the Gym" sequence, and rumble all use cinematic choreography to convey the growing conflict between the Jets and the Sharks. In "Cool," however, that conflict becomes internal. As the prologue demonstrates, the Jets rarely feel the need to control their actions or their emotions. Free Flow Effort, or an ongoing, often uncontrolled sense of motion, comes more naturally to them than control and composure. After the rumble, which leaves Bernardo and Riff dead, the Jets are leaderless and in panic. In a back alley they become more agitated as Action calls for revenge against the Sharks and tensions break out between the Jets and a man in an apartment above them. Ice steps in to take control, pushing the group of Jets and their girlfriends into an empty garage. Five minutes later they emerge again, now visibly more composed as they snap their fingers in unison. What caused this significant change?

Jerome Robbins's play between the physical tensions in the dancers' bodies kinesthetically integrates the number "Cool" into the causal progression of the narrative.[76] By the end of the sequence, the Jets are visibly too exhausted to be reckless or pick fights and have learned how to control their impulses—for the time being. This narrative integration comes specifically from the choreography, not just the song lyrics that cue us to notice these differences between getting cool and busting out. We are meant to understand that the Jets have succeeded in calming down by working themselves to physical exhaustion. Danced choreography shifts the Jets' performance into a diegetically plural space, and the kinesthetic, physical residue of the number registers in their bodies even after the number is over. The internal tension of the characters is apparent in their movement because of the choreography that emphasizes and juxtaposes layers of motion and emotion.

Being Cool

The lyrics of "Cool," sung by Ice at the beginning, emphasize that the Jets need to compose themselves. Action sets off the physical conflict by suggesting retaliation against the Sharks, whipping himself around to talk to different Jets, forming his hands into fists, and pulling and pushing others to convince them to join him. When their fighting draws the attention of a man in an apartment above, Action continues to escalate the situation. Now fully out of control, he yells at the man and threatens him. As he runs toward the man's window, he shakes free of the Jets who were restraining him and lashes out verbally and physically. His arms whip open, simultaneously engaging a sense of release, speed, and strength.[77] Through this brief shift through Flow, Time, and Weight Efforts together, Action's Effort Life moves him into what Rudolf Laban referred to as a Passion Drive, a moment of intensity where spatial awareness is absent, inner impulses dominate, and "bodily actions are particularly expressive of emotion and feeling."[78] Action's use of space is also expanding in this moment as he extends his arms and takes up sonic space by yelling and drawing attention to the Jets.[79]

Ice stops Action and pushes the Jets into the garage where the "Cool" number will take place. The dialogue that leads into the musical number emphasizes that the Jets are allowing their inner emotions to bubble up and

78 STORYTELLING IN MOTION

"bust" out. "You show it and you are dead," Ice warns, telling them they need to "play it cool" instead. Ice's song offers a dichotomy between being "hot" and "cool," with some specific guidance for what being cool would look and feel like. These words imply certain qualities of how the body should move, with associations to specific categories from Laban Movement Analysis's Effort Movement Factors. "Take it slow" evokes Sustained Time Effort and a more patient, serene attitude toward decision-making and the passage of time.[80] "Stay loose" suggests Free Flow Effort and a conscious release of control for instead a more relaxed progression of movement.[81] "Turn off the juice" implies less exertion of force to instead decrease pressure delicately with Light Weight Effort, while "go, but not like a yo-yo" encourages both Direct Space Effort to focus on a specific goal and Space Effort more generally through the activation of spatial awareness and the surrounding environment.[82] Together, the lyrics evoke dynamic qualities associated with all four of the LMA Effort Factors: Flow, Time, Weight, and Space.

Although Ice's guidance encourages a more restrictive movement range to maintain a low profile, "Cool" is ultimately about the Jets learning to control themselves. As *West Side Story*'s prologue sequence and Action's outburst before the start of "Cool" demonstrate, the Jets already move naturally with a sense of ongoing flux.[83] Staying loose is not a quality they usually lack. Rather, the number demonstrates their need to gain awareness about how they engage with their space and a better understanding of how a lashing out of their inner attitudes is putting them at risk. They achieve this through deliberate decision-making,[84] taking up less space,[85] and balancing their fluctuating control and inner sensing[86] with an awareness of how they are engaging with their environment.[87]

Robbins choreographs this contrast between "cool" and "busting" into the Jets' dance movements, making their emotional and kinesthetic progression legible to the audience through clear distinctions and redundancies. The performers express this difference in a few significant ways. "Cool" movements tend toward a smaller range of motion and a more contained Kinesphere with limbs pulling into the midline and a contraction and curving of the spine. Movements that "bust" out are more expansive, with limbs shooting away from the body center, particularly upward into verticality. "Cool" movements move the dancers into the ground through releases into gravity, a lowering of the body center, and a tendency toward stillness. "Busting" works against gravity by pulling the body away from the floor and through space. Finally, "cool" movements show the dancers more visibly moving through qualities that prioritize inner sensing, an awareness of the environment, deliberately slow decision-making, and an increase of fluidity.[88] Movements that "bust out," in contrast, are marked by their abruptness and power, often activating strength with quickness and stalled action.[89] Busting movements often occur with an erratic feeling that the body is moving without a clear spatial purpose to imply that the Jets are not in full control of their bodies. This impression is contrasted, of course, by the precise control of the professional dancers and their execution of Robbins's choreography, frequently performed in unison. As a result, these "busting" movements demonstrate a greater activation of a multifocused attention to space through Indirect Space Effort rather than a complete lack of control over the performers' orientation in space, which would result in a complete lack of Space Effort activation and fewer aesthetically pleasing and narratively legible shapes.

The early moments of the musical number, in which the Jets flutter in and out of diegetic plurality through an alternation of danced and pedestrian movements, introduce us to this choreographic approach and the Jets' struggle to compose themselves. Cinematographic choices reinforce the lack of control, with the movements of the dancers often splaying beyond the edge of the already expansive anamorphic frame as limbs extend away from the midline and the scene cuts to tighter framings. Action is the first to peel away from the group after Ice's verse, slamming his hands into the hood of a nearby truck. "Easy, Action," Ice warns, but without success. Baby John and Snowboy go next, walking with greater ease and fluidity toward the camera. They then quickly bust out in unison, kicking and stomping their feet in a downward motion before reversing direction into a spin and leap. Their momentum takes them back into the ground in a crouch, the ongoing flux controlled at the last moment to prevent their hands from slamming into the ground. A-Rab then repeats this style of alternation. In all instances, the Jets are only briefly able to sustain a sense of coolness before their pain bubbles up again. As the Jets' early, failed attempts to sustain a sense of control demonstrate, their bodies cannot easily make the switch. Getting cool will require some work.

Getting Cool

The Jets dance through their emotional turmoil in the heightened diegetic space of the musical number. At the beginning, Ice attempts to cool the

80 STORYTELLING IN MOTION

group down, as he does with A-Rab, and the choreography reflects a balance of movement that is temporarily controlled but that frequently busts out. However, after achieving a semblance of control[90] the Jets become more impassioned rather than immediately cooling off, moving through turbulent, traveling dance phrases that engage their strength and quick reflexes as they burn through their grief, anger, and frustration. Getting cool for them is an indirect process that occurs through multiple cycles of exertion and recuperation. Robbins's and Wise's staging of dancers and the camera reflects this nonlinear process. Rather than maintaining a consistent "frontal" facing, camera positions capture the dancers from all sides of the parking garage set, with an average shot length of 6.7 seconds. The adherence to continuity editing norms—matches on action, eyeline matches, and consistent screen direction—creates strong spatial clarity. Most significantly, the clear matches on action that connect the dancers' movements across shots create spatio-temporal contiguity to suggest that we are observing the Jets work through their grief in real time.

Initially, each individual must exert energy to be cool, and they recuperate from that exertion by busting out with more expansive choreography. As the number continues and the energy required to bust out wears them down, the Jets begin to recuperate instead with cool, controlled choreography. Unison (consensus) is also Ice's ultimate goal. Yet the Jets and their girlfriends rarely dance in full unison until the final moments of the number, emphasizing how each individual is moving through their grief and anger at their own pace. The shift between these two movement aesthetics and their subcomponents develops over the course of the number through an interplay among and within the dancers' bodies. As the early moments of "Cool" demonstrate, the Jets fluctuate often between these contrasting movement qualities. In addition, Robbins's choreography, which avoids extended unison phrases until the end of the number, juxtaposes contrasting qualities within a single composition. The complex choreography reflects this by combining multiple choreographic phrases simultaneously, using both lateral and depth staging to show the Jets' ripples of exertion and control throughout the frame.

The use of cinematic choreography here to demonstrate the Jets' tension is particularly visible in the segment that follows the initial attempts to get cool. After Action, Baby John, Snowball, and A-Rab fail to individually control their emotions, the Jets and their girlfriends move through a series of choreographic attempts in smaller clusters. This transitional section of the number juxtaposes groups of dancers in various stages of exertion and

AGENCY, CONTROL, AND SPACE 81

recuperation and ends with Ice effectively giving up on getting the Jets to cool down without first working through their frustration at a kinesthetic level.

A reframing camera shot transitions the number from A-Rab's solo to the first of these choreographic clusters. As the camera pans right to follow him, its movement reveals a trio of women, led by Graziella (Riff's girlfriend), as they begin to dance. Initially in the background, their more fluid and suspended unison phrase moves them into the foreground until they are centered in a medium long shot with the Jets watching them, but not dancing, in the background. They mostly block the Jets as they begin to quickly whip into rigid poses as they snap, their arms and shoulders tense. A cut matches their action as they shoot their arms straight up toward the ceiling before continuing to dance with "busting" movements, the camera now showing them in long shot in the right half of the frame as a trio of Jets begins to dance with more restraint in the left midground (figure 3.7). The remaining dancers are still mostly blocked by the trio of women in the foreground. The women's choreography grows more agitated as they swiftly change direction and take up space in the sagittal plane, tossing their heads backward, extending arms forward, and lunging legs backward. In contrast, the trio of Jets to the left hold a more hunched, contracted shape in their spines as they cautiously walk forward and snap.

As the shot ends, the trio of women lunge forward toward the camera and clap, beginning a phrase annotated on the music score as the "clap step" by Robbins or his assistant, Tommy Abbott.[91] A new shot reframes the group

Figure 3.7 The girls bust out in the right foreground as a group of Jets tries to stay cool in the left midground in *West Side Story*.
Source: The Mirisch Corporation.

82 STORYTELLING IN MOTION

Figure 3.8 The trio of girls perform part 1 of the "clap step" in the foreground in *West Side Story*.
Source: The Mirisch Corporation.

of dancers as the women begin the "clap step," setting up the staging in depth that will lead to the phrase rippling through the frame. The trio starts this dance phrase in a crouch, lunging forward with the left leg as the torso rounds forward (figure 3.8). They clap twice in this position and then quickly rotate their torsos and right legs outward (clockwise) into a layback position while vocalizing their exhalation, activating Far-Reach Sagittal movement through full extension of the arms and head into back-high space as the standing foot relevés and the right leg extends forward (figure 3.9). They then shift their weight onto the right leg as they return to verticality and continue the rotation, folding the left leg and curving the upper body in toward the body center in a suspended movement that shifts the dancers briefly back into a feeling of greater restraint. As the three women move into the second portion of this phrase (the layback) in the right foreground, the trio of Jets in the left midground begin the "clap step" phrase, and as soon as they reach the layback, a larger group of six Jets in the right background begin the phrase as well (figure 3.10). The three women move leftward in the frame to partner with the cluster of three Jets in a Lindy Hop–inspired phrase,[92] revealing the group of six Jets in the right background just as they extend their limbs in the second step of the phrase (figure 3.11). Because of the repeated clapping that initiates the phrase, our eye is drawn to each group of dancers as the "clap step" choreography ripples and weaves in canon through the frame.

The juxtaposition of movement qualities and conflicting gradations of control continues as the performers separate into "push theme and Lindy

AGENCY, CONTROL, AND SPACE 83

Figure 3.9 The trio of girls perform part 2 of the "clap step" in the right foreground as the trio of boys start part 1 of the "clap step" in the left midground in *West Side Story*.
Source: The Mirisch Corporation.

Figure 3.10 The "clap step" continues to ripple through the frame, with the girls finishing part 3 in the right foreground, the trio of boys performing part 2 in the left midground, and the remaining Jets preparing to begin part 1 in the right background in *West Side Story*.
Source: The Mirisch Corporation.

(partnered)" clusters (figure 3.12).[93] The latter pairs of dancers spill over the left edge of the film frame as the group of six Jets in the background begin to glide toward the camera while Ice coaches them, himself gliding backward in a crouch. Just as there is tension in the movement present on screen, sustained low notes play under more frantic movement in the upper register of the

84 STORYTELLING IN MOTION

Figure 3.11 The two trios begin their partnered Lindy Hop phrase in the left fore- and midground as the remaining Jets finish the "clap step" in the right background in *West Side Story*.
Source: The Mirisch Corporation.

Figure 3.12 The Lindy Hop group busts beyond the edges of the frame as the remaining Jets try again to get cool in *West Side Story*.
Source: The Mirisch Corporation.

music. In a strong visual moment of contrast punctuated by accented notes in the score, the "push theme" dancers then leap toward the ceiling, fingers extending beyond the top edge of the frame, just as the "Lindy (partnered)" dancers release into gravity. The groups then reverse movement qualities as the camera cuts to a high-angle shot of the two clusters; the "push theme" dancers roll their heads in a suspended motion as the partnered dancers rapidly spin and change direction behind them. A cut shifts to a new, low-angle facing of the "push theme" group in the midground, mostly blocking the "Lindy" dancers now behind them in the background. Ice is now only partially visible in the left foreground, the camera having cut around him.

Growing tensions lead to the end of this segment as each group increasingly loses their cool. The camera tracks back with the "push theme" group as they move forward. Their gliding phrase this time moves with greater control and sustainment as they extend their limbs far away from the body center.[94] Ice becomes more visible to their left as the camera tracks back and the "Lindy" dancers appear in flashes behind the group in the foreground, the men lifting the women as they slide toward and away from the ground. The flashes of color from the women's skirts make them more visible, especially as the "push theme" group moves out of the light filling the center of the room and into silhouette. A note in the music corresponds with the farthest extended reach of the "push theme" group, and the camera stops as the Jets spiral toward the floor, fully revealing the Lindy dancers. The segment ends as the twelve dancers hold their postures to watch Ice, who runs into the midground between the two groups and shouts "Cool!" as he jumps, twisting in the air as his hands extend to touch the low ceiling.

Notably, the dancers now visibly control their shifting movement qualities, observable in the ways that they move through more expansive dance phrases that emphasize sustainment rather than increasing speeds.[95] Now in greater control of their emotions, they become aware that in order to stay calm they need to burn through their desire to bust out. Much of the remaining choreography shows them taking up space through expanding movements as they leap, spin, and run. Yet even with more unison phrases, a sense of unity remains fleeting until the end of the number, reinforced by the cinematic style. The staging strongly avoids establishing a clear frontal direction at any point during the "Cool" sequence, as the number moves the dancers through the space and changes facings as the sequence progresses. Most notably, the final moments stage the dancers in a circle around Ice, with multiple performers turning their backs to the camera.

While the virtuosity of the choreography and the performers' execution create a feeling of spectacle in "Cool," the narrative intent is internal, with the characters moving toward greater inner awareness. In preproduction notes from 1958, Robbins describes a (eventually discarded) neutral territory, the "Crystal Cave," where the Jets and Sharks go to dance. There, the "attitude of these teen-agers is 'cool,' detached. They are lost in the dancing, rather than in each other."[96] Remnants of this space become the "Dance at the Gym"

86 STORYTELLING IN MOTION

sequence, filmed after Robbins was dismissed from the production, but the intent behind this environment is most visible in the final moments of "Cool." The dancers rarely turn their faces toward the camera and their eyes are often downcast or closed as they move, further drawing our attention to the movement of their bodies and the shifting movement qualities they embody (figure 3.12). The lighting reinforces this; the motivated car headlights create harsh lines of bright light that highlight the dancers at times, while the highly mobile choreography moves them through pockets of shadow, often silhouetting them against the brighter background when they dance toward the camera. The number ends, shifting away from diegetic plurality with a few more instances of busting movement, but it ultimately shows that the characters have themselves under control. The amount of exertion used for most of the piece emphasizes that the characters are able to pull themselves together only after they have expended all of the built-up energy, fear, and anger that was causing them to bust out.

Conclusions

West Side Story's producers arranged special contracts with overseas exhibitors to ensure that the film would run unaltered, as "U.S. distrib of a film musical always is faced with the possibility that the foreign exhib will decide to snip out the musical sequences, as was the case with 'The King and I' in France." Several numbers in *Can-Can* were designed with this possibility in mind according to Saul Chaplin, associate producer for both *Can-Can* and *West Side Story*.[97] For *West Side Story*, however, subtitles were created for the song lyrics as well as for dialogue scenes, an unprecedented policy[98] that *Variety* suggested "could well be a milestone in the international market for musical pix."[99]

Preparing such an insurance was a wise decision, as the prologue, "Cool," and many of *West Side Story*'s numbers are causally integrated with the larger film narrative. Jerome Robbins's choreography portraying the film's tensions between the Sharks and the Jets emphasizes the control and release of movement and space to demonstrate how the gangs are constantly holding on to what they have and reaching for what they need. The prologue establishes the heightened animosity between the Sharks and the Jets and emphasizes how much territorial overlap exists between the two gangs' spaces. The violence and tragedy of the rumble occurs within the confines of the heightened version of the diegesis, and both sequences rely almost entirely on choreography to communicate this narrative information. Despite their mutual hatred and prejudice, Robbins's choreography and the performers' movement reveal their inherent similarities in addition to their differences. In "Cool," the combination of filmic elements interact in dynamic ways with the dancers' bodies to move the story forward while still remaining within the Hollywood conventions of classical continuity. The lyrics of the number guide the audience to the conclusion that the Jets need to "get cool" to avoid apprehension by the police. Within the context of these lyrics, the meaning of being cool is more abstract and symbolic. The cinematic choreography, in contrast, provides the material evidence of the Jets' successful kinesthetic transformation. The frame's stylistic inability to contain the dancing ensembles also adds a claustrophobic, cramped feeling to the ensemble numbers, especially in contrast with the wide helicopter shots that open the film, revealing the expansiveness of New York City. The Jets and Sharks are practically forced on top of one another, the cinematic choreography suggests, unable to avoid each other's presence.

Steven Spielberg's 2021 adaptation of *West Side Story* draws further attention to the 1961 adaptation's limitations and strengths. Latinx/o/a performers were hired to play María (Rachel Zegler), Anita (Ariana DeBose), and the Sharks, with Rita Moreno returning as a coproducer and in the role of Valentina, a reimagined version of the shop owner, Doc, who employs Tony. Transgender nonbinary performer iris menas also plays aspiring Jet and liminal character Anybodys, and the role in the 2021 adaptation becomes more explicitly about a character exploring their gender identity.[100] Tony Kushner's screenplay makes María, Anita, and Valentina much more central to the narrative and further encourages the audience's allegiance with the Sharks by making the Jets more irredeemable characters steeped in the ugliness of white nationalism. Yet an uncomfortable 2018 town hall meeting between Spielberg, Kushner, and community members from the University of Puerto Rico in San Juan during preproduction emphasizes that the story's material continues to generate polymorphous reactions to its portrayal of Puerto Rican culture.[101]

Through these shifting priorities, the cinematic choreography of dance and choreographer Justin Peck's staging of musical numbers plays a different role in the 2021 film's narrative, with the characters' movement working to more clearly distinguish between the Jets and the Sharks. Spielberg and Peck's choices establish the Jets gang members as perpetuating patterns of systemic

88 STORYTELLING IN MOTION

racism while leaving the audience without much hope for their redemption. This is visible in Peck's new choreography for "Cool," which occurs earlier in the narrative as part of Tony's attempt to convince Riff and the Jets to call off the rumble. Unlike in the 1961 adaptation, in which Ice successfully calms everyone down, Tony's attempt in the 2021 version fails miserably. By taking away the gun Riff has acquired, Tony riles him up, and the number's choreography moves through a series of taunting postures and rounds of keep-away. Rather than de-escalating the situation, Tony's approach only adds fuel to the fire.

In 1962, composer Dimitri Tiomkin saw the "popular and Academy success" of *West Side Story* and several other film musicals as enough of a trend to declare a new "Golden Age of Hollywood filmusicals. . . . Trendspotters and bandwagon-jumpers take notice!"[102] Despite Robbins's anxiety (and the much-extended production period that resulted in his dismissal), he and Robert Wise were able to successfully explore their desires for a fresh perspective on filming musical numbers. The filmmakers also benefited from the remaining infrastructure and kinesthetic impact of the now-dismantled studio system. Robbins got the stylistic integration of movement and story he wanted, at the expense of any future career in Hollywood. His priority was learning how to use all the cinematic techniques at his disposal to tell the film's story through cinematic choreography, while ignoring the economic priorities of Hollywood's producers, who were increasingly risk averse.

West Side Story's cinematic choreography showed audiences new ways that figure movement could convey meaning in cinema and in so doing profoundly influenced future generations of musical filmmakers. Its careful integration of narrative and numbers was wildly popular with French audiences; whereas many other American musicals did not play well in French theaters, the 1961 film defied local expectations.[103] Its stylistic approach to diegetic plurality was an inspiration, particularly to French filmmaker Jacques Demy, who was developing his own musical projects inspired by the American form.

PART II
MUSICAL ECLECTICISM

4

Minimalism and Excess

Les Demoiselles de Rochefort (1967)

Jacques Demy's *Les Demoiselles de Rochefort* (1967) follows two sisters—the film's titular *demoiselles*—who live and work in the French port city of Rochefort-sur-Mer but dream of bigger things. Delphine (Catherine Deneuve) aspires to be a dancer at the Opéra national de Paris and Solange (Françoise Dorléac) seeks to be a professional composer. Both have yet to meet their *homme idéal*, but the film suggests that their ideal romantic pairing may be with one of the carnival workers who come to town for Rochefort's summer festival, or *kermesse*—Etienne (George Chakiris) or Bill (Grover Dale)—or the sailor Maxence (Jacques Perrin) and American composer Andy (Gene Kelly). We see the sisters prepare for a departure to Paris, agree to a last-minute performance, and interact with potential suitors over the course of several days. They also frequently visit their mother and café-owner Yvonne (Danielle Darrieux) who does not know that her former lover Simon (Michel Piccoli) has moved back to Rochefort and has not forgotten her. By the end, Simon and Yvonne have reunited, Solange and Andy have found each another, and Delphine and Maxence's paths will finally cross, the last shot implies, very soon.

Viewers familiar with *Les Demoiselles* will likely agree that the above paragraph provides an adequate plot summary. But they would also likely confirm that a plot description does not convey the film's broader appeal, which comes largely from its colorful visual design created by Bernard Evein, memorable music composed by Michel Legrand, and dynamic movement organized by choreographer Norman Maen and Demy as the main characters and pedestrians dance through the frame and Rochefort's bright streets. *Les Demoiselles* cannot be adequately described through a discussion of its narrative, despite the gratifying complexities in Demy's scenario regarding character relationships and coincidental encounters (and misses) as well as its connections to plot lines from other Demy films. Rather, Demy's stylistic

Storytelling in Motion. Jenny Oyallon-Koloski, Oxford University Press. © Oxford University Press 2024.
DOI: 10.1093/oso/9780197602669.003.0005

92 STORYTELLING IN MOTION

experimentation consistently exceeds the film's narrative motivations to keep the audience alert to formal flourishes.

The feature-length films that comprise the bulk of Demy's work, made between 1961 and 1988, do not fit neatly into one film tradition. Instead, they invoke conventions of various periods in classical French cinema, film animation, and classical American cinema (especially the tradition of the musical genre). Richard Neupert summarizes the appeal of Demy's work: "All [Demy's] films involve stylish narrative experimentation."[1] Despite beginning his career at the same time as many filmmakers associated with the French New Wave, Demy differed from his contemporaries. His relationship to the French New Wave is not the focus of this chapter, but where he fits into that movement remains a topic of discussion.[2] His alternate path to a filmmaking career impacted the narrative and aesthetic choices we can observe in his cinema. Demy did not get his start through film criticism, like Eric Rohmer, Jacques Rivette, Claude Chabrol, Jean-Luc Godard, or François Truffaut, the cinéphiles-turned-critics-turned-filmmakers best remembered for their participation in the French New Wave.[3] Nor did he have the bourgeois upbringing of Godard and Louis Malle or Truffaut's career-launching financial assistance.[4] Instead, Demy came from a provincial, working-class background, portrayed most clearly in Agnès Varda's *Jacquot de Nantes* (1991), a film based on Demy's memoirs of his childhood. Although several French New Wave directors chose to avoid the formal training available to film students at the renowned Institut Des Hautes Études Cinématographiques (IDHEC) in Paris,[5] Demy took an entirely different route by attending l'École technique de photographie et de cinématographie,[6] which stressed the acquisition of technical expertise in cinematography.[7] This technical training was crucial to his working methods. Demy remained closely involved in the detailed visual and auditory designs of his films through repeated collaborations with the artists overseeing the various components of his aesthetic vision, most significantly composer Michel Legrand and art director Bernard Evein.

Jacques Demy's films are filled with coincidental encounters and near misses between characters, convoluted mother-daughter relationships and absent fathers, unfulfilled or regretted romances, themes of father-daughter incest, geographic narrative specificity, intertextual references, implicitly and explicitly bisexual characters, and bold, conspicuous stylistic choices. They frequently display a fondness for the musical genre, Hollywood musicals in particular, and cinéphiles and scholars often refer to Demy's cinema as "magical."[8] Yet his films are also frequently odd or unsettling, blending a sense of wonderment with stylistic or narrative elements that feel out of place or out of touch with contemporary tastes. They also consistently use cinematic choreography as a primary form of expression.

Missing from discussions about Demy's aesthetic is the role that choreography plays in his work, both the collaboration with choreographers on the danced portions of his films and his staging of figure movement more broadly. The importance of these elements to his cinematic style is particularly visible in the staging choices for *Les Demoiselles'* musical numbers. Demy loved American musicals, and their influence on *Les Demoiselles'* aesthetic is unequivocal. But what makes his musical *à l'américaine* actually a musical *à la française*, or really, *à la Demy*? Through the repeated, patterned use of songs and the careful staging of dance and figure movement, Demy builds a movement vocabulary that functions narratively and aesthetically, created from both choreographic citations of Hollywood musicals and intrinsic movement phrases. The result of this extreme aesthetic variation— excessive even in relation to musical genre standards—is a deviation from classical storytelling modes and from the expectations of American critics and the Hollywood studio executives who helped to fund the film. Through his incorporation of figure movement, Demy and choreographer Norman Maen use an organization of figure and camera movement to undermine expectations of the musical genre and communicate character development through minimalist patterns of repetition, stylistic excess, and narrative obfuscation. Ultimately, Demy's desire to make a French film saturated with songs and dances in France during the 1960s was an industrial challenge that he and his crew could overcome only with international solutions.

The Problem of a French Musical (Production History)

Jacques Demy created his first sung-and-danced musical in a French context that did not have an established infrastructure for supporting such an ambitious musical production. He had already tried for years to make a musical featuring both sung and danced numbers; he wrote his first feature film *Lola* (1961) as a musical, to be shot in color, but producer Georges de Beauregard would only agree to make the film on a smaller budget. As a result, Demy shot *Lola* in black and white and removed most of the musical sequences.[9] The publicity surrounding his all-sung film *Les Parapluies de Cherbourg*

94   STORYTELLING IN MOTION

(1964) and its five Academy Award nominations launched the international reputations of its producer, Mag Bodard, its composer, Michel Legrand, and its star, Catherine Deneuve. It also increased Demy's cinematic credibility, and Demy made networking contacts in Hollywood that would lead to necessary financing for *Les Demoiselles de Rochefort*.[10] Much of the contemporary chatter in the trade press surrounding *Les Demoiselles de Rochefort* compares it to *Les Parapluies de Cherbourg* but notably emphasizes the addition of dance.[11] "Not a completely-sung film, as was 'Umbrellas,'" coproducer Gilbert de Goldschmidt told *Variety*, "'Rochefort' would be one-third song, one-third dance and one-third dialog."[12]

Although Demy's film is associated predominantly with France, producers de Goldschmidt and Bodard knew from the beginning that French financing would not cover the necessary budget. *Les Demoiselles de Rochefort* was therefore a transnational production from its inception. After negotiations with English producer Kenneth Harper stalled, Demy and the film's producers successfully caught American producer Norman Katz's interest instead, though the film's British connection would remain thanks to the film's largely English corps of dancers.[13] *Les Demoiselles*' status as an international coproduction reveals much about the budgetary needs of musical films and the priorities of the French film industry and French dance culture during this period.

Divergent Budgets

A coproduction and distribution deal with Norman Katz and Seven Arts Productions[14] would provide Demy's production enough of a budget to pay for Technicolor,[15] rehearsal time for the musical numbers, and a cast of dancer-actors—all expensive propositions. Labor and personnel aren't cheap, and the larger number of dancers required for Demy's musical numbers—as well as the time needed to rehearse those numbers—drove up the cost of his film projects. *Variety* specifically references "prohibitive dance rehearsals" as one of the many high costs of any film musical's production.[16] Demy echoes this in *Cahiers du cinéma*, in reference to his last feature *Trois places pour le 26*: "That's what is so horribly expensive: renting a rehearsal space, with fifty dancers present at each session."[17]

Given that the musical genre often requires more significant rehearsal periods (before and during production) and greater financial investments,

MINIMALISM AND EXCESS   95

a better understanding of Demy's relationship to money and funding is especially pertinent.[18] The final cost of the film was around 5.8 million francs, 2.5 million of which was provided by the agreement with Seven Arts.[19] The American distributor agreed to fund the project with the understanding that the film would be releasable to mainstream American audiences. One of the most important qualifications of this deal was that the film could be shown without subtitles. Their conditions were therefore that Demy shoot the film twice (once in French, once in English), so that an English-language version could be released for English-speaking markets, and that he hire a few American actors to increase appeal for US audiences. He agreed to both. The contractual obligation to hire three American actors—Gene Kelly, George Chakiris, and Grover Dale[20]—opened up new choreographic possibilities and options to make explicit citations or homages to American musicals. However, Demy was still working within budgetary and personnel constraints that distanced his film from a Hollywood mode of production.

Comparing budget ranges demonstrates the divergence between what Demy was working with and the resources available to musical productions occurring in Hollywood. *Les Demoiselles'* budget of $1.17 million[21] in 1967 is significantly higher than *Les Parapluies de Cherbourg's* $200,000 from three years earlier and is more expensive than the films Demy's French contemporaries were producing before and during this period.[22] But in comparison with Hollywood musicals, *Les Demoiselles* was relatively modest. In 1961, the $7.54 million budget for *West Side Story* (Robert Wise and Jerome Robbins) was considered "immensely expensive at the time."[23] However, two other 1967 musical releases, *Thoroughly Modern Millie* (George Roy Hill) and *Half a Sixpence* (George Sidney), had $6 million budgets—almost six times that of *Les Demoiselles*—which *Variety* considered a modest investment.[24] The musicals from the 1940s and 1950s that had a visible influence on Demy's film also all had budgets ranging from $2 million to $4 million: *The Band Wagon* (Vincente Minnelli, 1953), *Singin' in the Rain* (Stanley Donen and Gene Kelly, 1952), *An American in Paris* (Vincente Minnelli, 1951), *On the Town* (Stanley Donen and Gene Kelly, 1949), and *Meet Me in St. Louis* (Vincente Minnelli, 1944).[25] Comparing Demy's musical to those made in Hollywood without acknowledging this budget data does not take into account the different production modes between a Hollywood product and the resources available in France during the 1960s, even with financial assistance from Seven Arts. Additional industrial constraints existed as well. Shooting in studio interiors would have been prohibitively expensive for most French

96   STORYTELLING IN MOTION

film productions during this period, as rising rental costs in the 1950s led to the closing of many studio spaces.[26] The greater constraint, however, was the lack of a musical theater dance infrastructure in France to provide the caliber of dancers and choreographers needed for such a project.

Dancers (Not) for Hire

French dance culture in the late 1960s made finding the appropriate personnel in France for the choreography and dancing of *Les Demoiselles* a challenge. *Variety* mentions this difficulty, reporting that "dancers in France did not have the essential acting and singing backgrounds that are more prevalent in the U.S. and Britain. Besides, those who had such talent were usually tied up with the Opera here or ballet companies."[27] The novelty of Demy's choreographic choices for *Les Demoiselles* become clearer when we consider that ballet was the more popular dance form with audiences in France (independent of or connected to the operatic theatrical tradition). Unlike in the United States in the middle of the twentieth century, when many popular dance professionals had formal training in a range of dance traditions, French dance training at this time was primarily stratified into ballet and burlesque forms.

The 1950s and 1960s were a period of "neoclassicism" in French ballet, furthered particularly by the work of two important choreographers, Roland Petit and Maurice Béjart. Dance historians Marcelle Michel and Isabelle Ginot assign much agency to Petit's and Béjart's influence on French dance culture,[28] but we must also acknowledge the cultural significance of the Ballets Russes on European dance during this period.[29] These new forms embraced modern themes to reflect their historical times, while still maintaining the classical vocabulary long associated with ballet.[30] One of the influential minds responsible for propagating the popularity of ballet in France was Jean Cocteau, a major influence on Demy's aesthetic, who lent his hand to the creation of the Ballets des Champs-Élysées in 1945.[31] Roland Petit, appointed as the official choreographer for the aforementioned new ballet institution, was one of the few French choreographers of this period who also had some interaction with Hollywood and Broadway. Petit created filmed versions of some of his ballets while in the United States, compiled in the Hollywood-made *Black Tights* (Terence Young, 1961), and was Hollywood star Leslie Caron's ballet teacher. After a visit to New York City in the 1950s,

Petit's choreography began to incorporate some aesthetic influences from the Broadway musical, while remaining couched in the choreographic language and narrative conventions of ballet.[32] French cinema did not engage with classical dance to the same extent as Hollywood did, however, and Demy's production was no different.

Neither was it practical to turn to dancers working in the Pigalle-Montmartre nightclubs of the 1950s and 1960s that might have fit the bill for Demy's production. Paris had a vibrant vaudeville dance culture, some of which had died off in the middle of the century, that tourists and Parisians could take in at "leading niteries" like the Lido and Moulin Rouge.[33] A few differences exist between the vaudeville and cabaret dancers in the United States around the turn of the century and those professionals working in Paris, offering reasons why Demy's production did not (or could not) draw on that particular population. The dancing there was not the aesthetic Demy was looking for; the house styles of nightclubs like the Lido and Moulin Rouge were of a burlesque, striptease sort with some modern touches, as well as the cancan.[34] Such performers may not have had the ability or inclination to shift techniques, as most appear to have training in a single style. In addition, despite there being a number of individual acts and some repeated house shows and performers (like the man playing Valentin, Jean-Louis Bert, at the Moulin Rouge), such an impulse did not lead to the development of a more narrative-based, long-form musical theater structure as did occur in the US. Instead, operettas were more popular with French audiences, and filmic adaptations of theatrical works were common as well, especially from the 1930s to the 1950s.[35] *Variety* critic Gene Moskowitz suggests that even in the 1960s, French theatergoers' "tastes still seem to stay in the old operetta syndrome. . . . Attempts to do modern musicals in the Broadway vein have rarely made it."[36] French audiences therefore preferred operettas for their light, musical, dramatic entertainment at the turn of the century, the same period in which Broadway theater was gaining popularity in America and musical theater as we know it today was emerging as a new form.[37]

Similarly, French performers did not develop the same professional relationship between stage and screen performances that occurred between vaudeville, Broadway, and Hollywood. There were forms of nonballet theatrical dance in France like those performed at the Folies Bergères or the Moulin Rouge that gained popularity. But these shows did not result in the proliferation of schools to train dancers with professional aspirations to the same extent that Broadway musical theater encouraged the opening of dance

98   STORYTELLING IN MOTION

centers in New York City and Hollywood. By 1920, New York City chorus line dancers—the prevalent form of dancing in Broadway shows of this period— had access to the Ned Wayburn Institute of Dancing, which served as a dance studio but also a talent agency for chorus dancers. Aspiring performers were trained in a range of dance styles, including ballet, ballroom, tap, acrobatics, and musical comedy.[38] Once sound filmmaking became the norm in Hollywood, the incentive to appear in film musicals aided this trend. By the 1940s, performers trained only in tap dancing (often referred to as hoofers) found it more difficult to find employment given the plethora of dancers trained in a multitude of (high-brow and more popular) styles, supplemented by the availability of Agnes de Mille's "Acting for Dancers" class.[39]

In contrast, Moskowitz's descriptions of the popular shows at the Lido and Moulin Rouge in the 1950s and 1960s suggest that the specialization of performers around a particular style of dance or act was still common in France during this period, as well as the separation between the more popular, lower-brow fare available at nightclubs and the more elite performances of ballet at the Opéra. Britain, however, had a dance culture that more closely resembled that of the United States. France's neighbor also had highly trained classical and modern dancers during this period. A British style of ballet developed in the 1930s and 1940s,[40] and by the 1960s dancers auditioning for roles in West End musical productions were expected to be highly trained in both ballet and modern dance.[41]

Transnational Musical Solutions

The dance style that we see in *Les Demoiselles* was not, and arguably is still not, a preferred form in France, and the dancing in *Les Demoiselles* stands out against the expectations of theater and filmgoing French audiences in the late 1960s as a result. The choreography mixes modern jazz styles and some ballet inspired by Broadway and Hollywood musical traditions, Jerome Robbin's choreographic aesthetic in particular, and is performed by dancers who for the most part had ballet technique and figures. In addition, the dancers in the film are not French. Dirk Sanders, one of the few dancer-choreographers in France that could have fit such a role, had prior commitments.[42] The filmmakers hired the corps of dancers from England, which was supplemented with the dancing American leads for speaking parts: George Chakiris, Grover Dale, and Gene Kelly. French dancers with the sort of training the filmmakers were looking for were either not available or unwilling to participate in such a production.

Irish choreographer Norman Maen set the dances for Demy's film, with the help of assistants Maureen Bright and Pamela Hart and Gene Kelly's consultation for the numbers he appeared in. Maen's professional versatility made him a practical choice for the production, given his background choreographing for television and stage productions. He had worked with Hollywood choreographer Jack Cole, created dances for the Canadian Broadcasting Corporation, directed and choreographed for the Teilifís Éireann broadcast network in Dublin, and created choreography for a number of stage shows in Dublin, Edinburgh, and the West End.[43] As a result, Maen had experience working with a range of choreographic registers and had learned to create works quickly and efficiently, given the limited time and money in televised productions.

Even with *Les Demoiselles*' higher-than-average budget, rehearsal time was limited; Maen and Demy had only several weeks in London to rehearse the dancers and actors before production began on May 30, 1966.[44] The corps of dancers was also scheduled for only the first two months of the twelve-week production schedule. And the contrast between Kelly's, Chakiris's, and Dale's extensive dance training and the limitations of Deneuve and Dorléac meant that Maen's choreography needed to be flexible enough to positively portray each actor according to their own physical limitations. The resulting stylistic choices draw on simple choreographic parallels, strategically deployed through the film to help the viewer make inferences about romantic compatibilities between characters. But the sheer quantity of danced musical content throughout the film—by the lead characters as well as the corps of dancers sprinkled as pedestrians through the frame—stands out as stylistic excess of its own right, encouraging repeated viewings and distracting our attention from the narrative through-lines.

Decorative Parameters

To say *Les Demoiselles de Rochefort* contains many musical numbers is an understatement. They make up more than half of the film's total screen time. Some numbers serve direct narrative functions, but many exist as a joyful expression of decorative excess. This formal play exceeds what is normative, even for the aesthetic excess associated with the musical genre, to exist as

100 STORYTELLING IN MOTION

formal patterns that function adjacently to the film's narrative goals. Through parallel musical and choreographed phrases, Demy, Legrand, Maen, and others repeat stylistic parameters through the film, creating structures of perceptual play for the viewer. This approach shares traits with what David Bordwell and Kristin Thompson have described as parametric narration, in which the emphasis on formal patterns takes precedence over narrative proceedings.[45]

Consuming parametric filmmaking requires a different sort of work on the part of the viewer: a recognition of and willingness to go along with the film's stylistic patterning. Because of the emphasis on decorative, or ornamental, functions of style, the viewer's perceptual activity is more greatly engaged by the exhibition of "perceptual qualities or patterns" over narrative denotation.[46] Unlike the "comfortable set of viewing procedures" found in classical narration, Thompson argues that films of this sort create a level of "perceptual uncertainty" and forms of perceptual play through stylistic repetition and variation.[47] Paying attention to the way Demy shapes these formal parameters in *Les Demoiselles* is a significant part of the film's visual and sonic appeal. However, the musical genre complicates the question of stylistic parameters existing in excess of narrative motivations, given the genre's (partially earned) reputation for alternations between a conventional plot and musical numbers that arrest narrative progression.

Musical Excess

The extent to which musical numbers are seen as stylistically excessive to their narratives depends on critics and the films they consider to be core examples of the genre.[48] As my categorization of musical numbers in chapter 1 demonstrates, there is a range of subtle ways that musical numbers' content can relate to or further a film's narrative by conveying the expressivity of a character, communicating beneficial denotative information, or presenting content essential to a clear construction of the story. Many scholars emphasize numbers' narrative or stylistic disruptions as more significant to the genre than those sequences that emphasize narrative continuity between plot and number. They describe these numbers' relationships to the narrative as departures from realism,[49] self-contained, "parallel,"[50] "self-enclosed," "independent,"[51] or liberating.[52] Martin Rubin argues that these kinds of musical spaces allow for "spectacular expansions and distortions that can be clearly

MINIMALISM AND EXCESS   101

in excess of the narrative without necessarily disrupting it."[53] None of these writers, however, suggest that this tendency toward stylistic excess and diegetic distancing causes a radical break with the storytelling conventions of classical American cinema.

So where should the line be drawn between conventional iterations of the musical genre—generally understood to exist within the boundaries of classical narration—and what Bordwell and Thompson describe as parametric excess? Ultimately this is a question of scale. Thompson's discussion of classical (nonmusical) films' deflections toward excess suggests that, "to a limited degree, then, the Hollywood cinema can tolerate this slight departure toward the encouragement of the viewing that notes excess."[54] My aim here is not to definitively draw such a line but rather to emphasize that *Les Demoiselles* unequivocally crosses it.

Even if we acknowledge that certain Hollywood musicals contain greater stylistic excess than the average classical Hollywood film, a comparison of these American films to *Les Demoiselles* reveals that Demy's commitment to stylistic patterning exceeds that of the typical Hollywood musical. On a quantitative level alone, Demy's ability to experiment with his musical numbers is partly a result of volume. *Les Demoiselles* has twenty-four musical numbers, whereas the American musicals that influenced Demy's work have between fourteen and seven.[55] A higher percentage of the film consists of musical sequences as well. Of *Les Demoiselles*' two-hour screen time, the musical numbers comprise 69 minutes, or 57 percent. In comparison, despite the 17-minute dream ballet at the end of *An American in Paris*, the musical numbers in that film comprise only 47 minutes—or 42 percent of the film's just-under two-hour screen time. *On the Town*'s musical numbers comprise 39 minutes, or 40 percent of the film's run time, and *West Side Story*'s 49 minutes of musical numbers comprises only 32 percent.

Compared to the American musicals Demy admired, *Les Demoiselles* has musical numbers that feature longer average shot lengths, a higher repetition of locations, and staging choices in the exterior numbers that saturate the frame with figure movement. Although Demy expands on several intrinsic norms to experiment with more recognizable conventions from the studio-era musical genre,[56] he also plays with intrinsic stylistic patterns in subtle ways through his cinematic construction of diegetic plurality. Like the sheer scale of musical numbers in the film, Demy tends to hold his shots longer than his Hollywood counterparts where the musical numbers themselves are concerned. *Les Demoiselles*' musical numbers have an average shot length of

102 STORYTELLING IN MOTION

34.5 seconds. In contrast, the American films discussed in this chapter have an average shot length for their musical numbers of 25.2 seconds, which is close to the average (24 seconds) for Hollywood musical numbers more generally.[57] Vincente Minnelli's musical films studied here have, as a whole, an average shot length of around 20 seconds—higher than *Les Demoiselles'* average shot length of 16.5. Although Minnelli is known for his complex sequence shots, *Demoiselles'* musical number average of 35.5 is longer than the average of numbers from *Meet Me in St. Louis, The Band Wagon,* and *An American in Paris,* whose numbers combined average 31 seconds.

Demy's intricate camera work is also frequently compared to some of the filmmakers working in France that he admired, notably Jean Renoir and Max Ophüls. The averages of their films made in France are comparable or longer than *Les Demoiselles,* averaging between 15 and 20 seconds. In contrast, Renoir's *French Cancan* (1954) is cut more quickly, with an average of 9 seconds. Renoir describes the film in the credits as a "musical comedy" and "comédie musicale," and it functions as his "homage to the Belle Époque music hall."[58] While he does include some longer shots with simple panning camera movements to follow characters, Renoir chooses not to emphasize the intricate use of camera movement to create sequence shots for which he was known in the 1930s. In comparison, Demy maintains a use of lengthier shots and more complex camerawork—including some more elaborate sequence shots—in his experimentation with musical genre norms. One of these longer traveling shots that occurs as a transition between the end of the opening number on the square and an introduction to the sisters in their apartment also serves to signal that the sisters' apartment is also part of the location shooting and not a set (as is the case for the interiors of Demy's later musical, *Trois places pour le 26*).

Demy frequently reuses the Rochefort locations of his musical numbers. Two numbers occur in Lancien's art gallery, three occur in Simon's music store, three occur in the streets of the city, four occur in the sisters' apartment, five occur in Yvonne's café, and six occur on the central square. The only unique location for a number is the opening scene on the transporter bridge. In contrast, the American musicals mentioned here tend to rarely reuse diegetic locations more than once.[59] Two numbers in *On the Town* occur on the Empire State Building set, several numbers in *An American in Paris* use the café/street set, and several numbers in *West Side Story* take place on the (real) New York City streets and in the tailor's shop, but reusing a location in these films is more an exception than the norm. Lower budget Hollywood musicals may reuse sets more often for cost purposes, but many studio-era American musicals flaunt the variety of their set pieces. Several well-known musicals from the end of the Hollywood studio-era period also have sections and musical numbers filmed on location:[60] *West Side Story*, of course, but also *On the Town* and *Funny Face* (Stanley Donen, 1957), while *An American in Paris* and *Gentlemen Prefer Blondes* (Howard Hawks, 1953) both incorporate second-unit exterior shots of Paris. Demy's use of location shooting is novel, not only because his film may be the first French or American film musical to be shot entirely on location but also because of the ways in which he uses those locations in his construction of cinematic space. As cost was a concern for *Les Demoiselles'* production, the financial constraints opened up the opportunity for stylistic play in the creation of movement variations through a redundancy of on-location spaces.

Replete Framing

Demy consciously plays with multiple points of focus in the frame, frequently staging main characters or dancing pedestrians in all three planes—foreground, midground, and background. Demy's purpose in this spatial saturation is not to set up a multitude of visual and auditory gags, as French director Jacques Tati does through the use of parametric narration in *PlayTime*, also released in 1967. As both Kristin Thompson and Eric Faden argue, the perceptual pleasure of Tati's film comes from its replete stylistic patterning and the way our attention is drawn to different details on repeated viewings.[61] While Demy's stylistic patterning serves functions that differ from Tati's, the multiple points of interest necessitate a similar "scanning" of the image and multiple viewings to fully process all the content. Demy's attention to detail in the staging of these sequences, especially regarding the placement of the camera and the time of day (to account for different qualities of sunlight), is visible in the bird's-eye view maps of the space that Demy created (figure 4.1). The diagrams were sketched on paper from the Grand Bacha Hotel, where Demy and most of his cast and crew stayed while in Rochefort.[62] All of the existing overheads are for musical numbers, and most are for the danced numbers to organize and plan the space.[63]

One pattern that emerges from these replete compositions is the linking of outdoor spaces through the repetition of brief choreographic phrases. One such example is a little catch-step phrase that first occurs in "Andy

104 STORYTELLING IN MOTION

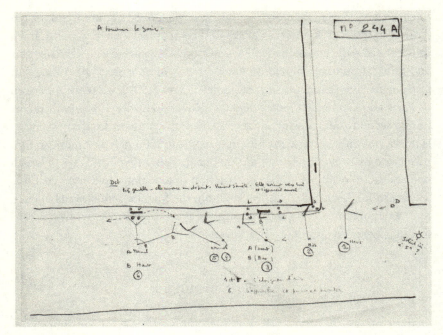

Figure 4.1 Plan décor from Demy's notes for the "Rencontres" number from *Les Demoiselles de Rochefort*. Note the symbols and notes indicating the location of the sun and the preferred time of day to shoot the scene ("A tourner le soir," "Soleil ici à 5h?").

Reproduced with permission from the Fonds Jacques Demy at the Cinémathèque française, © Ciné-Tamaris.

amoureux." Behind Andy, after he runs into a woman, we can see the four women and two sailors that he will eventually dance with. They approach the camera with a simple phrase: they plié (bend their knees) and extend one leg to the side, slightly off the ground, before placing it back on the ground in front of them. They repeat this motion on the other side, starting with the opposite leg. After one more repetition of this they take three little steps, alternating the feet, and undulate their spine from the waist up as their arms extend slightly to the side with a fluid, melting feeling.[64] The dancers continue to repeat this whole phrase, which I will call the "catch-step melt," one more time before the shot changes. This phrase returns, with a simpler series of walking steps before the "melting" portion, twice in "Les rencontres." Some sailors perform the phrase behind Andy and Maxence, and a couple performs the phrase again just before Andy runs into Delphine. Andy and

Figure 4.2 The "catch-step melt" phrase appears in the background of the "Andy Amoureux" number, *Les Demoiselles de Rochefort*.
© Ciné-Tamaris.

Figure 4.3 The "catch-step melt" phrase appears in the background of the "Les Rencontres" number, *Les Demoiselles de Rochefort*.
© Ciné-Tamaris.

Solange perform an even more parsed-down version of the phrase (without the undulating torso or arms) in the final number on the square (figures 4.2– 4.4). This simple phrase, one of several variations on walking in the film,[65] provides an efficient way to create repetition and variation in the frame without the time or financial resources Demy and Maen would have needed to choreograph completely new material for each musical number. It also choreographically links the diegeses of these musical numbers, creating a sense of continuity across the film's layers of diegetic plurality.

Demy activates off-screen space as well through frequent screen entrances and exits. People leap by in the foreground in several numbers, notably at

Figure 4.4 The film's leads perform a parsed-down version of the "catch-step melt" phrase in the midground of the "Départ des Forains" number, *Les Demoiselles de Rochefort*.
© Ciné-Tamaris.

the end of the "Arrivée des camionneurs" and "Les rencontres" numbers. He also activates the background space with groups of dancers in ways that depart from Hollywood films, and this stylistic trait is especially visible in numbers that take place in the street. The "catch-step melt" phrase, for example, most often occurs in the distant background of the numbers mentioned. In "Les rencontres" in particular, Demy has dancers performing multiple little choreographed phrases in the frame at the same time, creating many layers of movement at once that compete with the lyrics of the main characters for our attention. Some of the aesthetic impulse of adding choreography through the frame comes from *West Side Story*. We can see this in the use of tightly framed camera movement to reveal and hide characters in the off-screen space, as chapter 3 discusses. But the broader use of choreography in this way is not derivative of the Hollywood musical, the canonical films mentioned here in particular. In both "Andy amoureux" and "Les rencontres," Demy stages the dancers behind and around the main characters who are most often singing instead of dancing in these moments, and the subtle changes of staging allow the dancers in the background to be hidden and revealed at various moments. The four women and two sailors performing the "catch-step melt" in the background of "Andy amoureux," for example, become more visible as they slowly move in the center of the frame, in the lead space between Andy and the woman he has just bumped into. It is easy to miss these choreographic flourishes entirely if one's attention is focused on the singing protagonists in the foreground, but this "invisible" style[66] rewards repeated

MINIMALISM AND EXCESS 107

viewings by giving the audience additional visual stimulus as they shift their attention away from the foregrounded characters and scan the frame for additional stylistic and narrative details.

This incorporation of dancers throughout the frame creates a generic departure from the norms of classical numbers as well. Demy's musical influences in *Les Demoiselles* remain grounded in a cinematic setting that barely shifts diegetic levels. Unlike the Hollywood films he draws on, which frequently feature a dream ballet or other subjective sequence with implausible environments, Demy creates a heightened diegesis through coordinating colors but one that remains consistent across the film. The tight relationship between the content of the musical numbers and the narrative results in numbers that often skim the surface of diegetic reality. A spatial diegetic grounding, as a result, is one of the aesthetic constants on which Demy's other stylistic elements can play. In contrast, the frequent incorporation of dancing pedestrians means that Demy's musical numbers are constantly infused with shifting diegetic realities through the additional performances of the narrative city's bystanders. The result is a simultaneous mix of different levels, creating a contrast of diegetic plurality between pedestrians who are dancing and the characters who are singing, often in the same frame. A communal diegetic shift of this sort is also less frequent in the American musicals that influenced Demy, where pedestrians either do not experience such a shift or are absent from the space altogether during musical numbers.[67] Consider, for example, the other customers at the amusement stand when Fred Astaire dances in "A Shine on Your Shoes" from *The Band Wagon*, the other children playing basketball in the prologue from *West Side Story*, or the irritated policeman and the man Gene Kelly gives his umbrella to in the titular song from *Singin' in the Rain*.

The corps of dancers' larger movements—jumps and running steps[68]—become minimized somewhat because these motions frequently occur in the extreme background of compositions. Nevertheless, they add a sense of dynamism and energy to the frame and encourage the viewer to track the repetition of simple phrases as they reappear throughout the film. The redundancy suggests a sense of mundanity the relatively small world Rochefort can offer to the film's *demoiselles* and hints at the sort of (vibrant but limited) cycle that the sisters are trying to escape from, contrasted by the freedom and vitality embodied by the carnies. But there is also a perceptual pleasure on the part of the viewer to notice the patterns as they pop up over the course of the film and the emergence of new details that repeated viewings reward. The

108 STORYTELLING IN MOTION

heightened contrast between these levels encourages the viewer to be aware of both the dancing throughout the cinematic space as well as the actions of the film's main characters. The inclusion of a greater quantity of musical numbers gives Demy additional modules to play with patterns of repetition and variation. Yet his formal choices in *Les Demoiselles* also serve strong denotative and expressive functions to communicate information about potential romantic pairings between characters.

Romantic Play

Demy creates strong intrinsic movement norms and stylistic parallels across numbers to emphasize the formation of couples, tightly blending patterns of narrative and ornamental repetition.[69] One of the central narrative conceits of *Les Demoiselles* is romantic entanglements, and Demy cues the viewer to make inferences about who is meant to end up with whom in part through parallels of music scoring and cinematic choreography. In *Les Demoiselles*, Demy gives Solange and Delphine a set of romantic options and provides cues that delay a satisfactory pairing until the end of the film. The viewer must do much hypothesis testing and revising regarding the formation of couples in the film, and much of the evaluation of couple formations occur during musical numbers or from parallels between them. This occurs prominently during musical numbers in which characters sing about their romantic hopes and desires. The numbers eventually exceed their narrative function, however. The resulting "abnormal repetitiveness"[70] creates some playful indecision in the final formation of the story (who will Delphine and Solange pair up with?) but also allows the viewer to appreciate the choreographic patterns that connect these musical number subsets.

Demy's experimentation with genre conventions expands the concept of a dual-focus narrative that Rick Altman argues is the core of the American musical genre. In Altman's conception, the parallels between potential couples, rather than a conventional plot, moves the story forward.[71] Having multiple couples in a film musical is not unusual; *On the Town*, in particular, shows us the formation of three couples over the course of the film.[72] Each couple in the Hollywood film has a clear pairing from the moment the couples meet, however (Gabey and Ivy, Chip and Hildy, Ozzie and Claire), whereas what Demy proposes is several relationship alternatives for a few key characters. Nor is there the "personality dissolve" that Altman suggests couples undergo

MINIMALISM AND EXCESS   109

in musical films as each member of the couple takes on differential traits of the other to ultimately form a more compatible pair.[73]

Demy sets up several possible pairings for his main characters: Delphine could end up with Guillaume (Lancien), Etienne, or Maxence; Solange could be paired with Simon, Bill, or Andy. Viewer expectations of the Hollywood musical genre—generally a genre that ends happily—cue us to expect the sisters will end up with their ideal partner. In contrast, Demy's formation of couples in previous films could cue viewers to be more pessimistic about the likelihood of characters choosing a partner based on love rather than more practical considerations. This remains a valid possibility, given that *Les Parapluies de Cherbourg*—where Catherine Deneuve's character, Geneviève, settles for a man who will provide for her and her child financially but whom she does not love—was the film that gave Demy the directorial cachet that, in part, made it possible for him to put *Les Demoiselles* into production.[74] Two ideal pairings could be undermined in one move, the film hints, if Simon Dame ends up in a relationship with Solange instead of her mother, Yvonne. And the repeated numbers with Lancien keep alive the possibility that Delphine could rekindle her relationship with him. The film's plot more strongly suggests, however, that Delphine will partner up with Etienne or Maxence and Solange with Bill or Andy. The viewer's inferences surrounding these two possible matches are developed in part through extended stylistic play paralleling the twins and the carnies in musical numbers and creating grouped musical sequences, which I will refer to as "love numbers," that point the viewer toward each woman's ideal romantic pairing.

Love Numbers

Seven love numbers center on characters revealing information about their hopeful or lost loves through an interplay of melodic parallels and minimalist cinematic choreography. The kind of cellular dissection of the narrative that Bordwell and Thompson associate with parametric narration becomes particularly apparent in these numbers that Demy designs to show characters expressing their romantic hopes or disappointments. The repetition of musical scoring and the parallels between these sequences are easily apparent, but the viewer is hard-pressed to remember the order they occur in. In several instances, the ordering of these numbers could even be switched without dramatically affecting the viewer's ability to construct a coherent story. Nor are all these numbers causally essential; while much of the sung content serves a narrative function, due to the lyrics which are often tightly related to the film's content, many are not needed for narrative comprehension. Unlike Delphine and Maxence, whom we never see meet, or Simon and Yvonne, who recount story information that is not part of the plot, Solange and Andy's numbers recount information that occurs earlier in the film. Solange, in particular, recounts in vivid detail to Delphine the way she and Andy met in the street, resulting in content that is both narratively specific but also excessively redundant. A classical musical would either show a meet-cute followed by an expressive number or a number in which characters remember past events that the plot elides.[75] *Les Demoiselles* does both.

These seven numbers have a strong expressive function but also frequently provide narrative information about the characters' ideal relationships. Demy's narrative and stylistic choices bear similarities to the sort of narratively relevant musical numbers in Hollywood in which characters are ruminating about their love interests. Judy Garland's "The Boy Next Door" from *Meet Me in St. Louis* (Vincente Minnelli, 1944) is a canonical example of this, in large part because Esther's song's lyrics (performed by Judy Garland) are so closely tied to plot. Much of the song is predominantly expressive, a recounting of Esther's romantic desires, but the opening verse, thanks to some particularly film-specific narrative information, reveals her so-far-unsuccessful attempts to get John's attention, even though she "[lives] at 5135 Kensington Avenue, and he lives at 5133." Demy takes this idea for a musical number further, however, by building an extended network of romantic desires that the viewer must untangle in part thanks to the information provided by these seven songs. Much of the film's exposition about the characters' romantic pasts and futures occurs predominantly in these musical numbers.

Through this particular subset of musical numbers, Demy creates parallel love sequences only for the members of the romantic couples that finally coalesce and that most viewers would likely consider to be the appropriate romantic pairing: Delphine and Maxence, Solange and Andy, and Yvonne and Simon. There are strong stylistic and narrative parallels between them as a set, and additional connections between the numbers that link the characters who are an ideal match. These similarities add to the complex formal play of stylistic devices in Demy's film, but they also serve to cue the spectator to infer the ideal romantic pairings that will occur over the course of the film.

Each member of the pair (Maxence and Delphine, Simon and Yvonne) sings along to their own musical melody that helps the viewer notice the match. The last two numbers (Solange and Andy's songs), are the only exceptions. The numbers occur in only a few interior spaces of this diegetic universe, creating an additional sense of parallelism: Maxence and Yvonne's songs occur in the café, Delphine and Solange's songs occur in their apartment, Simon and Andy's songs occur in the music store, and Maxence's reprise occurs in Lancien's gallery and ends in the sisters' apartment. Many feature a single sequence shot with fluid camerawork that follows their movement and reframes them in the space. All provide narrative information of sorts through the strongly content-specific dialogue. All feature the characters singing to other characters—recounting their desires or experiences—rather than an isolated expression of emotion (as we see in *Meet Me in St. Louis*) or a part of a larger sung conversation (as we see in other musical numbers in *Demoiselles*).[76] And, importantly, the numbers are staged in deliberate, consistent ways. All the numbers share a simple choreographic structure that emphasizes a similar physical approach. Strong repetition of figure movement cues suggest that Demy staged his actors to create a sense of repetition in figure movement across these numbers. And certain shared movement characteristics between the numbers that link the "correct" partners also help the viewer to make subtle inferences about their romantic compatibility.

All of the numbers involve the characters walking through the space they are currently occupying. Their meandering, curved pathways add an energy to the otherwise often melancholy nature of their singing. As the characters sing, their movement qualities alternate in varying degrees between two primary states of being. Sometimes we see an internalization of their emotional expression that causes their gaze to be less focused and their attention to turn inward[77] as their movement dynamics take on a more delicate feeling, suggesting an attention to self.[78] This quality often occurs as the characters begin to walk around the space without any clear direction (narratively speaking) in mind. In contrast, we can see frequent movements of the head that are often an initiation of a deliberate attention and eye contact with other characters to whom they are recounting their stories, desires, or romantic memories.[79] These numbers emphasize an alternation between these states of inner and outer focus.

Simon and Yvonne's numbers demonstrate the unique ways each actor embodies the shifts between these movement qualities.[80] Simon moves his head occasionally with small shakes to engage his inner focus,[81] but his head

112   STORYTELLING IN MOTION

Figure 4.5 Simon moves into Indirect Space Effort as he looks back at Solange in his "Love Numbers" sequence in *Les Demoiselles de Rochefort*.
© Ciné-Tamaris.

movements are more often oriented in relation to his setting (figure 4.5).[82] His shifts into an inner state are more often apparent thanks to his movement of hands and feet. He frequently turns and tilts his head on an angle, creating a sense of mobility[83] and his phrasing is more even, without many quick accents at the beginning of a gesture or movement.[84] This absence of Time Effort correlates with an avoidance of decision-making in Laban/Bartenieff Movement Studies, indicating that perhaps Simon is leaving himself open to a relationship with Solange even as he is remembering his love for her mother Yvonne.

A particularly distinct example of Simon's patterns occurs when he shifts his weight to the right foot and scuffs the ground with his left, using a feeling of lightness and control as he traces a curved pathway on the ground as the foot moves toward and away from his midline (figure 4.6).[85] He uses a similar movement dynamic a few seconds later when he reaches absent-mindedly for the staircase railing before turning back to look at Solange.[86] This pattern of dynamic change correlates with Laban Movement Analysis's Dream State, activating Weight and Flow Efforts, and an emphasis on attention to the inner self through a sensing of one's weight and ongoing movement through the space. This shows us Simon's conflicted emotional state: that he is both remembering fondly a former love interest and discovering his affection for Solange.

Similarly, Yvonne frequently moves her head as part of her inner attention[87] and complements this focus with a direct address that alternates eye contact with Dutroux and Maxence (figure 4.7).[88] Like Simon, her attention

Figure 4.6 Simon's Shape Flow with Light Weight Effort and Bound Flow as he scuffs his foot in his "Love Numbers" sequence in *Les Demoiselles de Rochefort*.
© Ciné-Tamaris.

Figure 4.7 Yvonne's head movements with Direct Space Effort in her "Love Numbers" sequence in *Les Demoiselles de Rochefort*.
© Ciné-Tamaris.

to self[89] is often frequently visible from her arm and hand gestures; she interlaces her fingers, brings her hands to her side, and absent-mindedly twists a handkerchief (figure 4.8). As she reflects and her movements turn to inner impulses, she moves with frequent lightness, quick shakes of the head, and a sense of ongoing progression.[90] These qualities flit in and out and intensify as Yvonne reaches the peak of her memory and we see her framed in a medium close-up. She moves into a dynamic combination of these qualities that reveals how she is dominated by her emotions in a brief absence of external awareness,[91] an intensification that quickly diminishes as she turns back to look off-screen in Dutroux's and Maxence's direction.

Figure 4.8 Yvonne's Shape Flow movements with the handkerchief in her "Love Numbers" sequence in *Les Demoiselles de Rochefort*.
© Ciné-Tamaris.

Within these broader patterns and individual performance nuances emerge micropatterns that further link together the pairs of numbers between the intended lovers, even though each actor's unique physicality means that the simple movements and gestures appear with variations in each number's instance. Maxence and Delphine's numbers have the fewest distinguishing features that set them apart from the rest (partially because Andy and Solange's numbers end with a refrain from their musical theme), while Simon and Yvonne's numbers share the most unique characteristics. Solange and Andy's parallel numbers also share some figure movement qualities, but Solange's performance is the most divergent of the seven numbers. The melody of her song is unique; no other love number shares it.[92] The tempo of her song is livelier than the others in this set, and her movements parallel this. She is more animated, changing levels and the volume of space her body occupies in a postural shift that takes her from standing to crouching as she recreates the events that lead to her and Andy's meeting.[93] The repetition of narrative information serves to justify the stylistic figure movement differences between Solange's "love number" and the other six, as it introduces additional variation.

A closer look at the parallels Demy creates between Simon and Yvonne's numbers helps to show the compatibility between the characters despite their earlier parting, due to Yvonne's reluctance to adopt the name "Madame Dame." Her number occurs after his in the plot, and their similar melody and parallels in the phrasing and content of Demy's lyrics make it quickly apparent to the viewer that Yvonne is singing about Simon. Certain gestures

MINIMALISM AND EXCESS 115

and a similar fluid camera movement during the single sequence shot of each number helps to reinforce this. Both smile as they are remembering past experiences, unlike Delphine and Maxence, who are more often solemn. Both employ a gestural sort of inner focus[94] with a distal initiation coming from the ends of the limbs as they recount their memories: Simon scuffs the ground with his foot and reaches a hand for the stair railing, Yvonne twists a handkerchief in her fingers and raises them to her face as she sits. Unlike Solange and Maxence, who cross their arms across their bodies to narrow their physical space,[95] or Andy and Solange who frequently spread their arms to widen theirs, Yvonne and Simon move somewhere in between. They both widen somewhat as they reach for the staircase (Simon) or the table (Yvonne), but they also walk with their hands in their pockets, creating a distinct shape than none of the other characters share. In fact, of the three women's dresses, Yvonne's is the only one to include pockets. These are used to hide the handkerchief prop she later draws out, and the costume design helps to reinforce the intentional differences between each set of couples.

Both Simon and Yvonne circle around the space as they sing, and the camera movements alternate between following their figure movement and reframing to position them in closer or more distant shot scales. This general movement pattern is present in each of the love numbers, but the parallels between these two, with their single sequence shot, are especially striking. In the "Chanson de Simon," after an initial pause, Simon walks forward and the camera tracks back to keep him in the same medium shot scale. After an initial turn back to Solange (who is now behind him), he turns to his left and crosses the frame, the camera panning left slightly to reframe. The camera continues to move, tracking right and panning left to slightly change our perspective on the characters. When Simon continues to walk toward the left side of the frame (turning to look at Solange as he does so) the camera pans left to follow him, and he slowly increases in size to a medium close-up as he approaches the camera. After both pause in the center of the room, the camera tracks back to reframe Simon (and Solange, who reenters the frame) in a long shot. The camera remains still as he scuffs the ground with his foot and reframes slightly as he walks to the left toward the staircase, after which the camera continues to track forward to reframe him in a medium close-up, the camera also panning to the right as Simon walks back to Solange.

In the "Chanson d'Yvonne," we begin with a medium close-up of Yvonne, who perches on a table and turns her head as she alternates looks at Maxence and Dutroux who are off-screen to the left and right of the frame, respectively.

116   STORYTELLING IN MOTION

Soon, however, the camera begins to track back to reframe the space, ending on a long shot of the three at the tables. After a brief pause, Yvonne rises and begins to walk toward the left side of the frame past Maxence, and the camera pans slightly to keep her in the shot, then pans right as Yvonne walks back to the table. She then begins walking a third time, and this time the camera pans to keep her in the frame as she walks to the left, ending up in a medium close-up before she stops and turns to look back at the men. The camera continues to pan left and begins tracking back, however, to slowly circle Yvonne. After a few beats she continues to walk toward the left side of the frame and the camera continues to move with her until she reaches Dutroux and Maxence's table and is framed between them.

By the end of each number the camera has circled around the space in such a way that it ends facing the opposite direction from the one it started in, the characters having changed their orientation in the space as well. The camera is as involved in Demy's staging of the space as the figure movement, with the patterned repetition of cinematic choreography working symbiotically to cue narrative comprehension. An overhead Demy drew in preparation of filming seems to portray the staging of Simon's scene and the deliberate movement of characters and camera through the space (figure 4.9). The simplicity of this figure movement carries over into the other musical numbers, as the in-teraction between couples and acquaintances supports most of the musical numbers in the film. The specific ways that Demy repeats and shapes these movements, however, creates strong similarities between key characters and their emotional expressions. He takes this narrative complexity further, how-ever, obfuscating our efforts at narrative clarity by introducing contradictory cues through a second set of romantic musical numbers.

Dual Focus Distraction

Demy uses four numbers to explore the parallels between and interactions of Solange and Delphine with the two main carnival workers, Bill and Etienne. We can observe a more conventional dual-focus coupling in these potential pairings and the way they play out over the course of the plot. Throughout his film, Demy hints at the dual-focus nature of the pairing between these two groups by emphasizing some similarities between them but also strong differences, and these musical numbers allow the viewer to evaluate their

MINIMALISM AND EXCESS 117

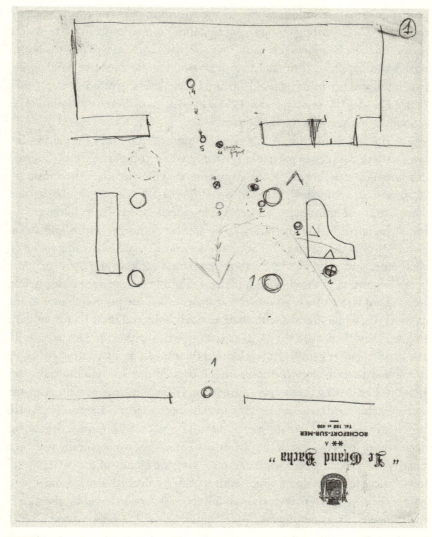

Figure 4.9 An overhead drawn by Jacques Demy that appears to portray the staging changes for the "Chanson de Simon" number from *Les Demoiselles de Rochefort*.

Reproduced with permission from the Fonds Jacques Demy at the Cinémathèque française, © Ciné-Tamaris.

potential romantic union. While in the love numbers the music cues do most of the heavy lifting by signaling romantic compatibility through shared melodies, these numbers rely more on patterned figure movement to accomplish a similar effect. Ultimately, they also point to the narrative parallels between Bill and Etienne's relationship and Lorelei and Dorothy's in *Gentlemen Prefer Blondes* (Howard Hawks, 1953), in which any heterosexual union is secondary to their love for each other.[96]

The dual-focus nature of this relationship and the hint of a pairing between these couples is particularly visible when comparing the "Chanson des jumelles" number to "Nous voyageons de ville en ville." The music for "Chanson des jumelles" is based on a simple alternation of chorus and verses, and the minimalist choreography parallels this. The choreography for each chorus is, like the lyrics, fairly similar each time with slight variations. Throughout most of the song the sisters alternate between a focus on each other and a direct address to the camera. Delphine and Solange pause at the beginning of the chorus, sometimes slightly raising a shoulder, before turning a quarter of a rotation so that their bodies are perpendicular to the camera. They plié slightly, with their arms straight and their hands on their thighs. They then walk forward, executing half turns with each step, with their hands either gently clasped behind their backs or alternating swinging forward with each step. The color inserts of their dresses help the skirt portion fly open during these steps, the costume design further accentuating the turns. Each time the chorus returns, the sisters change the direction in which they begin the phrase, creating an additional variation. The end of the chorus varies more than the rest of the phrase but consists of some combination of a pose—either leaning backward or embodying the quality of the "whimsy galore" lyric, "de la fantaisie à gogo," with repeated balanced poses—and a twirl before they walk to a new portion of the room for the next verse. The movement in the verses emphasizes poses and staging that often create a sense of symmetry in the frame, as we can see when the sisters sit on the couch with their arms draped similarly on the edges of the arm and their outer legs wrapped around their inner legs, a pose that they hold as they sing. The choreography also emphasizes stability; the sisters often hold poses for longer periods and their movements are more vertical,[97] without much movement off-center.[98] Throughout the number, much of the phrasing is impulsive,[99] with quick, light accents.[100] We can observe a sense of determination and decision-making in the song that is supported by their movement choices. The choreography is simple, but the actresses' movements are also controlled and externally oriented.[101] The straightforwardness of their dancing parallels the unambiguous nature of the lyrics as they sing about their plans for the future.

The carnies' number, "Nous voyageons de ville en ville," shares a number of structural similarities to the sisters' song to indicate their romantic compatibility, while variations—in dual-focus narrative fashion—suggest differences that must be overcome or reconciled for a successful coupling. Like the sisters' song, the carnies' later duet, "Nous voyageons de ville en ville," also alternates between a chorus ("nous voyageons . . .") and verses, with an additional bridge in the middle for an extended dance sequence. The choreographic variations are greater than in the earlier number and more complex to accommodate the performers' (Chakiris's and Dale's) more refined dance technique. The movement vocabulary of the number consists primarily of turns, locomotion through the space with accented movements in the upper body, leaps (sometimes while turning), and extensions of the arms and legs outward and upward away from the body. Their movement phrases are occasionally phrased with an initial accent, but they also move with more suspension,[102] resulting in impactful phrases that often end with an increase of strength[103] as the arms or legs extend into verticality. Although the specific iteration of those steps does not usually repeat in the same way, a brief similar phrase ends each verse before the return of the chorus. The two briefly pause and hold their current pose, rapidly spread their arms outward,[104] and gather their arms back toward the midline in order to rotate in a full turn, after which they again begin to extend their arms outward in a more lingering fashion[105] before moving into the next chorus.

Some of Bill and Etienne's movements create a choreographic continuity from the sisters' number. There is an emphasis on turns and on locomotion toward and away from the camera on the z-axis of the mise-en-scène,[106] as well as the holding of poses at the end of a phrase. One of the crouched cross-leg poses the carnies hold parallels the shape of the sisters' symmetrical crossed-leg pose they hold while sitting on their couch (figures 4.10 and 4.11). Some of the carnies' choreography is also mirrored, like that of the sisters, but more often their movements are performed in union on the "same side," and the choreography for their number creates a greater expansion of their bodies[107] and is more mobile, with a greater use of phrases that intensify into a quickly executed movement.[108] The greater sense of fluidity in the men's movements,[109] the speed with which they cover the space, their greater change of movement levels as they leap and spin around the café, and their

Figure 4.10 Delphine and Solange's bent arm and leg positions create symmetry in the frame in *Les Demoiselles de Rochefort*.
© Ciné-Tamaris.

Figure 4.11 Bill and Etienne's extended arm and bend leg positions parallel those of the sisters from figure 4.10 in *Les Demoiselles de Rochefort*.
© Ciné-Tamaris.

fuller forceful extension of their limbs with balled fists[110] deviate from the sisters' movement qualities and vocabulary. The larger movements of the carnies hints that their world is more mobile and dynamic than that of the sisters, and we can see parallels with the similarly expansive movements of outsiders in the film: the other carnies, Andy, and to a certain extent, the sailors stationed in Rochefort.[111] Choreographic similarities create inferences about their romantic compatibility, while differences—and the potential that the couples can overcome them—adhere to the traditional dual focus model.

The film's similar editing and framing patterns also firmly link these numbers. In both the sisters' song and the carnies' song, Demy has his cinematographer Ghislain Cloquet frequently shift to closer framings during the verses, alternating between two shots and singles of the men or the sisters, who in both numbers alternate between glances toward one another and a direct address of the camera.[112] The closer framings of the sisters is more easily justified stylistically, given the simplicity of the choreography. However, the larger movements of the men during their number, which requires more distant shot scales to be fully visible, could make the closer framings feel more obstructive to our continued appreciation of the cinematic choreography. Given that Cloquet does not film the other dance numbers with this sort of patterned repetition between closer singles and two shots of the characters, this stylistic choice in "Nous voyageons de ville en ville" reinforces the parallelism between the carnies' and the sisters' musical numbers. To further this connection, the scene that follows "Nous voyageons de ville en ville" returns us to the sisters' apartment, where Solange plays the chorus of the sisters' song on a recorder before improvising on the tune. Similarly, after the sisters' number Delphine leaves the apartment, and we see her walking through the square where she almost runs into Etienne and Bill, one of the many close, coincidental encounters that the film creates through careful staging and blocking.

The sisters and carnies also share two numbers later in the film, which continues to posit the possibility of their eventual romantic union and the foursome's overall compatibility. When the two sisters perform their song again for the carnies in "De Hambourg à Rochefort," we see an initial repetition of the earlier choreography. Both stand and plié again in the beginning of the chorus, but this time they lean against the piano. Instead of walking forward, they twirl in a full circle, Delphine first, then Solange. Delphine then sits on the piano stool, and they both move into poses for the "fantaisie à gogo" lyric. Delphine's movement is fairly similar to the original number, and she moves into the pose with a similar dynamic quality as she did in the earlier number,[113] whereas Solange extends an arm into verticality while she sinks slightly into a plié, with a greater sense of prolonged fluidity.[114] When Bill and Etienne stand to join them, they also alternate turns as they move through the space toward the sisters. The alternation and depth staging echoes the carnies' earlier number, but the complexity of their initial choreography is simplified to match Deneuve and Dorléac's technical capacities. Later on, the men's suspended, strong high kicks[115] return from their earlier sequence. However, most of the choreography for this number consists of simple turns and steps through the space, blending the choreographic

122 STORYTELLING IN MOTION

impulses of the two earlier numbers. This sense of harmonious combination, as well as the eventual pairing of the couples (Delphine dancing with Etienne and Solange dancing with Bill) points to the possibility of their romantic union.

The final number between the sisters and carnies, "Toujours, jamais," occurs after the men have admitted their carnal desires to the sisters and continues the use of parallelisms and symmetry in the frame from the earlier numbers. However, this number serves instead to emphasize the endurance of Bill and Etienne's relationship. As in the earlier two numbers, Demy uses many closer framings that create parallel, balanced compositions as the sisters sing to, and then stand and walk toward, their rejected lovers. The similarity of costumes and color choices helps to reinforce the mirroring that occurs as the carnies stand in the middle of the frame, their backs to one another, as they face the women. Soon after, the sisters walk toward each other and the facings switch, creating a simple variation in the symmetrical staging that continues as the men reach out to the women, who turn their upper bodies to exchange glances and to accept being kissed (also at the same time). No dancing occurs in the beginning of the number, but after the sisters have left, the two men run and leap around the now-empty stage and square before exiting the frame. The latter dancing section, with its fast locomotion and balletic jumps, also parallels the "Marins, amis, amants, ou maris" number where the carnies are similarly rejected by a pair of women. In both instances, the men shrug off the dismissals with a knowing glance and a smile. Women come and go in their lives, but Etienne and Bill's relationship remains a constant. These additional stylistic parallels between the carnie's numbers reinforces that their bond is more profound and substantial than the fleeting pairings with the women they encounter in their travels.

Conclusions

Demy and his crew filmed two versions of *Les Demoiselles de Rochefort* as planned: one in French and one in English. The English-language version of the film was never released, but it is worth remembering that Demy and his crew shot the film twice—much of which involved the corps of dancers hitting their marks consistently in both versions—on a budget that was already lower than the Hollywood average for the time. The now recently merged Warners–Seven Arts did not distribute *Les Demoiselles* in American theaters until April of 1968, where it had a "very poor" first two weeks at the box office, earning only $15,000 during that period.[116] *Les Demoiselles* received 1.5 million theater entries in France during its run[117] but was not in the top twenty most-seen films in France during 1967, a year dominated largely by Louis de Funès comedies and James Bond.[118]

The American company did not market the film aggressively enough from the point of view of its French producers. Eliot Hyman countered producer Gilbert de Goldschmidt's accusation of Seven Art's lost faith with the reassurance that the distributor "used every effort available to us and the expenditure of substantial sums in advertising to try and make it work, but it just didn't."[119] The delayed American release and perceived lack of interest in *Les Demoiselles* from its American distributors may have stemmed from the company's state of flux, as Eliot Hyman acquired the assets to Warner Brothers Pictures Inc. on July 15, 1967, creating the newly merged Warners Bros.–Seven Arts Ltd.[120] Hyman's correspondence to de Goldschmidt in April 1967 suggests as much, referencing the "overall Warner Bros. situation" as one of the reasons why Seven Arts had yet to make arrangements to distribute the film in the US.[121] Their reaction to the English-language version played a part in the decision as well. Norman Katz had no objections to it, and there do not appear to be records of what other decision-makers at Seven Arts thought, despite the existence of memos from de Goldschmidt repeatedly asking for their reactions.[122] But the silence speaks volumes. The American company likely decided the English-language version of *Les Demoiselles* would not play well with American audiences and released the French subtitled version, marketed as an art-house film, instead.[123]

Les Demoiselles de Rochefort failed to live up to Seven Arts' expectations of what a mainstream Jacques Demy movie would be like because Demy's films are consistently unconventional. The film's complex and unusual formal structure challenges its audience, subverting expectations of musical genre conventions by forcing the viewer to continuously revise their narrative hypotheses. Demy and Norman Maen's choreographic choices are key drivers of this playful process. *Les Demoiselles de Rochefort* emphasizes how important cinematic choreography is as a stylistic tool in Demy's idiosyncratic, cinematic worlds.

After finishing *Les Demoiselles de Rochefort*, Demy spent two years in Los Angeles with his partner and fellow filmmaker Agnès Varda. These years introduced Demy to a "new artistic and cinematographic scene."[124] While in California, he made *Model Shop* (1969) for Columbia Pictures, a film

124 STORYTELLING IN MOTION

with a strong anti-Vietnam war sentiment that incorporates Demy's fascination with the city of Los Angeles and his immersion in the American countercultural aesthetic of the late 1960s. Despite his desire to continue working in Hollywood, Demy was unsuccessful in getting another American film project off the ground, not being one to accept the Hollywood rule of "one for you, one for me." Columbia's producers were expecting a big, colorful musical *à la Demy*, not the brooding, slow reflection on Los Angeles culture that was *Model Shop*. The film's financial failure made Demy a risky investment to Hollywood executives,[125] and his project pitches—including an adaptation of Perrault's fairy tale "Peau d'âne" in English[126] and a musical about Californian counterculture based on the "Tristan and Isolde" myth—were turned down. With Catherine Deneuve on board to star in a musical fairy tale, he returned instead to France to make *Peau d'âne* (1970).

In this musical that also features extensive choreographed figure movement, Demy blends the medieval and Renaissance aesthetics of the French fairy tale with anachronistic details and musical genre norms, contrasts that are paralleled in Legrand's score and Demy's choreographic choices. Unlike his close collaboration with Gene Kelly and Norman Maen on *Les Demoiselles de Rochefort*'s choreography, Demy largely organizes *Peau d'âne*'s expressive movement himself. By making his princess an active agent in her fate, unlike the more passive princesses of classic fairy tales, *Peau d'âne* explores a hybrid genre form to reflect the values of the French Women's Liberation Movement that was at its height in 1970 and to draw attention to the physical labor of domestic tasks. The expressive diegetic shifts associated with musical numbers are distinguished from magically motivated moments largely through a distinction between stationary, gesture-based choreography (for the former) and full-body traveling through the cinematic space, often combined with in-camera effects (for the latter). Demy's adaptation of Perrault's tale plays out in part through the polarized figure movement choices between the film's fairy tale and musical number moments, developed through references to classical Disney animation, postmodern American dance, and 1940s French art cinema.[127] This penchant for aesthetic eclecticism would continue in his last feature and only other sung-and-danced musical, *Trois places pour le 26*.

5

Musical Unease

Trois places pour le 26 (1988)

Halfway through Jacques Demy's *Trois places pour le 26* (1988), popular French actor and singer Yves Montand is in rehearsal with a corps of dancers. Dressed in a black vest, slacks, and a pressed white shirt, he sings about his days working in the Marseille shipyard. Montand's iconic voice mixes with his simple movements as he walks among lines of dancers. In contrast, the corps of male dancers around him are dressed in stained workmen's clothes, and their choreography is expansive, angular, quick, and functional, emphasizing their muscular bodies and the working-class status of their characters. Composer Michel Legrand's electronic music that links these sung and danced phrases, the latter choreographed by Michael Peters, is a departure from both Montand's and Demy's known aesthetics. The film deviates significantly from Demy's other musicals as well as American musicals of the 1980s through a number of its aesthetic and narrative choices. It is also a culmination of the French filmmaker's formal experimentations with the musical genre and his use of figure movement to communicate narrative information.[1]

Trois places draws significantly on biographical details about Yves Montand's rise to fame. The film opens with Montand, in character as himself, arriving in his hometown of Marseille to premiere a new stage show, *Montand Remembers*. The narrative we see unfold on the stage is largely autobiographical and traces Montand's rise to fame, complete with references to his relationships with Simone Signoret, Edith Piaf, and Marilyn Monroe. But the plot that takes place off-stage is of Demy's fabrication. In this frame story, Marie-Hélène or Mylène (Françoise Fabian)—once Montand's lover, now the wife of a corrupt aristocrat—disapproves of her daughter Marion's (Mathilda May) desire to become a performer and her idolatry of Montand. The unusual twist of fiction off-stage and reality on-stage is destabilizing, as Demy's films tend to be, and the lines between these worlds get blurrier as the film progresses, especially once Marion joins the show when the original

Storytelling in Motion. Jenny Oyallon-Koloski, Oxford University Press. © Oxford University Press 2024.
DOI: 10.1093/oso/9780197602669.003.0006

126 STORYTELLING IN MOTION

actress abandons the touring company. We gradually learn that Montand's romantic lead, Maria, now played by Marion, is based on Marie-Hélène. After the show's successful opening night, Montand and Marion sleep together, but—unlike the audience—they do not realize they are father and daughter until the next day. Rather than condemning the unintentional incest with a tragic ending, Demy ends his film with a happy reunion between Montand and Marie-Hélène—who still love each other—as the theater troupe leaves Marseille to go on tour.[2]

Trois places pour le 26 is a perturbing film; it is at once meticulously designed and uplifting while also leaving the viewer uneasy and having to make a moral judgment about Montand and his (fictional) daughter's actions. It equally fits uncomfortably into the backstage musical subgenre. Demy deviates from French film acting conventions, contemporary dance styles, and genre expectations to deliberately construct an unsettling aesthetic. More so than his earlier dance-filled musical *Les Demoiselles de Rochefort* (1967), *Trois places* confronts its viewers' expectations and challenges their assumptions about musical genre form. The film also went into production with significant financing after France's dance culture had exploded, fostering Demy's ability to further link a cinematic choreographic aesthetic to his storytelling demands.

Shifting Constraints and Expectations (Production History)

Twenty-one years separate *Trois places pour le 26* from *Les Demoiselles de Rochefort*. Demy's career moved through a number of shifts between the two films, and his aesthetic activities varied widely during this time. In the years after his fairy-tale musical *Peau d'âne* (1970), Demy struggled to get script projects off the ground, leading to a professionally dry period. While working in Los Angeles in the late 1960s, he and Yves Montand attempted to finance some musical collaborations, called "Les Folies Passagères" and "Dancing," without success. Demy wrote four scenarios in the 1970s that were all refused.[3] The films Demy did complete often didn't earn enough money to make him a safe bet for producers, creating difficulties in getting other projects financed. The international coproduction *Lady Oscar* (Jacques Demy, 1979) was very popular in Japan and Eastern Europe but not in France, where Demy sought financing.[4] In 1976 and 1977, he was set to direct a Russian-French musical coproduction.[5] The musical drama *Anouchka* told the story of a French film crew making a musical film adaptation of Leo Tolstoy's *Anna Karenina* in Russia. In an elegant blend of cinematic reality and fiction, Demy and Michel Legrand were to play the director-composer team at the helm of an international coproduction, with dancers for a large ballet about the daily routine of merchants in Leningrad provided by the Bolchoï Ballet. Russia's Mosfilm was prepared to cover most of the cost, but the refusal on the part of French distributors to guarantee a French exhibition contract resulted in the project's dissolution.[6] Investing even a fraction of the production costs for a Demy film was seen as a risky investment in the 1970s, and the filmmaker was unable to find an investor for the three million French francs required.[7]

Out of necessity, Demy shifted his professional interests to other forms of media, developing his skill for staging performers outside of cinema. During the 1970s, he worked as a director and staged performances for several French theatrical productions. He also made frequent trips between the US and France, especially in 1976 and 1977, when he seemingly served as a consultant or creative collaborator for the stage production of *The Umbrellas of Cherbourg*, an adaptation of his 1964 film that played at the Public Theater in New York during 1979.[8] Demy was also involved with several opera productions during this period, for which he provided the mise-en-scène. In 1972 he staged a production of Igor Stravinsky's *Le Rossignol* for La Maison de la culture d'Amiens (opening at Venise and then playing at the Théâtre de la Ville in Amiens, France).[9] Demy told *Cinéma 76* he was offered the chance to do the mise-en-scène for the 1977 revival adaptation of Jean-Philippe Rameau's opera *Platée*, a few years later, a position that he seems to have declined, as no evidence exists of his collaboration on that project.[10] He also staged the performances for the first ever French César awards ceremony on April 3, 1976.[11]

The range of Demy's theatrical exposure during this period emphasizes that he had more experience working with choreography and dancers than his filmography alone conveys. He brought this experience to *Trois places* at a time when governmental investment in the movement-based art form was growing and French dance culture more closely matched the styles he sought for his musical productions. Thanks to the interest of producer Claude Berri in the project, *Trois places*'s filmmakers had a generous budget to exert even greater stylistic control. Once again the production looked internationally for its choreographer, hiring American Michael Peters, and Demy chose once

128   STORYTELLING IN MOTION

more to use his relative financial freedom to make unconventional choices for his final feature film.

France Dances

In the period between *Les Demoiselles* and *Trois places pour le 26*, French dance culture was evolving. Government initiatives helped to create regional choreographic centers that fostered the development of a more postmodern approach to dance in France, called *danse contemporaine*, adopted around the 1970s.[12] The form has parallels to the modern and postmodern dance traditions that developed in the United States in the twentieth century that Demy likely experienced while living in Los Angeles in the late 1960s. Unlike postmodern dance in the United States, which was largely a reaction to modern dance,[13] *danse contemporaine* in 1970s France was a departure from the ballet works of Maurice Béjart.[14] By the 1980s, *danse contemporaine* was an established part of French dance culture, spurred in large part by government subsidies.

In the early 1980s, dancers in Paris could also experience forms of hip hop dance, though Felicia McCarren points out that French hip hop had different origins than its American counterpart, which began in Black communities of the South Bronx. The term refers more to a specific dance form rather than a broader, multimedia artistic movement, as it does in the United States.[15] French hip hop dance forms were "taken up first in [French] suburban and immigrant communities, becoming a forum for debate on assimilation and multiculturalism."[16] The same regional, state-funded centers for dance that aided in the establishment of *danse contemporaine* assisted its development, and the form built off both pan-African and American jazz dance vocabularies and traditions.[17] However, French hip hop became more pervasive in the late 1980s and early 1990s,[18] so while it may have been available to dancers as they auditioned for Demy's film, it would not yet have been an engrained part of a professional movement training. Professional French dancers during this period were still primarily classically trained, or studying *danse contemporaine*, but they also had greater access to American choreographic training. Teachers would come from the United States to give Broadway-style dancing workshops, sponsored by regional dance centers. Several American dancer-choreographers—Matt Maddox, Molly Molloy, and Rick Odums— also emigrated to France and established modern jazz dance companies there during the 1970s and 1980s, organizations which directly impacted the movement practice of some of the dancers hired for *Trois places*.[19]

Demy initially had several French choreographers in mind for his film. Planning notes have the French ballet choreographer Roland Petit's name scribbled on the side, and Demy's planner suggests he tried to get in touch with Petit on or around August 24, 1987.[20] Demy also entertained the idea of a more avant-garde look to the dancing. He thought there to be a number of "magnificent choreographers, like Pina Bausch" in Europe at the time[21] and he tells *24 Images* that he considered her before deciding that her work was "too anguished, too tortured."[22] In an interview from 1988, he mentions the name of French choreographer Maguy Marin, a significant figure in the contemporary dance world.[23] Her works are known for their destabilizing and grotesque qualities, while also remaining grounded in the ballet tradition she acquired as a dancer for Maurice Béjart.[24] Yves Montand and Michel Legrand rejected the idea of an avant-garde aesthetic, and Montand suggested American choreographer Michael Peters, a choice that Demy ultimately also supported.[25]

The 1980s were a prolific period for Michael Peters. He choreographed Pat Benatar's "Love Is a Battlefield" music video (1983) and was a co-choreographer (with Michael Bennett) for the original 1981 Tony-winning Broadway production of *Dreamgirls*. He also choreographed several of Michael Jackson's early music videos, "Beat It" (1983) and "Thriller" (1983). Although hip hop dancing began in the 1970s, widespread exposure to (and a greater commercialization of) this new dance form occurred in part thanks to the popularity and aesthetic choices made by the creative teams, including Peters, involved in the "Beat It" and "Thriller" videos.[26] Both were significant catalysts in the music video industry and are held responsible for the increase of music record sales in 1983, including eight million copies of Michael Jackson's *Thriller* album.[27] Peters's choreographic versatility from working in a range of choreographic modes and media industries, like that of *Les Demoiselles de Rochefort*'s choreographer Norman Maen's, was a good fit for the eclectic range of music and dance styles that *Trois places* would encompass.

Cost-attainable

For the only time in his filmmaking career, Demy had the resources to make a musical—in color, with songs, dances, large set-pieces, and long rehearsal

130   STORYTELLING IN MOTION

periods—without prohibitive monetary limitations. *Trois places* owes its existence in large part to producer Claude Berri who, after the financial success in 1986 of his two-part film *Jean de Florette* and *Manon des sources* (starring Montand, Daniel Auteuil, and Gérard Depardieu), offered to fund the project that Demy and Montand had failed to finance twenty years earlier. A cost estimate from April of 1988 puts the total cost at just under 56 million francs.[28] Budget comparisons from the perspective of equivalent purchasing power in 1988 show that *Trois places pour le 26* cost approximately twice as much as *Les Demoiselles'* 29.6 million.[29] The budget disparities become more interesting when comparing itemized costs for production design, which reinforces the importance of a carefully crafted visual look to Demy's films. If we compare the costs of set design (with labor included), we can better see how Demy was able to devote additional resources to creating his desired visual look. Taking inflation into account, the set design for *Les Demoiselles* was budgeted at 2.5 million francs and the estimated budget for *Trois places*'s set design was 10 million. In addition, Berri's funding for *Trois places* meant Demy could shoot all his interior scenes on studio lots, allowing him a greater level of control over his mise-en-scène. *Les Demoiselles'* set design budget was 8.5 percent of the film's total cost; *Trois places*'s set design costs (with studio rentals included) accounted for 25 percent of the film's total budget.[30]

Additional funding also paid for a larger corps of dancers and longer rehearsal times. Twenty-five English dancers were hired for *Les Demoiselles*, plus the three Americans whose presence was designed to attract US audiences (George Chakiris, Grover Dale, and Gene Kelly). *Les Demoiselles'* shooting schedule suggests a production period of about twelve weeks, with two weeks of rehearsal beforehand for the dancers in England. *Trois places* had a similar production period of just under twelve weeks, but this time with a group of thirty-seven dancers—hired from England, the United States, and France—and three months of rehearsals with the full corps.[31]

Berri's offer provided Demy with generous financial resources to make his film. Because Berri and Montand were the primary impetus for initiating the production, it also brought his lead actor into the filmmaking process earlier than was normal for Demy, which led to some collaborative friction. Montand was more involved in the minute details of preparation than the film's publicity suggests,[32] leading to conflict between the filmmaker and his lead just before the start of the film's principal photography.[33] The choice to incorporate more popular music and dance styles into the musical also stemmed in part from the more elevated budget and the need to attract a wider audience demographic. Despite the filmmakers' hope that a contemporary feel to the songs and dances would attract younger audiences, the resulting eclectic blend of visual and sonic aesthetics and their relationship to the narrative and the musical genre creates a disconnect between *Trois places* and other musicals from the 1980s.

A cursory look at stylistic decisions made in American musicals from the time period emphasizes that the dance and music styles in *Trois places* are not in sync with contemporary trends. This is apparent from the film's greater reliance on movement vocabulary from musical theater, jazz, and ballet as opposed to hip hop or the more aerobic jazz (and corresponding costumes) seen in *Flashdance* (Adrian Lyne, 1983) or *Breakin'* (Joel Silberg, 1984) that were especially popular in American media of this period. Peters' work on the film deviates from his own choreography for the music videos he made with Pat Benatar—"Love Is a Battlefield"—and Michael Jackson— "Beat It" and "Thriller." Peters's choreography from *Trois places* shares some similarities to his work on music videos in 1983, but overall his work for Benatar and Jackson stands apart, as each video develops its own choreographic logic to parallel the musical rhythms and reinforce the narratives of the music videos. In both the videos and the film we can see a use of spinal undulations, isolations of the hips and torso, and a rapid extension and contraction of the arms towards the body center.[34] This versatility is what drew Demy to Peters in the first place, both his flexibility as a choreographer and his ability to shape a performance to fit the context at hand.

Differences in editing patterns also make *Trois places* stand out from contemporary American musicals, like *The Blues Brothers* (John Landis, 1980) or *Little Shop of Horrors* (Frank Oz, 1986), which most often have an overall shot length average of around 5 seconds.[35] Compared to *Les Demoiselles'* average shot length of 16.5 seconds, *Trois places's* average shot length of 9.8 seconds continues a downward trend and is cut quite quickly within the context of Demy's career. Comparing the average lengths of musical numbers in *Les Demoiselles*—35.5 seconds—to *Trois places*—25 seconds—also shows an increase in editing-based pacing. But in relation to other musical examples from the 1980s, Demy's film is cut quite slowly. The figure movement-heavy numbers in *Xanadu* (Robert Greenwald, 1980) have an average shot length of 11.6 seconds. The numerous dance numbers in the musical-science fiction hybrid *Earth Girls Are Easy* (Julien Temple, 1988) have an average shot length of 4 seconds. The three music videos Peters worked on in 1983 have a combined average shot length of 3.9 seconds.[36] Demy intentionally wanted

132 STORYTELLING IN MOTION

to distance himself from the music video aesthetic, which he told *Cahiers du cinéma* too closely resembled a "super montage, madness . . . it's another language that has nothing to do with our cinematographic expression."[37] The editing pace of Demy's films may have sped up, but his numbers in *Trois places* are quantitatively closer to the editing norms of the studio era[38] than of contemporary 1980s averages.

By 1988, however, dance culture in France was more closely aligned with Demy's choreographic preferences. In addition to seeing more than six hundred dancers for the corps,[39] Demy suggests that in casting the role of Marion he auditioned dozens of talented actors, "which proves that there would be the necessary talent in France to produce musical comedies."[40] For the first time, Demy had a French lead trained professionally in both song and dance (Mathilda May), allowing him to further develop the storytelling potential of figure movement and dance in his filmmaking practice.

Choreographing Character Development

There are narrative continuities across Mathilda May's performance in *Trois places* that reveal the subtle work May, Demy, and Peters executed to shape the physicality of her character. Demy's choices for May's performance as Marion are particularly pertinent for an analysis of figure movement given her character's arc within the conventions of the genre. As Rick Altman discusses, it is common for a lesser-known or more amateur performer to take over for a star who is "injured, recalcitrant, or absent" in the show or backstage musical subgenre.[41] Altman suggests that in Hollywood musicals this switch more often occurs in the final moments before the last performance of the film and that the replacement is a "non-performer," which "symbolically merges the stage world . . . and reality"[42] while also emphasizing the diegetically heightened qualities of the performance. In contrast, Demy chooses to have the female lead of Montand's show quit earlier in the film (forty-five minutes in), allowing us to observe the process of Marion stepping into the role progressively over the course of the plot.[43] Unlike the sort of heightened diegetic performances we would observe in a Hollywood film, where it is somewhat implausible that a different performer could execute such flawless performances at the last minute, Demy provides many narrative cues to suggest the labor and effort put into Marion's growth as an artist.

MUSICAL UNEASE   133

We can observe a carefully structured, deliberately choreographed performance that spans May's dancing and her figure movement. As Erin Brannigan discusses, paying attention to the "distinct performance modalities" that occur in musical stars' performances, not only in the musical numbers but throughout the film, can reveal a richer understanding of their role in the film and the continuities between their unremarkable and danced movements.[44] Demy's choices in this regard provide nuance to Marion's character and allow us to observe the shifts in her physicality once she joins Montand's show and matures as a performer. The contrast between May's physicality in *Trois places* and her movement in earlier starring film roles further reinforces the deliberate choices that the pair made to provide character development through figure movement.

Movement Baselines

We can see clear differences in May's performance when we compare her physicality in *Trois places* to her work in Tobe Hooper's *Lifeforce* (1985) and Claude Chabrol's *Le Cri du hibou* (1987), two films in which she had leading roles soon before making Demy's film. In *Lifeforce*, May plays a space vampire who sucks the vitality out of the unsuspecting male victims caught in her spell. There is a clear sexualization of her (nude) body through more distant camera framings, but her movements are more limited to help suggest an alien, inhuman nature. Occasionally her movements are quicker[45]—the first time we see her open her eyes, for example, and when she turns her head to look at someone—but overall she moves with an unchanging slowness.[46] This is fitting, given her role as an alien vampire ensnaring her prey; Rudolf Laban considered expressive movement fluctuations that engaged Flow, Space, and Weight Effort with unchanging Time Effort to shift into brief trance-like moments called Spell Drives, implying a feeling of controlling others or being controlled. May's focus is usually pinpointed, especially when she is engaged with a victim.[47] Her movements are also usually flourish-free, besides the frequent widening of her eyes; her most expansive movements are the arcing gestures of her arms as she raises them to the sky or toward her victims to draw them to her.

May's performance in Chabrol's *Le Cri du hibou* is more nuanced but still austere. Here she plays Juliette, a woman who becomes obsessed with Robert, whom she finds spying on her from the woods behind her home.

134   STORYTELLING IN MOTION

Her movements as she interacts with him for the first time are reserved and cautious;[48] she walks slowly as they talk and raises her hand gradually to drink her coffee.[49] Her body appears shrunken and small;[50] she holds her arms crossed in front of her, her torso is bowed slightly toward the front, and she holds her head down, jutting her chin forward when she looks up. Later in the film, when she grows in confidence, she smiles more frequently and holds her head higher, but her dynamic movement qualities[51] do not change dramatically. Even when she is upset later in the film and she speaks quickly as she cries, she sits still and moves very little. Chabrol's staging choices also affect our ability to see much of her physicality. Throughout much of the film, cinematographer Jean Rabier presents May in medium shots or close-ups, and much of the film takes place at night, in cars or darkened rooms. In both *Lifeforce* and *Le Cri du hibou*, the range of her movement is more limited, and what we do see appears restrained through Bound Flow Effort.

In contrast, May's character in *Trois places* moves with greater Free Flow Effort, demonstrating a fluid baseline and playful confidence. When we first see Marion in her apartment, she walks with a more relaxed quality than her previous roles, which we can observe through the small reverberations that move into her shoulders and torso. Her consistent expressive baseline combines a frequent engagement of quickness and a sense of ongoing motion,[52] qualities that relate to Laban Movement Analysis's Mobile State when they manifest in combination. Expressivity of this kind suggests an active, deliberate progression through the world. May's physicality in the film suggests an impulsive nature and a dislike of stasis or delay, which fits with Marion's character and her desire to advance her performance career.

We can observe this pattern of impatience after Marion's musical number, "Au concert," in her apartment. Marie-Hélène (her mother) scolds her for the performance and leaves the living room. The film then cuts to Marie-Hélène in the kitchen as Marion walks toward her from the background; she leans against the kitchen doorway, and as her shoulder comes into contact with the edge, her arms, hips, and foot ripple in response to the weight shift (figure 5.1). This example demonstrates that a controlled exertion of pressure[53] is not a main part of Marion's baseline at this point in the film—she falls into the wall more than she deliberately shifts her weight into it—but moments of delicate touch and a multifocused awareness do appear in her movements,[54] especially when she dances. Although she does not frequently employ larger gestures as she talks or moves, May frequently rotates and turns her wrists

Figure 5.1 We see Marion's Free Flow Effort as she rebounds slightly when she leans on the doorframe in *Trois places pour le 26*.
© 1988 – PATHE FILMS.

with this lighter flexibility, which we can see when she withdraws her hand from the perfume case as she is talking with her friends at work. May often moves her shoulders expressively into verticality to punctuate phrases or as she turns her head as well, bringing a cheek to her shoulder as she looks off to the side. When sitting, however, she sometimes slumps in her shoulders, especially in her apartment. These movement patterns combined point to a confidence in her decisions—bordering on stubbornness—that allows her to successfully navigate her environment to her advantage, while her lack of self-awareness can sometimes eclipse that outer clarity, especially when her nerves get the better of her.

Marion's mood shifts this baseline in narratively significant ways. In her first encounter with Montand, she appears visibly more agitated and nervous. May still performs little gestures with her hands, but they are more restrained and forceful as she twists her fingers and grasps her hands together,[55] inadvertently revealing her nervous excitement (figure 5.2). When she sits, she does not collapse quite as much in her upper torso, but she initiates small movements forward as she talks,[56] and her small gestures convey a sense of urgency.[57] May's figure movement is also distinguishable thanks to Demy's choice to favor more distant framings—medium long shots and long shots—than Chabrol. Jean Penzer's cinematography in Demy's film allows us to observe how May acts with her whole body as well as her face. As a result, we can see the clear choices Demy made in her performance, especially in contrast to May's roles earlier in the 1980s.

Figure 5.2 We can observe Marion's nervous agitation from the tension in her hands in *Trois places pour le 26*.
© 1988 – PATHE FILMS.

Movement Evolution

We can observe a progression of professional performance and maturity in Marion's physicality, both in how she dances and how she moves elsewhere in the film. Some of these cues come from actions Marion performs in the film's broader narrative. Most apparently, Demy builds a slight clumsiness into her character. The first time we see her in the perfume shop, Marion knocks over a perfume box as she is opening a drawer and telling her friends about her plan to get them tickets for Montand's show. She pulls the drawer with a clear directionality,[58] but her focus is on her story rather than her work and she does not notice the box until it falls. Only at that moment does her movement quality shift to a more multifocused sense of urgency indicating an awareness and responsiveness to the environment as she notices her error.[59] Similarly, when Marion leaves Montand's dressing room for the first time, she is focused on Montand and her movements are tight and restrained as she backs away from him,[60] smiling and still processing the compliment he just paid her. She does not look where she is going in her excitement, walks in reverse, bumps into a chair, and stumbles before leaving (figure 5.3). Her exit in reverse from the dressing room repeats when she leaves for the second time, after Montand agrees to test her in the role now available due to Betty's departure. This time she leans forward slightly in excitement before retreating to leave, but she twists toward the chair and gently catches herself by placing a hand on the edge, which prevents her from fully repeating her earlier clumsy exit.

Figure 5.3 Marion backs into a chair leaving Montand's dressing room in *Trois places pour le 26*.
© 1988 – PATHE FILMS.

This clumsiness—and Marion's later avoidance—is in Demy's scenario, a further indication of the early attention devoted to the character's physicality. For Marion's first exit from Montand's dressing room, Demy writes, "MARION leaves walking backwards. She hits the coffee table, drops her bag, mumbles something resembling an excuse."[61] For her second exit (after Montand agrees to test her in Betty's old role), Demy writes, "She leaves walking backwards, avoids the table, smiles, and closes the door."[62] There are differences from the scenario to the film—the shift from a table to a chair and the elimination of additional details, like the bag dropping and some business about closing doors—but the intent and the reflection on Marion's character remains the same.

Marion's earlier musical numbers—"Au concert" and "La parfumerie"—also largely emphasize relatively simple, though virtuosic, steps, like single-unit turns,[63] leaps, and leg extensions. In "Au concert," in which she dances by herself, Marion usually remains on center, moving through jazz-infused balletic choreography and extended, suspended movements that keep her predominantly stable and vertical or pull her briefly off-center.[64] "La parfumerie" draws on movement vocabulary from the film's first two diegetically heightened sequences, "Interview" and "Au concert," but with strong choreographic departures from both. This number is more predominantly expressive than the earlier numbers; the choreography reflects the women's excitement about seeing Montand's show (Marion's friends Alice and Nicole) or about becoming a star (Marion). Much of the dance draws on ballet—pirouette turns, leaps, traditional arm shapes and leg extensions—and modern jazz—isolations and extensions of the hips and torso, quick direction changes, and angular shapes. There is also a brief evocation of hip hop dance, when the girls bind their flow and isolate the movement of their bent arms from their torsos, creating a "robot" effect.

Peters also emphasizes symmetry in his choreography of the "Au concert" number, a symmetry that serves primarily to draw viewer attention back to Marion. In Rudolf Laban's conception of symmetry operations, spatial configurations in the body can be transposed or moved to repeat specific shapes and patterns. Carol-Lynne Moore develops four of these transpositions: "In *reflection*, a given shape is reversed to produce a mirror image. In *rotation*, the shape is moved a certain number of times around an axis. In *translation*, the shape is moved a set distance and repeated; while *glide reflection* combines the movements of translation and reflection, moving a shape a constant distance and also reversing it."[65] A key example of symmetry operations and interactions—between individual figures, the mise-en-scène, and camera movement and placement—occurs in the section of the dance where there is no singing. The girls' singing ends in the fifth shot of the number as they raise their arms (figure 5.4). Marion's arms, extending fully into verticality,[66] create a reflection in her body. Alice's and Nicole's exterior arms are also extended in a similar direction, but their inner arms create opposition and balance in their bodies as they rest by their sides. Within the frame, however, their opposition enhances the reflection created by Marion's body. Here the slower gesture is emphasized with a gradual pace,[67] combined with an increase of a fine touch as the arms rise.[68]

Figure 5.4 Alice, Marion, and Nicole's arms create symmetry in the frame in *Trois places pour le 26*.
© 1988 – PATHE FILMS.

MUSICAL UNEASE   139

The women then transition to their extended unison phrase, where the repetition of movement across bodies creates a translation of the movement in the frame. Their transition creates a moment of lovely opposition and reflection between bodies, as Marion transitions by lowering and folding her right arm to her torso, whereas Alice and Nicole raise and fold their right arms to their torsos moving with quick backward bourrées[69] in order to create a greater play with depth in the frame. The difference in Marion's movement and her now larger appearance in the frame as she moves forward also helps draw further attention to her.

Peters's choreography in this number is highly invested in the sort of symmetry operations that Laban and Lynne-Moore identify. This is aided by the clarity in Demy's conception of the musical number's space and the symmetrical layout of the chosen setting. The space reflects itself lengthwise, thanks to the three counters, the rectangular empty space in the center, and the two staircases that frame the back portion of the room, and there is a clear sense of repetition of pathways and positions as the three performers move through the space, all ultimately serving to repeatedly bring our focus back to Marion. Unlike in *Les Demoiselles de Rochefort*, which had to use existing locations for interior shoots, *Trois places*'s production had access to studios for interiors. The use of a studio space to create the perfume shop and the street in front of it gave the filmmakers complete control over the spatial layout and arrangement.

The "La parfumerie" number shifts the performances away from the diegesis and plausible motivations, shifts that reach their height when a translucent Montand appears for a brief duet with Marion. However, Demy playfully has the shop owner catch the women on the counter as they hold their final poses, the ringing bell of the opening shop door overlapping with the final chord of the music on the soundtrack. The number functions to show us Marion's singing and dance abilities, which cues us to understand her confidence when she offers to replace Betty in Montand's show, however ostentatious that suggestion seems in the moment. In rehearsals, we see Marion struggle to embody her parts, but her performances in the musical numbers that follow those setbacks suggest a professional maturation.

A significant performative development occurs in Marion's last heavily danced number, "Saint-Germain-des-Prés," in which the choreography she performs with the other show members is more syncopated and complex.[70] Her expressive qualities shift from her earlier dance phrases, which often emphasized suspension[71] to draw attention to the classical shapes created by her body and the long lines of her arms and legs. The choreography in "Saint-Germain" still requires May to extend her limbs into far space,[72] but the motions are often shorter and more quickly executed. Rather than traveling through space, as she frequently does in "Au concert" and "La parfumerie," here Marion stays more in one place, swinging her limbs and torso forward and backward (figure 5.5).[73] In addition, May moves with even more of a fluent quality than she has previously while dancing, the choreography encouraging a rebounding in her shoulders and limbs from the quick jumps and weight shifts that create small waves of movement through her body.[74] In this diegetically motivated number, Peters more frequently moves her off-center, creating a greater sense of mobility and pulling her away from vertical as she dances.[75] Given the verticality and stability of Marion's earlier dances, these shifts—and her ability to execute them—suggests a progression and development in her training.

Finally, when Marion and Montand emerge to take their bows at the end of the show's premiere, her physicality has transformed from her earlier baseline of clumsier, quicker shifts and simpler[76] movements. Montand's show ends with the pair immobile on stage, Marion's weight shifted forward onto one foot, as extras pass behind them. Marion bounces with excitement as she hugs Montand once the curtain is down, but when they enter for their bows she appears more grounded, relaxed, and confident. As she walks toward Montand, she moves with little fluid steps and greater initiation from her center. Her movements flow from one body part to another,[77] her hips and

Figure 5.5 Marion's movement qualities shift to incorporate greater mobility through off-center choreography in "St-Germain des Près" from *Trois places pour le 26*.
© 1988 – PATHE FILMS.

shoulders twisting ever so slightly in a quick, shimmying motion, and she poses, without wobbling, with her body twisted, for her bows. The more angular and off-center poses are paired with more lingering arm extensions and bows that display a lessened fine touch and fewer smaller, fidgety gestures.[78] As Marion initially reaches for Montand, she does rotate her wrist once, but the gesture is more subtle, a fluid continuation of her arm movement and a function of her nimbly navigating the space as she reaches toward Montand,[79] which contrasts from her earlier internally focused hand gestures.[80] Despite her nervousness before the show, Marion's curtain call demonstrates that she has mastered a sense of theatrical presence, something she struggles to embody earlier in the film. Marion's character development is a minor aspect of *Trois places*'s plot, yet it reveals a prominent use of an actor's ability to display expansive physicalities in acting and dance performance that were not available to Demy in his earlier musicals.

Labor and the Disrupted Show Musical

Because of its close ties to the backstage (or show) musical subgenre, *Trois places pour le 26* is Demy's film that most resembles a classical musical form. This is apparent even in a simple examination of the numbers' diegetic affiliations. In contrast to earlier Demy films like *Les Demoiselles de Rochefort* or *Peau d'âne*, which feature more heightened diegetic sequences, most of the numbers in *Trois places* are motivated by Montand's show or other diegetic situations. But the film also includes multiple narrative disruptions, causing it to deviate from many of the subgenre's norms and to ultimately throw into question our categorical certainty about the stage-bound numbers' diegetic plausibility.

Neither *Les Demoiselles* or *Trois places* is a conventional example of the subgenre,[81] but unlike the former, much of the plot in *Trois places* is "primarily concerned with putting on a show"[82] and therefore shares numerous semantic elements with the show musical that Altman considers crucial, professional performers and the stage setting especially. However, Demy's film is offset from three of Altman's core aspects of the show musical subgenre: the relationship between the reality found in the world of the city and the fiction found in the world of the stage; the focus on the "white-collar" aspects of the show's production (those elements relating to, for example, performance and directing, as opposed to the construction trades or janitorial

142 STORYTELLING IN MOTION

work); and the narrative culmination of the film's main romance with the show's achievement. [83] The narrative structure of *Trois places* also obliquely undercuts generic norms of the show musical, drawing attention to the play of expectations between genres and their audiences and emphasizing that Demy consistently undermines these in his experiments with the musical. In addition, we can observe more subtle ways that Demy blurs the lines between his reversal of reality and fiction and the ways that he uses certain musical numbers to do so. This storytelling choice ultimately draws attention to the labor of the show musical and assigns greater narrative significance to the choreography of figure movement.

Flipping the Script

Demy flips the duality of reality and fiction in *Trois places* by including largely biographical information about Montand's rise to fame in the stage show while building a fictional plot to surround it that includes Marion, Marie-Hélène, and their relationships to the star. The realities we see on stage are mediated through the filmic diegesis, but the details about Montand's experiences during the periods represented are historically verifiable. In contrast, in the American show musical, the "real" of the city is juxtaposed with the "ideal" of the stage.[84] We can see this carry over early on in the subtle ways that Montand's mannerisms bleed into the broader script. Executive producer Pierre Grunstein remembers that in the moment of tension between Montand and Demy before the film's production period began, "it was constantly 'don't you believe that,' 'don't you think that,' etc."[85] We can observe a similar, albeit less tension-ridden interaction between Montand and Toni, the show's director, as the cast and crew gather for notes after the "Ciné qui chante" number. Toni's first comment is "the second number is ready" ("le deuxième numéro est au point") to which Montand responds that he thinks the end drags a little. Toni insists that the ending plays perfectly, but Montand looks unconvinced. In the hallway outside his dressing room, Montand tells Toni, "It's how I work, you know that" ("c'est ma façon de travailler, tu le sais bien").

The line between reality and fiction begins to further break down when Marion joins the production, which notably occurs after the three most diegetically distanced numbers have occurred in the plot—"Interview," "Au concert," and "La parfumerie." Although she also portrays characters like

Edith Piaf in the show, her main role is Maria who, unbeknown to her until the end of the film, portrays her mother. Demy intended to take the play of fiction and reality even further. The separation between reality and fiction was undone in the original, more diegetically ambiguous ending. His script had the interactions between Montand, Marion, and Marie-Hélène remain the same, as the latter two arrive at the train station and Montand is reunited with his former lover. However, after this reconciliation, Demy had an additional reveal planned for the audience:

> At this moment the camera moves backwards and we discover we are at the theater. The set represents the Saint-Charles station stairs. Dancers dressed as travelers with luggage walk up and down the stairs to the "Interview" melody heard at the beginning of the film. The red velvet curtain falls slowly.[86]

After the credits scroll, Demy planned to add a postscript: "Deep down, all this, is cinema.[87] But cinema and life is the same. J.D."[88] The crew filmed the scene on the staircase set; director Olivier Ducastel, who worked as an assistant on *Trois places*, remembers editing it for the original cut. Production stills suggest that the film even ended with the three of them taking a bow, hands held. The producer (presumably Berri) was confused, however, by Marie-Hélène's presence in the scene, given that she was not part of Montand's show. As a result, Demy refilmed the final scene to show Marion and her mother meeting Montand on the same train station steps we see at the beginning of the film.[89] Production stills of the stairs emphasize how it is likely that audiences could be momentarily fooled by the set if the actors were filmed in tighter shots before the reveal as the camera tracks back; the rising stairs make it difficult to initially identify the set as such, given that the abstract background is barely visible (figures 5.6 and 5.7). The more ambiguous version that ends on stage completes the unraveling effect between Demy's reversal of reality and fiction. The ultimate ending on the stairs, however, makes it more difficult for audiences to deny the denotative details of the story: that Montand does actually spend the night with his daughter and that we end with a happy familial reconciliation in spite of this taboo. The more ambiguous ending equally blurred the line between the members of the show and nonprofessionals, like Marie-Hélène, whereas throughout the film Demy stresses the rigor of stage productions and the labor involved in such a process.

Figure 5.6 Yves Montand and Françoise Fabian on the studio train station steps in a production still showing Demy's original ending.
© 1988 – PATHE FILMS, reproduced with permission from the Fondation Jérôme Seydoux-Pathé.

Figure 5.7 Yves Montand and Françoise Fabian embracing in the final moments of the film, reshot on the actual Gare de Marseille Saint-Charles steps.
© 1988 – PATHE FILMS.

Musical Labor

In his take on this musical subgenre, Demy emphasizes the work that goes into the theatrical creation process, labor that is usually elided in Hollywood accounts. Studio-era show musicals focus on the white-collar aspects of putting on a show, and Altman argues that "the show musical takes for granted most of the activities normally performed by the working class, masking the blue-collar work of production."[90] Demy devotes much of the film's story to

MUSICAL UNEASE 145

these white-collar concerns, but he also addresses the blue-collar aspects and the physical and technical labor involved in staging a show. This becomes apparent from the first moment Toni and Montand go to visit the theater where the premiere will take place. When they arrive, the only person present is a cleaning woman, who vacuums the balcony carpet as they inspect the space. Montand takes the mic, plugs it in, and speaks into it as he tells Toni about Mylene (Marie-Hélène) and their history. The quality and reverberation of his voice changes once the mic is on, and we hear interference as Montand untwists the cable. Toni walks into the auditorium and the two men test the sound, reminding us of the technical labor required for all aspects of production.

Demy continues to remind the viewer of the labor—blue or white collar— involved in creating a show, to a greater extent than we would expect from a Hollywood musical.[91] Before the "Ciné qui chante" number, we see the final pieces of the set lowering into place, a worker carrying a ladder, and another sweeping the stage floor. There are tensions over costumes not fitting properly, an actor leaving his hat lying around, and the testing of the mics. Later a scene transition is delayed due to a "technical dove issue" ("un petit problème technique de colombe"). Demy does not portray these as narrative obstructions or insurmountable challenges but rather as inevitable, expected parts of show business. The emphasis on fixing technical glitches before and after stage performances also draws attention to the film's unusual presentation of musical numbers in relation to the show musical subgenre.

Including the technical labor involved in the show's creation also prompts us to consider the crafting of the stage-bound musical numbers in a similar light, which sheds further doubt on their diegetic plausibility. In a more significant departure from generic tradition and in a destabilizing narrative move, *Trois places* situates its stage-bound musical numbers within the plot in ways that make us ultimately question what version of the show we have actually seen. Demy frames the numbers from Montand's show in such a way as to reveal less of the stage's edges than he does in stage-bound numbers from his first feature, *Lola* (1961), or *Les Demoiselles de Rochefort*, creating more of a spatial segmentation between the content portrayed in the stage performances and the frame narrative. And, with a few exceptions, Demy does not include shots of the audience to remind us that this is a stage number. This occurs in the "Saint-Germain-des-Prés" number, as Montand walks into the theater to watch the rehearsal. This shot is somewhat ambiguous, however, since within the context of the show rehearsal, Montand is

146   STORYTELLING IN MOTION

frequently shown watching or interacting with a younger version of himself on stage. The eyeline match between Montand and Marion (still performing) accentuates the possibility that Montand's entrance is part of the show. The camera's infrequent departure from the stage production as it plays out makes it easier for the spectator to downplay the contrast between the (by all appearances) polished musical numbers and their appearance in the plot during the rehearsal process. It is not until the end of the film that we realize that we have seen most of the stage numbers before the show's opening night.

Hollywood studio-era musicals tend to present the numbers from the final stage show towards the end of the plot, as we can observe in Busby Berkeley numbers from the 1930s, *Singin' in the Rain* (1952), and *The Band Wagon* (Vincente Minnelli, 1953).[92] There are exceptions; the stage-bound numbers in *Kiss Me Kate* (George Sidney, 1953) begin earlier in the plot, but we see them in the context of the show's opening night. To illustrate this idea, we can take *The Band Wagon* as a point of contrast, a film that is mentioned frequently in comparisons to *Trois places*.[93] This film's stage numbers are shown as finalized, actual performances and as part of the show, instead of as rehearsals. When in *The Band Wagon* we do see a rehearsal version of a number to the song "You and the Night and the Music," it is to emphasize all the things that are going wrong in the initial show attempt. We see Tony (Fred Astaire) and Gaby (Cyd Charisse), in rehearsal clothes and states of distraction, as they attempt to rehearse their dance while fireballs go off unexpectedly around them. The numbers we later see—"New Sun in the Sky," "I Guess I'll Have to Change My Plan," "Louisiana Hayride," "Triplets," and the "Girl Hunt" ballet—are established as the versions that the diegetic audiences see (an exception being the diegetic plurality of the "Girl Hunt" ballet) and are meant to be understood as part of the repeated performance the cast gives as they tour their show, complete with program names for each number. Although we do not see evidence of a diegetic audience until the New York performance, the numbers are signaled with an abstracted shot of the orchestra for the first number and with inserts of the show number titles from the program.

In *Trois places*, rehearsals for Montand's show begin in earnest twenty minutes into the film, and we see almost all of the show's numbers—"Ciné qui chante," "L'esprit frappeur," "Moulin Rouge," "Libération," and "Saint-Germain-des-Prés"—before opening night. We see each number in full, without interruptions, and in each instance the cast is in full costume and makeup, despite being up to several weeks away from the first performance.

Come opening night, we see two scenes on stage: the very beginning of the show in which dancers perform a brief phrase before acknowledging Montand's entrance (to enthusiastic applause) and the reprise of "Douce folie" between Montand and Marion which is immediately followed by the curtain call. In the brief plot moments between these scenes we see the the-ater owners in the office, with a television monitor showing a section from Marion's dance in "Saint-Germain-des-Prés," which repeats exactly the staging, choreography, and costuming from the earlier scene that shows the cast rehearsing the number. We see the beginning and end of Montand's show on opening night, but not the middle.

Diegetic Reassessments

"Douce folie," the one stage number we see as part of opening night, is a key component of Demy's narrative obfuscation. The ambiguity of what is "real" and what isn't heightens when we see Marion perform the reprise of "Douce folie" with Montand in the final number of the show and we recall Montand's dance with Marie-Hélène to the same song earlier in the plot. The first itera-tion of this number occurs when Montand and Marie-Hélène meet at the bar Le paradis and the song "Douce folie" begins to play. Marie-Hélène comments that the song is in his show, and he tells her "when I sing this song, it's you I'm thinking about" ("Tu vois, en scène, quand je chante cette chanson, c'est à toi que je pense"). Montand then invites Marie-Hélène to dance with him, and they walk to the dance floor. They move through a simple choreographed dance: he takes her by the hand and then spins her in so that they sway with Marie-Hélène facing away from him. She turns back to Montand and pulls away before letting him draw her toward him as she tosses her head back (figures 5.8 and 5.9), and they move to a closer embrace (a closed framing in social dancing) and spin slowly as they talk. After a single full rotation, Marie-Hélène spins herself out, extends her arm to the background, and spins back in; they sway a few more times before the number ends.

The same song returns at the end of the stage show when Montand and Marion's character (Maria) meet after years of separation. Montand's earlier comment about the intention behind the song reinforces that "Maria" is meant to evoke Marie-Hélène. Montand begins to dance with Marion, and the parallels between Marion and her mother are reinforced by similar, albeit pared-down, choreography. As Montand starts to sing, he pulls Marion in

Figure 5.8 Marie-Hélène and Montand sway together, both facing forward, as they begin to dance in "Douce Folie" from *Trois places pour le 26*.
© 1988 – PATHE FILMS.

Figure 5.9 Marie-Hélène relaxes and tosses her head as Montand pulls her toward him in "Douce Folie" from *Trois places pour le 26*.
© 1988 – PATHE FILMS.

but she faces away from him, which creates a similar shape as the beginning of his dance with Marie-Hélène. They take a few steps forward. Marion turns toward Montand and he takes her hand, stepping away from her to create space between them, like Marie-Hélène did earlier (figures 5.10 and 5.11). After a few steps in this position, the number ends, and the pair holds the last pose until the curtain falls.

The basic structure is the same, as is Montand's performance in both (though of course he sings in the second version). The smaller choreographic details and the women's performances, however, emphasize the differences between the two sequences. Marion's version is significantly pared down: her

MUSICAL UNEASE 149

Figure 5.10 We see a similar choreography as in figure 5.8 but different expression in the reprise of "Douce Folie" between Montand and Marion, as they dance close together in a frontal facing in *Trois places pour le 26*.
© 1988 – PATHE FILMS.

Figure 5.11 Marion and Montand replicating the shape seen in figure 5.9 as Marie-Hélène pulls away from Montand, but without Marie-Hélène's head toss, in the reprise of "Douce Folie" from *Trois places pour le 26*.
© 1988 – PATHE FILMS.

movements do not include subtle movements of the head and Montand does not spin her quickly around as he does with Marie-Hélène. The two numbers are also shot differently, the first in three shots to vary the shot scale and the second in a single crane shot that slowly pushes in on the couple as they dance. More telling, however, are the dynamic movement differences[94] between Françoise Fabian and Mathilda May's performances.

Demy has the actresses in both iterations of the "Douce folie" number modify their movements to create a contrast in their acting styles elsewhere

150 STORYTELLING IN MOTION

in the film. During the first number, Marie-Hélène visibly relaxes and her expressive baseline[95] changes. In her previous and subsequent exchanges with Montand in the bar, her gestures are small and quick and her movements are more constricted in her arms and torso.[96] This is especially noticeable when she lies to Montand about her husband's whereabouts before the number begins. The shift once the pair begins to dance cues us to understand that she still has affection for Montand despite her earlier suggestion that she is happy in her current marriage. Marie-Hélène's movements are freer and less constricted as she dances; her torso sways as an extension of the gestures in her head and arms.[97] And she allows herself to go off-balance,[98] trusting Montand to hold her. She leans her head onto his shoulder as she faces away from him and leans her whole torso into back space when she tosses her head back. As they dance and talk their bodies press together. When the two walk back to their seats, she is visibly more relaxed, allows her arms to swing freely, and takes his hand. Once seated, however, her baseline of quicker restrained movements returns,[99] as does the more limited range of motion in her arms and torso.

In contrast, Marion's movement during the second number remains cautious and her steps small.[100] She does not allow herself to go off-balance, remaining more upright and stable and maintaining a greater distance between herself and Montand.[101] There are no spins or flourishes, and Marion plays the number as more impersonal and distant, especially in contrast to the first iteration where Marie-Hélène lets down her guard. Her performance as Maria matches the discomfort the character demonstrates when running into Montand one final time at the end of the stage play. Once the curtain falls, however, we see Marion relax as she smiles and bounces with resilient urgency[102]—a variation of the same expressive modality her mother reverts to after her dance with Montand[103]—that causes reverberations of movement through her body.

The choreographic choices create a feeling of discomfort around this particular pairing, especially when compared to the compatibility apparent in the first number. Marion and Marie-Hélène's baselines are somewhat flipped—Marion's tendencies outside of numbers are more inclined toward an ongoing quickness,[104] while Marie-Hélène's are toward an accelerated restraint.[105] Both dynamic combinations align with what Laban Movement Analysis describes as Mobile State, an expressive state that implies a determination for progressing through the world with less of an inner focus, which subtly creates a choreographed family resemblance. The choreographic

MUSICAL UNEASE   151

parallels narratively reinforce that Marion's role portrays her mother and that Montand remains in love, but the movement patterns also destabilize the diegetic grounding of the earlier number. The simplicity of the choreography makes the first "Douce folie" number appear fully diegetically motivated, but the improbability of such strong stylistic similarities between numbers throws this retroactively into doubt once we see the repeated duet between Marion and Montand. This in turn cues the viewer to question the diegetic status suggested by Montand's whole show.

The numbers in *Trois places* are rehearsals for a later show that we never see. This raises questions about the film's narrational reliability. Did we see the final versions of each number earlier in the plot? Or should we assume that the show continued to change in its last few weeks of rehearsal? Rather than being swept away in one last grand stage performance, as is expected of a backstage musical, we are left wondering if we ever saw the show in the first place. The narrative choices to place the diegetically heightened numbers early in the plot, show the stage numbers during rehearsal, and have the "Douce folie" stage number reference figure movement from earlier in the film disrupts our seemingly clear understanding of the film's story and the norms for diegetic plurality that it has established. It is credible to believe that we are seeing the final numbers from Montand's show, but the placement of these numbers in the plot creates ambiguity through the violation of the show musical's narrative norms.

Conclusions

Trois places pour le 26 undermines the show musical's core conventions by emphasizing a range of labor practices, creating a contrast between a "real" stage world and the surrounding fictionalized city life and establishing low stakes for the show's success relative to romantic realizations. These choices drive the film's unsettling tone as much as the narrative's revelation, and ultimate downplaying, of incest. Demy's subtle manipulation of musical genre norms—particularly visible in his ambiguous rendering of the stage numbers in Montand's show—causes his audience to question the viewing practices mobilized by a knowledge of the show musical subgenre, adding to the tonal malaise *Trois places* creates.

The demanding aesthetic and narrative cocktail that was *Trois places* did not sit well with the moviegoing public, and the film ultimately failed

152 STORYTELLING IN MOTION

financially. Despite positive reviews in the French press,[106] audiences largely avoided it.[107] *Trois places* was made in financial and collaborative conditions that differ, often greatly, from Demy's previous cinematographic experiences. Not all these experiences were positive for Demy, but changes in France's dance culture allowed Demy to hire Mathilda May, a French triple-threat actress capable of acting, singing, and dancing, with whom he could develop a more nuanced performance within and across the musical numbers and the film's plot. The result is a development of expressive cinematic choreography from Michael Peters, particularly noticeable in the shifts of characters' Effort Lives, that evolves over the course of the film to emphasize both the range of danced material as well as Marion's improvement as a performer. This led to new aesthetic and narrative choices for Demy's final feature. *Trois places pour le 26* presents a more fragmented and unsettling aesthetic while revealing the ways that Demy experimented with the backstage musical subgenre to obfuscate the diegetic status of his stage performances.

Jacques Demy's films force us to confront our tastes and expectations. As such his work engenders admiration, contempt, and bewilderment, but rarely indifference. Understanding the conditions that led to the creation of *Trois places pour le 26* reveals his career-long formal strategy to experiment with genre norms and challenge audience assumptions of what a musical should look like. Demy's use of choreographed figure movement enriches the viewer's understanding of plot and character. His films experiment with the diegetic motivation of musical numbers, a geographic specificity through location shooting, a functionality of movement, and the physical labor of his characters in ways that distinguish his work from American musicals made during the same period.

The differing industrial conditions of French and American filmmaking profoundly affected Jacques Demy's approach to a historically expensive film genre. As Kelley Conway notes, France "never developed the industrial infrastructure necessary to sustain a Hollywood-style genre system, musical or otherwise."[108] In France, Demy only had access to higher budgets, large studio lots, extensive rehearsal time, and a corps of versatile trained dancers and singers for his final film, *Trois places pour le 26*. The nature of French film and dance culture meant that Demy's films consistently drew on international financing, casts, and crews, but his persistence in working in a genre that was never prominent in France meant that his work left a legacy of the French musical form. By situating Demy's films within an understanding of these industrial constraints, we see that he adapted to work in a transnational

MUSICAL UNEASE 153

mode of filmmaking that demanded choreographic attention during a time when the necessary French infrastructure was lacking.

The aesthetic payoff of such financial constraints—through Demy's emphasis on location shooting and geographical specificity, in particular—is the filmmaker's investment in a spatial grounding of his musical numbers. With the exception of the "Rêves secrets d'un prince et d'une princesse" number from *Peau d'âne* (1970), Demy's musicals predominantly avoid diegetic spatial shifts. As a result, Demy's films float above the diegetic norms of realism more popular in France during this period rather than completely departing from them. In addition to geographical specificity, Demy's aesthetic grapples with the tensions between cinematic realism and spectacle. His musicals are invested in functional movements, which frequently draw on simple, repeated choreography to emphasize working class and domestic labor. Many of the performances in his filmmaking at large are focused on tasks, and many of his film plots involve themselves with the portrayal of labor, particularly working-class labor. We can see a clear continuity across Demy's films to emphasize the technical aspects of labor, regardless of the profession. *Les Parapluies de Cherbourg* (1964) opens with Guy fixing a car, we see the carnival workers assembling stages for the *kermesse* in the background of the shots on Rochefort's main square in *Les Demoiselles de Rochefort*, the princess and the women of the village perform a variety of domestic tasks in *Peau d'âne*, Catherine Deneuve's character works as a hairdresser in *L'événement le plus important depuis que l'homme a marché sur la lune* (1973), Calaïs adjusts sound levels in the recording studio as Orphée records a new song in *Parking* (1985), we see the physical work that provides the foundation for Yves Montand's stage show in *Trois places pour le 26*, and Demy would have portrayed the technical details of filmmaking and setting up shots on set—while playing himself—in *Anouchka* if the film had been produced. Demy was a realist filmmaker as much as he was an escapist one and was invested throughout his career—not just in his musical films—in portraying the labor and activities of the French working class.

By mixing dancing and musical styles, bending the musical genre framework, and blending fictional narrative elements with autobiographical details and historically rich locations, Demy creates a feeling in his films that is designed with a formal rigor to balance his audience on a tightrope between entertainment and bewilderment. Here lies the paradox of his filmmaking career, a paradox greatly clarified through a study of figure movement. Demy always sought to appeal to a broad, popular audience; his films consistently

154 STORYTELLING IN MOTION

follow the realities of everyday, working-class people and evoke well-known genre traditions. Unlike many of their French filmic equivalents, Demy's characters do not sit and philosophize about their existence. Instead, they talk or sing about their daily lives as they and the camera meander and dance through their environments.[109] But the filmmaker equally wanted to challenge his audiences by blending disparate aesthetic traditions, undermining generic expectations, and putting his characters in uneasy situations.[110] Demy's films concurrently confirm viewer tastes and generic expectations and challenge our stylistic and moral values through his cinematic choreography.

Jacques Demy's films, the later ones especially, received poor reception from contemporary audiences, but he remains a pivotal figure in the history of the French musical and a significant influence on filmmakers intent on experimenting with the genre's form. Contemporary filmmakers like Christophe Honoré, Olivier Ducastel, Jacques Martineau, Gérome Barry, Paul Calori, Kostia Testutand, and Damien Chazelle continue to be inspired by the innovative, and at times contradictory, ways that he negotiated his distinctive aesthetic within the genre expectations of the musical form.

6

Endless Conversations

Reflexive Musical Clusters

Figure 6.1 Title screen and analytical sample from the "Endless Conversations" videographic chapter. Video duration: 10 minutes. Images courtesy of the author.

The videographic essay accompanying this written statement can be found on this book's companion website: www.oup.com/us/storytellinginmotion.

A core aspect of genre studies consists of tracing commonalities across media forms and practices to consider the stability and evolution of genre conventions.[1] One consistency of the musical genre is reflexivity:[2] reusing songs, cinematic choreography, and elements of the mise-en-scène (costuming and sets in particular) to reappropriate recognizable musical elements, historically with various degrees of acknowledgment toward the original creators.[3] This videographic chapter[4] visualizes the ways musicals cite their predecessors' cinematic choreography and evoke stylistic norms of practice. While these films' sonic correspondences are noticeable, the piece highlights the movement-driven relationships between the chosen clips, drawing attention to the ways that the characters twirl, travel, run, meander, imitate, confront, and escape together.

The musical genre is dependent on rhythm and movement, qualities that can dissipate under the constraints of written, text-based argumentation.

156 STORYTELLING IN MOTION

By engaging with performative and parametric approaches to research and scholarship,[5] this chapter uses the poetic potential of the audiovisual form to generate knowledge effects.[6] Videographic methods can aggregate, visualize, and analyze to draw attention to stylistic continuities and departures. The multiscreen, clustered approach of this video essay emerges from an ongoing videographic exploration of musical grids, in which I display every musical number from a film simultaneously.[7] These grids function as a multiscreen supercut, an effect that this videographic chapter replicates in more subtle ways as well. As opposed to supercut videos using chronological or topical organization that allows the viewer to appreciate each instance individually, the order and duration of the musical numbers in these examples take on spatialized qualities instead to allow for side-by-side comparisons.

This videographic chapter opens with an epigraph, inspired by Jane Feuer's work on the reflexive potentials of the musical, and is indebted in form to the audiovisual epigraph genre pioneered by Catherine Grant.[8] My formal videographic choices performatively materialize these ideas both by demonstrating Feuer's articulation of this generic reflexivity and by adding to the instances of this videographic genre. I present selected reflexive musical moments as conversations, illustrating the stated citations of filmmakers discussed throughout this book as well as my own analysis of stylistic similarities. The introduction and conclusion of this videographic work playfully uses excerpts from musical numbers that function reflexively through music and song, while the main content's focus is on examples from the cinematic choreography of *West Side Story* (Robert Wise and Jerome Robbins, 1961), *Les Demoiselles de Rochefort* (Jacques Demy, 1967), *Trois places pour le 26* (Jacques Demy, 1988), *Jeanne et le garçon formidable* (Olivier Ducastel and Jacques Martineau, 1998), and *La La Land* (Damien Chazelle, 2016). The use of synchronized sound from selected clips creates an effect of correspondence with the other images playing simultaneously, what Michel Chion calls a "forced marriage." "By observing the kinds of music the image 'resists' and the kinds of music cues it yields to," Chion argues, "we begin to see the image in all its potential significance and expression."[9] This piece emphasizes how the characters in these films move harmoniously with each other's rhythms. Rather than taking a comprehensive approach with these citations,[10] this chapter includes examples that draw on the central films of this book and that encourage a flow from topic to topic, as an engaging conversation would. To performatively enhance the cyclical, reflexive effect of this chapter, I have designed the video to play in a loop.[11]

PART III
MUSICAL REALISM

7

Diegetic Flutters

Views from the Bridge

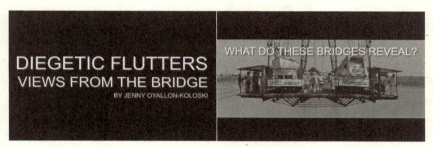

Figure 7.1 Title screen and analytical sample from the "Diegetic Flutters" videographic chapter. Video duration: 5 minutes, 30 seconds. Images courtesy of the author.

The videographic essay accompanying this written statement can be found on this book's companion website: ww.oup.com/us/.

This videographic chapter[1] explores a specific aspect of the musical genre's predilection for "bursting" into song and dance in five post-studio–era films discussed centrally in this book: *West Side Story* (Jerome Robbins and Robert Wise, 1961), *Les Demoiselles de Rochefort* (Jacques Demy, 1967), *Trois places pour le 26* (Jacques Demy, 1988), *Jeanne et le garçon formidable* (Olivier Ducastel and Jacques Martineau, 1998), and *La La Land* (Damien Chazelle, 2016). The impacts and effects of diegetic plurality carry through research on the genre,[2] yet most accounts focus on the distinctions between number and narrative or the functions of the number itself. This chapter lingers on the transition between these more stable units, what choreographer Mandy Moore describes as a bridge.[3] Unlike Erin Brannigan's work, which theorizes the significance of these transitional moments as adding greater meaning to the overall narrative,[4] I want to sit a bit longer with the musical moments themselves.[5] Some of these

160 STORYTELLING IN MOTION

transitions occur as a brief moment of diegetic instability before the musical number solidifies. In other instances, particularly in the central films discussed in this book, these musical moments diegetically flutter between narrative and number, either through the presentation of contradictory diegetic information in the frame or a formal refusal to entirely shift toward a full musical number and its utopian potentials.[6] What can these flutters reveal?

8

Imperfect Bodies

Jeanne et le garçon formidable (1998)

American studio-era musicals present an idealized and largely uniform dancer: young, white, thin, and classically trained.[1] The desire for technically dazzling choreography performed by attractive dancers persisted during this period, even as Hollywood standards of beauty and virtuosity evolved.[2] After the convention of keeping large corps of dancers on retainer declined with the industrial changes to the American studio system, choreographers and filmmakers wanting to use figure movement as a key element of their storytelling had to evolve the norms of practice to incorporate figure movement and dance on screen. Bringing in new forms of movement expression and new performers was a key aspect of this shift. Dance found ways to continue flourishing in Hollywood, from the more casual social dancing in the *Beach Party* musicals, to Elvis's solo hip swivels (also parodied in 1963 by George Sidney's *Bye Bye Birdie*), to choreographer-directors Bob Fosse's and Kenny Ortega's extension of conventional musical forms blended with newer popular dance styles.[3] Dancing was central to the narratives and marketing of exploitation musicals like *Saturday Night Fever* (John Badham, 1977), *Flashdance* (Adrian Lyne, 1983), *Footloose* (Herbert Ross, 1984), and *Breakin'* (Joel Silberg, 1984), before such popular dance forms found a new platform in the music videos broadcast on MTV.[4] *Flashdance* is also famously remembered for its use of dance doubles for the final audition number, combining the labor of several male and female performers.[5]

The French cinema industry, in contrast, has had limited enthusiasm for musicals that feature extensive dance sequences.[6] French musicals evolved largely around the *chanson*, popular music, and the operetta form;[7] dance rarely drives these narratives. As earlier chapters in this book on Jacques Demy's *Les Demoiselles de Rochefort* (1967) and *Trois places pour le 26* (1988) demonstrate, this lack of emphasis on figure movement–driven storytelling was impacted by the shape of French concert dance culture and its relationship to the film industry. France's lack of a robust relationship between the

Storytelling in Motion. Jenny Oyallon-Koloski, Oxford University Press. © Oxford University Press 2024.
DOI: 10.1093/oso/9780197602669.003.0009

162   STORYTELLING IN MOTION

art worlds of cinema and dance meant that Jacques Demy worked with international choreographers and dancers for most of his career to ensure his musical stories could be replete with figure movement. Subsequent French filmmakers had broader access to choreographic collaborations for their musical projects, in part thanks to Demy's expansion of French musical norms and production practices as well as his influence on filmmakers prioritizing staging and dance as narrative devices.

In the several decades since Demy's final dance-filled feature film, French filmmakers produced over a dozen musicals,[8] several of which feature significant genre experimentation. Alain Resnais's *On connaît la chanson* (1997) syncs prerecorded songs with musical moments in the image track to play with conventions of the genre, echoing the style of the US-produced *Pennies from Heaven* (Herbert Ross, 1981). François Ozon's *Huit femmes* (2002) includes performances of famous songs by the performers—many of whom are known for their musical performances in other films—while adhering to a tight formal symmetry: eight actresses, eight musical numbers. Demy's films also had a powerful influence on French musical filmmakers, notably Christophe Honoré (visible in *Les Chansons d'amour*, 2007 and *Les Bien-aimés*, 2011), and Olivier Ducastel and Jacques Martineau's first feature, *Jeanne et le garçon formidable* (1998).

Dance is pivotal to *Jeanne et le garçon formidable*'s musical aesthetic and crucial to its narrative logic. In place of the more established choices of jazz, ballet, partnered social dancing or, more recently, hip hop, *Jeanne* foregrounds *danse contemporaine*, a French dance form that shares qualities with both modern and postmodern dance in the United States. *Jeanne* also remains a significant cinematic portrayal of the AIDS epidemic. The film focuses on the constantly changing love life of its high-spirited eponymous protagonist (Virginie Ledoyen). Jeanne finds her ideal match with Olivier (Mathieu Demy, Jacques Demy's son with Agnès Varda). Their joyful relationship is short, as Olivier is HIV positive and dies of an AIDS-related illness soon after they meet. *Jeanne*'s narrative deals explicitly with the political struggles surrounding AIDS and devotes a significant portion of screenplay time to ACT UP, the organization committed to ending the AIDS epidemic, including filming footage of ACT UP demonstrations in Paris as part of the fictional narrative. Ducastel's and Martineau's film is one of the earliest French films, along with François Margolin's *Mensonge* (1992) and Cyril Collard's *Les Nuits fauves* (1992), to depict HIV positive characters. At the time of its release, it was heralded as "perhaps the greatest French film created about, or rather with, AIDS."[9]

Jeanne et le garçon formidable challenges musical film conventions through its tragic-political narrative. Its filmmakers integrate contemporary dance forms into and around the musical numbers. These choices situate the work in a unique place in musical genre history; *Jeanne* reconciles cinéphilic links to established musical norms—predominantly those within the classical Hollywood model and the French musicals of Jacques Demy—with a more experimental stylistic incorporation of contemporary dance forms. The film also engages with both objective and subjective forms of cinematic realism[10] through its inclusion of quasi-documentary moments of ACT UP protests and its portrayal of the experiences of HIV positive people, respectively. The resulting aesthetic of musical realism uses choreographed figure movement to draw our attention to bodies' fragility and complexity through the juxtaposition of musical numbers, performance styles, and movement forms.

Contemporary French Musicals (Production History)

French-financed film production was increasing steadily during the 1990s, thanks largely to aggressive investments and governmental reforms from Minister of Culture Jack Lang. The 1986 Audiovisual Law arranged distribution and funding agreements with French television channels, in particular with Canal +, France's first pay-TV cable station established by Lang in 1984.[11] A number of new filmmakers were entering the space of French film production during the 1990s, increasing the number of first films by up to 30 percent over the course of the decade.[12] *Jeanne et le garçon formidable's* codirectors, Olivier Ducastel and Jacques Martineau, benefited from the timing of these governmental initiatives for first filmmakers and the expansion of investments in French film production more generally. *Jeanne et le garçon formidable* had a budget of 24 million francs,[13] a high figure especially for a first feature, aided in part by an investment from Canal +. The average budget for a French film in 1997 was 31 million francs, up 30 percent from the year before; the median production budget in 1997 was 18.6 million francs.[14] Ducastel and Martineau suspect that their relatively straightforward access to funding came from some lingering guilt on the part of French distributors for not funding Jacques Demy's musicals,[15] as well as some guilt relative to

164   STORYTELLING IN MOTION

the overall lack of French films addressing the AIDS epidemic.[16] They used this funding to support their choices in physical and generic emphasis.

Physical Emphasis

Despite their willingness to fund the film with knowledge of the subject matter, *Jeanne*'s distributors remained reticent about its content, in particular the explicit inclusion of ACT UP protests. Jacques Martineau changed the final title for the film to *Jeanne et le garçon formidable* after its potential financiers balked at his original title, *Olivier a le sida (Oliver Has AIDS)*.[17] Explicit political messaging, however, was common to French cinema of this period. France saw mass demonstrations in the mid-1990s to protest the right wing policies of Jacques Chirac's presidency, especially those surrounding questions of immigration and *les sans papiers*.[18] A commonality of *le jeune cinéma* of this period, Guy Austin argues, is an "attempt to voice the exclusion and suffering of its protagonists in ways that might potentially go beyond 'simply' witnessing, to retrieve some element of the political."[19] For Martineau in particular, who was a founding member of ACT UP Paris, including protests in the narrative was essential and also a crucial link between the fight against AIDS and the film's emphasis on dance, given that "ACT UP's fight is a fight very much linked to the body, in that the body itself becomes a political object."[20] *Jeanne*'s financiers' resistance to the film's movement—both the portrayal of ACT UP's political momentum and the dancing in the musical numbers—is a constant thread throughout its production history.

The film's elevated budget made it possible for choreographer Sylvie Giron to devote significant preproduction time to crafting *Jeanne*'s dance sequences as well as the overall physicality of the actors. Cost was a key aspect of the distributors' objections to *Jeanne*'s inclusion of dance, as they found the movement sequences to be of secondary importance to the songs. For Ducastel and Martineau, however, dancing was essential to the film for both its political as well as its aesthetic value, for "a musical has no purpose without dancing."[21]

In addition to rehearsal time for the dance numbers, the film's preproduction included separate workshops with the professional dancers and the actors (who had little formal dance training) to develop physical personae for the film.[22] During this process, the actors were also encouraged to create movement sequences that emerged from their own movement aesthetic, to "build confidence in the actors and help them find the movement quality that is their own."[23] For Giron, Martineau, and Ducastel, there was a real luxury in having the time to work with the performers in a context separate from the specific needs of the narrative. This emphasis on crafting the physical aspect of performance places the filmmakers in the company of French directors like Jacques Demy and Jacques Tati or comedic actor Louis de Funès, where physical expression was a central stylistic focus. Unlike this smaller corpus, much of French sound cinema places priority on expression through dialogue (or through the *chanson* in French musicals). In contrast, silence was a major element in the preproduction workshops. For Giron, that environment was especially important in helping the professional actors, who were amateur dancers, learn how dance could communicate and evoke sensations independently of the cinematic and theatrical elements they were accustomed to.[24]

Genre Emphasis

Telling their story in musical form was essential to Olivier Ducastel and Jacques Martineau, who thought the film would be too sorrowful without the uplifting aspects of the genre. Dancing characters were equally essential. Their formal decisions were motivated by this narrative logic, as well as a desire to pay homage to Jacques Demy and his films, which were a significant influence on both filmmakers.[25] As a whole, *Jeanne* evokes more musical conventions associated with Jacques Demy than those associated with Hollywood. More so than with the American musical form, *Jeanne* shares qualities with the style of the French musicals that Demy developed, films that themselves depart from Hollywood norms, as I have discussed in previous chapters. As distinct from the citations of American musicals, in which there are links to specific narrative situations or gags, Ducastel and Martineau's numbers tend to evoke Demy's aesthetic more generally. Instead of consistently contrasting a realistic diegesis with a heightened one in the musical numbers, Demy's musical numbers tend to hover between these realities. They maintain a heightened level of style through music, movement, costuming, and set design that is simultaneously countered with location shooting and an aesthetic that is partially grounded in contemporary cultural forms (art, fashion, music, dance). And in his musical numbers, Demy includes choreography that ranges from virtuosic danced phrases performed by professional dancers to more pedestrian (everyday) movements that blur the line between narrative and number. Jacques Demy was a catalyst in developing a French variety of the genre, *Jeanne*'s filmmakers argue, in "acclimating the form to the specificity of our cinematographic style and the particularities of the French language."[26]

To Ducastel and Martineau, by "working exclusively with original music, in writing his own lyrics, and in preferring expressivity over virtuosity," Demy "gave to his songs a specific status that we attempted to recover."[27] Ducastel's and Martineau's incorporation of Demy's musical aesthetic is clear, but those stylistic choices also function narratively with greater sincerity rather than an ironic or winking distance, as their citations of Hollywood musical aesthetics do. One such latter moment is the final number, "La vie à crédit." The lead-up to and choreography in *Singin' in the Rain*'s "Make 'Em Laugh" number "served as a distant reference for the "La vie à crédit" number, clearly positioned as an imitation of the Hollywood musical."[28] As the last musical number in the film, "La vie à crédit" serves as comic relief—as well as a commentary on consumer culture—in the otherwise tragic final act of the film.

Ducastel, like Demy, uses staging in depth during the musical numbers to fill the frame with dancing characters that perform adjacent to the leads and whose movement pulls the viewer's eye through the frame. In Demy's "Les Rencontres" number from *Les Demoiselles de Rochefort* (1967), pairs of protagonists exchange witty banter through song as pedestrians dance behind and past them (figure 8.1). Delphine (Catherine Deneuve) collides with Andy (Gene Kelly), and he kneels to help her collect her fallen parcels in the foreground as walking, dancing, and cycling pedestrians cross the

Figure 8.1 The leads in the foreground are contrasted with dancers in the midground in *Les Demoiselles de Rochefort*.
Source: Ciné-Tamaris.

frame behind them in the midground. As the pair walks and continues their conversation in a single extended sequence shot, a pair of sailors breeze past them in the close foreground, creating a temporary blur between the performers and the camera. These kinds of spatial relationships between primary and secondary characters repeat throughout the film. We see a similar treatment of space in *Jeanne et le garçon formidable* (figure 8.2), directly inspired by Demy's aesthetic.[29] As Jeanne and Olivier sing in the beginning of the "Java du séropo," in which Jeanne learns of Olivier's illness, we see flashes of dancers appear and disappear in the off-screen space of the background, hidden and revealed by the trees in the park and the blocking of the leads as they walk in the foreground. Over the course of the final sequence shot of the number, the camera dollies leftward to follow Olivier and Jeanne as they dance in the foreground and midground and the dancing pedestrians progressively fill the background with movement.

Ducastel and Martineau use a walk-and-talk set up (really, a "walk-and-sing") for many of their musical number and conversation scenes, including the "Java du séropo," using tracking, dolly, and handheld cameras to follow the characters with little editing. While Steadicam technology was available in France at the time, the filmmakers and their director of photography, Matthieu Poirot-Delpech, chose not to use it for their first film, citing "a very dogmatic choice on the part of filmmakers who wanted to pull a Jacques Demy and certainly not do whatever with a Steadicam."[30] Ducastel and Martineau adopt a long-take aesthetic for their musical numbers, using follow shots and staging in depth to convey information, instead of the more

Figure 8.2 The leads on the left are contrasted with dancers on the right in *Jeanne et le garçon formidable*.
Source: Les Films du Requin.

168 STORYTELLING IN MOTION

rapid editing style adopted by contemporary Hollywood musicals. With musical numbers averaging a shot length of 33 seconds, *Jeanne*'s filmmakers hold shots ten times longer, on average, than US musicals released soon afterward like *Moulin Rouge!* (Baz Luhrmann, 2001) and *Chicago* (Rob Marshall, 2002). This aligns *Jeanne*'s editing pace with the numbers from *Les Demoiselles de Rochefort* instead, which also average close to 30 seconds.[31]

Ducastel and Martineau intentionally avoided what they refer to as an "ultra-edited" aesthetic, even if they acknowledge that, because of contemporary editing norms, "it's very difficult to explain that you can film music [musical numbers] in long takes because people have the impression that if the film doesn't change shots every two seconds, people will get bored."[32] However, *Jeanne*'s editing pace for musical numbers is close to double that of its French musical contemporaries, *On connait la chanson*[33] and *Huit femmes*. Their average shot lengths for musical numbers at 20 and 14 seconds, respectively, are also long by contemporary American musical standards. *Jeanne et le garçon formidable* uses the emphasis on staging in these longer takes and the whole frame to offer contradictory visual information. The result is that our attention is drawn to multiple places in the frame as we attempt to process the various pieces of choreographic information, particularly in the numbers that juxtapose sequences with the main characters and a corps of dancers.

At the end of the "Java du séropo" number, for example, our attention is divided between Jeanne and Olivier in the foreground, the band in the midground, and the dancers who are performing at least three different phrases simultaneously, one in the near midground, a second in the distant midground, and a third in the background (figure 8.3). Our attention is drawn to Jeanne and Olivier, in part because they are the protagonists but also because they are in the foreground, and often film viewers' eyes are drawn to objects that appear larger in the frame. But our eyes are also drawn to motion and brightness, and not only are the dancers in the background in constant motion, which draws our attention, they are also lit more brightly than the characters in the foreground.[34] Our ability to alter our attention and scan the frame is possible because of Ducastel and Martineau's decision to use longer takes, instead of controlling our focus through editing. This also results in greater ambiguity, of focus and of diegetic clarity. The musical number blends levels of diegetic distance, creating a heightened sense through dancing and singing performance on the part of the main characters and dancing pedestrians. The setting remains diegetically grounded, however, and this impression is heightened as the camera dollies left, eventually

Figure 8.3 Dancers fill the foreground, midground, and background in *Jeanne et le garçon formidable*.
Source: Les Films du Requin.

revealing a band performing live in the park. This addition troubles the diegetic status quo and forces us to reassess our expectations.

These filmmaking choices, in staging and camerawork especially, evoke those made by Demy and French filmmaker Jean Renoir, whose long-take aesthetic influenced the former. It aligns with the realist aesthetic championed by André Bazin, used by filmmakers who put their "faith in reality" by adopting stylistic choices like staging in depth, deep focus, and sequence shots over the juxtaposition techniques inherent to Soviet Montage and faster editing rates.[35] But it is also a choice often made by choreographers of contemporary dance: to present to the audience a plethora of phrases and movement qualities in different spaces of the stage, pulling the audience's eye in multiple directions and making it nearly impossible to absorb every detail in a single viewing. *Jeanne*'s incorporation of cinematic choreography draws significantly from Demy's impulses in *Les Demoiselles de Rochefort*, in which the film's staging has characters dance, rather than walk, through scenes to move the narratives forward. Yet Ducastel and Martineau did not adopt Demy's continuity with the Hollywood tradition of using ballet and jazz choreography, choosing instead to incorporate *danse contemporaine* for its stylistic and political implications.

Cinematic *Danse Contemporaine*

French concert dance was thriving in the 1990s. Choreographers were more easily able to financially support their work during this period thanks to

170   STORYTELLING IN MOTION

greater government investments into the arts and culture. President François Mitterrand doubled the French Ministry of Culture's budget in the early 1980s, and Minister of Culture Jack Lang grew and decentralized investments in dance through the creation of the *Centres chorégraphiques nationaux* (national choreographic centers). This investment in the cultural development and preservation (*patrimoine*) of dance in France culminated in the creation of the *Centre national de la danse* in 1998 as a subunit to the French Ministry of Culture. As a result, the period in which Ducastel and Martineau were making their film was a rich one for dance in France. *Jeanne*'s filmmakers use *dance contemporaine* as a key storytelling device for communicating character relationships. Their use of the form was unusual in the musical genre, both in its style and in the ways that Ducastel and Martineau use the pedestrian nature of its choreographic approach to blur the lines between narrative and musical numbers.

Against the Norm

The choice to include dancing in *Jeanne et le garçon formidable* was nonnegotiable. The filmmakers had to fight to keep portions of choreography in their film, as their distributor did not see the necessity of dancing in a musical comedy, something Ducastel and Martineau considered "heretical."[36] Ducastel and Martineau's choice to use primarily *danse contemporaine* in their musical provides an additional departure from the dance norms in French cinema as well as those established by the classical Hollywood musical. A few other French films incorporate the form,[37] but its use, like the inclusion of dance in French musicals more generally, is uncommon.

American musical films have similarly never widely incorporated modern or postmodern dance. The work of Valerie Bettis, Katherine Dunham, and Twyla Tharp establishes a precedent that nonetheless is a departure from choreographic norms.[38] Bettis, a modern dance choreographer, worked briefly in Hollywood, choreographing Rita Hayworth's numbers for *Affair in Trinidad* (Vincent Sherman, 1952) and *Salome* (William Dieterle, 1953).[39] Dunham's dance company, the Dunham School, and her codification of Dunham technique were significant contributions to modern dance study as well as a foundational aspect of jazz dance and studies of Caribbean, African, and African American dance traditions.[40] In addition to her concert dance and educational work, Dunham choreographed numbers for several Hollywood musicals during the studio period including the titular dream ballet in *Stormy Weather* (Andrew L. Stone, 1943). Tharp's training in modern dance is visible in her choreography for *Hair* (Miloš Forman, 1979), the American musical that most influenced Ducastel and Martineau's formal choices for *Jeanne*. They saw Tharp's choreography in the film as "distinctly [freeing] itself from the classical codes of the musical."[41] Generally, however, because of the professional divergence between commercial and concert dance in the United States, the overlap between commercially driven Hollywood and the modern/postmodern dance communities remains rare.

Danse contemporaine encompasses the more contemporary styles of dance adopted in France around the 1970s. It has parallels to the modern and postmodern dance forms that developed in the United States in the twentieth century. Modern dance in America emerged as a "recognizable dance genre" by the 1950s, predominantly rejecting the conventions of ballet and those of popular entertainment, Broadway and Hollywood in particular. Instead, modern choreographers used "stylized movements and energy levels in legible structures (theme and variations, ABA and so on) to convey feeling tones and social messages."[42] Emotional expression and the conveyance of a specific expressive or thematic message were strong currents of the form. Postmodern dance should be considered primarily an American form, dance historian Sally Banes argues,[43] and as such is largely acknowledged to have emerged from the performances of the Judson Dance Theater in New York City in the early 1960s.[44] Choreographers like Yvonne Rainer, Steve Paxton, and Simone Forti strove to reject the imperatives of modern as well as classical American dance forms. Their association with postmodern dance came less from a united aesthetic and rather from a common desire to rethink the choreographic process and to emphasize medium-specificity and function (movement for the sake of movement) over the emotional expression central to modern dance choreographers.[45]

Danse contemporaine shares qualities with both American forms. Unlike postmodern dance in the United States, which was largely a reaction to the modern dance movement, *danse contemporaine* in 1970s France was a departure from the ballet works of Maurice Béjart. His choreography, in turn, provided a departure from the (itself complex) established ballet tradition of post-war French culture, epitomized by the works of choreographers like Roland Petit. Béjart's work provided new perspectives in the use of

172   STORYTELLING IN MOTION

costuming, music, and performance spaces[46] with a continuity of classical ballet's choreographic lexicon.[47] According to dance historians Marcelle Michel and Isabelle Ginot, *danse contemporaine* has roots in earlier dance traditions that made their way to France in the 1930s and 1940s—the work of Rudolf Laban, François Delsartre, Mary Wigman, and Kurt Jooss—but the impulse for new dance forms remained marginalized in France until the events of May 1968 propelled an impetus for change.[48]

In addition to the earlier influence of German choreographers like Wigman and Jooss, part of the impulse for choreographic change in France leading to *danse contemporaine* was the result of American influence, specifically works by choreographers like Merce Cunningham, Alwin Nikolaïs and members of his company, and Trisha Brown.[49] These choreographers reinforced "the idea that modernity is linked to invention and to the renewal of a choreographic language" and brought with them a "more advanced level of technique," providing additional credibility to the growing French form.[50] Michel and Ginot argue that "French dance took from Germany a taste for drama, and from the United States the important lesson of composition."[51] The latter refers especially to the rupture that Cunningham created in moving away from narrative-based choreographic composition,[52] a strategy favored by classical, and sometimes modern, choreographers. German choreographer Pina Bausch's bridging of theatrical and dance forms also had a strong presence on French stages and was a favorite of *Jeanne*'s director Olivier Ducastel because of the way she would incorporate narrative elements into her choreography.[53] Emerging French choreographers also drew from their own artistic history, inheriting a rich theatrical tradition that resulted in movement that "offers itself rather as a mirror onto the interiority of the dancer."[54]

By the 1980s the period of "high masters" in France was over, and a second generation of young choreographers began exploring different strands of the new form.[55] One important figure who emerged from this transitional period in French choreography was Dominique Bagouet. Two important strands of Bagouet's work were the use of "dance, pure and abstract, as a space for invention of movement and for composition, and a theatricality favoring the creation of characters often inspired from cinema."[56] *Jeanne*'s choreographer Sylvie Giron was one of Bagouet's students, and the legacy of his interest in the development of unique physical characters is visible in Giron's work for the film.

Musical *Danse Contemporaine*

The filmmakers' choice to use *danse contemporaine* was in part aesthetically driven. Olivier Ducastel had for a long time been an avid attendee of theatrical dance, in particular Pina Bausch's narratively driven works. Working with the actors to create a clear physical embodiment of their characters was of paramount importance to Ducastel and Martineau. For them, "contemporary dance allows for the creation of interesting and beautiful choreography that does not necessarily call upon virtuosity or technique."[57] Professional dancers trained in this form of course have advanced technical proficiency. Because *dance contemporaine*, like postmodern dance in the United States, is invested in a sense of democratizing dance by making the form more inclusive—of those performing the movements as well as of what kinds of movements can be considered dance—often the movement vocabulary of its choreography incorporates everyday, functional, pedestrian movements. This approach was appealing to the filmmakers, because of the way it could stylistically ensure a continuity of character through narrative integration, instead of transforming the characters of Jeanne and Olivier into dancers.

To achieve this function, one of Giron's tasks was choreographing movement that created a natural continuity. This includes an extensive use of what Sally Banes calls "natural movement," also a common part of the postmodern dance aesthetic. Basic actions like running, jumping, falling, or walking are presented as "undistorted for theatrical effectiveness, drained of emotional overlay, literary reference, or manipulated timing . . . executed without regard to grace, visual appeal, or technical skill."[58] From Giron's perspective, "the actors were singing with their non-professional voices, dancing with the fragility of amateurs, so it was important that the dancers were in ordinary bodies, non demonstrative, men and women who dance, and not technicians trying to prove something."[59] We cannot fully equate the amateur training of Ledoyen and Demy's dancing to that of their singing, however, as Demy had more extensive vocal training and Ledoyen was primarily dubbed by singer Elize Caron. The leads' singing performances, as a result, pull the characters farther from the diegesis with their greater professional polish. The dancing acts more as a diegetic tether; Olivier's and Jeanne's choreography conforms rhythmically with the music of the numbers, but their movement vocabulary remains simple, especially in comparison to that of the professional dancers performing with them.

174 STORYTELLING IN MOTION

A description of fragility, timidity, and apprehensiveness, in relation to both the dancing and the lead performers themselves, runs through the discourse from Giron, Ducastel, and Martineau about the film's choreography. The filmmakers were cognizant that having nonprofessional dancers performing in the film could trouble a sense of diegetic continuity, an idea that they committed to by having diegetically heightened dancing flutter in and out of the musical numbers, choreographing little moments of diegetic plurality that could shatter at any moment. In discussing her choreographic choices for the film, Giron emphasizes that "I thought of the dances as soap bubbles, like all that can still be light in life even when the latter is going badly."[60] As a result, the dancers are never too far from the film's diegetic realities, relating to the desired aesthetic of narrative continuity through the musical numbers, in which flickers of the tragic story and the limits of the human body peek through even in the most fantastical of moments.

This rhetoric of fragility is misleading, however, because the movement quality of the choreography is also built on a foundation of strength. The physical personae that Giron created for the dancing in *Jeanne et le garçon formidable* draws on pedestrian movement in the contemporary dance portions. Weight shifting is a key aspect of the dances' aesthetic, both an individual performer's shifting of their weight in all three dimensions as well as sharing the weight of others and allowing oneself to be supported through partnering, lifts, and touch-based phrases. There is also a strong aesthetic of dancing in partnerships, in part inspired by Steve Paxton's work in Contact Improvisation: pulling, pushing, and sharing the weight of others.[61] For Laban/Bartenieff Movement Studies, the presence of Weight Effort—both the delicateness of Light Weight Effort and the solidness of Strong Weight Effort—suggests a sense of intentionality and an active emotional investment.[62] In the "Java du séropo" number, especially, Giron's choreography makes use of fluid weight shifts, both as the dancers move through all three dimensions of space and as they give their weight to be supported by another dancer. There is a sense of continuous flow in the dance, with few moments of stillness and an emphasis on interiority rather than a sense of the dancers projecting outward.[63] The greater fluidity of weight shifting, in addition to moments of more complex choreography—either through more extended dance sequences or more multi-unit postural movements— also distinguishes the professional dancers from the amateur ones. This is

Figure 8.4 Jeanne flirts with an unnamed office cleaner who lifts and dances around her in *Jeanne et le garçon formidable* as the other office cleaners sing.
Source: Les Films du Requin.

especially apparent in the tango and the java, when the dancers are acutely aware of the subtleties in their partners' movements, and their focus remains on the pair or the individual rather than the larger environment.

Giron's choreographic emphasis on weight sensing and shifting reinforces an investment in awareness of one's body and in the narrative's focus on the body's pleasures as well as its finiteness. This is especially visible in the film's prioritization of character relationships through an emphasis on duets instead of solos. Jeanne's dances are heavily contact-driven and make use of lifts, weight shifts, and partnered traveling through space. This pattern is prevalent in the contact-driven duets between Jeanne and the men in her life: one of the office building cleaners, her early boyfriend Jean-Baptiste, Olivier, and the street artist. We can see these strong similarities by comparing Jeanne's first duet with the office cleaner (Fabrice Ramalingom) and last duet with the street artist (Sylvain Prunenec). Both make use of walking and running through the space, spins, lifts, and jumps as each couple comes together and separates in choreographic flirtations.[64] The choreography of the first and last of Jeanne's duets with potential romantic partners distinguishes between the technique of Ledoyen and her dancing partner; in both instances the men dance around her with greater prowess (figures 8.4 and 8.5).

Jeanne's duet with Olivier in the "Java du séropo" echoes these patterns as well, but in a more parsed down, somber fashion appropriate to both the tone of the number and to Demy's more limited dance experience. Like the differences between Ledoyen and her professional dancing partners, Giron's

Figure 8.5 Jeanne flirts with an unnamed street artist who lifts, spins, and dances around her in *Jeanne et le garçon formidable*.
Source: Les Films du Requin.

Figure 8.6 Jeanne and Olivier dance, feeling each other's weight as he spins her around in *Jeanne et le garçon formidable*.
Source: Les Films du Requin.

choreography for the "Java du séropo" has the professional dancers parallel the pared-down dancing of the leads. Their choreography similarly occurs frequently in pairs and with an emphasis on weight sensing and sharing weight (figure 8.6). For example, a couple in green and purple on the left of the frame, midground, perform head supports and jumping lifts behind Jeanne and Olivier. Also, as Olivier pauses in the middle of his final lyrical sentence, a group of dancers in the background suspend an upward arm reach as they fall forward.[65] As Olivier resumes singing, they catch the fall by bending the arm and quickly leaping into a turn,[66] a movement that echoes

Figure 8.7 Jeanne and Jean-Baptiste dance, with little enthusiasm, in *Jeanne et le garçon formidable*.
Source: Les Films du Requin.

Jeanne's bent-arm initiated turn from a few seconds earlier. This connects the decision-making connotations of Time Effort to Olivier's acceptance, explicitly voiced in his lyrics, of his terminal illness.

Jeanne's tango scene with Jean-Baptiste, choreographed by Francisco Miranda Terto, differs the most from her other duets, signaling the romantic incompatibility of the pair (figure 8.7). Their tango performance differs from the more sophisticated couples moving around them, in part because much of their duet occurs in medium and medium-close shots, drawing attention to Jeanne's voiced-over song, the dourness of Jeanne and Jean-Baptiste's expressions, and the contrast with the other more passionate duets occurring simultaneously in which the full bodies of the dancers are visible in the background. The tighter framing also draws attention to the subtle ways in which the couple's weight shifting is not in sync. Unlike the other tango dancers, who glide through the space and use the close contact of the tango's frame to move as a single unit, we can see Jeanne and Jean-Baptiste unevenly pouring weight into each other. This is especially visible at the start of the medium close-up of the couple, which allows us to see how their heads move independently, their foreheads gently sliding against the other. The other couples use head contact as another stable, physical contact point to move through the space as a single unit. Some of this difference likely comes from the contrast between the professional and amateur dancers. Narratively, however, it reinforces the incompatibility between Jeanne and her partner, something she acknowledges to herself in song later in the number.

Dancing Through the Diegesis

The choice of setting for many of Jeanne's numbers unifies the three major aesthetic influences that Ducastel and Martineau chose to evoke in their take on the musical genre: specific instances of the Hollywood musical, Jacques Demy's filmmaking, and *danse contemporaine*. Even though Maurice Béjart's choreography departed from existing French ballet tradition by using nontraditional spaces like a circus tent or sports arena to present dance,[67] contemporary choreographers took this shift a step further, displaying their works in more unusual settings: parks, skyscraper rooftops, art galleries, airport runways, or abandoned factories.[68] A significant feature of *danse contemporaine*—one it shares with postmodern dance in the United States—is the use of nontraditional performance spaces,[69] often for political (democratic) as well as aesthetic purposes.[70] Musical conventions frequently lead characters to dance beyond the confines of the proscenium and diegetic groundedness, and the musicals that influenced Ducastel and Martineau—*Hair* and *Les Demoiselles de Rochefort* in particular—also rely heavily on location shooting and diegetically heightened figure movement for their musical numbers.

Not all the examples of *Jeanne*'s heightened figure movement occur in the musical sequences; the film also incorporates brief choreographed dance phrases throughout the setting of Jeanne's workplace, Jet Tours. When Jeanne is at work, we often see moments in which these phrases appear in the background plane of the frame (figure 8.8). In the opening shots of the film, all the

Figure 8.8 Diegetically ambiguous dancers appear in the background of Jet Tours in *Jeanne et le garçon formidable*.
Source: Les Films du Requin.

IMPERFECT BODIES 179

pedestrians dance their way in and out of the Jet Tours building. In the first shot, the camera cranes down and dollies back from the side of the building to reveal the main revolving door, with Jeanne visible at her desk in the background through the glass. Two pedestrians approach the door from opposite sides of the frame; a woman in a yellow outfit gets there first and engages the door, causing the man to slow his movement, suspending his step as he shifts his weight backward a step before he in turn engages with the revolving door. Both look at each other as this occurs, but as the first woman moves into off-screen space the man's attention is drawn to a new pedestrian, all in red, exiting the building. The scene cuts to Jeanne at her desk, answering phone calls. She is centered in the frame, and behind her we can see the large glass windows of the office building and the Parisian city street behind her. A suited office worker enters the shot from the right and skips as he rotates away from Jeanne toward the camera in the foreground and extends a hand forward, which another suited office worker takes as she enters the frame. He gently pulls her toward him while waving at Jeanne, a gesture which Jeanne returns as the couple exits frame left. The camera begins to push in on Jeanne as she continues to answer the phone, and a new couple, one of whom is the woman wearing red who exited the building earlier, walks rightward behind Jeanne on the street outside. As they pass behind her, the woman turns and puts her arms around her companion's neck. She then slices her arms behind her in a wide arcing motion and reverses the pathway.[71] The couple maintains physical contact as they continue to walk down the street, out of frame. In the next shot we see one more couple exiting an elevator; a suited man guides the woman in yellow who entered the building earlier through a full-rotation spin before putting his arm around her as they continue walking.

Such brief danced phrases continue to flutter in and out of the diegesis throughout the scene as Jeanne engages in conversation with her office boyfriend, Jean-Baptiste, and the plumber, Mr. Martin. The brief moments of heightened figure movement provide additional visual information for our eyes to process in the space of the frame around Jeanne as she goes about her business at the end of the workday. In each instance, dancers perform brief, largely pedestrian phrases without the scene ever developing into a full musical number. Neither do they move in rhythm to a song, as the orchestral music on the soundtrack ends partway through the scene. Each time, the more mundane business of a couple coming together is paired with a single more embellished movement that often emphasizes weight shifts and touch between the members of the pair.

180 STORYTELLING IN MOTION

These moments that include contemporary dance create additional flutters of diegetic plurality outside of movements that are more clearly articulated as musical numbers. Like Demy's musicals, which seem to float above any fully realistic grounding outside of the musical numbers, these moments emphasize a diegesis in which dance, and bodily awareness, is an inherent part of everyday life. What we see in these moments are the remnants of a more explicitly developed number that was to occur in conjunction with the opening film credits. The sequence's intent was to better establish these dancing pedestrians as characters in the diegesis by exposing the energy and specificity of each dancer within this group of secondary protagonists.[72] However, the film's use of *danse contemporaine*, as well as the inclusion of ACT UP demonstrations, was a point of tension between the filmmakers and the film's distributors, leading to some aesthetic compromises.

Political Choreography and the Imperfect Body

Incorporating dance into *Jeanne et le garçon formidable*'s form had a strong aesthetic value to Ducastel and Martineau, but it had a significant political importance as well. *Jeanne*'s narrative expresses discontent about social and political issues in the musical numbers through a consistent juxtaposition of realist and escapist impulses. Martineau's script addresses the politics of the AIDS epidemic and ACT UP demonstrations, but the filmmakers were not fully aware until postproduction of the extent to which their choreographic choices also had political implications that would impact the film's final form. This led to narrative changes in order to maintain the political potentials of the figure movement.

Choreographic Objections

The fleeting glimpses of dancers in Jeanne's workplace that appear in the film's opening and at brief moments later in the plot were meant to feature more prominently in the opening sequence as "a sort of micro-choreography interspersed with the credits."[73] According to Martineau, they wanted to create an aesthetic where "at Jet Tours, everyone dances." Half a dozen couples exited the building, each with their own dance phrase that made use of the revolving glass doors of the building, a concept that the filmmakers found "absolutely magnificent." But Martineau explains that the sequence led to one of the major battles he and Ducastel had with their distributor over the final cut:

> We sensed that the choice we had made, and the very free sort of chore-ography, and the dancers, created a problem. [The distributors] had so strongly in mind the idea that a musical comedy would be like what you would see on television . . . , variety shows and such, that they were going to have beautiful dancers with huge smiles, and we brought them people who were funny, with unusual appearances. . . . Our distributor did not tolerate the dancers . . . or their bodies.[74]

Both uses of figure movement—the incorporation of a more inclusive definition of a dancing body and the presentation of ACT UP protests—made the film's producers uncomfortable, according to Ducastel's and Martineau's recollections of the postproduction period.[75] The result was a compromise that led to eliminating most of the opening dance sequence in order to save the ACT UP content, none of which was cut for the final version of the film.[76] Although *danse contemporaine* was an established and respected form in France by the late 1990s, it did not fit the distributors' expectations of musical conventions. The final version, with only minimal remnants of the longer cinematic choreography, instead establishes the film's musical realist aesthetic by committing to neither a fully escapist nor a fully grounded diegesis.

The film's ACT UP scene, however, avoids any suggestions of a heightened diegetic space. The filmmakers considered a version of the protest scene in which the fictional characters sang as they marched, akin to Jacques Demy's approach to the striking workers in *Une Chambre en Ville* (1982). Instead, the staged scenes with the film's characters are combined with footage of one of ACT UP's "*journée du désespoir*" protest marches that shows, in a wide shot, the magnitude of the crowd participating in the real-life protest. The distributors' discomfort likely came from the documentary aesthetic of these moments in which the musical fantasy elements are absent, reinforcing the seriousness of the AIDS epidemic. For Martineau, these portions of the film needed to have a solidly documentary tone to them.[77]

Musical Resistance

Jeanne juxtaposes realist and fantastical formal elements to express sociopolitical discontent, and much of the information with extra-narrative political resonances occurs in musical sequences. These numbers address the consequences of the AIDS epidemic, but Ducastel and Martineau draw attention to questions of immigration and labor as well. The opening number establishes the pattern of Jeanne's danced duets with her potential romantic partners. Singing and dancing as Jeanne and her partner flirt are Amy Bamba, Mohamed Damraoui, Jean-François Deleray, and Gino Sitson, four singers of color playing the cleaning staff. The number implies the characters are of North African and Arabic descent, and the lyrics address *sans papiers* tensions and frustration over current French immigration policies.[78] Jeanne's duet with one of the cleaning staff (Fabrice Ramalingom) occurs within the number's broader vocalization of the challenges facing immigrants in France through the number's lyrics. Jeanne, notably, takes no part in the sung portions of the number, and her attention is only for the man she is dancing with (figure 8.9). Her character, played by the white actor Virginie Ledoyen, cynically serves as a spectator surrogate for Ducastel and Martineau's audience, engaging with the issues that affect the people she interacts with daily only when they begin to directly impact her happiness.

Another frequent visitor to the Jet Tours building lobby is a plumber, Mr. Martin, who sings and dances as he inspects the toilets, marveling in song about how they always seem to be clogged. The number is a comical take on the kind of choreographed staging attributed to Busby Berkeley and

Figure 8.9 Jeanne has eyes only for her partner in *Jeanne et le garçon formidable*.
Source: Les Films du Requin.

Figure 8.10 The plumber Mr. Martin is seen from a Busby Berkeley–style top shot, bending his legs while fixing a toilet in *Jeanne et le garçon formidable*.
Source: Les Films du Requin.

his abstract dance choreography for Warner Bros. in the 1930s. It features Berkeley's signature high-angle top shot of the bathroom the plumber is fixing, with the set from above revealed to be a purple yin-yang (figure 8.10). As he sings about the advantages and pitfalls of the plumbing profession, professional actor but amateur dancer Michel Raskine kicks and swings his legs from side to side as he lies stretched out on the ground. The movement is highly functional, reflecting the changes a plumber's body would undergo while twisting to reach a pipe, but his body is also positioned in such a way that evokes the chorus girls' movements in the "Young and Healthy" number (figure 8.11) from *42nd Street* (Lloyd Bacon, 1933). Of course, the abstract, kaleidoscopic shapes that occur in Berkeley's films do not create such an effect when only one person is performing them, so the number in *Jeanne* comes across as whimsical instead of lavish and spectacular, drawing attention to the stylized labor of the single performer as opposed to the abstracted objectification of bodies into shapes seen in Berkeley's aesthetic.

Jeanne, like most of Ducastel and Martineau's films, seeks to educate its public about the AIDS epidemic and humanize its fictional narrative's HIV positive characters. The expression of injustice occurs in the musical numbers, whereas action to combat that injustice occurs in the grounded (albeit fictional) diegesis. Jeanne learns about the personal impact of the AIDS epidemic from François's (Jacques Bonnaffé's) solo sung number, in which he sings about losing his partner to AIDS and society's indifference to the suffering of gay men. His sung number over, François tells Jeanne about his

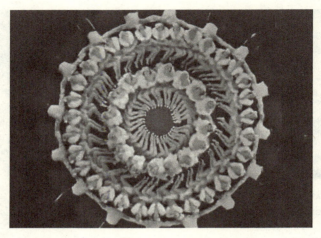

Figure 8.11 The dancers in *42nd Street* execute similar shapes as Mr. Martin, creating abstract shapes through the repeated aggregation of their movements.
Source: Warner Bros.

work with ACT UP to fight for a cure and against the stigma associated with the disease. Jeanne similarly learns that Olivier is HIV positive as the "Java du séropo" number begins and he tells her, in song, about his stages of grief in learning about his illness and his past struggle with drug addiction that led to his infection. He also redirects her question about who "contaminated" him, telling her that those in society who would reject his life as valuable are the ones to blame.

The "Java du séropo" number pulls together several aesthetic contrasts. Olivier sings about his diagnosis while dancing with Jeanne, and despite the seriousness of the (sung) conversation, they are also still thinking about their attraction, as they continue to seek out the other's touch. The emphasis on physical closeness also draws attention to the work of destigmatizing physical contact with HIV positive people. The number contrasts the simpler partnered choreography for amateur dancers Ledoyen and Demy with the corps of professional dancers, whose dancing grows in the background as the main couple sings, eventually pulling the couple into the dance as well. This combines with the diegetic pulls, discussed earlier, between the contrast of the heightened performances of the singers and dancers with the groundedness of the orchestra playing in the park and the diegetic stability of the mise-en-scène. The complex staging and diversity of stimuli pull our eye through the depth of the frame and force us to juxtapose Olivier's tragic acceptance of his situation—that he will die of AIDS—with the joyful lives of the dancers behind him and Jeanne, who, like most of the other characters in the film, live in ignorance of his condition and the struggles of the many HIV positive people like him.

The choreographic emphasis on touch and weight sharing in the musical numbers also draws attention to Olivier's absence from the narrative once he becomes sick. Rather than cinematically represent his physical decline, Ducastel and Martineau choose to have him disappear entirely from the narrative. This disappearance and rapid decline in health was, for Martineau, reflective of how he lost friends to AIDS before more effective treatments became available in the mid-1990s.[79] Narratively, this echoes François's telling Jeanne through song about his experience losing his partner to AIDS early in the plot. Whereas we hear about François's experience, we see Jeanne experiencing the same physical absence. Jeanne also learns about Olivier's death through staging choices that echo their meet cute.

Olivier and Jeanne meet in the Paris Métro. As a cinematic location, the moving trains are an ideal parallel to a choreography that emphasizes weight shifting and sharing, as the movement of the cars requires the body to constantly make small adjustments through weight sensing to maintain balance, and we see the characters swaying slightly throughout these scenes as a result.[80] Jeanne races to open the métro door before the train departs and narrowly avoids a collision with the man by the central pole. As she is making her way through the train car, an abrupt jolt of the train throws her off balance and she falls into Olivier's lap, lingering in place to apologize before taking the seat opposite him.

Near the end of the film Jeanne once again catches a métro car as the train is about to depart, but this time she collides with the passenger who is holding on to the car's central pole, and their bodies separate more rigidly as he berates her.[81] As she moves once again through the car she recognizes Olivier's friend, who was with him during their first meeting and who informs her of Olivier's death. In both scenes, Jeanne's interactions occur through accelerated movements as she either rushes or is thrown through space.[82] The absence of a deliberate engagement with sensing her weight or an attention to orienting herself in space through Weight or Space Effort has her interacting with characters in a Mobile State,[83] which emphasizes a sense of changing one's progression through the world but without a clear inner focus on self. The parallels of mise-en-scène draw attention to Olivier's absence as Jeanne's posture remains frozen in place at the shock of her loss,[84]

186 STORYTELLING IN MOTION

even as the gentle sway of the métro rocks her, and the world around her moves on.

Conclusions

Olivier Ducastel and Jacques Martineau, through a combination of documentary techniques, realist impulses, and escapist aesthetics, use musical genre conventions to express the anguish of those impacted by the AIDS epidemic. The choices of staging and choreography draw attention to figure movement and dancing for the sake of aesthetic pleasure but also to emphasize the political importance of the body. The emphasis on the figure through dance makes our realization of the fragility of Olivier's body as he succumbs to the AIDS virus even more devastating.

Instead of serving primarily as a means of aesthetic escapism, dancing in *Jeanne* serves important narrative and political functions. Contemporary dance in France and the United States is often associated with political positions as its choreographers fight against expectations of what the medium of dance and dancers' bodies should look like. Beyond *danse contemporaine*'s aesthetic complementarity to Ducastel and Martineau's narrative, its history as a democratizing dance form also parallels the political symbolism of the body in *Jeanne*'s story and the film's production history. While maintaining ties to the conventions of the musical, Ducastel and Martineau's film ultimately pushes us to rethink the boundaries of the genre by re-examining how a film musical can expand the narrative and stylistic possibilities of musical numbers.

Since *Jeanne et le garçon formidable*'s release, *danse contemporaine* in French musical sequences has become more common. Later films, like *On va s'aimer* (Ivan Calbérac, 2006) and *Sur quel pied danser* (Paul Calori and Kostia Testut, 2016) continue the incorporation of this French movement form as a central narrative element. However, unlike Ducastel and Martineau's foregrounding of these more experimental dance styles as an important force for political and social change, these later films use *danse contemporaine* more as a stylistic curiosity. Reviews and descriptions for the 2016 film *Sur quel pied danser* connect the film's aesthetic to Jacques Demy as well as classical Hollywood, paralleling descriptions of American musical *La La Land*'s transnational influences, released the same year (Damien Chazelle,

2016).[85] *Sur quel pied danser* certainly references Demy's musical tendencies through minimalist choreographed figure movement and an emphasis on the working class and the performance of physical labor. Yet within the history of the French musical, Olivier Ducastel, Jacques Martineau, and Sylvie Giron's cinematic choreography in *Jeanne* deserves credit for pioneering the formal and political worth of *danse contemporaine* to cinematic storytelling.

9

Rhythmic Realism

La La Land (2016)

The musical genre has always played with the tension between fantasy and realism. For Olivier Ducastel and Jacques Martineau in *Jeanne et le garçon formidable* (1998), the fantastical elements of the musical genre tempered the tragic realities of their narrative about the HIV/AIDS epidemic. They were similarly inspired by Jacques Demy's proclivity for musical sequences that maintain close ties to the stylistic rules of the diegesis. An aesthetic of realism also serves as an important counter to musical fantasy in *La La Land* (Damien Chazelle, 2016). Audie Cornish's interview with Chazelle, "Showbiz Dreams Collide with Reality in 'La La Land,'" is telling in the title's focus.[1] *La La Land*'s form is invested in the genre's convention of shifting from diegesis to fantasy and in how those transitions and their rhythmic patterning can challenge the audience's narrative comprehension of the film's realist components.

All choreographed movement has rhythm, driven by patterns of duration and pause. Rhythm, though linked to the perception of time, is also connected to body motor sequences: movement.[2] In Laban Movement Analysis, rhythm and pacing, acceleration and deceleration, are linked to decision-making and Time Effort.[3] As a percussionist, *La La Land* director Damien Chazelle is no stranger to rhythm. The way he paces musical numbers—through repetitive figure movement, fluid long-take cinematography, and sequence duration—reinforces the film's narrative emphasis on career stagnation and decision-making tensions between personal and professional life. *La La Land* follows Mia (Emma Stone), an aspiring film actor, and Sebastian (Ryan Gosling), a jazz musician who wants to open his own club, as they struggle to make careers for themselves in Los Angeles. Multiple chance encounters in the city bring them together as they support each other to achieve their dreams, but pursuing those dreams ultimately pulls them apart.

La La Land was a financial success, earning a worldwide gross of $450 million on a $30 million budget.[4] Heralded as revitalizing the musical, it drew

Storytelling in Motion. Jenny Oyallon-Koloski, Oxford University Press. © Oxford University Press 2024.
DOI: 10.1093/oso/9780197602669.003.0010

attention for its stylistic inventiveness, its nostalgic reverence for the genre's conventions, and its emphasis on jazz in the storytelling. Much of the focus of existing research—and criticism—about *La La Land* centers on its portrayal of jazz and its place in the inequitable racial history of the form, particularly the choice to cast white actors (Emma Stone and Ryan Gosling) as the leads in a film that is so focused on an African American tradition of music.[5] These critiques continue an important conversation about the erasure of Black artists—and artists of color more generally—in American history. The singing and dancing vernacular of the American film musical, in particular, is still frequently associated with white European styles only despite owing much of its form to the work of African American, Mexican, and Jewish artists.[6]

Because of the emphasis on jazz to their arguments, analyses of the film tend to focus more on Sebastian's half of the story, downplaying Mia's importance to the narrative and to its patterns of stagnation and momentum. To position *La La Land*, despite these valid critiques, as reinventing the musical genre without centering its female lead, relationship to French musical aesthetics, and approach to cinematic choreography misses its more generative contribution to the genre's evolution. French filmmaker Jacques Demy's style of musical cinema influences the choreography of Mia's movement, in particular, through an emphasis on repetition and stasis that guides her movement and (lack of) progression through the story.

La La Land thematically aligns with contemporary media's emphasis on transmedial aesthetics, remakes, and reflexivity through its extensive use of musical citations. "A film like *La La Land*," writes Desirée Garcia, "reaches back in order to move forward."[7] *La La Land* is invested in the symmetries of its jazz, of old and new, of realism and fantasy, of duration, and of relationships between performers and the mobile camera. By engaging with established and innovative stylistic options, *La La Land* deviates from many norms of recent Hollywood musicals by emphasizing long-take cinematography, complex staging, and choreography that drives narrative purposes over showstopping functions to ultimately challenge audience expectations through the resulting narrative ambiguity.

La La Land picks up on the tension of the imperfect body that we see in *Jeanne et le garçon formidable* but to a different effect. Gosling's and Stone's casting as the film's leads comes largely from their embodiment of Hollywood star power and their reputation as highly trained professional actors, juxtaposed with their nonprofessional status as dancers and their characters'

190 STORYTELLING IN MOTION

inability to succeed professionally. These patterns of repetition, stagnation, and dreams for a more fulfilling future play out through Chazelle's deliberate stylistic shifts away from the diegesis in musical numbers, creating detailed layers of tension between aesthetics of realism and fantasy. *La La Land*'s filmmakers could have adopted the highly edited aesthetic common in contemporary Hollywood musicals to create a flashier feel to the dancing and downplay any physical limitations of its performers. Instead, they chose to work with sequence shots and Steadicam-driven cinematography. This musical approach connects the realist aesthetic evoked by these cinematographic choices with director Damien Chazelle's love of classical Hollywood musicals and Jacques Demy's cinema. In *La La Land*, the camera awakens and stretches, engaging cinematographic muscles weakened by editing's dominance over the contemporary cinematic landscape.

Contemporary Musical Norms (Production History)

Contemporary discourse at the time of *La La Land*'s release lauded the film as reviving the musical, echoing an often-repeated lament (or celebration) that the genre is dying off.[8] Declaring the death and rebirth of the genre is a time-honored tradition in film musical criticism. The classical Hollywood musical norm of sincere, narratively integrated song and dance numbers fell out of favor in the 1970s alongside the rise of New Hollywood aesthetics. Rather than dying off, the genre adapted to take advantage of contemporary tastes and industrial priorities in order to maintain financial and cultural viability.[9] In addition to finding ways to repackage their classical film output and draw audiences in with the convention of sung musical numbers, studios greenlit films on the periphery of the genre like *Saturday Night Fever* (John Badham, 1977), *Flashdance* (Adrian Lyne, 1983), or *Breakin'* (Joel Silberg, 1984) that could exploit the synergistic potential of film and record sales and compete with music videos' increasingly popular form through quickly edited musical sequences, tight framings on flashily dancing performers, and extractable content.[10]

As with earlier claims of the genre's death in the 1960s, there were plenty of musicals—both Broadway adaptations and cinematic originals—being produced in Hollywood in the decades preceding *La La Land*. The year 2014 saw the theatrical release of Will Gluck's *Annie*, Clint Eastwood's *Jersey Boys*, and Rob Marshall's *Into the Woods*. In 2012 came Tom Hooper's *Les*

Misérables, Salim Akil's *Sparkle*, and Jason Moore's *Pitch Perfect*. A big year for musicals was 2007, with theatrical releases of Julie Taymor's *Across the Universe*, Kevin Lima's *Enchanted*, Adam Shankman's *Hairspray*, John Carney's *Once*, and Kenny Ortega's made-for-television *High School Musical 2*, whose sequel (*High School Musical 3: Senior Year*) would have a theatrical release in 2008. And earlier in the century, films like *Moulin Rouge!* (Baz Luhrmann, 2001) and *Chicago* (Rob Marshall, 2002) significantly impacted the stylistic choices filmmakers made in portraying dance on screen.

Intensifying (Dis)continuity

Director Baz Luhrmann amplified an editing-driven musical aesthetic in *Moulin Rouge!* while returning to earlier conventions of narratively integrated numbers balanced with showstopping spectacle through an "unashamed and unapologetic" style.[11] Luhrmann deliberately creates an overwhelming, overstimulating aesthetic to simulate the experience of attending the famous nitery that subsequent filmmakers drew on without the same narrative motivation. The film's financial success convinced Miramax to fund Rob Marshall's adaptation of choreographer Bob Fosse's *Chicago*, which subsequently encouraged studios to greenlight other stalled musical projects. Numerous studios also released films during this period that emphasize dance sequences and narrative conflicts between dance styles and the communities that perform them, like *Save the Last Dance* (Thomas Carter, 2001) and *Step Up* (Anne Fletcher, 2006).[12]

Editing rates for musical numbers during this period were faster than ever. Classical Hollywood musical numbers have an average shot length of 24 seconds,[13] whereas both *Moulin Rouge!* and *Chicago*'s musical numbers have an average shot length around three seconds—3.2 and 2.9, respectively—and their numbers that feature dancing are edited even more quickly, averaging 1.4 seconds for *Moulin Rouge!* and 1.9 seconds for *Chicago*. Subsequent Hollywood musicals are closer to *Moulin Rouge!* and *Chicago*'s editing range than classical Hollywood's. Rob Marshall's *Mary Poppins Returns* (2018) and Steven Spielberg's adaptation of *West Side Story* (2021) both have musical number average shot lengths of around 10 seconds. The inclusion of at least a few musical numbers with average shot lengths of under 5 seconds is now standard in contemporary Hollywood film musicals and even more common in musical television series like *Glee* (Fox, 2009–2015).[14]

192 STORYTELLING IN MOTION

Moulin Rouge! also draws from popular Indian cinema in its use of fast cutting, stylistic excess, and repeated or overlapping action. *Moulin Rouge!* relies not only on rapid editing to create a dynamic quality. Many of the shots are set up to create invisible edits, as we see at the beginning of the number introducing Christian (Ewan McGregor) to the night club, where the courtesans sing a line from "Lady Marmalade" as the camera pans away from one courtesan's face only to cut to a steady framing of the next. Cinematographer John O'Connell often adjusts the shutter speed, creating blurred movement or slow-motion effects. Extensive special effects and matte effects are also used to create composite images of the various parts of the Moulin Rouge set and to create crossfades and overlapping images, adding even more stimuli to the screen.

Moulin Rouge!'s stylistic debt to popular Indian song aesthetics is visible through its fast editing pace, large corps of dancers, visual excess, and figure movement influences (most visible in the "Hindi Sad Diamonds" number),[15] yet in the cinematic choreography for Hindi-language films like *Dhoom 2* (Sanjay Gadhvi, 2006) there is also an amplified attention to spatiotemporal continuity and contiguity paired with fast editing paces. Take, for example, *Dhoom 2*'s song "Dil Laga Na," choreographed by Shiamak Davar, which brings together the film's five main characters near the end of the narrative as they gather in Rio de Janeiro to execute or attempt to stop a major heist. Surrounding them are hundreds of extras and dancers, with choreography that blends movement styles from popular Indian cinema with Brazilian movement forms like Capoeira. The number is quickly edited, with an average of 2.5 seconds, and the cinematic choreography is complex. The moments of faster editing occur primarily through jump cuts that change to subtly different framings along a single axis (horizontal, sagittal, or vertical), maintaining clear spatial legibility as a result. However, some shots hold longer on the action, creating compositions in which the camera rack focuses or glides through the space to follow or shift attention to a different protagonist.

One such shot immediately follows a split-screen composition of the five main characters walking in slow motion toward the camera. This 37-second take begins with Aryan (Hrithik Roshan) in the right midground standing by several extras; some out of focus dancers in the left foreground twirl out of frame to reveal Jai (Abhishek Bachchan) walking toward Aryan. As Jai sings and Aryan turns to face him, the camera arcs around them to the left to position them in the center of the frame. Jai finishes his verse and the two walk past each other and out of frame, revealing Monali (Bipasha Basu) in the background. She sings and moves rightward as the camera follows her until she reaches Ali (Uday Chopra) and pulls him close as he tosses the drinks he was holding to reciprocate. They twirl off-screen right in the foreground to reveal the stage behind them, where Sunehri (Aishwarya Rai Bachchan) begins to sing and dance, flanked by a dozen dancers. As she moves, her gaze is consistently focused off-screen left, and she walks off the stage and to the left as the camera dollies back to reveal Aryan facing her. She reaches for him as her verse ends and he begins to sing, dancing away from her touch and turning to face the camera as she watches him. He reverses his movement to face Sunehri and spins to kneel before her as the camera cranes up and arcs right to frame them in profile. The multiple camera angles and rapid editing in "Dil Laga Na," alternated with more complex sequence shots, add to the kinetic feeling of the sequence without sacrificing spatiotemporal clarity or the intelligibility of the dancing. This is contrary to the norm for danced numbers in contemporary Hollywood, which often eschew spatiotemporal clarity for a more generalized feeling of energy through quick cutting.

Faster cutting, multicamera shooting, and often fleetingly seen choreography became the norm in the contemporary Hollywood musicals that preceded *La La Land*. David Bordwell's analysis of Hollywood storytelling and style points to an intensification of classical continuity conventions after the studio era. Stylistically, this has resulted in more mobile framing, lens length bipolar extremes, a greater use of tighter framings, and faster editing paces.[16] When shots have longer durations they are usually saved for intricate traveling shots, made possible in part by lighter camera equipment and Steadicam stabilizer technology.[17] Filmmakers are able to maintain spatial coherence through this style of intensified continuity, but Bordwell emphasizes that "some action sequences are cut so fast (and staged so gracelessly) as to be incomprehensible."[18] A similar effect is noticeable in contemporary musical norms; at times spatial clarity in these numbers is sacrificed for a more abstract sense of dynamic kineticism or as a cost-saving measure. This aesthetic is particularly visible in later seasons of Ryan Murphy's musical television series *Glee* (2009–2015), in which musical numbers featuring dance are produced quickly and filmed with multiple cameras, offering little time for choreographer Zach Woodlee or the show's directors and editors to plan clear continuity across shots. Faster editing paces do not inherently fracture classical rules of spatiotemporal continuity, as Bordwell demonstrates: "Close-ups and singles make the shots very legible. Rapid

194   STORYTELLING IN MOTION

editing obliges the viewer to assemble many discrete pieces of information, and it sets a commanding pace: look away, and you might miss a key point."[19] Yet the norms of intensified continuity and the use of dance can conflict when seeing the full figure or understanding where the performer is in space is necessary to the meaning-making process.[20]

Editing is a powerful tool for guiding audience attention; it is also a tool for contemporary filmmakers to hold onto that attention. "Television-friendly, the style [of intensified continuity] tries to rivet the viewer to the screen,"[21] Bordwell writes. Sean Griffin adds that "the rapid, disjunctive editing and flashy visuals [of music videos] are used to draw viewer attention, in recognition of the distracted nature of television watching (at home, in a bar/club, etc.)."[22] Mandy Moore, *La La Land*'s choreographer, is also a frequent choreographer for the television series *So You Think You Can Dance* (2005 – present) and *Dancing with the Stars* (2005 – present). She emphasizes how the filming style for those shows is designed to match the intensity of the commercials that interrupt them: "It's fast, it's big, because you don't want the people to turn off, they should be visually stimulated, just like the ads. . . . It aligns with the very idea of television and commercialism."[23] Prioritizing a style of intensified (dis)continuity in musical numbers impacts how the dancing figure functions as a storytelling element. Choreography of characters in contemporary Hollywood communicates emotion, dynamism, and community first, and narrative and character development second. As a practical reality of such a strong industrial shift to editing-dominated style, the craft of long-take cinematography for filming choreography has dwindled in contemporary American cinema.

Extending a Franco-American Style

One reviewer of *La La Land* writes, "Chazelle put his faith in dancing as good storytelling. As a result, dance makes a triumphant return as an expressive cinematic language."[24] As we've seen, dance never stopped being a part of the musical equation. The way *La La Land*'s filmmakers capture figure movement, however, gives the moving and dancing performers greater narrative responsibility and, as a result, greater attention. For Chazelle, in much of contemporary Hollywood, including in his previous film *Whiplash* (2014), movement is created by editing: "Editing is substituting for body language and the face is substituting for the body. And so the whole style of this entire movie, of *La La Land,* was a reaction to that [to intensified continuity],[25] was to try to have every scene, whether it was a dance number or not, be shot the way the dance numbers were shot."[26] *La La Land*'s overall average shot length is 10 seconds, right in the average range of 8–11 seconds for classical Hollywood films, whereas contemporary features average more than half that cutting rate.[27]

La La Land's "Start a Fire" number has a more quickly edited aesthetic to match contemporary norms; its average shot length of 2.6 seconds mirrors the averages of both *Moulin Rouge!* and *Chicago*'s musical numbers. Mia, in the audience, is literally pushed away from the stage by the enthusiastic concert attendees, and Sebastian's presence is downplayed in multiple shots that show him in the background behind lead singer/guitarist Keith (John Legend) or blocked from audience view by the four dancers who appear midway through the song. Thanks to Keith, Sebastian's career at this moment speeds ahead and leaves Mia behind, and the difference of staging and editing reinforces this. By contrast, most of the film's sung and danced numbers focus on the leads—Mia especially—to convey their romantic development and Mia's professional stagnation. The remaining numbers overwhelmingly occur in long takes, with an overall number shot length average of 60 seconds, close to three times the average for classical Hollywood numbers. Three sequences—"Another Day of Sun," "Sebastian's Theme," and "City of Stars"—have three or fewer shots, while both "A Lovely Night" and Mia's audition number are a single take. Rather than isolating fluid, extended shots as a stylistic flourish, Chazelle and cinematographer Linus Sandgren make them a central part of the film's visual construction.

La La Land's style deviates from contemporary Hollywood norms in favor of a new approach to the Franco-American cinematic choreography seen in earlier chapters of this book. *La La Land* follows in the tradition of *cinéma vérité* documentaries like *Chronique d'un été* (Jean Rouch and Edgar Morin, 1961), ethnic folk musicals,[28] and jazz shorts like "St. Louis Blues" (Alfred N. Sack, 1929), "Black & Tan" (Dudley Murphy, 1929), and "Jazz Dance" (Robert Tilton, 1954), the latter of which show communities of audiences, dancers, and musicians coming together around jazz performance.[29] *La La Land*'s style is also driven by the influence of long-take musical filmmakers like Vincente Minnelli and Stanley Donen, the director-choreographers like Fred Astaire and Gene Kelly who worked with them, and the French musicals of Jacques Demy. To Chazelle, Demy's musicals are "resolutely stories about

196 STORYTELLING IN MOTION

ordinary people, shot where they're set, and have this quality of real life that seeps through the artificiality of the genre,"[30] shot with a camera that never seems to stop moving.[31]

La La Land was made on a $30 million budget; its crew had a ten-week pre-production period[32] and a forty-two-day shoot.[33] That time gave choreographer Mandy Moore the opportunity to rehearse with Gosling and Stone four or five times a week for three months before production began, which was significant training time for a Hollywood film production of this period.[34] Moore was brought in very early in *La La Land*'s preproduction process, allowing her to be closely involved in foundational creative conversations. In her already extensive career choreographing for film and television, being a creative collaborator early on rather than a facilitator later in the process was an anomaly, as was having two dance assistants—Jillian Meyers and Michael Riccio—for the film, rather than one.[35] Director of photography Linus Sandgren and Steadicam operator Ari Robbins were also closely involved in the preproduction dance rehearsals, frequently attending or reviewing mobile phone footage captured by Chazelle or Moore. For Moore, the crew's choice to shoot the complex dance sequences without coverage would not have been possible without Robbins, in particular, studying the choreography before arriving on set and without the time to train Gosling and Stone to dance, not just memorize steps. Yet she emphasizes that, despite the production's aesthetic commitment to having nonprofessional dance leads and her satisfaction with the choreographic results, having more time to work with the performers would have allowed them to go even deeper into the movement material.[36]

Strikingly, there are strong parallels between the time Chazelle had to make a musical in 2016 and those Demy had in France the summer of 1966 while working on *Les Demoiselles de Rochefort* (1967). *La La Land*'s filmmakers had sixteen weeks with their cast: ten for preproduction and rehearsals and six for production. *Les Demoiselles de Rochefort*'s filmmakers had fifteen weeks: three to rehearse and twelve to shoot. Demy's resources in the late 1960s were limited compared to those available to Hollywood filmmakers a decade earlier.[37] The parallels to *La La Land*'s production emphasize how much the American industry's resources for musical production have changed. And, as with Demy's early musicals and Olivier Ducastel's and Jacques Martineau's decisions for *Jeanne et le garçon formidable*, the choice in *La La Land* to cast nondancers in the lead roles was a combination of stylistic preference and industrial necessity.

Ordinary Dancing

The choice of Emma Stone and Ryan Gosling for the lead roles in *La La Land* rankled some critics, not only because of the issue of racial (non)representation already mentioned but also because of Hollywood's continuation in casting professional actors, but nonprofessional singers and dancers, in musical productions.[38] *La La Land's* producers were not original in choosing to cast white A-list stars in musicals rather than prioritizing more diverse or lesser-known triple-threat actors. Films like *Moulin Rouge!*, *Chicago*, *Les Misérables* (Tom Hooper, 2012), and the *Mamma Mia* films (Phyllida Lloyd, 2008 and Ol Parker, 2017) make similar casting choices, as did Francis Ford Coppola for *One from the Heart* (1982).[39] Casting actors with adequate but not virtuosic musical talents and surrounding them with professional singers or dancers is common enough in this period to be a parameter of contemporary Hollywood musical conventions, much to the dismay of those who appreciate the musical first and foremost for its spectacular, showstopping solos and duets.

Decisions to cast nonprofessional dancers in lead roles can be the result of a preference for a more realism-driven style, as the previous chapter demonstrates with *Jeanne et le garçon formidable*. But they also come from producers' resistance to financial risk and Hollywood's devaluation of versatility in actors' training. Desirée Garcia and Karen Backstein both argue this point, emphasizing that contemporary Hollywood producers view pitching a musical without a star as too financially risky.[40] Mandy Moore points to this tension as well when she says "so many films [from earlier periods in American filmmaking] had dance in them and so people knew how to shoot it, people knew how to create it, people knew how to write for it. . . . And I think when it went away, we lost a generation of people or we skipped a generation of people knowing how to do it."[41]

The period between the Hollywood studio system and the time of *La La Land's* production saw a significant loss in choreographer-filmmakers and dancer-actors because of industrial changes, lessened incentive for actors to train as dancers, and the devastation of the HIV/AIDS epidemic on the choreographic community. Moore sees the latter as particularly impactful on the changes to cinematic choreography in Hollywood, as "so many people that would have moved on to being choreographers/directors were just gone," from a community that is already relatively small and so heavily dependent on embodied forms of knowledge transfer.[42] Several decades of this

198 STORYTELLING IN MOTION

practice meant that the industry no longer had a vast repertory of actors with song or dance training. This echoes Backstein's articulation of changes to the poststudio musical: "Along with *New York, New York* [(Martin Scorsese, 1977)], *One from the Heart* is a plaintive reminder of why large-scale musicals became so hard to produce after the studio system had vanished. Everything Coppola and Scorsese had to create from scratch previously existed (seemingly) permanently on MGM's back lot."[43] *La La Land*'s filmmakers similarly had to reestablish many of these foundations.

For Chazelle, the choice to cast Gosling and Stone in the lead roles was motivated in part by their star charisma and previous on-screen chemistry. Aesthetically he also sought, in collaboration with choreographer Mandy Moore, to consistently emphasize the diegetic "slippage" from ordinary into danced movement "so [the lead's] non-dance movements could never be too un-dance-like, and their dances could never be too polished or too un-lifelike." He adds, "I think I always saw it [dancing] as an inextricable part of the same equation, that was the visual equivalent of singing. So if this is a world where talking can slip into singing, then walking can slip into dancing."[44] Nonprofessional dancing was a practical constraint, but it also became a central aspect of the film's musical aesthetic, drawing attention to relationships and an acting continuity across numbers instead of show-stopping movement virtuosity.

The mobilization of pedestrian, choreographed movement is particularly visible in the pattern of Mia's traveling through the film. We frequently see her walking in extended follow shots, either alone or as a point of contrast to those around her and visible in medium to long shots. She walks through the apartment with her roommates in "Someone in the Crowd," the only one not immediately excited about the potential of a night out. She walks away from a bad audition through a hallway waiting room of near-identical, white, red-headed women waiting their turn. She slowly walks alone through pairs of dancing couples toward the end of "Someone in the Crowd," having lost her roommates in the fray. After her car is towed, she walks alone at night through empty Los Angeles streets toward the club where Sebastian is playing, limping a bit from a night of wearing heels and slowing to a stop when his music reaches her. She quickly walks away from another failed audition in frustration, the usually steady camera shaking with a handheld feel. After emailing invitations to her one-woman show, she walks home alone at night again, this time to her and Sebastian's apartment where she slows down as she hears jazz music wafting out of the room inside. And she twirls with a smile on her face as she walks to work after the "A Lovely Night" number and after she leaves the stage she has rented for her play. At times she is unchanging in her speed[45] and at others she rushes,[46] either to hurry to an audition, as she does leaving the coffee shop where she works, or to storm away from one after it goes badly. The film shows that Mia is constantly on the move, doing what seems expected of her to propel her acting career, but it gets her nowhere. Instead, it is by changing her rhythm—slowing down and pausing—that she succeeds. Her final (successful) audition with Amy Brandt (Valarie Rae Miller) starts like the others, as she walks into the room to greet the casting directors, but her movement turns to stillness once she reaches the center of the room. She sings her audition in place, rooted to the spot with her memories as the set around her fades to black and the camera slowly circles her. Looking back allows her to move forward.

La La Land's filmmakers embraced the inherent performance imperfections of their nonprofessional dancers. A more diegetically ambiguous, realist aesthetic that uses the singing and dancing talents of amateur singers and dancers (who are professional actors) is one evolution of the genre's norms and a deliberate stylistic choice for filmmakers interested in more realism-driven renderings of the genre, as Demy's, Ducastel's and Martineau's musicals demonstrate. In *La La Land*, Moore, Chazelle, and Sandren use subtle choreographic work to play with the relationships between camera and performer movement and to establish the narrative's tensions between realism and fantasy.

Diegetic Slippage and Ambiguous Realism

La La Land's musical numbers have a one-minute average shot length. There is a perceived tether between cinematographic duration and cinematic "truth" or realism, one that frays when we examine the musical's proclivity for undermining diegetic realities as sequences shift into and out of musical numbers. Daniel Morgan analyzes the often implicitly assumed affinities between objective realism and long-take, mobile cinematography. Especially in the wake of André Bazin's legacy on theories of cinematic realism, this kind of "unbroken duration" often stands "as a guarantor of truth: a preservation of the image's fidelity to the world," a viewpoint Morgan argues is misleading in its simplification of the formal potentials of long-take cinematography.[47] The relationship between shooting continuously and spatiotemporal unity

200 STORYTELLING IN MOTION

is a frequent consideration in cinematographic craft since, Serena Ferrara argues, "the physical perception of time is given by the space that is actually crossed by the camera. In other words, the time of the action is made real by the space that we cross through completely."[48] Despite this perception of continuity, musical sequences allow diegetic fluctuations to occur within the seeming spatiotemporal stability of a continuous action in addition to shifting that action completely away from plausible diegetic settings. The musical sequences known as dream ballets particularly illustrate this point. Accordingly, musical moments emphasize how the image's sense of fidelity can be ruptured within a single shot, through the genre's conventional practice of deviating from diegetic norms in complex, myriad ways.

Diegetic Instability

One of the strongest draws of the musical genre for director Damien Chazelle is the expectation of diegetic deviations: "It breaks the whole idea of the bond of reality in a movie . . . I love the idea of how radical musicals can be while being so mainstream."[49] In *La La Land*, Chazelle was particularly invested in the idea of the diegesis "slipping" in and out of musical numbers rather than shifting abruptly into a new diegetic situation. Jacques Demy and earlier studio-era musical directors were a central influence on this approach, in "that idea of a through-line, an environment where song and conversation coexist and slip in and out, and the idea of things slipping as opposed to right-turning. It was at the core of what I wanted to play with in [*La La Land*]."[50] The film achieves this with gradual transitions into the musical sequences by having heightened movements flutter in and out rather than steadily shifting away from the diegesis,[51] often through long-take cinematic choreography. The latter in particular draws attention to duration and the film's portrayal of time and professional stagnation, at times in ways that add narrative ambiguity to the action portrayed by the moving camera.

For Chazelle, the moments of diegetic slippage were a chance to play with the formal subversion of reality through shifts toward escapism: "With *La La Land*, I wanted to get at reality in an indirect way. It's an emotional portrait of L.A., not a realistic one. . . . I wanted to push back against the strict reliance on realism."[52] The musical numbers often disrupt this sense of aesthetic realism and diegetic unity within extended sequence shots that begin well before the number does. Except for the "Planetarium" and "Epilogue" numbers, which shift the whole diegesis into implausible spaces, the settings in *La La Land* remain more grounded; diegetic plurality emerges more often from the performers' song and dance. Cinematographer Linus Sandgren molds the light of golden hour in Los Angeles to bathe the characters with vibrant blues, oranges, pinks, and purples in musical numbers like "A Lovely Night" and "City of Stars," adding to the feeling of an unreal environment, but these light characteristics do not shift throughout the numbers.

Both "Another Day of Sun" and Mia and Sebastian's duet, "A Lovely Night," use extended sequence shots to establish the performers in space before shifting into musical content. "Another Day of Sun" begins with a crane down from the bright sky to dolly laterally along rows of cars stuck in traffic, and the soundscape shifts as we hear the sounds from each blending together. Twenty seconds into the shot we get our first diegetic flutter, as we hear Desirée Garcia's voice emanating from a car radio, singing a song originating from Damien Chazelle's first feature, *Guy and Madeleine on a Park Bench* (2011). The moment fades as the camera continues to travel past the car and new song segments blend into the soundtrack. Thirty seconds into the shot we hear *La La Land* composer Justin Hurwitz's music for "Another Day of Sun" begin and the camera glides over the traffic median and toward the first woman who begins to sing and dance (Reshma Gajjar), soon joined by the rest of the commuters on the freeway.

"Another Day of Sun" is filmed in three shots, stitched together to appear as a single take; all of "A Lovely Night" occurs in a single sequence shot. The latter number's shot begins with Mia and Sebastian walking up the hill searching for her car, over a minute before the first notes of the melody begin and Sebastian spins himself around the lamp post, evoking Gene Kelly's iconic pose in the titular number from *Singin' in the Rain*. The dancing does not take off, however, and the first few minutes of the sequence emphasize the pair's reluctance to be drawn into the number, Mia especially. Each speaks responses to the other's initial sung verses, and their movements shift into staged choreography before continuing into dancing, as Sebastian childishly kicks dirt at Mia on the bench and she, in response, crosses her legs away from him and tosses her head with irritation in rhythm to the music. Even in these moments, however, Moore and Chazelle incorporate moments that pull at the changing diegesis in subtle ways, as Mia changes out of her stiletto sandals and puts on more sensible Oxfords (that match Sebastian's) before the two shift into the dancing sequence. Choreographer Mandy Moore and Damien Chazelle reference the Fred Astaire and Ginger

202 STORYTELLING IN MOTION

Rogers number "Isn't This a Lovely Day" from *Top Hat* (Mark Sandrich, 1935) as an important influence on the number. Moore calls the Astaire-Rogers duet "beautifully tempo-ed" in the way it moves from pedestrian to danced movements without drawing attention to the switch, while also incorporating the act of flirtation into the choreography.[53] Functionally, however, "A Lovely Night" also echoes the narrative purpose of Astaire's duet with Cyd Charisse in *The Band Wagon*, "Dancing in the Dark," as it is by finding common ground through dance and synchronizing their movements, after an initial period of hesitation and hostility, that the first sparks of romance are ignited.

In production, Chazelle was making deliberate stylistic choices that he felt helped to smooth the shifts between the film's diegetic reality and musical fantasy. One of these choices involved recording sound on set when possible instead of syncing to playback, less for the need of a "liveness" or realism in capturing the performers singing and more about the subtle sonic textures that resulted from recording sound on set. Chazelle's aesthetic preference was for a "closer" sonic feel between the sound texture of the singing and speaking voices: "We wanted to make the feel [of songs and nonsongs] as close to each other as possible, and so that's where doing some stuff that we could do live came from, tiny things like how we would mic the singers with much further mics, and more room mics than you would tend to do these days instead of close mics, not putting reverb on. All the sort of things you tend to do to songs today, to make them sound more polished or better or cleaner, we would not do."[54] In "A Lovely Night," the sounds of the body in space do not disappear from the soundtrack. Instead, we hear Mia clicking her car keys, Sebastian kicking dirt on her, her slapping him on the arm in return, and the tapping and sliding of their shoes on the road as they dance. Rarely do these sounds disappear completely in *La La Land*'s sound mix.

Returning to the Dream Ballet

La La Land's final musical number, the "Epilogue," is a subjective musical sequence that shifts fully away from the grounded diegesis and is one of the few instances of a Hollywood dream ballet since they fell out of favor in the 1950s.[55] It was a common enough convention, at the studios that could afford it, for Hollywood musicals during the late studio era to include what are commonly referred to as dream ballets or sequences as a major set piece.

Choreographer Agnes de Mille frequently gets credit for originating the dream ballet convention of dance-based thematic reflection for her "Laurie Makes Up Her Mind" sequence in the stage musical *Oklahoma!* (1943), but there are numerous instances of film musicals experimenting with this form of number prior to the play's debut. Filmmakers were exploring the heightened diegetic potentials of this form concurrently, as we can see in Katherine Dunham's titular choreographic sequence for *Stormy Weather* (Andrew L. Stone, 1943) or Busby Berkeley's "Web of Dreams" number in *Fashions of 1934* (William Dieterle, 1934).[56] These numbers frequently eschew singing in favor of more complex dance sequences (often ballet) and elaborate set pieces. They usually showcase expansive sets and employ some level of abstraction in their set design. And they often are motivated as a subjective experience of a character in the narrative (whether through an actual dream or not) and are frequently self-contained, with internal narratives, conflict, and resolution.

The "Epilogue" is *La La Land*'s ultimate blend of realist and fantasy aesthetics. Chazelle wanted the film to include a dream ballet because of its powerful evocation of classical Hollywood musical conventions. The inclusion of a dream ballet in *La La Land* is an obvious reference to the classical Hollywood norm of lavish, dance-driven set pieces and specific MGM musical numbers. Chazelle considers Gene Kelly's dream ballet at the end of *An American in Paris* (1951) as one of the most avant-garde moments from later classical Hollywood musicals, in part because of its extreme approach to duration.[57] The "Epilogue" also echoes Gene Kelly and Stanley Donen's dream ballet sequence in *Singin' in the Rain*, with its multiple diegetic shifts into increasingly abstract environments.

Beyond its clear evocation of Hollywood's most extravagant musical convention, the sequence carries significant narrative weight as well. Unlike the focus of *An American in Paris*'s dream ballet, and many others choreographed by Gene Kelly, *La La Land*'s final fantastical number does not just recap the events of the narrative in choreographic, balletic form. Nor does it primarily serve to feature virtuosic dancing. Instead, the number offers a view of an alternate future in which Mia and Sebastian stay together while achieving professional success. The sequence offers a neatly resolved Hollywood ending only to snatch it away by returning us to the original diegesis for the final few moments of the film. Like Demy's original ending to *Trois places pour le 26* (1988), in which characters from the diegesis were to join the stage actors in a final meeting revealed to take place on theatrical, rather than diegetic, train

204 STORYTELLING IN MOTION

steps, Chazelle's dream ballet deliberately obfuscates the film's intrinsic diegetic norms.

Ambiguous Realities

La La Land's "Epilogue" sequence follows the rarely broken genre rule of lyrical silence in dream ballets; no words are sung or spoken. All diegetic sounds of the body, frequently heard elsewhere in the film—like the rustling of clothing, mouth sounds, or the shuffling of feet on the ground—similarly fade from the sound mix once Mia and Sebastian leave the restaurant space. Yet as we move deeper into the sequence, and farther from the grounding tethers of the diegesis, the stylistic cues provide contradictory information to cast doubt over whether this sequence of events is the true one.

The transition into the heightened musical sequence connects Sebastian's performance of "Mia and Sebastian's Theme (Late for a Date)" for a crowd that includes Mia and her husband (Tom Everett Scott) to the moment he plays the same theme earlier in the film in defiance of his boss (J. K. Simmons) who insists that he "play the set list" only. Instead of brushing past Mia in anger, as he did before, he interrupts her compliment with a passionate embrace. Even in these first few moments, the film's precedent for temporal repetition calls into question the diegetic status of their meeting. *La La Land*'s first act repeats Mia's entrance into the restaurant as she hears Sebastian play, the first time at the end of a sequence following her after the couple's meet cute on the freeway, the second time after the sequence following Sebastian after he drives away from her. Seeing Mia enter the restaurant in her same blue dress as she approaches Sebastian briefly hints that perhaps, once again, we are back where we started. Some shots, the ones of Mia approaching Sebastian in particular, appear to be shot duplications instead of new set-ups (figures 9.1 and 9.2). This expectation quickly dissipates, however, as the spectators around them, including Sebastian's boss, begin to dance in their spots, encouraging the couple as Sebastian spins Mia before they run out of the building and into a utopic[58] montage of their early relationship.

After Mia's play is a roaring success, they run out of the theater and into an abstract, white set-piece that evokes the lavish MGM sound stages used in Gene Kelly's dream ballet sequences from the 1950s and that we also see a hint of earlier in the film (figures 9.3 and 9.4). Whereas Chazelle stages the musical numbers in *La La Land* with sincerity rather than an ironic or reflexive distance, here the film breaks with that precedent. Mia and Sebastian

RHYTHMIC REALISM 205

Figure 9.1 Mia approaches Sebastian to compliment his playing in the beginning of *La La Land*.
Source: Summit Entertainment.

Figure 9.2 Mia approaches Sebastian again as the "Epilogue" dream ballet begins.
Source: Summit Entertainment.

Figure 9.3 Mia and Sebastian admire a sound stage while walking through the backlot in *La La Land*.
Source: Summit Entertainment.

Figure 9.4 As part of their dream ballet, Mia and Sebastian dance through the mise-en-scène they had admired earlier in *La La Land*.
Source: Summit Entertainment.

pause and look around in confusion at their new surroundings, further splintering the diegesis. As they continue to move into the increasingly colorful space—which blends abstracted sets evoking California, Hollywood musicals, the freeway from the opening musical number, and the gas station from *Les Parapluies de Cherbourg*—they are swept back into the fantasy. In a single, lateral-moving crane shot, they wind and slide through the set and a corps of dancers before Mia is pulled out of Sebastian's grasp by the casting director, Amy, whom she auditions for earlier in the film. Amy walks into the busy frame toward Mia and freezes the dancers in place with her presence, shifting the couple into the next portion of the sequence.

Mia and Sebastian's professional success is now more diegetically grounded by the narrative plausibility of the characters' actions. Mia nails her audition, she and Sebastian move to Paris, Mia pursues a career in acting while Sebastian finds success as a jazz musician, and their romance continues. Sebastian following Mia to Paris is a logical choice for their relationship as well as for his career, especially for audiences familiar with extradiegetic French culture, as the form of jazz that he seeks to champion continues to thrive there. This portion of the dream ballet also lingers on trumpeter Wayne Bergerson's solo, pulling focus away from the fantasy toward the musician and his music while evoking the jazz shorts Chazelle discusses as an influence. Stylistically, however, the segment is still heightened through set design and choreography. Mia's audition occurs in silhouette, while the remaining sets evoke a painted aesthetic that echoes *An American in Paris* and Impressionist painting. Mia, Sebastian, and the performers dance or move rhythmically to the music. After walking along an artificial Seine, through pedestrians frozen in place, Mia and Sebastian waltz into a twinkling blue space that evokes their earlier starry planetarium dance in which they fly into the stars. The camera once again laterally tracks their progression before craning up as they twirl, swooping past them as the scene changes once more.

The dream ballet transitions to the penultimate segment as Mia and Sebastian sit on the floor of a dark space while a screen plays a projected image in front of them, revealing flickering home movie images. The camera pushes past them and into the lower gauge filmstock footage, showing them presumably having moved back to Los Angeles to start a family. One shot of Sebastian and Mia walking through a field of flowers evokes the idyllic and psychedelic dream ballet from Jacques Demy's *Peau d'âne* (1970). The desaturated shots are grainy, jumpy, and shaking, however, evoking the realist aesthetic frequently associated with handheld, amateur, or documentary filmmaking.[59] Similarly, the staging and movement of the characters are not heightened or rhythmically linked to the music. They smile and wave for the camera, engaging with their baby and one another and casually touching their faces, seemingly self-conscious of the camera's presence.

A cross-fade shifts the scene to the same child reading books with a babysitter as Sebastian and Mia leave for an evening out, paralleling Mia and her husband's departure earlier in the film that led them to Sebastian's club. Sebastian's and Mia's house is more modest, but they similarly exit through a door in the midground right, saying goodbye to their child and the sitter on the couch in the foreground (figures 9.5 and 9.6). The rest of their

Figure 9.5 Mia kisses her daughter goodnight as she and her husband head out for the evening in *La La Land*.
Source: Summit Entertainment.

Figure 9.6 Mia and Sebastian say goodbye to their son and sitter as they head out for the evening in *La La Land*.
Source: Summit Entertainment.

evening parallels the earlier sequence, minus the conversation, until Mia and Sebastian end up in the same jazz club, sitting in the audience listening to a pianist on stage. The cinematography, staging, and performance, which mirrors the style of the scene preceding the fantasy sequence, adds doubt to whether this version of Mia and Sebastian's life actually occurred, until we cut to a close-up of the piano as the final note is played and the camera tilts up, away from the pianist's hand, to reveal Sebastian's face. *La La Land*'s final shots unambiguously reestablish how Mia and Sebastian's choices have pulled them in different directions.

The "Epilogue" sequence suspends the viewer in doubt until the final minutes through its seven-minute duration and slow shift away from the peak of fantastical diegetic plurality to more realism-based stylistic cues. Whereas the sequence's blending of realist and fantastical stylistic choices creates a narrative ambiguity that challenges the authenticity of the main plotline, the transition out of the musical number is definitive. The camera circles in the sequence's final shot, panning across the audience in the club to the stage where a pianist (not Sebastian) is playing and back toward the audience where Mia and Sebastian are sitting. Chazelle could have staged the transition out of the number as an ongoing shot as he does in earlier musical numbers, where the camera continues its arc to reveal the stage once more, with Sebastian now at the instrument. Instead, a cut demarcates diegesis from musical number. Throughout *La La Land* the camera moves fluidly to connect spaces and lines of action, but here the diegetic separation is unequivocal. The fantasy is over.

The Dancing Camera

Camera movement, like figure movement, is both functional and expressive. *La La Land* is as much about the movement of characters through space and their environment—Los Angeles—as it is about those characters themselves. The use of Steadicam stabilizer technology and fluid camera movement throughout the film and musical numbers ties into the film's stylization of the environment. Director Damien Chazelle and cinematographer Linus Sandgren describe the camera as a "unifying" element between narrative and number "which needed a consistent personality."[60] *La La Land*'s filmmakers frame and stage their subjects to reveal more than their simple presence.

What does it mean, expressively and materially, to consider the camera as a character in the space? The introduction to this chapter playfully personifies the camera, as Chazelle and Sandgren do in their discussion of *La La Land*'s cinematographic aesthetic. However, while stylistically the resulting relationship is between a human performer and the mechanical camera, the artistry of the latter is also the result of human motion. In *La La Land*, much of the craft and labor of the fluid camera comes from Steadicam and A camera operator Ari Robbins, guided by cinematographer Linus Sandgren, director Damien Chazelle, and choreographer Mandy Moore's choices for the cinematic choreography.

The Camera as Dancer

La La Land's filmmakers frequently discuss the camera as if it were a dancer or a character in the space, assigning it a person-like agency. Chazelle describes the "A Lovely Night" number as a trio: "I think the third dancer in this number that you don't see onscreen is the camera."[61] Mandy Moore recollects that "Damien [Chazelle] from the beginning really wanted the camera to be choreographed as well,"[62] whereas Chazelle describes the camera aesthetic for the film as "constantly moving," "dancing," having "its own internal metronome," and "always lilting and weaving."[63] Serena Ferrara, in analyzing the camera's role in establishing cinematic space, argues that "space, presented as a character with qualities and functions, is thus considered one of the agents of the action."[64] More broadly, stabilizer technologies like Steadicam used in *La La Land* evoke associations of a cinematography that is "smooth, highly mobile, dynamic, curious, and constantly capturing nonstop action."[65] The

210 STORYTELLING IN MOTION

fluidity of such movement possibilities comes through in Katie Bird's description of Garrett Brown's early Steadicam work, where she describes the shot from *Bound for Glory* (Hal Ashby, 1976) as floating and weaving through the space.[66]

What would it mean, from a movement analysis perspective, to consider the camera as an active agent, whose movements are narratively meaningful?[67] We cannot assign full human-like control or range of motion to a machine,[68] but it is interesting to explore what agency the camera does have and what role it plays in the action. Theories of cinema frequently imply an anthropomorphized or subjective camera that determines the film spectator's point of view, an idea that Daniel Morgan pushes back against. He articulates that particularly in film phenomenology and the writings of Vivian Sobchack and Jennifer Barker, "the connection between spectator and camera—the idea that the camera functions as our surrogate—is inextricably tied to a belief in the camera's fundamental anthropomorphism."[69] As Morgan argues, this connection is not predetermined, and our spectatorial perception of moving through the diegesis is an illusion: "This dual perception, of at once moving and not moving, is key to what makes cinema an *aesthetic* experience, an illusion capable of visceral and kinetic pleasures that in everyday life would produce a vastly different response."[70] Patrick Keating's descriptions of mobile cinematography also point to the ways that we can assign person-like significance to the movement in question and the ways in which the mobile camera's "meanings are ever shifting."[71] At times he describes the referential functionality of the camera movement (it cranes, dollies, pans, tilts), while elsewhere he assigns it a semantic expressiveness, as the filmmakers he studies describe their own craft: the camera spins "dizzily," becomes " 'restless,' " and moves " 'irresponsibly' " by "imitating [characters'] affective gestures."[72] He calls this form of camera movement "participatory," arguing that these stylistic choices deliberately contribute to our understanding of character emotion.[73]

There are parallels, therefore, between the expressive contributions of the camera that Keating and Morgan describe and the analysis of human movement's expressive essences that drives the work in Laban Movement Analysis. There are inherent limitations to studying camera movement from the perspective of the LMA movement taxonomy, given that the system is designed for human movement, built on observations of primarily white European bodies. Yet applying its vocabulary to the mechanics of the camera reveals the strengths and limitations of cinematographic movement and the ways such mobility in *La La Land* parallels and complements the figures it frames.

Like human movement, the camera's progression through space can be both functional and expressive. Laban Movement Analysis's target vocabulary to functionally describe Space, where the body moves, and a description of the Kinesphere, the body's stance or personal space, parallel existing descriptors for camera movement. They share distinctions between axis-based movements—tilting and panning—and movement through space along the three dimensions—dollying horizontally or sagittally and craning vertically. The resulting movement expression, however, is inherently focused outward, as any movement is perceived based on the frame's relationship to the environment. A camera moving without a subject to capture (say, with the lens cap on) would manifest as total darkness and lack spatial context. As a result, questions of Shape, or how the body is moving in relation to its environment, are more focused on that external relationship rather than an internally focused attention to self.[74]

Considering the vocabulary of Body from LBMS or the movement patterns from Bartenieff Fundamentals are meaningless in this context, as there are no body parts to move: no joints to rotate, no limbs to grow or shrink, no muscles to flex and extend. Handheld cinematography is often aligned with perceptual realism because of the shakiness of the footage and the perceived link between that instability and the multidimensional motion of human walking patterns.[75] The boom and Steadicam cinematography in *La La Land* deliberately eliminates this affective instability, however. The closest correlations to the fundamental changes of body shape would be the ways that the frame's aspect ratio suggests a fixed resting shape,[76] one which in a cinematic context is generally fixed for the duration of the film. *La La Land* playfully exploits this assumption, however, opening on the Summit production logo in the Academy ratio before extending the frame horizontally to the CinemaScope aspect ratio while drawing attention to the changing shape of the frame.[77] Chazelle and Sandgren worked closely with Kodak on the choice of anamorphic film stock to give the film the subtle optical distortion (as well as the narrower aspect ratio) that Chazelle wanted in order to evoke the aesthetic of early Cinemascope features. The pair were equally deliberate in their choice of predominantly 30 mm (wide-angle) lenses to achieve a specific depth and field of view.[78]

Studying Effort's movement qualities, or how the body moves, offers the most fruitful language for cinematographic expressiveness. Because the

212 STORYTELLING IN MOTION

camera in this context is single-focused (I delegate the agency of multifocus staging to the mise-en-scène), the camera is frequently locked in Direct Space Effort. There is no body to exert increasing or decreasing pressure, so the camera's expression also minimizes perceivable changes in Light and Strong Weight Effort, particularly in *La La Land*'s use of stabilizer technology.[79] The most noticeable changes in the camera's expressive range of motion[80] are in changes of speed through acceleration with Sudden Time Effort or deceleration with Sustained Time Effort and in the controlled resistance of movement with Bound Flow Effort or a fluid progression through space with Free Flow Effort. LMA associates Time Effort with decision-making and Flow Effort with progression. When manifesting simultaneously, these effort factors result in Mobile State, associated with moving through the world.[81] As a result, a Labanian analysis of the camera's inherent expressiveness in *La La Land* would suggest its psychological agency relates to decisive mobility: deciding when the time is right to move on, whom to follow, and knowing when it is best to stay put.

Mobility, Stability, and Aesthetics of Camera Movement

La La Land's musical numbers are filmed with crane and Steadicam shots, the former used when shots needed to move vertically for expressive effect ("A Lovely Night") or functionally to avoid physical obstacles ("Another Day of Sun," which used both camera technologies).[82] Chazelle moves his hands in curving motions to describe the ongoing feel of movement he wanted the camera to have, as if "the camera is this balloon that could float up and down when it wants, it can weave this way and that way, and push in and pull out, and very rarely is completely stuck in one place, and going at right angles. . . . *La La Land* I wanted to always be curved."[83]

The film's emphasis on extensive sequence shots with complex choreography between dancers and camera movement hearkens back to the work of musical filmmakers like Vincente Minnelli, Stanley Donen, and Jacques Demy. We can see such attention to subtle reframings, fluid follow shots, and complex staging as John Truett helps Esther Smith turn out the lights throughout the house after a party in *Meet Me in St. Louis* (1944), as the six younger Pontipee brothers listlessly complete chores in the "Lonesome Polecat" number from *Seven Brides for Seven Brothers* (1954), and as Delphine interacts with pedestrians on the street while dancing on her way

RHYTHMIC REALISM   213

to end a relationship in "De Delphine à Lancien" from *Les Demoiselles de Rochefort* (1967). None of these films were shot with stabilizer technology like Steadicam rigs, first used in the 1970s. While *La La Land* evokes these earlier musicals' aesthetics, the filmmakers also innovate the form, in enclosed sets in particular, through the use of Steadicam cinematography.

Comparing the sequence shot aesthetic in the "Lonesome Polecat" number from *Seven Brides for Seven Brothers*, whose visual aesthetic was one of Chazelle's inspirations, to the camera movement in one of the sequence shots from "Someone in the Crowd" demonstrates how camera mobility and stability anchors these numbers in different ways. The "Lonesome Polecat" number focuses on the six younger Pontipee brothers' romantic melancholy. Michael Kidd's choreography and George Folsey's cinematography for the number, shot in a single three-and-a-half-minute take, moves them in an embellished fashion through their outdoor chores as they think about the women they met in town.

The number begins with a static, establishing wide shot that reveals all six brothers at work. Gideon (Russ Tamblyn) and Frank (Tommy Rall) saw away at a log in the left midground. Benjamin (Jeff Richards) sharpens an axe in the center midground as Dan (Marc Platt) and Ephraim (Jacques d'Amboise) walk to the right carrying a log in the background. Caleb (Matt Mattox) chops wood in the right midground, framed by Dan and Ephraim. Stanley Donen and Michael Kidd's cinematic choreography in this number uses camera movement to reframe the characters nine times, with distinct pauses in between each mobile camera shift. The movements of the camera emphasize Caleb's centrality in the number by often staging the other brothers in the background on either side of him in the frame and panning and dollying to the left in one moment to feature him individually while his brothers continue to sing off-screen. The camera pauses as Caleb spins and swings his axe for a brief solo, playing with the weight and momentum of the axe. While the number moves through the space with the characters, its range of motion is predominantly lateral. The use of a sound stage and painted backdrop rather than the on-location shooting Donen had hoped for likely influenced Kidd's choreography to emphasize more frontal facings, while the separation of characters in the frame emphasizes their isolation and melancholy. The number includes one minute and 45 seconds of stillness, which covers about half of the number's total duration (figure 9.7).

By contrast, the camera only flirts with stillness in the first half of the "Someone in the Crowd" musical number, filmed by Ari Robbins with a

Figure 9.7 A visualization in Adobe Premiere Pro of the extended moments of camera stillness in "Lonesome Polecat" from *Seven Brides for Seven Brothers*. The expanded markers in the middle of the image indicate when the camera is not moving.
Source: Metro-Goldwyn-Mayer.

Steadicam rig. Taking place in Mia's apartment, the sequence begins with Mia in her bathroom as she leaves the shower and hums to herself in the mirror. She is preparing for a quiet night at home before her three roommates convince her to join them on a wild night out that conjures the atmospheres of *Singin' in the Rain*'s "Broadway Melody" rise-to-fame montage and Bob Fosse's choreography for the "Rich Man's Frug" from *Sweet Charity* (1969). The opening Steadicam shot whip pans between Mia and her roommates as they interrupt her singing and move one by one into the bathroom—Tracy (Callie Hernandez) in a red dress, Alexis (Jessica Rothe) in a green dress, and Caitlin (Sonoya Mizuno) in a yellow dress—before Mia returns to her bedroom to change for a night in. Three brief shot-reverse-shot set-ups follow as Tracy confronts Mia at the bedroom doorway about her evening plans before barging into the room. The subsequent Steadicam shot follows Mia and her roommates through the whole apartment as they attempt to sway Mia with their musical exuberance. Ari Robbins's camerawork follows the four women through a complex series of reframings as Mandy Moore's, Linus Sandgren's, and Damien Chazelle's staging has them dance, run, pose, and wind their way through the apartment. In line with an exploration of the camera as having

RHYTHMIC REALISM   215

character-like agency, the following descriptions playfully use Ari Robbins's first name, rather than "the camera," to describe the cinematography of this sequence.

This 90-second sequence shot begins with a few moments of stillness as the characters talk and sit on Mia's bed. Once the sequence shifts into a full musical number, Ari rarely stops moving. This pattern is particularly noticeable after the four women pose with a tissue box awards "statuette" and separate from one another to spread through the apartment. Ari chooses to stick with Alexis as she runs toward the kitchen in the background of the shot. Ari dollies to follow her, outpacing her speed to center her in a medium close-up in the doorway as she poses with her arm against the doorframe and faces to the right, the other three roommates now off screen. Alexis continues moving through rooms deeper into the background, walking sideways to stay in profile to Ari, who follows and matches her pace. Ari slightly reframes right and left, without changing speed, following Alexis while weaving through the off-set doorways to each room. She picks up a fan from an off-screen table and whips it open, holding it up in profile as she backs out of frame to the left, revealing Tracy pulling Mia into the dining room in the background-right through the front of the room's two doorway arches. As Tracy pulls her, Mia is posing with her hand to her head as Caitlin did earlier in the sequence. Ari's forward momentum smoothly shifts to follow Mia and Tracy as Alexis exits the frame. Tracy leans against the wall between the arches and hangs the dress hanger on Mia's neck as Ari approaches them, moving from a long shot to a medium close-up right as Tracy completes the action and Mia sticks her tongue out in response. Tracy pats Mia on the shoulder as Mia walks away from her, into the background and out of the room through the farmost doorway arch. Without changing pace, Ari dollies rightward to follow her, moving into the hallway through the front-most doorway arch. As Ari moves, the wall that Tracy leans against and that separates Ari from Mia briefly obscures the frame before revealing Mia in the hallway in a medium shot as Ari dollies backward to match Mia's forward walking pace. After a few of Mia's paces, the front-most archway is visible in frame and Tracy passes through it to walk alongside Mia. They and Ari continue for a few more paces before Alexis enters from frame left and poses in the hallway in front of them with her arms outstretched to touch the hallway walls. Undeterred, Ari, Mia, and Tracy continue their locomotion, the latter two ducking beneath Alexis's arms. Caitlin then appears from the bathroom doorway to the right, using a hairdryer to blow glitter at Mia. Both Mia and Tracy pause slightly in

216   STORYTELLING IN MOTION

response, as Mia briefly but fully gives in to the playful glitz of the number's diegetic plurality.

As the shot comes to a close, the three roommates prepare to leave without Mia. Ari pauses briefly on Caitlin in the foreground, who turns to look over her shoulder and sings directly to Ari (encouraging Ari to join them?) before twirling toward the door as Mia's three friends leave without her. Rather than following them, Ari continues to move leftward, panning and tilting down to bring into frame a mirror. It reveals Mia, who is still looking out of her bedroom French doors, right as we see the last roommate move out of frame and hear the door close off-screen behind the mirror. Ari lingers on Mia's reflection in the final moments of the shot, slowing pace and dollying forward toward the mirror. The scene then cuts to a high-angle shot of Mia as she lies down on her bed and changes her mind about staying in, joining her roommates outside as the number continues.

Enormously complex choreography connects the movements of the four performers and the mobile framing created by Robbins's Steadicam cinematography for this single shot. Enormous, but not immeasurable; Robbins moves through over twenty distinct reframings and speed adjustments to capture the four roommates' movements into, out of, and across the cinematic space. The camera pauses only eight times, rarely for more than a second. Mia and her roommates playfully repeat one another's shapes throughout the number as they strike poses and lean against walls in moments of "red-carpet-play-acting,"[84] feign outrage and excitement, carry around Mia's borrowed blue dress, and follow and pull each other as they race through rooms. Rather than attempt to follow all four performers at once, Robbins's camerawork flows between the women as they move separately through the apartment. Robbins's dancing camera expressively functions as a fifth roommate, who like Mia is indecisive about staying in or going out. More timid and shy than the others, perhaps, they follow the excursion through the apartment before excitedly swooping into the hallway ahead of Mia and Tracy as the women follow them down the hall in the final moments of the number, eventually sweeping Robbins-and-camera and Mia into the musical fun.

Unlike in *Seven Brides for Seven Brothers*, ongoing movement in *La La Land*'s sequence shots is more dominant than held framings. Whereas the camera is in full stillness for roughly half of the "Lonesome Polecat" number, complete stillness in the 90-second sequence shot from "Someone in the Crowd" occurs for only 18 seconds, less than 15 percent of the total shot's duration (figure 9.8). *La La Land*'s Steadicam cinematography in "Someone

Figure 9.8 A visualization in Adobe Premiere Pro of the limited moments of camera stillness in "Someone in the Crowd" from *La La Land*. The expanded markers in the middle of the image indicate when the camera is not moving.
Source: Summit Entertainment.

in the Crowd" emphasizes movement and an ongoing flow, interrupted by moments of stillness, whereas the crane shot from *Seven Brides for Seven Brothers* in "Lonesome Polecat" leans more toward a stationary foundation with moments of reframing. *La La Land*'s Steadicam shots are not inherently more fluid than its other cinematographic methods; the single crane shot in "A Lovely Night" is similarly moving throughout most of the sequence. Yet the tight spaces of the apartment in "Someone in the Crowd" and the camera's quick reactions to the women's movement emphasize the Steadicam's stylistic potentials through Robbins's execution.

The Dancer as Camera

Of course, in a practical sense, the camera is not moving purely mechanically. It is the physicality and artistry of the camera operator, in Steadicam shots especially, that determines the final rhythm and flow of the shot.

218 STORYTELLING IN MOTION

Steadicam operation is physically intense, requiring extensive training with the rig akin to learning a dance technique in which "the operator's own body must not only literally fall away from the Steadicam but also have both the strength to guide and the flexibility to be moved by the Steadicam."[85] Katie Bird's videographic examination of archival and test footage demonstrates how the Steadicam operator must employ significant core stability and a rigidity in the torso and controlling arm to guide the camera on the rig.[86] The labor involved in operating such stabilizer technologies is significant, and the artistry required to execute the kinds of precise correspondences with on-screen figure movement that occurs in *La La Land* requires training that aligns closely with the kind of technique seen in dance.

For *La La Land*'s camera operator, Ari Robbins, Steadicam operation is profoundly intimate. Robbins tells Tiffen, the company that makes the Steadicam rig he uses:

> It is just this intimate connection with something, which may sound strange as it just a bunch of steel, metal and electronics, however it really is a very deep connection. When most people put on a rig for the first time they will more than likely feel the physical burdens of the machinery on their body. They will feel the weight as it pushes and pulls on against them, making their first experience quite uncomfortable. However, the very first time I put the rig on with [Steadicam Operator Nick Franco] I didn't feel that burden, it didn't feel strange to me. It is difficult to describe, but my initial reaction was one of complete amazement and comfort, it felt natural having the rig on. Although it seems strange to say about an object, it was love at first sight.[87]

Robbins describes his connection with his Steadicam rig as very personal, a part not only of his body but of his life.

Discussions of Steadicam operation emphasize this sense of intimacy and also individualism. Just as casting different actors in a film will impact the final performance, a different Steadicam operator will provide a different cinematographic performance. Bodily uniqueness, like that of a dancer's, comes through in a Steadicam take. "This intuitive recognition is built on a knowledge of personal quirks (ways of moving in space), as well as the weight and placement of load by the operator's body," Katie Bird explains. "In other words, no Steadicam shot performed by different operators would look alike even if filmed under the exact same shooting conditions, flight path, and start and stop marks."[88]

Steadicam operators will at times refer to their rigs as dance partners,[89] emphasizing the close physical relationship involved. Really, though, this partnership is a trio: between the camera rig, the operator, and what (or whom) they are filming. The relationship Bird describes between the Steadicam operator and the rig is akin to that of ballroom dancing partners, in which the movement is defined and executed through the mastery of a relatively rigid physical connection (the frame). Like ballroom dance training, Steadicam trainings and manuals have identified patterns with dance names like "walking the line"[90] and include step diagrams. By contrast, the relationship between the camera/operator and their filmed subjects is closer to the partnering seen in Contact Improvisation, in which the weight sensing relationship changes as dancers pour weight into and pull away from their partners, maintaining a physical connection that is in constant flux.[91] While this relationship exists in any camera operation, the sort of moment-by-moment, layered shifts we see in Contact Improv are most palpable in Steadicam shots where, as Bird articulates, "the daily labor of a stabilizer operator involves a kind of skillfully trained dance improvisation."[92]

In discussing his choice of emphasizing Steadicam shots in *La La Land*, Damien Chazelle echoes the parallels between dancing and operating stabilizer technology, saying that "it felt like the closest you can get a camera to a dancer would be with a great Steadicam operator."[93] Considering the labor and physical exertion of the technician emphasizes inherent contradictions of movement quality involved in creating Steadicam takes. The impulse toward continuous motion and a disinclination toward stillness in the movement of Steadicam shots evokes an aesthetic of ongoing progression,[94] which contrasts with the necessary restraint and control[95] the camera operator must embody to work with the equipment. Like a talented dancer, a skilled Steadicam operator makes the work look effortless.

Conclusions

In music and in life, timing is essential. *La La Land* uses rhythmic patterns of realism through a cinematic choreography of duration, exploring this idea stylistically—through the interplay of human and camera movement in sequence shots—and narratively—through Mia's career stagnation and the

220 STORYTELLING IN MOTION

narrative ambiguity created by the film's final dream ballet number. Despite *La La Land's* extensive use of fluid sequence shots, director Damien Chazelle and editor Tom Cross also use cutting to clearly distinguish between narrative reality and fantasy, as we see in the cut separating Sebastian at the piano from his earlier (imagined) seat next to Mia in the audience. The film's dream ballet, and its promise of the perfect life, ends abruptly. The film blends various stylistic elements and diegetic levels in service of its cinematic choreography and figure movement's meaning-making potential.

Stylistic realism, as a counterbalance to the musical's heightened aesthetic, has always been a thread running through the genre. Musicals for Damien Chazelle are an "ecstatic state of being" more than anything else, "where everything is a little pitched between fantasy and reality, and music and non-music."[96] Inspired by the long-take cinema of earlier musical filmmakers, like Vincente Minnelli, Stanley Donen, and Jacques Demy, Chazelle's film deviates from the norms of intensified (dis)continuity seen in most contemporary Hollywood musical films. It was a financial risk in 2016 to release an original screen musical that stylistically deviated from the attention-grabbing, editing-driven style of contemporary cinema that was influenced by New Hollywood aesthetics and adjacent exploitation cinema, Hollywood musicals of the early twenty-first century, music videos, and media commercialization. *La La Land's* filmmakers were able to move forward thanks to the support of key producers and financial investors who saw promise in the film's formal premise, as well as the marquee pull of A-list stars Ryan Gosling and Emma Stone as the film's leads, despite their not having prior screen musical experience.

In 2017, another original screen musical, *The Greatest Showman* (Michael Gracey), was also a financial success, earning more than $400 million at the world-wide box office. The financial payoff of two successive original screen musicals, both featuring song and dance, was a contemporary precedent for future aspiring musical filmmakers to point to when justifying the financial viability of what Hollywood often considers a risky prospect. *La La Land* and *The Greatest Showman* also shared key creative talents. Lyricist team Benj Pasek and Justin Paul wrote the lyrics, Tom Cross edited, and Ari Robbins was the Steadicam operator for both. Chazelle recounts the luck he felt in getting to work with Robbins on *La La Land's* cinematic choreography, in particular, saying that "it's being able to dial into the most tender, observant thing that really takes the eye of someone [like Robbins] who's really musical and really visual at the same time to do. It's that combo of athlete and micro-attuned artist."[97]

La La Land deviates from the contemporary norms of editing-based screen choreography to emphasize symmetry and ambiguity instead through the subtle correlations between Chazelle's staging, Mandy Moore's choreography, and Robbins's camerawork, overseen by cinematographer Linus Sandgren. *La La Land*'s stylistic use of durational ambiguity also impacts the viewer's experience with the film. Because the spectator's eye is given more freedom to wander through the frame during the film's extended sequence shots, determinations of the numbers' purposes may vary more widely than in numbers where editing guides the eye to salient details, as we see in *West Side Story* (Jerome Robbins and Robert Wise, 1961). *La La Land*'s songs, composed by Justin Hurwitz with lyrics by Pasek and Paul, are broader in design, through sung material that relates broadly to the narrative events but often plays in counterpoint to the figure movement. Viewers focusing on the music to the exclusion of the choreography, therefore, may see the musical numbers as less narratively integrated and more directed exclusively toward entertainment. The musical sequences' figure movement, in contrast, serves to guide our attention to character and story nuances. Shifting that attention to cinematic choreography—in *La La Land* and all film musicals—impacts our perception of musical numbers' formal impact.

Early in the summer of 2021, critics expressed discontent online over the colorism of *In the Heights*, director Jon M. Chu's cinematic adaptation of Lin-Manuel Miranda's 2008 Broadway musical of the same name. Echoing the reception of *La La Land* and the 1961 film adaptation of *West Side Story*, this led to mixed reviews from critics who loved the film but were frustrated by Hollywood's continued lack of racial and ethnic inclusivity.[98] In another corner of Twitter, and in a clear subtweet of Chu and *In the Heights*, critic Josh Spiegel wrote, "Movie-musical directors, hold a shot for more than two seconds of dancers performing choreography. You can do it. I believe in you."[99] In both instances, criticism of the film points to the continued reluctance of Hollywood executives to invest financially in filmic approaches that deviate from convention. That winter, after the release of *West Side Story* (Steven Spielberg, 2021) hit movie theaters, the film's choreographer Justin Peck praised the cast and crew's commitment to choreographic realism and longer shot lengths:

> One of the things I'm most proud of about our @westsidestorymovie is that the entire cast gives a fully authentic and genuine performance in their dancing. There's no smoke & mirrors. There's no body-doubling. There's

222 STORYTELLING IN MOTION

no face-replacement technology used. It's just some über-talented dance-artists laying it bare on camera, often times for very long-held extended takes. ◑◑ It's incredibly rare for a modern film and filmmaking team to embrace, support, and prioritize this approach—frankly, it's the opposite and requires extra care and investment.[100]

As it turns out, the average shot length of *In the Heights*'s musical numbers (13.5 seconds) is similar to that of Spielberg's *West Side Story* (10.3 seconds), since the former's filmmakers used longer takes in several non-danced musical sequences. The 10-second average shot length of *West Side Story*'s numbers is still a faster cutting rate for musical sequences than any of the films that anchor this book's chapters,[101] and sixfold more quickly cut on average than *La La Land*'s. The 2021 *West Side Story*'s shots may be extended relative to most contemporary Hollywood musicals but not relative to the ones discussed here that also center dance and figure movement. Peck's discussion of his work is a reminder that our individual perceptions of pacing and stylistic norms are specific to our viewing practices. Yet what Spiegel does not acknowledge—and Peck does—is that choreographing the camera with the dancers in musical numbers is a choice but is also a skill. The ability to create effective cinematic choreography must be learned. Observing all the narrative richness and aesthetic virtuosity this craft offers is also a learned viewing practice. Both skillsets have gotten rusty, as industries and audiences shift their attention elsewhere. What we gain by focusing our attention back to this practice is an understanding of the extraordinary ways that filmmakers have used figure movement to tell stories and a front-row seat to its expressive subtlety.

Song is auditory. Movement is visual. Overlooking the latter omits half of the cinematic whole. Musicals are fantastical and often antirealist, but they are also practical. More than any other genre or filmmaking form, musicals are driven by the material, kinesthetic performances of song and dance and their interconnectedness through filmmaker craft practices. With decreasing investment in daily dance class, song and dance trainers, and personnel with the institutional knowledge of how to stage, film, light, edit, and choreograph musical numbers, there grows a gap in the embodied transfer of knowledge. Contemporary filmmakers interested in centering the choreography of figure movement now must often start from scratch or reinvent the craft. Despite this, there continue to be powerful instances of figure movement and dance guiding narrative filmmaking. Cinematic choreography, despite all odds, continues to thrive.

APPENDIX 1

Laban Movement Analysis "Cheat Sheet"

Semantic Fields

Inner/Outer | Exertion/Recuperation | Mobile/Stable | Function/Expression

Effort: How the Body Moves

Various components can describe people's Effort Lives, or the "complicated networks of changing effort qualities" and the "rhythms and the structures of their sequences." Effort qualities are constantly in flux.[1]

Effort Movement Factors are individual manifestations of expressive qualities. Effort States occur when two movement factors manifest simultaneously. Effort Drives occur when three movement factors manifest simultaneously. Drives are intense and are defined by the movement factor they lack.

Effort Element Descriptions and Associations

Table 1.1 Individual Effort Movement Factors, Qualities, and Associations

Movement Factors	Bipolar Qualities	Association (Laban / Yung)
Weight: "the effort exerted to apply the right amount of pressure"[a]	**Strong**: increasing pressure, firm, forceful, solid **Light**: decreasing pressure, delicate, fine touch, sensitive	Intention / Sensing
Space: "the effort exerted to aim and orient movement"[b]	**Direct**: specific, pinpointing, straightforward, single-focused **Indirect**: flexible, scanning, pliant, multifocused	Attention / Thinking
Time: "the effort exerted to pace movement adroitly"[c]	**Sudden**: quick, accelerating, speeding up, urgent, simultaneous **Sustained**: decelerating, slowing down, gradual, lingering, prolonging	Decision-making / Intuiting
Flow: "the effort exerted to control movement"	**Bound**: binding, careful, controlled, restrained **Free**: relaxed, ongoing, fluent	Progression / Feeling

[a]Moore "Introduction," 55.

[b]Ibid.

[c] Ibid.

[d] Ibid.

224　APPENDIX 1

Table 1.2　Effort State Names, Linked Factors, and Associations

Name	Movement Factors	Semantic Association
Stable State	Weight and Space	Grounded (to self), connected to the space
Remote State	Space and Flow	Deliberate navigation of the environment
Dream State	Weight and Flow	Inner state, ongoing feeling of flow, sensing of weight
Mobile State	Time and Flow	Going, moving through the world
Rhythm or Near State	Weight and Time	Presence; more about the mover than the environment
Awake State	Time and Space	Outer state, aware and responding to the environment

Table 1.3　Effort Drive Names, Absent Movement Factors, and Associations

Name	Absent Movement Factor	Semantic Association
Action Drive	Flow	Task-oriented
Passion Drive	Space	Inner impulses dominate
Vision Drive	Weight	Outer connection without emotional investment
Spell Drive	Time	Trance-like, controlling or being controlled

Effort Phrasing, from Vera Maletic's *Dance Dynamics*

Impulsive/Decreasing-Intensity: "changes the movement quality in that it decreases its initial intensity."[2]

Resilient: "result of repetitive, rebounding qualities that can be performed with three different emphases," elastic, buoyant, weighty.[3]

Vibratory: "consists of sudden repetitions that continue over a shorter or longer period of time."[4]

Impactful/Increasing-Intensity: "the performance of a quality that changes in that it increases in intensity."[5]

Space: Where the body Is Moving

The Kinesphere is "the sphere around the body whose periphery can be reached by easily extended limbs without stepping away from that place which is the point of support when standing on one foot" also known as the stance or one's "personal space."[6]

APPENDIX 1   225

Spatial Subdivisions

Dimensional or Axial movement: Movement with a single Spatial Pull (six total):

- Along the vertical axis: movement up (toward the head) and movement down (toward the feet)
- Along the horizontal axis: movement closing across the midline or opening away from the midline (right and left)
- Along the sagittal axis: movement forward (in front of the body) or movement backward (in back of the body)

Planar movement: Movement in planes/along diameters with two uneven Spatial Pulls, one primary and one secondary (twelve total):

- In the vertical plane: predominantly up or down, with a secondary, lesser pull into horizontality
- In the horizontal plane: predominantly closing or opening (right and left) with a secondary, lesser pull into sagittal space
- In the sagittal plane: predominantly forward or back, with a secondary, lesser pull into verticality

Diagonal movement: Movement along diagonals, with three equal Spatial Pulls, one along each of the three dimensions: vertical, horizontal, and sagittal (eight total):

- Right forward high
- Left back low
- Left forward high
- Right back low
- Left back high
- Right forward low
- Right back high
- Left forward low

Spatial Stability and Mobility

Laban describes Axial movement as inherently more stable and Diagonal movement as inherently more mobile.[7]

Body: Which Parts of the Body Are Moving

Key Concepts

- Movement: any distinguishable change or individual movement
- Stillness: arrested movement, suspension
- Body attitude: the resting shape a body takes (erect, hunched, leaning to one side, etc.)
- Single-unit movement: one primary movement occurring at a time

226   APPENDIX 1

- Multi-unit movement: secondary movements occurring at the same time as a primary movement
- Body part phrasing:
    - Simultaneous: all body parts move at once
    - Successive: movement flows from one body part to another
    - Sequential: unconnected body parts move one after the other

Basic Body Actions

The Basic Body Actions are fundamental movement options.

Table 1.4 Descriptions of the Basic Body Actions[a]

Name	Description
Traveling	Any pathway (straight or curving)
Change of Support	A weight shift leading to a new place of support
Rotation	A full or partial revolution in any dimension, of any body part
Flexion	A narrowing, contracting, folding, or adducting motion
Extension	A widening, extending, unfolding, or abducting motion
Spring	Any movement in which all limbs leave the ground
Falling	A loss or release of balance in any direction

[a] Yoo, "Body Actions Handout."

Shape: How the Body Moves in Relation to Its Environment

Shape studies the changing dimensions of the Kinesphere in relation to the environment. The Modes of Shape Change are three dominant categories of movement in the Shape category:

- Shape Flow: Movement that is more internally focused, attentive toward the self. The Columbia College Chicago GLCMA faculty combine conflicting accounts of Shape and define it as "the growing and shrinking of the actual kinesphere [*sic*] as manifested in growing and shrinking of the body shape."[8]
- Carving/Shaping: a molding, dynamic, multidimensional relationship to the environment.
- Directional movement: a more straightforward relationship to the environment, which can be either Spoke-like or Arc-like:
    - Spoke-like Directional: "movement tracing a linear pathway to a point."[9]
    - Arc-like Directional: "movement tracing a flat arc through space."[10]

APPENDIX 2

Analytical Data

Budget Data (for Case Studies and Cost Comparisons from Existing Data)

Table 2.1 Budget Data for Core Films

Film	Year	Budget (in millions, local currency)	Budget Source
Singin' in the Rain	1952	2.50 ($)	AFI catalog
West Side Story	1961	6.75 ($)	Mirisch
Les Demoiselles de Rochefort	1967	5.76 (Fr)	Fonds Jacques Demy
Trois places pour le 26	1988	56.00 (Fr)	Fonds Pathé
Jeanne et le garçon formidable	1998	24.00 (Fr)	Ducastel/Martineau
La La Land	2016	30.00 ($)	Box Office Mojo

Table 2.2 Comparative Budget Data for *Les Demoiselles de Rochefort*

Film Categories	Year	Cost (original, in millions)	Comparative Cost (in 1967 millions of dollars)	Country (financing)	Source
Demy Films					
Les Demoiselles de Rochefort	1967	5.76 (Fr)	1.17	France/USA	Ciné-Tamaris
Les Parapluies de Cherbourg	1964	.90 (Fr)	0.20	France	Hill
US Musicals					
Thoroughly Modern Millie	1967	6.00 ($)	6.00	USA	Farmer
Half a Sixpence	1967	6.00 ($)	6.00	USA	*Variety*
West Side Story	1961	6.75 ($)	7.54	USA	Mirisch
The Band Wagon	1953	2.87 ($)	3.59	USA	Fordin
Singin' in the Rain	1952	2.59 ($)	3.24	USA	Fordin
An American in Paris	1951	2.72 ($)	3.50	USA	Fordin
On the Town	1949	2.13 ($)	2.99	USA	Fordin
Meet Me in St. Louis	1944	1.19 ($)	2.25	USA	Fordin

228   APPENDIX 2

Table 2.3 Comparative Budget Data for *Trois places pour le 26*

Film Categories	Year	Cost (original, in millions)	Comparative Cost (in 1988 millions of dollars)	Country (financing)	Source
Demy Films					
Trois places pour le 26	1988	56.00 (Fr)	9.35	France	Pathé
Peau d'âne	1970	5.28 (Fr)	29.60	France	Ciné-Tamaris
Les Demoiselles de Rochefort	1967	5.76 (Fr)	23.20	France/USA	Ciné-Tamaris
Contemporary Films					
Earth Girls Are Easy	1988	10.00 ($)	10.00	USA	IMDb
School Daze	1988	6.50 ($)	6.50	USA	IMDb
Who Framed Roger Rabbit	1988	70.00 ($)	70.00	USA	IMDb
Le grand bleu	1988	80.00 (Fr)	13.40	France	IMDb

Quantitative Film Data: Average Shot Lengths and Musical Number Durations

General Hollywood Data

Film average shot length (1930–1960): 8-11s[1]
Musical number average shot length (1933–1961): 24.3 s[2]

Quantitative Average Shot Length (ASL) Data

Table 2.4 Stylistic Data for Core Films

Film	Year	ASL (total film)	ASL (musical numbers)
Singin' in the Rain	1952	16.4	19.8
West Side Story	1961	11.7	13.9
Les Demoiselles de Rochefort	1967	16.5	34.5
Trois places pour le 26	1988	9.8	25.1
Jeanne et le garçon formidable	1998	13.4	32.8
La La Land	2016	10.0	59.6
Average:		**13.0**	**31.0**

APPENDIX 2   229

Table 2.5 Classical Hollywood Musical Number Stylistic Data for *Les Demoiselles de Rochefort*

Film	Year	Number ASL	Musical Number Quantity
Meet Me in St. Louis	1944	28.4	11
On the Town	1949	35.6	14
An American in Paris	1951	28.7	11
Singin' in the Rain	1952	19.8	13
Gentlemen Prefer Blondes	1953	14.9	7
The Band Wagon	1953	33.7	14
West Side Story	1961	11.7	14
Average		**25.2**	**12**

Table 2.6 Music Video Stylistic Data for *Trois places pour le 26*

Music Videos	Year	ASL
"Love Is a Battlefield"	1983	3.45
"Beat It"	1983	4.90
"Thriller"	1983	3.40
Average		**3.90**

Table 2.7 Contemporary Hollywood Stylistic Data for *Trois places pour le 26*

Musicals	Year	ASL
All That Jazz	1979	2.20* (full film)
Xanadu	1980	11.60 (dance numbers)
Blues Brothers	1980	4.80* (full film)
Little Shop of Horrors	1986	5.30* (full film)
Earth Girls Are Easy	1988	3.95 (dance numbers)
Average:		7.80

* Data from Cinemetrics

230   APPENDIX 2

Table 2.8 Comparative Stylistic Data for *Jeanne et le garçon formidable*

Film	Date	ASL (total film)	ASL (musical numbers)
Les Demoiselles de Rochefort	1967	16.5	34.5
On connait la chanson	1997	22.4*	19.5
Jeanne et le garçon formidable	1998	13.4	32.8
Moulin Rouge!	2001	2.0*	3.2
8 femmes	2002	7.9**	14.1
Chicago	2002	2.8*	2.9

* Data from Cinemetrics
** Average of multiple ASL database entries

Table 2.9 Comparative Stylistic Data for *La La Land*

Film	Year	ASL (musical numbers)
Moulin Rouge!	2001	3.2
Chicago	2002	2.9
La La Land	2016	59.6
The Greatest Showman	2017	3.6
Mary Poppins Returns	2018	10.7
West Side Story	2021	10.3
In the Heights	2021	13.5

Notes

Introduction

1. Guillermo del Toro (@RealGDT), "Extremely hard to execute. Pure, masterly clockwork precision and a lot more complex than 'seamed' shots or steadicam-to-crane 'relay' shots . . ." Twitter thread, February 26, 2022, https://twitter.com/realgdt/status/1497625522041352192?lang=en.
2. Zaumer, "Oscars."
3. Mandy Moore, in conversation with the author, May 23, 2019.
4. Appadurai, "Disjuncture and Difference," 296.
5. Ruyter, *Cultivation of Body and Mind*, 66; Pearson, *Eloquent Gestures*, 22–23.
6. Foster, *Choreographing Empathy*, 2.
7. Bordwell, *Figures*, 11.
8. For these categories I rely on existing literature from dance studies to distinguish among major dance forms. See, in particular Harris, *Making Ballet American*; Banes, *Terpsichore in Sneakers*; Ginot and Michel, *La danse au 20e siècle*; Guarino and Oliver, *Jazz Dance*.
9. McLean, *Dying Swans*; Brannigan, *Dancefilm*; Iyer, *Dancing Women*.
10. Bordwell, *Figures*, 8.
11. See Foster, *Reading Dancing*; Mackrell, *Reading Dance*; Preston-Dunlop, *Looking at Dances*; Smith-Autard, *Dance Composition*.
12. Chapter 2 and appendix 1 both expand on the movement taxonomy from Laban/Bartenieff Movement Studies (LBMS).
13. See Bird, "Feeling and Thought"; Haraway, "Manifesto for Cyborgs," 7–46.
14. Mandy Moore, in conversation with the author, May 23, 2019.
15. See Banes, *Terpsichore in Sneakers*; Ginot and Michel, *La danse au 20e siècle*; Philippe Noisette, *Danse contemporaine mode d'emploi*; Harris, *Making Ballet American;* McCarren, *French Moves*; Reynolds and McCormick, "Dance in the Movies"; Guarino and Oliver, *Jazz Dance*; Bales and Eliot, *Dance on Its Own Terms*; Butterworth and Wildschut, *Contemporary Choreography*; Carter, "Destabilising the Discipline"; Carter and O'Shea, *The Routledge Dance Studies Reader*; Layson, "Dance History Source Materials."
16. See Rosenberg, *Screendance*; Brannigan, *Dancefilm*; Dodd, *Dance on Screen*; Bench, *Perpetual Motion*; Brooks, "From Méliès to Streaming Video"; Centre national de la danse, *Danse/Cinéma*; Kappenberg, "Does Screendance Need to Look Like Dance?"
17. See McLean, *Dying Swans*; Genné, *Dance Me a Song*; Delamater, *Dance in the Hollywood Musical*; Iyer, *Dancing Women*; Mueller, *Astaire Dancing*; Rubin,

232 NOTES TO PAGES 7–11

Showstoppers; Franceschina, *Hermes Pan*; McLean, *Being Rita Hayworth*; Ovalle, *Dance and the Hollywood Latina*.

18. Parker and Sedgwick, "Introduction," 1–18.

19. See Naremore, *Acting in the Cinema*; Phelan, *Unmarked*; Taylor, *Theorizing Film Acting*; Baron and Carnicke, *Reframing Screen Performance*; Lovell and Krämer, *Screen Acting*; St. John, *Victor Turner*.

20. See Moore and Yamamoto, *Beyond Words*; Argyle, *Bodily Communication*; Hawhee, *Moving Bodies*; Birdwhistell, *Kinesics and Context*; Goffman, *The Presentation of Self in Everyday Life*.

21. McLean, *Dying Swans*, 6–10.

22. For further discussion of the distinctions between denotative and connotative meaning, see Thompson, *Breaking the Glass Armor*, 12.

23. See Bordwell, *Making Meaning* and Bordwell, "The Viewer's Share," 30.

24. Runick, Cutting, and DeLong, "Low-Level Features of Film," 133.

25. Thompson, *Breaking the Glass Armor*, 32–33.

26. Bordwell, *Figures*, 36.

27. Caroll and Seeley, "Cognitivism, Psychology, and Neuroscience," 59.

28. Ibid., 60.

29. See Brunick, Cutting, and DeLong, "Low-Level Features," 134; Carroll and Seely, "Cognitivism, Psychology, and Neuroscience," 60; Bordwell, "The Viewer's Share," 30–31; and Smith, "Watching You Watch Movies," 174, 178.

30. Bordwell, "The Viewer's Share," 30.

31. Carroll and Seeley, "Cognitivism, Psychology, and Neuroscience," 61–63, 70–71.

32. Faden, "Visual Disturbances."

33. Schonig, *Shape of Motion*, 4.

34. Keating, *Dynamic Frame*, 75, 76. For additional discussion of the relationships between the moving body and camera, see Morgan, *Lure of the Image*; Delamater, *Dance in the Hollywood Musical*; Mueller, *Astaire Dancing*; Martin, *Showstoppers*; Bordwell, *Figures*; Bird, "Feeling and Thought"; Schonig, "The Follow Shot."

35. Moore, *Harmonic Structure*, 84. Carol-Lynne Moore sees similar ties between Bergson's categorizations of intellectual and intuitive perception and the various ways of distinguishing between and discussing movement systems at the core of Laban/Bartenieff Movement Studies.

36. Schonig, *Shape of Motion*, 6.

37. Keathley, Mittell, and Grant elaborate on the methods of generating videographic research and scholarship in *The Videographic Essay: Practice and Pedagogy*.

38. Mittell, "Videographic Criticism," 226.

39. Haseman, "Manifesto for Performative Research," 102; Grant, "Audiovisual Essay," 14.

40. Grant, "Audiovisual Essay"; O'Leary, "Workshop of Potential Scholarship."

41. Mackrell, *Reading Dance*; Preston-Dunlop, *Looking at Dances*; Smith-Autard, *Dance Composition*; and Foster, *Reading Dancing* provide methods in this regard. McKechnie and Stevens, "Visible Thought" and Foster, *Choreographing Empathy* also provide useful guidance for ways to understand dance structure more broadly.

NOTES TO PAGES 11–17   233

42. This community of practitioners recently decided to start calling this work Laban/Bartenieff Movement Studies rather than Laban Movement Analysis to better acknowledge Irmgard Bartenieff's contributions. I find it useful to continue using LMA to reference this work's central movement taxonomy and to use LBMS in reference to the broader field of study associated with these concepts.

43. For additional literature on the Laban systems, see in particular: Laban and Ullmann, *Choreutics*; Laban and Ullmann, *Mastery of Movement*; Studd and Cox, *EveryBody Is a Body*; Bartenieff and Lewis, *Body Movement*; Bradley, *Rudolf Laban*; Dell, *A Primer for Movement Description*; Hutchinson Guest, *Motif Notation*; Maletic, *Dance Dynamics*.

44. Bradley, *Rudolf Laban*, xi.

45. Moore, *Harmonic Structure*, 84.

46. Rudolf Laban and his students did develop a symbol-based notation system called Labanotation that is used today to record a series of movements comprehensively, but that system is dependent on a mastery of a notation language, requires separate training, and does not take into account the more qualitative aspects of movement that are central to Laban Movement Analysis.

47. Some of Laban's most influential contributions to research on human expression developed from studying the repetitive motions of factory workers. See Bradley, *Rudolf Laban*, 34.

48. For more on the various populations Laban worked with, see Bradley, *Rudolf Laban*.

49. McLean, "Feeling and the Filmed Body," 5.

50. Schonig, *Shape of Motion*, 3.

51. For more on these major modes of historical inquiry, see Allen and Gomery, *Film History*, 20.

52. Bordwell, *Film Style*, 148, 151.

53. Ibid., 150.

54. Allen and Gomery, *Film History*, 109.

55. Altman, *American Film Musical*.

56. For a more detailed history of early stabilization technology, see Bird, "Feeling and Thought."

57. See Keating, *Dynamic Frame*, 1–14.

58. Bordwell, *Figures*, 8–9.

59. See Weis and Belton, *Film Sound: Theory and Practice*, especially 1–73, for a history of studio-era sound technology.

60. Bordwell, *Poetics*, 281–325.

61. Delamater, *Dance in the Hollywood Musical*, 218.

62. Damien Chazelle, in conversation with the author, July 20, 2018.

63. See Clover, "Dancin' in the Rain," 157–167; Jones, "Jazz Dance and Racism," 231–239.

64. For more on the evolution of the French musical, see Powrie and Cadalanu, *The French Film Musical*.

65. Kessler, *Destabilizing the Hollywood Musical*, 10.

66. Neale, *Genre and Hollywood*, 17–18.

67. McLean, *Dying Swans*, 23–26.

68. Allen and Gomery, *Film History*, 68.

234 NOTES TO PAGES 18–31

69. Ibid., 131.
70. See Schatz, *Boom and Bust*, 329–352.
71. Bazin, "*Umberto D*," 82.
72. Cohan, "Introduction: How Do You Solve a Problem Like the Film Musical," 5.
73. Plantinga, *Alternative Realities*, 65. See also Thompson, *Breaking the Glass Armor*, 35; Smith, "Bridging the Gap," 4.

Chapter 1

1. Cohan, *Incongruous Entertainment*, 196, 200.
2. Notable examples include Genné, *Dance Me a Song*; Cohan, *Incongruous Entertainment*; Griffin, *Free and Easy?*; Delamater, *Dance in the Hollywood Musical*; Feuer, *The Hollywood Musical*; Basinger, *The Movie Musical!*; Balio, *MGM*; Clover, "Dancin' in the Rain." Jason Mittell also uses the film as a case study for the deformative potentials of videographic criticism ("Deformin' in the Rain").
3. Genné, *Dance Me a Song*, 183; Cohan, *Incongruous Entertainment*, 200–202; Clover, "Dancin' in the Rain," 159.
4. Balio, *MGM*, 76, 176; Cohan, *Incongruous Entertainment*, 200; Griffin, *Free and Easy?*, 143.
5. Genné, *Dance Me a Song*, 126–183.
6. Griffin, *Free and Easy?*, 152.
7. Cohan, *Incongruous Entertainment*, 222–223.
8. Reynolds, *Debbie*, 86–91.
9. Delamater, *Dance in the Hollywood Musical*, 210, 245, 246.
10. Ibid., 250.
11. Griffin, *Free and Easy?*, 143.
12. Ibid., 152, 155.
13. Balio, *MGM*, 152–153.
14. Sean Griffin also discusses the greater nuance between the Freed and Pasternak units (*Free and Easy?*, 134).
15. Steve Neale describes the musical as a "mongrel genre. In varying measures and combinations, music, song and dance have been its only essential ingredients" (*Genre and Hollywood*, 105). Jane Feuer emphasizes the musical as a set of ideological contradictions (Feuer, "Self-Reflective Musical"). Richard Dyer emphasizes the contrast between the realistic and utopian qualities of narrative and numbers, respectively (Dyer, "Entertainment and Utopia"). For John Mueller, how closely the musical sequences are causally linked to the narrative is of paramount importance ("Fred Astaire"). For Rick Altman, narrative integration is less important than the clear shift from the film's diegesis to the musical number, which he discusses as existing in a "supradiegetic" space. Altman prioritizes his concept of the audio dissolve in his discussion of style and a dual-focus emphasis in his discussion of narrative (*American Film Musical*, 59–89). Martin Rubin, like Altman, prioritizes numbers that move the film away from the narrative's diegetic realities, and his discussion of this shift is based

on an evaluation of plausibility; his concept of numbers that contain "impossible" elements given the diegetic context is more helpful in getting at this sense of a shift ("Busby Berkeley," 57).

16. Steven Neale echoes this, writing that, "most uses of the term [integration] are rather vague" (*Genre and Hollywood*, 107).

17. All of the following draw on the category of integrated musicals: Balio, *MGM*, 152–153; Griffin, *Free and Easy?*; Kessler, *Destabilizing the Hollywood Musical*; Cohan, *Incongruous Entertainment*; Garcia, *Migration of Musical Film*; Cooper, "The Body Censored."

18. Cohan acknowledges that "with the exception of revues, no single musical purely adheres to one form or the other, of course" (*Incongruous Entertainment*, 43–45).

19. Garcia, *Migration of Musical Film*, 11.

20. Griffin, *Free and Easy?*, 134.

21. Jerome Delamater uses integration to refer to the way a number relates to the narrative but also whether the number (and the dancing especially) is designed to be film-style specific, a criterion that is inherently problematic. Delamater argues that "the nature of integration of the film musical lies not simply with the idea that the musical numbers and the dances, in particular, should advance the plot but also suggests an integration of the entire cinematic process" (*Dance in the Hollywood Musical*, 98). Simply by existing as a performance within a filmic production, all dancing in musical films is by definition already integrated with the cinematic process.

22. Meuller's work, in particular, champions causal narrative integration as central to the genre ("Fred Astaire").

23. Garcia, *Migration of Musical Film*, 11; Cohan, *Incongruous Entertainment*, 61; Waldron, *Jacques Demy*, 61–62; McLean, *Dying Swans*, 208–209. Guido Heldt flips this, considering this kind of number as "barely integrated," positioning instead a typical backstage, "purely diegetic," number as more highly integrated (*Music and Levels of Narration*, 139).

24. Some scholars also discuss racial integration in the musical and Hollywood, but this is a rarer use of the term in relation to the musical genre. See Griffin, "Gang's All Here," 21–45; Garcia, *Migration of Musical Film*, 11.

25. See also Herzog, *Dreams of Difference*, 5–8; Brannigan, *Dancefilm*, 160–161.

26. For more on the distinction between plot (syuzhet) and story (fabula), see Bordwell, *Ozu*, 51.

27. Mueller's taxonomy of musical numbers ("Fred Astaire," 28–40) and Bordwell's discussion of narrative theory and stylistics (*Figures*, 33–35) provide guiding frameworks to situate a musical number in relation to its surrounding narrative.

28. For more on the various categories of stylistic functions, in relation to staging in particular, see Bordwell, *Figures*, 33–34.

29. This relates to John Mueller's category of "integrated" musical numbers, in which the characters' singing or dancing serves an essential purpose and advances the narrative ("Fred Astaire," 28–30).

30. Mueller, "Fred Astaire," 33–35.

236 NOTES TO PAGES 36–46

31. Mueller's second category, "numbers which contribute to the spirit or theme," would be applicable here as well ("Fred Astaire," 28).

32. Cohan, *Incongruous Entertainment*, 43, 44.

33. Mueller emphasizes dance in his taxonomy of integration because, as he convincingly articulates, song and music continue to receive greater scholarly attention ("Fred Astaire," 31).

34. Mueller, "Fred Astaire," 35.

35. Altman suggests that this shift occurs in musical numbers to emphasize opposition on multiple levels (technical, thematic, narrative). This is accomplished with the help of the audio dissolve, in which the soundtrack shifts priority from the diegetic dialogue track to the music track, resulting in a "reversal of the image/sound hierarchy" (*American Film Musical*, 62–67).

36. Rubin's determination of a film's status as a musical depends on the inclusion primarily of numbers that are "persistently contradictory in relation to the realistic discourse of the narrative" (*Showstoppers*, 37).

37. Cohan, *Sound of Musicals*, 3.

38. Rubin, *Showstoppers*, 12.

39. For more on examining cinematic techniques from the perspective of filmic space and time, see Bordwell, *Narration in the Fiction Film*, 74–130; Deleuze, *Cinema 1* and *Cinema 2*; Jacobs, *Film Rhythm*, 112, 141; and Kappenberg, "Does Screendance Need to Look Like Dance?"

40. Smith, "Bridging the Gap," 7.

41. Rubin, *Showstoppers*, 39.

42. Altman, *American Film Musical*, 62–73.

43. See also Iyer, *Dancing Women*, 9–14; Brannigan, *Dancefilm*, 158–163.

44. A notable exception would be *Earth Girls Are Easy* (Julien Temple, 1988), a musical-science fiction blend in which the alien characters are able to perfectly mimic the sounds created by inanimate objects as well as human voices.

45. Cohan argues that "this is why the genre gives pride of place to performing; great stars like Fred Astaire, Judy Garland and Barbra Streisand can hold one's attention on screen while singing or dancing, even if their voices are pre-recorded and the sounds of their tapping feet achieved in post-production" (*Sound of Musicals*, 4).

46. Carol Clover mentions that Betty Noyes's last name may have been Royce. Clover, "Dancin' in the Rain," 158.

47. Recording the voice separately from the filmed performance (as is the norm for most musical genre modes of production) does not alter these categorizations of diegetic change. Dubbing is a technological craft practice that is not normally meant to be noticed in the context of the diegesis (exceptions exist, of course, as we see with *Singin' in the Rain*). Vocal dubbing is not usually meant to draw attention to itself; rather, it adds to the illusion of perfection and virtuosity that is frequently present in musical numbers, in Hollywood musicals especially. The same idea is applicable to the practice of dance doubles, which is less common.

48. Smith, "Bridging the Gap," 6.

49. Ibid., 22.

NOTES TO PAGES 47–55   237

50. Beth Genné describes Gene Kelly's watery tap sounds as "deliciously squishy" (*Dance Me a Song*, 120).
51. The "and dancin'" portion of the lyric is also absent from earlier iterations of the Freed/Brown song (Cohan, *Incongruous Entertainment*, 222).
52. Genné, *Dance Me a Song*, 183.
53. Griffin, *Free and Easy?*, 137.
54. Quick Time Effort in Laban Movement Analysis terms. Capitalized phrases refer to the more precise descriptive-analytical language from Laban/Bartenieff Movement Studies. See chapter 2 and this book's appendix 1 for an overview of the Laban Movement Analysis system.
55. Smith, "Watching You Watch Movies," 174, 178.
56. Cohan, *Incongruous Entertainment*, 187.
57. Genné, *Dance Me a Song*, 183.
58. Delamater, *Dance in the Hollywood Musical*, 211.
59. Ibid.
60. Passion Drive.
61. Strong Weight Effort and Time Effort.
62. Space Effort.
63. Effort Life.
64. Bound Flow Effort.
65. Free Flow Effort.
66. Space Effort is absent.
67. Gene Kelly is, of course, still performing for the film audience in this moment, so his distancing from an outer focus is a matter of degree.
68. Remote State with Bound Flow and Direct Space Efforts.

Chapter 2

1. A captioned version of this video chapter is available on Vimeo at https://vimeo.com/cinemajok/seeingmovement.
2. Laban and Ullmann, *Choreutics*; Laban and Ullmann, *Mastery of Movement*; Studd and Cox, *EveryBody Is a Body*.
3. Capitalized terms or phrases refer to the more precise descriptive-analytical language from Laban/Bartenieff Movement Studies. See also this book's appendix 1 for a summary of the Laban Movement Analysis system.
4. Laban, *Choreutics*, 10.
5. Ibid., 27–30.
6. Ibid., 27.
7. Much of this work grew from the research of Irmgard Bartenieff, who studied with Laban and pioneered the field of dance therapy.
8. For an apt discussion of the difference between human and mechanical (robotic) figure movement using LBMS frameworks, see LaViers and Egerstedt, "Style Based Robotic Motion."

238 NOTES TO PAGES 57–62

Chapter 3

1. Letter from Jerome Robbins to Robert Wise, April 4, 1960. Jerome Robbins Papers. New York Public Library for the Performing Arts.
2. Robbins restaged his choreography for *The King and I* (Walter Lang, 1956), and Deborah Jowitt's biography suggests that he was given considerable control over the filming of the numbers. It is not surprising that Robbins's desire for artistic control and his experience on that production motivated him to demand a directorial role in *West Side Story*. See Jowitt, *Jerome Robbins*, 184–185.
3. It is likely that his desire to create the perfect film counterpart, maintaining the coordination among artistic components—notwithstanding the hours of rehearsal that delayed the shooting schedule or the cost of shooting numerous takes on expensive 70mm film stock—resulted in his dismissal from the project partway through production. Harold Mirisch, one of the producers, voices these concerns in several memos to Robbins and Wise. Letter from Harold Mirisch to Robert Wise and Jerome Robbins, October 11, 1960; Letter from Harold Mirisch to Robert Wise and Jerome Robbins, September 15, 1960. Jerome Robbins Papers. New York Public Library for the Performing Arts.
4. Delamater, *Dance in the Hollywood Musical*, 98.
5. Altman, *The American Film Musical*, 167. See also Mueller, "Fred Astaire," 28–40.
6. See Delamater, *Dance in the Hollywood Musical*, 98.
7. Ibid., 173.
8. Acevedo-Muñoz, *West Side Story*, 9–10.
9. Ibid., 30.
10. Ibid., 34; Mirisch, *I Thought We Were Making Movies*, 125.
11. Memo from Harold Mirisch to Robert Wise and Jerome Robbins. September 12, 1960. Jerome Robbins Papers. New York Public Library for the Performing Arts.
12. Letter to Robert Wise from Jerome Robbins, April 4, 1960. Jerome Robbins Papers. New York Public Library for the Performing Arts.
13. Letter from Robert Wise to Jerome Robbins, April 8, 1960. Jerome Robbins Papers. New York Public Library for the Performing Arts.
14. Letter from Robert Wise to Jerome Robbins, April 8, 1960. Jerome Robbins Papers. New York Public Library for the Performing Arts.
15. See appendix 2 for quantitative data.
16. The five-second average shot length of the final can-can contradicts this idea somewhat, but it is possible Pan did not have final say on the editing. See Franceschina, *Hermes Pan*, 224.
17. Letter from Robert Wise to Jerome Robbins, April 8, 1960. Jerome Robbins Papers. New York Public Library for the Performing Arts.
18. Letter from Jerome Robbins to Robert Wise, n.d. Jerome Robbins Papers. New York Public Library for the Performing Arts.
19. Acevedo-Muñoz, *West Side Story*, 10.
20. Berson, *Something's Coming*, 159–160.
21. Ibid., 162.

NOTES TO PAGES 62–65 239

22. Moreno had worked for MGM, Warner Bros., 20th Century Fox, and independent productions. Chakiris briefly signed with Paramount in the 1950s before working on Broadway and playing Riff in the London production of *West Side Story*. Tamblyn had an extensive career in Hollywood as a child actor and signed a long-term contract with MGM in the 1950s (Hopper, "Russ Tamblyn," D1).

23. Acevedo-Muñoz, *West Side Story*, 10.

24. See ibid., 150–152.

25. Ibid., 10–12. Elizabeth Wells discusses similar parallels for the original theatrical production (*West Side Story,* 99–140).

26. In his autobiography, Walter Mirisch acknowledges that Natalie Wood was "not ideal as a Hispanic" character (*I Thought We Were Making Movies*, 124).

27. Herrera, *Latin numbers*, 116. See also Beltrán, *Latina/o Stars*, 79, 80.

28. Acevedo-Muñoz, *West Side Story*, 152–153.

29. Negrón-Muntaner, *Boricua Pop*, 60.

30. Esteban Muñoz, *Disidentifications*, 3–6.

31. Herrera, *Latin Numbers*, 98–99.

32. White "ghost singers" Marni Nixon and Betty Wand contributed vocals to Rita Moreno's songs as well as Natalie Wood's (Acevedo-Muñoz, *West Side Story*, 53–54). For more on this practice, see also Smith, "Black Faces, White Voices."

33. Garcia, *Movie Musical*, 4.

34. Garcia, *Migration of Musical Film*, 1–17.

35. Carol Clover analyzes this practice in relation to *Singin' in the Rain* (Clover, "Dancin'," 160–164).

36. Grant describes an association between the Sharks and mambo and the Jets and jazz (*Hollywood Film Musical*, 104).

37. Acevedo-Muñoz, *West Side Story*, 168, referencing Cohan, "Introduction: Musicals of the Studio Era," 1.

38. Acevedo-Muñoz, *West Side Story*, 169.

39. *West Side Story* sectioned annotated script, 1958. Jerome Robbins Papers. New York Public Library for the Performing Arts.

40. Dyer, *White*, 44–45.

41. See McLean, *Dying Swans*; Cohan, *Incongruous Entertainment*; and Doty, *Flaming Classics*.

42. McLean, *Dying Swans*, 16.

43. The section title is a play on the lyrics in the parodic musical number from *Silk Stockings* (Rouben Mamoulian, 1957) in which a character sings about the need to attract audiences with "glorious Technicolor, breathtaking CinemaScope, and stereophonic sound."

44. The Panavision Corporation's anamorphic lenses, developed in 1958, resolved many of the optical distortions and limitations associated with the earlier CinemaScope lenses. For a more detailed analysis of CinemaScope's historical significance, see Belton, "Cinemascope," 244–253.

45. Bordwell, *Poetics*, 291.

46. Delamater, *Dance in the Hollywood Musical*, 218.

240 NOTES TO PAGES 65–73

47. Bordwell, Poetics, 284.

48. Ibid., 307–308.

49. Cohan, *Incongruous Entertainment*, 43–45.

50. Herrera, *Latin Numbers*, 107.

51. See Bordwell, *Poetics*, 310.

52. Ibid.

53. The 1961 Japanese poster for the film features the pose prominently.

54. See Acevedo-Muñoz, *West Side Story*; Grant, *The Hollywood Film Musical*.

55. Gap uses this pose briefly, along with more extensive choreography from "Cool," in a 2000 ad spot for jeans and khakis.

56. See, in particular, Jacques Demy's *Les Demoiselles de Rochefort*, discussed in Becker and Williams, "What Ever Happened," 303–321.

57. See, in particular, Acevedo-Muñoz, *West Side Story*, 150–169; Negrón-Muntaner, *Boricua Pop*, 63–67; Berson, *Something's Coming*, 207–221, and Grant, *Hollywood Film Musical*, 102. For a discussion of Hispanic representation in the theatrical original, see Wells, *West Side Story*, 99–140.

58. Not quite adults, not quite children; Robbins's description of the prologue in preproduction documents includes the note, "It must be noted that they are all kids and are not aware of the seriousness of what they are involved in, let alone to what it may lead." Sectioned annotated script, 1958. Jerome Robbins Papers. New York Public Library for the Performing Arts.

59. Berson, *Something's Coming*, 154.

60. Bordwell, Staiger, and Thompson, *Classical Hollywood Cinema*, 31–32.

61. Far-reach Kinesphere. Capitalized phrases in text or in notes summarize my analysis using the more precise descriptive-analytical language from Laban/Bartenieff Movement Studies; for more on that taxonomy or the usage of specific terms see chapter 2 and appendix 1.

62. Indirect Space and Free Flow Efforts, or Remote State.

63. Laban's description of Bound Flow Effort combining with other elements like Strong Weight or Direct Space (Laban, *Mastery of Movement*, 76).

64. All move through Direct Space and Bound Flow Efforts.

65. Herrera, *Latin Numbers*, 113–114.

66. The section title references the Prince's response to the news of Mercutio's murder (Shakespeare, *Romeo and Juliet*, 68).

67. Garcia, *Migration of Musical Film*, 137.

68. Acevedo-Muñoz discusses this at length, arguing that "*West Side Story* 'creates' Puerto Rican identity within the confines of a particularly performative genre in which references to reality are extremely mediated at best and, more often than not, respond only to its own generic, formal, and structural rules" (*West Side Story*, 154).

69. A Far-Space Kinesphere with a tendency for Indirect Space and Free Flow Efforts.

70. A Mid and Near-Space Kinesphere.

71. Near-Reach Space.

72. Bound Flow Effort and Direct Space Effort.

73. Body Attitudes.

74. Remote State.

NOTES TO PAGES 74–86   241

75. Dyer, "Entertainment and Utopia," 19–30.
76. Although Robbins was fired before all *West Side Story*'s musical numbers were filmed, shooting schedules confirm that he was still on set during the filming of "Cool," as it was one of the first numbers to be completed after the New York location shots. Anecdotal reports also confirm this, suggesting that the dancers piled the burned remains of their kneepads—essential for dancing on the concrete floor of the parking garage—in front of Robbins's office after they finished filming the number. Shooting schedule memo from Robert Wise to Al Wood, July 27, 1960. Jerome Robbins Papers. New York Public Library for the Performing Arts; Berson, *Something's Coming*, 165.
77. Free Flow, Quick Time, and Strong Weight Efforts.
78. Laban, *Mastery of Movement*, 80.
79. Far-Reach movements in the Kinesphere.
80. Studd and Cox, *EveryBody*, 85–86.
81. Ibid., 82–83.
82. Ibid., 83–84, 86.
83. Free Flow Effort.
84. Sustained Time Effort.
85. Moving with a Mid-to-Near Space Kinesphere.
86. Flow and Weight Efforts.
87. Space Effort.
88. An Effort Life consisting of Light and Strong Weight Effort, Space Effort (both Direct and Indirect), Sustained Time Effort, and Free Flow Effort.
89. An Effort Life characterized by Strong Weight, Quick Time, and Bound Flow Efforts.
90. The result of a deliberate engagement with Bound Flow and Sustained Time Efforts.
91. *West Side Story* Libretto, 1958. Jerome Robbins Papers. New York Public Library for the Performing Arts.
92. The Lindy Hop is a social dance, a form of swing dance, originally developed by African American artists. There are different styles of Lindy Hop, but all maintain a strong frame between partnered dancers—that is to say, a fixed position of the arms and torso in relation to one another that allows the dancers to move fluidly together while maintaining a similar spatial relationship between their bodies. It is the frame in social dancing that allows a lead (traditionally a man) to direct his partner through subtle changes in pressure on her upper back.
93. *West Side Story* Libretto, 1958. Jerome Robbins Papers. New York Public Library for the Performing Arts.
94. Bound Flow and Sustained Time Efforts combined with Far-Reach Space.
95. Far-Reach Space and Bound Flow Effort with Sustained Time Effort rather than Quick Time Effort.
96. Sectioned annotated script, 1958. Jerome Robbins Papers. New York Public Library for the Performing Arts.
97. "Saul Chaplin," 17.
98. An earlier *Variety* article mentions that *Porgy and Bess* would have "just the general meaning of song numbers flashed on screen as subtitles from time to time" ("O'Seas Chill," 3).

242 NOTES TO PAGES 86–95

99. "Subtitle Plot," 4.
100. Horst, "West Side Story."
101. Abramovitch, "Steven Spielberg."
102. Tiomkin, "Filmusicals' 2d 'Golden Age'," 43.
103. Moskowitz, "'West Side Story'," 2.

Chapter 4

1. Neupert, *History of the French New Wave Cinema*, 360.
2. See, especially, Hill, "Demy Monde"; Hill, "The New Wave," Hill, "The Films of Jacques Demy," Neupert, "Jacques Demy's *Bay of Angels*," Lazen, "'En Perme à Nantes.'"
3. Neupert, *History of the French New Wave Cinema*, 29.
4. Ibid., 86, 87, 165, 208.
5. Ibid., 65, 87. The IDHEC, still in Paris, is now La Fémis.
6. The École technique de photographie et de cinématographie (then on the rue de Vaugirard in Paris) is now the École supérieure nationale Louis-Lumière (in Saint-Denis).
7. Berthomé, *Jacques Demy*, 39.
8. The sense of a fantastical or holistic aesthetic often guides the titles of works about his filmmaking. See Duggan, *Queer Enchantments*; Taboulay, *Le cinéma enchanté de Jacques Demy*; Berthomé, *Jacques Demy et les racines du rêve*; Orléan, *Le monde enchanté de Jacques Demy*; Hill, "Demy Monde."
9. Berthomé, *Jacques Demy*, 110.
10. Ibid., 189, 190.
11. Moskowitz, "Les Demoiselles," 6; Hawkins, "'Filmmusicals," 78; "'Rochefort' First Big Scale French Tunepic'," 20.
12. Frederick, "French Film Youths," 5.
13. Berthomé, *Jacques Demy*, 191. Kenneth Harper's wife, dancer Pamela Hart, plays Judith in the film.
14. Discussions of *Les Demoiselles*'s American distributor frequently refer to the company as Warners–Seven Arts, but Eliot Hyman would not merge the two companies until 1967, notably right during the film's distribution period (Hoyt, *Hollywood Vault*, 191).
15. The Technicolor estimate was a cost of nearly £5,000 (Galea "Letter to P. Dussart"). Fonds Jacques Demy, La Cinémathèque française.
16. "Demy Succeeds With Filmmusicals," 25.
17. Clech et al, "D'un port à l'autre," 58. Translation by the author.
18. Throughout his career, Demy expressed distaste for the monetary aspects of filmmaking. Unlike Demy's partner, Agnès Varda, or Claude Berri, *Trois places pour le 26*'s producer, Demy did not create his own production company or become deeply invested in the financial aspects of his films. Berthomé suggests that some of Demy's financial issues stemmed from this reluctance to involve himself more deeply in the money behind his projects (*Jacques Demy*, 418).

NOTES TO PAGES 95–98   243

19. *Les Demoiselles de Rochefort* "Devis"; *Les Demoiselles de Rochefort* "Devis Estimatif." Fonds Jacques Demy, La Cinémathèque française.

20. Dale is less well known for his film work, but both he and Chakiris appeared in early theatrical runs of *West Side Story*.

21. All the budget data in this paragraph is converted to 1967 equivalent purchasing power in US dollars for more accurate comparison. More information is available in the budget data charts in appendix 2.

22. For more on this comparison, see Hill "Demy Monde: Jacques Demy," 55–100 and "Demy Monde: The New-Wave Films." Berthomé suggests that a film coproduction in 1966 would cost on average 3.48 million francs, or $700,000 (*Jacques Demy*, 192). Jean Renoir's 1954 *French Cancan*, also a musical of sorts with songs and a long dance set piece at the end, was one of several "big-budget quality productions" during this period (Williams, *Republic of Images*, 281), yet it still was presumably less expensive—accounting for inflation—than *Les Demoiselles* over a decade later. Crisp suggests that an average French film in 1954 cost 100 million francs, giving it an equivalent purchasing power of $353,000 in 1966 (*Classic French Cinema*, 86, 87). Even if Renoir's film cost three times above average for the period, his film would have still cost less than Demy's.

23. Mirisch, *I Thought We Were Making Movies*, 127.

24. Farmer, "The Singing Sixties," 125; "Tunepix," 15.

25. Fordin, *The Movies' Greatest Musicals*, n.p.

26. Crisp, *Classic French Cinema*, 123.

27. "Demy Succeeds," 25.

28. Michel and Ginot, *Danse au 20e siècle*, 51.

29. Ibid., 47; Stilwell, "Le Demy-monde," 124.

30. Michel and Ginot, *Danse au 20e siècle*, 47.

31. Ibid., 49.

32. Ibid., 50, 51.

33. "French Producer," 5. Although still performed regularly, the cancan had an artistic revival of sorts at nightclubs like the Lido and Moulin Rouge in 1953 ("Cancan Again Kicks Up Stir," 11).

34. Gene Moskowitz's reviews for *Variety* of the Lido and Moulin Rouge performances suggest that the house dancers of both nightclubs would perform simple choreography based on cabaret styles, some acrobatics, and older popular dances like the cancan, all in flashy costumes and surrounded by elaborate set dressings and other groups of "undraped girls" (Moskowitz, "Moulin Rouge, Paris," 101; Moskowitz, "Lido, Paris," 59). The descriptions of the Lido and Moulin Rouge shows suggest they were fairly similar, the Lido featuring content that benefited (or suffered) from better funding and more class.

35. Conway, "France," 32.

36. Moskowitz, "French Like Cow and Gang Films," 30.

37. Grant, *Rise and Fall*, 215.

38. Ibid., 230.

39. Ibid., 259.

244 NOTES TO PAGES 98-104

40. Reynolds and McCormick, *No Fixed Points*, 183.
41. "Boy and Girl Dancers," 15.
42. Berthomé, *Jacques Demy*, 191.
43. "Choreography," 18; Stewart, "Music as Written," 30, 31; "The Stage: 'Carrie,'" 15; Mac., 67; Kauf., 64. In later decades, Maen would also provide choreography for *The Muppet Show* (1976–1981) and would collaborate again with Gene Kelly for the latter's numbers when he guest starred on the show in Season 5, Episode 1.
44. Rehearsals started May 9, about three weeks before principal photography (de Goldschmidt "Telegram to Seven Arts"). Fonds Jacques Demy, La Cinémathèque française.
45. See Bordwell, *Narration in the Fiction Film*, 274–310.
46. Bordwell, *Poetics*, 377–380.
47. Thompson, *Breaking the Glass Armor*, 251.
48. For more on this topic, see chapter 1 of this book.
49. Dyer, "Entertainment and Utopia," 23.
50. Cohan, "Introduction: Musicals," 9.
51. Rubin, *Showstoppers*, 36.
52. Altman, *American Film Musical*, 70, 71.
53. Rubin, *Showstoppers*, 36.
54. Thompson, *Breaking the Glass Armor*, 260.
55. See appendix 2 for quantitative film data.
56. For a more in-depth exploration of these networks of cinematic citations, see chapter 6.
57. See appendix 2 for quantitative data. I distinguish between the average shot lengths of whole films and their musical numbers as the resulting averages often differ.
58. Conway, *Chanteuse*, 124.
59. *Meet Me In St Louis* does this more than my other American examples, because so much of the narrative action occurs in the Smith's house.
60. Henneton and Waldron point to location shooting as an important difference between *Les Demoiselles* and Hollywood productions (Henneton, "Jacques Demy's Musical Comedies," 231; Waldron, *Jacques Demy*, 61).
61. Thompson, *Breaking the Glass Armor*, 252; Faden "Visual Disturbances."
62. *Les Demoiselles de Rochefort* "Plans décor." Fonds Jacques Demy, La Cinémathèque française.
63. The sections in which dance would appear in the film was an early part of Demy's writing process. In some notes Demy made in preparation for the film, next to descriptions of the action occurring at "La Maison du Crime," as the location is described, Demy has written "DANSE" in red next to the description. This occurs at several places in his notes ("Notes diverses," Fonds Jacques Demy, La Cinémathèque française).
64. Successive Phrasing with Free Flow Effort. Capitalized phrases in text or in notes summarize my analysis using the more precise descriptive-analytical language from Laban/Bartenieff Movement Studies; for more on that taxonomy or the usage of specific terms see chapter 2 and appendix 1.

65. One of these phrases is the repeated quick straight-leg kicks that groups of dancers perform, with their hips in flexion, in the opening and closing numbers on the square, as well as in the background of the "Rencontres" number. The *West Side Story*-inspired leg suspension is another.
66. Faden, "Visual Disturbances."
67. And when bystanders do join in, they tend to sing instead of dance. Take, for example, Lorelei and Dorothy's guests in "Bye Bye Baby" from *Gentlemen Prefer Blondes*.
68. Springs and Travelling.
69. For more on the often close relationships between structure and ornamentation in art, see Gombrich, *Sense of Order*, 163–168.
70. Bordwell, *Narration*, 286.
71. Altman, *American Film Musical*, 21.
72. Stilwell, "Demy Monde," 134.
73. Altman, *American Film Musical*, 80–89.
74. Demy did initially consider a different ending to *Les Demoiselles*, in which the carnies leaving Rochefort accidentally hit Maxence with their truck rather than picking him up (Taboulay, *Cinéma enchanté*, 66).
75. Imagine, for example, if instead of Cosmo cheering Don up with "Make 'Em Laugh" in *Singin' in the Rain* after Don expresses his career doubts, Don instead sang to Cosmo about his car ride with Kathy, the cause of his professional and emotional turmoil.
76. The exception to this rule is the second-to-last of these numbers, the "Chanson de Solange," when Delphine joins Solange in singing the refrain that we originally hear in the "Chanson de Maxence."
77. Shape Flow.
78. Light Weight Effort.
79. Direct Space Effort.
80. Figures 4.5–4.8 serve as a reference point to find the precise moment I am discussing within each number.
81. Shape Flow.
82. Activation of Direct and Indirect Space Effort.
83. Diagonal Spatial Pulls.
84. Avoiding activation of Time Effort.
85. Light Weight Effort and Bound Flow Effort.
86. Activating Indirect Space Effort.
87. Shape Flow.
88. Direct Space Effort.
89. Shape Flow.
90. Light Weight Effort, Quick Time Effort, and Free Flow Effort.
91. Passion Drive.
92. The melody from the beginning of Andy's love number is also not shared by any of the other love numbers, but his uses the same melody as Solange's "Concerto," which he has found in the street after their meet cute.
93. Growing and shrinking Kinesphere.
94. Shape Flow.

246 NOTES TO PAGES 115–123

95. Narrowing of the Kinesphere.
96. See Doty, *Flaming Classics*, 131–154.
97. Axial spatial pulls.
98. Little movement into Planar or Diagonal spatial pulls.
99. A movement that initiates with an accent has an impulsive phrasing quality, whereas a movement that increases into an accent has an impactive phrasing quality. For more information about phrasing of movements and the relationship to Laban's Effort qualities, see Maletic, *Dance Dynamics*, 59–60.
100. Quick Time Effort and Light Weight Effort.
101. Bound Flow Effort and Direct/Indirect Space Effort, or Remote State.
102. Sustained Time Effort.
103. Strong Weight Effort.
104. Quick Time Effort.
105. Sustained Time Effort.
106. Sagittal movement.
107. Expansive Kinespheres.
108. Quick Time Effort and Impactful phrasing.
109. Free Flow Effort.
110. Strong Weight Effort.
111. This breaks down over the course of the film; as the carnies leave the townspeople continue to dance (including Yvonne and Solange and their romantic and dance partners, Simon and Andy).
112. Engaging both Indirect and Direct Space Effort.
113. Quick Time Effort and Bound Flow Effort, especially.
114. Sustained Time Effort and Free Flow Effort.
115. Engaging Sustained Time Effort and Strong Weight Effort.
116. Joseph M. Letter from Joseph M. Sugar to Gilbert de Goldschmidt, April 26, 1968. Fonds Jacques Demy, La Cinémathèque française.
117. Simsi, *Ciné-Passions*, 162.
118. Simsi lists *Les grandes vacances*, *Oscar*, *The Dirty Dozen*, and *You Only Live Twice* as the most-seen films in France for 1967 (Simsi, *Ciné-Passions*, 32). *Variety* also reports that *Les Demoiselles* didn't do particularly well in France or abroad (Moskowitz, "French Like Cow and Gang Films," 30).
119. A series of memos back and forth during the exhibition period suggests the French producers' frustration: Letter from Gilbert de Goldschmidt to Eliot Hyman, April 9, 1969; Letter from Eliot Hyman to Gilbert de Goldschmidt. May 8, 1969. Goldschmidt's disappointment comes after an agreed $200,000 buyout of his interest in the film in July 1967 (Letter from Norman Katz to Eliot Hyman, July 12, 1967.) Fonds Jacques Demy, La Cinémathèque française.
120. Greg G Morrison, "News About SEVEN ARTS" press release, July 17, 1967. Fonds Jacques Demy, La Cinémathèque française. Hoyt, *Hollywood Vault*, 190, 191.
121. Letter from Eliot Hyman to Gilbert de Goldschmidt, April 20, 1967. Fonds Jacques Demy, La Cinémathèque française.
122. Norman Katz received a copy of the American version in April 1967, and Eliot Hyman received a copy in late April or early May 1967 (Letter from Gilbert de

NOTES TO PAGES 123–127   247

Goldschmidt to Eliot Hyman, April 24, 1967; Letter from Gilbert de Goldschmidt to Eliot Hyman, May 31, 1967. Fonds Jacques Demy, La Cinémathèque française).

123. Letter from Joseph M. Sugar to Gilbert de Goldschmidt, March 22, 1968. Fonds Jacques Demy, La Cinémathèque française.

124. Orléan, "Los Angeles Trip," 114, translation by the author.

125. Ramaeker, "Demy in the New Hollywood," 44, 45.

126. Demy initially considered making the film in Hollywood and wrote to Columbia Pictures Division president Stanley Schneider to ask for his help on the film, without success (Letter from Jacques Demy to Stanley Schneider. N.d. Fonds Jacques Demy, La Cinémathèque française).

127. Oyallon-Koloski, "A Dance in Disguise," 59–74.

Chapter 5

1. For more on Jacques Demy's early filmmaking aesthetic, see chapter 4.

2. The subject was a popular trope of French cinema; Noël Burch and Geneviève Sellier suggest that of the thousand French film productions between 1929 and 1939, about a third touched on incestuous relationships between fathers and daughters (18–23).

3. Haustrade, "Jacques Demy," 77.

4. Several of the films Demy did make during this period received limited distribution in France or did not recoup their costs. *The Pied Piper* (1972) played only briefly in French theaters four years after its initial distribution, and *L'événement le plus important depuis que l'homme a marché sur la lune* (1973), although made on a modest budget, was a commercial failure (Amiel, "Jacques Demy," 103, 104). *Lady Oscar* (1979) was one of Demy's biggest commercial successes and earned back its investment after eight weeks in Japanese theaters. French distributors remained uninterested in screening the film or investing in subtitles for the English-language production (Haustrade, "Entretien (Jacques Demy)," 78).

5. Demy's planners from 1976 and 1978 have references to the "Anouchka" script and indicate trips to Russia to visit St Petersburg and Moscow. Jacques Demy collection, Ciné-Tamaris.

6. Tremois, "Film Invisible de Jacques Demy," 15.

7. Haustrade, "Entretien (Jacques Demy)," 78.

8. Demy's 1977 planner has notes about "Sheldon" on January 15 and September 26; this is likely Sheldon Harnick, who translated the lyrics for *The Umbrellas of Cherbourg*. In addition to any professional meetings, Demy also attended several Broadway shows in October and November 1976, seeing *Guys and Dolls*, *Pippin*, *The Wiz*, *Shenandoah*, *My Fair Lady*, *Grease*, and *Porgy and Bess*, as well as a magic show (Demy 1976 agenda). Jacques Demy collection, Ciné-Tamaris.

9. Amiel, "Jacques Demy," 106.

10. Ibid.

11. Thirty-five hundred people attended the Césars, which was also broadcast on the television station Antenne 2. Jean Gabin presided over the ceremony, Jean-Pierre

248 NOTES TO PAGES 127–130

Spiero directed the program, Michel Legrand provided musical accompaniment, and Demy staged the performers ("France's Oscar," 7; "Radio-Télévision," 12; La Bardonnie, "Les Césars d'Antenne 2," 26).

12. See chapter 8 for a broader history of *danse contemporaine* and French government initiatives during this period.

13. Banes, *Terpsichore in Sneakers*; Banes, *Democracy's Body*.

14. Michel and Ginot, *La danse au 20e siècle*, 175.

15. See Aprahamian, *Birth of Breaking* for a broader history of dance in American hip hop.

16. McCarren, *French Moves*, xii.

17. Ibid., xvi, xviii.

18. Ibid., 53.

19. Katy Varda, in conversation with the author, 2015.

20. "*Trois places pour le 26* production notes." Fonds Jacques Demy, La Cinémathèque française. Demy 1987 planner. Jacques Demy collection, Ciné-Tamaris.

21. "Jacques Demy, ou l'arbre gémeau." Translation by the author.

22. Grugeau, "Entretien avec Jacques Demy," 60. Translation by the author.

23. "Jacques Demy, ou l'arbre gémeau."

24. A note in Demy's planner from November 21, 1987, suggests that he was interested in American postmodern choreographers as well, as he attended at least one of Trisha Brown's shows. Jacques Demy collection, Ciné-Tamaris.

25. Clech et al., "D'un port à l'autre," 10.

26. Shore, *Rolling Stone Book*, 285.

27. Ibid., 14, 15. The cinematic interest in hip hop grew more significantly in 1984 when Hollywood studios, afraid that it would be a short-lived phenomenon, attempted to capitalize on the movement that was gaining awareness and popularity. Two studios released competing break dance-centered films that year: Orion's *Beat Street* and Cannon Films' *Breakin'* (Oyallon-Koloski, "Danceploitation," 15–27).

28. "Devis Récapitulatif (*Trois places pour le 26*)," April 5, 1988. Fonds Pathé, Jérôme Seydoux-Pathé Foundation.

29. "Devis (*Les Demoiselles de Rochefort*)," March 24, 1966. Fonds Jacques Demy, La Cinémathèque française.

30. None of the budget documents for these films specifically reference costs for location shooting, which would give an even clearer comparison for the overall production design of each film. Unfortunately, *Trois places*'s cost estimate is also vague on the total cost of choreography and dancers.

31. The total for the corps of dancers, plus the four Americans, was estimated at 2 million francs ("Devis Récapitulatif (*Trois places pour le 26*)," April 5, 1988. Fonds Pathé, Jérôme Seydoux-Pathé Foundation.). Michael Peters arrived beforehand with his assistants and four American dancers; Demy suggests that "the physical work began at the beginning of the year, I called Michael Peters in Los Angeles in January, he arrived in February, and until May we were preparing" (Clech et al., "D'un port à l'autre," 58. Translation by the author).

32. *Trois places pour le 26* Press Book, 1988. Fonds Jacques Demy, La Cinémathèque française.

NOTES TO PAGES 130–136 249

33. The tension came to a head on May 1, 1988—nine days before filming was to start—as Demy has a note in his planner about an argument with Montand, one that seems to have emerged after a long day of prerecording songs for the film (Demy planner, 1988. Jacques Demy collection, Ciné-Tamaris). In a recent making-of documentary about the film, this subject is mentioned by multiple people involved in the project: Mathilda May, executive producer Pierre Grunstein, and costume designer Rosalie Varda ("Dans les coulisses").

34. Engagement of the arms along the Vertical Plane diameters with Quick Time and Direct Flow Efforts. Capitalized phrases in-text or in notes summarize my analysis using the more precise descriptive-analytical language from Laban/Bartenieff Movement Studies; for more on that taxonomy or the usage of specific terms see chapter 2 and appendix 1.

35. See appendix 2 for this quantitative data.

36. For information on individual musical numbers or music videos, see data charts in appendix 2.

37. Clech et al., "D'un port à l'autre," 58. Translation by the author.

38. See appendix 2 for more quantitative data.

39. Clech et al., "D'un port à l'autre," 10.

40. *Trois places pour le 26* Press Book, 1988. Fonds Jacques Demy, La Cinémathèque française.

41. Altman, *American Film Musical*, 231.

42. Ibid.

43. We see something closer to this structure in *Easter Parade* (1948) when Ann Miller's character leaves and is replaced by Judy Garland, but this film seems to be the exception rather than the rule according to Altman's analysis (Altman, *American Film Musical*, 248).

44. Brannigan, *Dancefilm*, 141, 142.

45. Quick Time Effort.

46. An absence of fluctuating Time Effort.

47. Direct Space Effort.

48. Bound Flow Effort.

49. Sustained Time Effort.

50. A Near-Reach, compressed Kinesphere.

51. Effort Life.

52. Quick Time and Free Flow Efforts.

53. Weight Effort.

54. Light Weight Effort and Indirect Space Effort.

55. Bound Flow Effort and Strong Weight Effort manifesting as Shape Flow.

56. Activating the Sagittal plane.

57. Quick Time Effort and Impulsive phrasing. Vera Maletic describes Impulsive phrasing as that movement with an initial accent that decreases in intensity (*Dance Dynamics*, 59).

58. Spoke-Like Directional movement.

59. Indirect Space Effort and Quick Time Effort manifesting in an Awake State.

250 NOTES TO PAGES 136–145

60. Bound Flow Effort.
61. Demy "Découpage technique relié," 47. April 8, 1988. Fonds Pathé, Jérôme Seydoux-Pathé Foundation. Translation by the author.
62. Demy "Découpage technique relié," 70. April 8, 1988. Fonds Pathé, Jérôme Seydoux-Pathé Foundation. Translation by the author.
63. A single-unit turn would occur when the whole body moves simultaneously.
64. Engaging Sagittal Plane Spatial Pulls, in particular.
65. Moore, *Harmonic Structure*, 249.
66. Activating Vertical Plane Spatial Pulls.
67. Sustained Time Effort.
68. Light Weight Effort.
69. Locomotion with Vibratory Effort Phrasing. Maletic suggests Vibratory phrasing "consists of sudden repetitions that continue over a shorter or longer period of time" (*Dance Dynamics*, 60).
70. Multi-Unit.
71. Sustained Time Effort.
72. Expanding her Kinesphere.
73. Moving in the Sagittal Plane.
74. Free Flow Effort and Resilient Phrasing.
75. Activating Planar and Diagonal Spatial Pulls.
76. Single-Unit.
77. Successive rather than Simultaneous or Sequential movement.
78. Sustained Time Effort with a reduction of Light Weight Effort and Shape Flow.
79. Shaping.
80. Shape Flow.
81. For more on Demy's activation of backstage musical conventions, see Père and Colmant, *Jacques Demy*, 268; Taboulay, *Cinéma enchanté*, 142; Berthomé, *Jacques Demy*, 386; Angiboust, "Chanter le jour," 64; Henneton, "Jacques Demy's Musical Comedies," 227.
82. Altman, *American Film Musical*, 200.
83. Additional analysis of show musicals from the 1940s, 1950s, and 1960s would help to nuance the shifts in genre norms. Altman discusses later filmic examples, but the bulk of his analysis is based on films from the 1930s.
84. Altman, *American Film Musical*, 206, 208.
85. "Dans les coulisses." Translation by the author.
86. Demy "Découpage technique relié," 148. April 8, 1988. Fonds Pathé, Jérôme Seydoux-Pathé Foundation. Translation by the author.
87. The French expression "c'est du cinéma," means "it's all an act" and does not have an equivalent in English that maintains the pun.
88. Demy "Découpage technique relié," 148. April 8, 1988. Fonds Pathé, Jérôme Seydoux-Pathé Foundation. Translation by the author.
89. Olivier Ducastel, in conversation with the author, April 23, 2013.
90. Altman, *American Film Musical*, 208, 209.
91. One notable exception is *Singin' in the Rain* (1952), which devotes a whole scene to the technical complications involved in the shift to talking pictures.

NOTES TO PAGES 146–156 251

92. Altman suggests this as well (*American Film Musical*, 212).
93. Berthomé, *Jacques Demy*, 386; Père and Colmant, *Jacques Demy*, 268.
94. Effort qualities.
95. Effort Life.
96. Quick Time Effort and Bound Flow Effort.
97. Free Flow Effort.
98. She moves into Sagittal and Horizontal Planar Spatial Pulls.
99. Quick Time Effort and Bound Flow Effort.
100. Bound Flow Effort and a smaller Kinesphere.
101. Movement primarily along Axial Spatial Pulls.
102. Free Flow Effort and Quick Time Effort.
103. Mobile State, or Flow and Time Effort.
104. Free Flow Effort and Quick Time Effort.
105. Quick Time Effort and Bound Flow Effort.
106. *Le Monde* and *Cahiers du cinéma*'s reviews of the film were positive overall (Sicilier, "L'amour toujours," 13; Magny, "Les mi-lieux de Demy," 6–9). *Variety*'s reviewer found the film to be in "surprisingly poor taste" (Len., "Review," 19).
107. Berthomé suggests the film received only 54,000 entries in its first week (Berthomé, *Jacques Demy*, 403), and Simon Simsi's *Ciné-Passions* indicates that *Trois places* did not top more than 500,000 entries in its entire French run (Simsi, *Ciné-Passions*, 272).
108. Conway, "France," 29.
109. We could compare, for example, Yves Montand's character in *Trois places pour le 26* to his role in Marcel Carné's *Les Portes de la nuit* (1946).
110. Regarding *Trois places pour le 26*, Demy found that some audience members even tried to convince themselves that the act of incest had not occurred, despite explicit narrative cues (Clech et al., " D'un port à l'autre," 57).

Chapter 6

1. Klein, "Genre," 195.
2. Feuer, "The Self-Reflexive Musical," 31–40.
3. We can consider, for example, the uncredited imitation of Cole Porter's "Be a Clown" song in *Singin' in the Rain*'s "Make 'Em Laugh," and Hollywood's extensive track record of incorporating music and dance traditions from African American labor, often without industrial acknowledgment or financial compensation. See Clover, "Dancin' in the Rain," 157–167; Igartuburu, "Fugitive Plots."
4. This video essay is also available on Vimeo at https://vimeo.com/cinemajok/endle ssconversations.
5. Grant argues for the academic value of audiovisual, practice-led scholarship ("The audiovisual essay," 255–265), and O'Leary argues for the research value specifically of parametric and constraint-based practices, less in a hermeneutic or explanatory way and more in a performative one ("Workshop of Potential Scholarship").
6. Keathley, "La Caméra-stylo," 181–182.

252   NOTES TO PAGES 156–162

7. Oyallon-Koloski, "Musical Grid Videographic Deformations."
8. Keathley, Mittell, and Grant, "Videographic Epigraph."
9. Chion, *Audio-Vision*, 189.
10. Some omissions are deliberate; in order to make space for less-emphasized connections, for example, *Singin' in the Rain* is absent.
11. To create the looped effect, the video repeats the five-minute piece once.

Chapter 7

1. This video essay is also available on Vimeo at https://vimeo.com/cinemajok/diegeticf lutters.
2. See chapter 1 and Altman, *American Film Musical*, 42; Cohan, "Introduction," 3; Dyer, "Entertainment," 19; Feuer, "Self-Reflexive Musical," 34; Rubin, "Busby Berkeley," 56.
3. Mandy Moore, in conversation with the author, May 23, 2019.
4. Brannigan, *Dancefilm*, 160–161.
5. For a broader theorization of musical moments, see Herzog, *Dreams of Difference*, 5–8.
6. Dyer, *Only Entertainment*, 19–35.

Chapter 8

1. McLean, *Dying Swans*, 15, 24.
2. McLean, *Dying Swans*; McLean "Flirting with Terpsichore," 70.
3. Jeanine Basinger sees animated- and documentary-inflected musicals as the dominant forms during this period, and dance was certainly present in these iterations of the genre as well (*The Movie Musical!*, 531–580), though Sean Griffin argues that during the 1970s, in particular, dance in musicals was a lesser presence (*Free and Easy?*, 253). See Griffin, *Free and Easy?* and Kessler, *Destabilizing the Hollywood Musical* for a broader history of the post studio system American musical.
4. Oyallon-Koloski, "Danceploitation," 15–27.
5. Griffin, *Free and Easy?*, 298.
6. See Powrie and Cadalanu, *The French Film Musical*, for a broader history of French musicals.
7. See Powrie and Cadalanu, *French Film Musical*; Lacombe and Porcile, *Musiques du cinéma français*; Dauncey and Cannon, *Popular Music in France*; Conway, *Chanteuse in the City*.
8. This list includes *On connaît la chanson* (Alain Resnais, 1997), *Jeanne et le garçon formidable* (Olivier Ducastel and Jacques Martineau, 1998), *Huit femmes* (François Ozon, 2002), *Les choristes* (Christophe Barratier, 2004), *Crustacés et Coquillages* (Olivier Ducastel and Jacques Martineau, 2005), *On va s'aimer* (Ivan Calbérac, 2006), *Les Chansons d'amour* (Christophe Honoré, 2007), *Agathe Cléry* (Etienne Chatiliez, 2008), *Faubourg 36* (Christophe Barratier, 2008), *Les Bien-aimés* (Christophe Honoré,

NOTES TO PAGES 162–165   253

2011), *Sur quel pied danser* (Paul Calori and Kostia Testut, 2016), *Swing Rendezvous* (Gérome Barry, 2023). For more on musical shorts made during this period, see Cadalanu, "Expérimenter le film musical," 265–284.

9. Martin, "Cinéma." Translation by the author.

10. See Plantinga for further distinctions between objective and subjective forms of ontological realism (*Alternative Realities*, 22, 23).

11. Michael, *French Blockbusters*, 9, 34.

12. Frodon, *L'âge moderne du cinéma français*, 888.

13. Olivier Ducastel and Jacques Martineau, in conversation with the author, April 23, 2013.

14. Bouzet, "1997."

15. For more on the later part of Demy's filmmaking career and his struggle to secure financing for his later projects, see chapter 5.

16. Olivier Ducastel and Jacques Martineau, in conversation with the author, June 2, 2021.

17. Raja, "'Jeanne et le garçon formidable.'"

18. Frodon, *L'âge moderne du cinéma français*, 889; Austin, *Contemporary French Cinema*, 219.

19. Austin, *Contemporary French Cinema*, 220.

20. Olivier Ducastel and Jacques Martineau, in conversation with the author, June 2, 2021. Translation by the author.

21. Ibid.

22. Even on their nonmusical films, Ducastel and Martineau organize similar workshops, budget permitting, with Sylvie Giron and their actors to develop each character's physical aesthetic. For *Drôle de Félix* (2000), especially, they found that "over the course of the workshops, Sami Bouajila [the lead] found a movement quality specific to his character that we made frequent reference to during the shoot. Sami, in certain shots, dances with the camera" (Olivier Ducastel and Jacques Martineau, in conversation with the author, October 2, 2011).

23. Olivier Ducastel and Jacques Martineau, in conversation with the author, October 2, 2011.

24. Sylvie Giron, in conversation with the author, April 26, 2013.

25. *Jeanne's* connection to Jacques Demy is aesthetic but also personal. Olivier Ducastel was an assistant editor on *Trois places pour le 26* (1988), Demy's final feature. Demy's editor for *Trois places* and several of his other later features, Sabine Mamou, was the editor for *Jeanne* as well. And Demy's son with filmmaker Agnès Varda, Mathieu Demy, plays the male lead in the film, though this casting was never a foregone conclusion, as the filmmakers have discussed on multiple occasions (Raja, "'Jeanne et le garçon formidable,'" as well as Martineau's introduction to a screening of *Jeanne* at the Cinémathèque française on January 3, 2019). Ducastel and Martineau, along with Jacques Demy's family and other members of the French filmmaking community, knew that Demy had died of complications from AIDS in 1990, but this was not known to the general public or the French press until Agnès Varda's discussion of the topic in her 2008 film *Les plages d'Agnès*. It was Mathieu Demy who first approached

254 NOTES TO PAGES 165–170

Ducastel and Martineau about playing the part; the filmmakers indicated that they had him in mind as a possible lead but had not wanted to create an indelicate situation, given that the film would already evoke Demy's aesthetic. Demy's family has chosen not to speak about how he contracted the virus.

26. They describe *Jeanne* as "a project directly inspired by Demy's work and thought of as an homage and as a proposal to continue the kind of musical film that Demy initiated." Olivier Ducastel and Jacques Martineau, in conversation with the author, October 2, 2011. Translation by the author.

27. Olivier Ducastel and Jacques Martineau, in conversation with the author, October 2, 2011. Translation by the author. For more on *Jeanne*'s references to Hollywood and Demy's cinema, see Oyallon-Koloski, "Genre Experimentation," 91–107.

28. Olivier Ducastel and Jacques Martineau, in conversation with the author, October 2, 2011. Translation by the author.

29. Olivier Ducastel and Jacques Martineau, in conversation with the author, April 23, 2013.

30. Olivier Ducastel and Jacques Martineau, in conversation with the author, June 2, 2021. Translation by the author.

31. See appendix 2 for all the statistics discussed in this section.

32. Olivier Ducastel and Jacques Martineau, in conversation with the author, April 23, 2013. Translation by the author.

33. It should be noted that Resnais's inclusion of songs in his film resemble musical moments, as theorized by Amy Herzog (*Dreams of Difference*, 5–8), more than musical numbers. The moments of characters lip syncing to popular French songs usually occur midshot and midconversation and last no more than half a minute on average.

34. See Brunick, Cutting, and DeLong, "Low-Level Features," 134; Carroll and Seely, "Cognitivism, Psychology, and Neuroscience," 60; Bordwell, "The Viewer's Share," 30–31; and Smith, "Watching You Watch Movies," 174, 178.

35. Bazin, "Evolution of Film Language," 88.

36. "A film with songs," to them, "is not a musical comedy, which for us must always associate the pleasure of music, song, and movement." Olivier Ducastel and Jacques Martineau, in conversation with the author, October 2, 2011. Translation by the author.

37. See *On va s'aimer* (Ivan Calbérac, 2006), *Les Bien-aimés* (Christophe Honoré, 2011), and *Sur quel pied danser* (Paul Caolri and Kostia Testut, 2016).

38. Modern dance forms are also visible in Robert Alton's "Choreography" number from *White Christmas* (Michael Curtiz, 1954), which parodies Martha Graham's technique, Michael Kidd's choreography for "Lonesome Polecat" in *Seven Brides for Seven Brothers* (Stanley Donen, 1954) which in part anticipates postmodern choreographers' interest in pedestrian movements and everyday tasks, and Louis Johnson's choreography for *The Wiz* (Sidney Lumet, 1978), shaped by his choreography for the Alvin Ailey American Dance Theatre and his studies with Katherine Dunham and Jerome Robbins.

39. McLean, *Being Rita Hayworth*, 172–197.

NOTES TO PAGES 170–180 255

40. Corbett, "Katherine Dunham," 89–95.
41. Olivier Ducastel and Jacques Martineau, in conversation with the author, October 2, 2011. Translation by the author.
42. Banes, *Terpsichore in Sneakers*, xiii.
43. Ibid., xxxvi.
44. Banes, *Democracy's Body*.
45. Banes, *Terpsichore in Sneakers*, xiv–xvi.
46. Noisette, *Danse contemporaine*, 20, 34
47. Michel and Ginot, *Danse au 20e siècle*, 47.
48. Ibid., 175.
49. Ibid., 178; Noisette, *Danse contemporaine*, 22–23.
50. Michel and Ginot, *Danse au 20e siècle*, 178. Translation by the author.
51. Ibid., 183. Translation by the author.
52. Noisette, *Danse contemporaine*, 18.
53. Olivier Ducastel and Jacques Martineau, in conversation with the author, June 2, 2021.
54. Michel and Ginot, *Danse au 20e siècle*, 187. Translation by the author.
55. Ibid., 186. Translation by the author.
56. Ibid., 190. Translation by the author.
57. Olivier Ducastel and Jacques Martineau, in conversation with the author, October 2, 2011. Translation by the author.
58. Banes, *Terpsichore in Sneakers*, 17.
59. Sylvie Giron, in conversation with the author, April 26, 2013. Translation by the author.
60. Ibid.
61. Contact Improvisation is an improvisation-based dance form initiated in the 1970s that explores the relationship between two or more moving bodies. Participants play with the relationship to gravity as they sense, share, and transfer the weight of their bodies and their partner(s).
62. Capitalized terms and phrases in the text and notes summarize my analysis using the more precise descriptive-analytical language from Laban/Bartenieff Movement Studies; for more on that taxonomy or the usage of specific terms see chapter 2 and appendix 1.
63. Free Flow Effort and Shape Flow.
64. Traveling, Rotation, Changes of Support, and Springs.
65. Sustained Time Effort Falling along the High/Low Sagittal diameter.
66. A Rotated Spring in Quick Time Effort initiated by Flexion of the right elbow.
67. Michel and Ginot, *Danse au 20e siècle*, 54.
68. Noisette, *Danse contemporaine*, 15.
69. Ibid.
70. Banes, *Democracy's Body*, 133.
71. A Far-Reach Peripheral Pathway along the Front-High to Back-Low Sagittal Plane Diameter.
72. Olivier Ducastel and Jacques Martineau, in conversation with the author, June 2, 2021.

256 NOTES TO PAGES 180–191

73. Olivier Ducastel and Jacques Martineau, in conversation with the author, April 23, 2013. Translation by the author.
74. Ibid.
75. Ducastel and Martineau remain discreet about the specific figures who objected to the film's content.
76. Olivier Ducastel and Jacques Martineau, in conversation with the author, April 23, 2013.
77. Olivier Ducastel and Jacques Martineau, in conversation with the author, June 2, 2021.
78. The film also includes reference to Chinese immigrants in France by having the woman in the Chinese restaurant sing about Tsingtao beer while handing Jeanne and her sister Sophie their lunch order, a moment that lands more clumsily.
79. Raja, "'Jeanne et le garçon formidable.'"
80. Weight Effort and Free Flow Effort.
81. Bound Flow Effort.
82. Quick Time Effort.
83. Time Effort and Flow Effort.
84. A held Body Attitude with Resilient Effort phrasing.
85. Mandelbaum, "'Sur quel pied danser.'"

Chapter 9

1. Cornish, "Movie Interviews."
2. Locatelli, "Paul Fraisse," 85.
3. Capitalized terms and phrases in the text and notes indicate the more precise descriptive-analytical language from Laban/Bartenieff Movement Studies. For a summary of the Laban/Bartenieff Movement Analysis vocabulary, see chapter 2 and appendix 1.
4. Box Office Mojo, "La La Land."
5. See Madison, "*La La Land*"; Gabbard, *La La Land*, 92–103; Abdul-Jabbar, "How 'La La Land' Misleads"; Cohan, *Hollywood Musicals*, 204.
6. For a more in-depth study of this history, see Garcia, *Migration of Musical Film*.
7. Garcia, *Movie Musical*, 20.
8. Powers, "*La La Land*"; Delorme, "Hollywoodland," 42.
9. See McQueen, "After 'The Golden Age.'"
10. Griffin, *Free and Easy?*, 279–291; Oyallon-Koloski, "Danceploitation," 16–18; Smith, "Ancillary Markets," 143; Kessler, "Gone in a *Flash(dance)*," 129–149.
11. Griffin, *Free and Easy?*, 319. Griffin also emphasizes Disney's role in prioritizing narratively integrated musicals in the 1980s and 1990s through their live-action and animated films (*Free and Easy?*, 308, 309).
12. Griffin, *Free and Easy?*, 320–321; Backstein, "Stayin' Alive," 300.
13. See appendix 2 for quantitative data.
14. See Hunting and McQueen, "A Musical Marriage," 289–308.

NOTES TO PAGES 192–200   257

15. While not disconnected from the film plot, "Hindi Sad Diamonds" also shares similarities to the item number in popular Hindi cinema through its emphasis on female bodies and spectacle; see Iyer, *Dancing Women*, 200–201.
16. Bordwell, *Way Hollywood Tells It*, 121.
17. Ibid., 134–135.
18. Ibid., 123.
19. Ibid., 180.
20. See also Lewis, "The Virtuosic Camera."
21. Bordwell, *Way Hollywood Tells It*, 180.
22. Griffin, *Free and Easy?*, 291
23. Mandy Moore, in conversation with the author, May 23, 2019.
24. Kaufman, "Triumphant 'La La Land.'"
25. In our interview, Chazelle explicitly used Bordwell's term in an earlier moment to describe his understanding of contemporary Hollywood aesthetics (Bordwell, *Way Hollywood Tells It*).
26. Damien Chazelle, in conversation with author, July 20, 2018.
27. Bordwell, *Way Hollywood Tells It*, 121–123.
28. Garcia, "*La La Land*."
29. Damien Chazelle, in conversation with the author, February 20, 2020. "St. Louis Blues," "Black & Tan," "Jazz Dance," and *Chronique d'un été* were among the films Damien Chazelle curated for the University of Wisconsin Cinematheque in 2018 ("Damien Chazelle in Person!" *The Cinematheque* website).
30. Dillon, "La La Land."
31. Damien Chazelle, in conversation with the author, February 20, 2020.
32. Dillon, "La La Land."
33. Feinberg, "'Awards Chatter.'"
34. Mandy Moore, in conversation with the author, May 23, 2019; Murphy, "Damien Chazelle Narrates."
35. Mandy Moore, in conversation with the author, May 23, 2019.
36. Ibid.
37. For more on *Les Demoiselles de Rochefort*'s industrial history, see chapter 4.
38. See in particular the discussion of *La La Land* in Basinger, *Movie Musical*. Emma Stone did have some professional experience, as she made her Broadway debut as Sally Bowles in the 2014 revival of *Cabaret*.
39. Backstein, "Stayin' Alive," 297.
40. Garcia, "*La La Land*"; Backstein, "Stayin' Alive," 294.
41. Mandy Moore, in conversation with the author, May 23, 2019.
42. Ibid.
43. Backstein, "Stayin' Alive," 296.
44. Damien Chazelle, in conversation with the author, July 20, 2018.
45. An absence of Time Effort.
46. Sudden Time Effort.
47. Morgan, *Lure of the Image*, 18.
48. Ferrera, *Steadicam*, 87.

258 NOTES TO PAGES 200–211

49. Damien Chazelle, in conversation with the author, July 20, 2018.
50. Ibid.
51. For more on the ways that musicals play with this concept of diegetic fluttering, see chapter 7.
52. Powers, "La La Land."
53. Mandy Moore, in conversation with the author, May 23, 2019.
54. Damien Chazelle, in conversation with author, July 20, 2018.
55. Gene Kelly created most of his dream ballets during this decade; see Genné, *Dance Me a Song*, 193–228.
56. De Mille's choreography popularized a style, Rick Altman argues, pioneered by the modern dance choreographer Martha Graham and ballet choreographers Léonide Massine and Eugene Loring (who worked for Hollywood in the 1940s): Altman, *American Film Musical*, 283. Jane Feuer argues that these sequences had their roots in 1930s Broadway musical comedies (Feuer, *The Hollywood Musical*, 73–74). Adrienne McLean suggests that George Balanchine's "Slaughter on Tenth Avenue" number from the Broadway musical *On Your Toes* (1936) was also influential in this regard (McLean, *Dying Swans*, 134).
57. Damien Chazelle, in conversation with the author, February 20, 2020.
58. See Dyer, *Only Entertainment*, 19–35.
59. Plantinga, *Alternative Realities*, 3; Ramaeker, "New Hollywood," 120.
60. Dillon, "La La Land."
61. Murphy, "Damien Chazelle Narrates."
62. Mandy Moore, in conversation with the author, May 23, 2019.
63. Damien Chazelle, in conversation with the author, July 20, 2018.
64. Ferrara, *Steadicam*, 83.
65. Bird, "Dancing, Flying Camera Jockeys," 50.
66. Ibid.
67. For broader investigations of this question, see Morgan, *Lure of the Image*; Keating, *Dynamic Frame*; Schonig, *Shape of Motion*.
68. See LaViers, "Style Based Robotic Motion," for an in-depth, LBMS-derived analysis of human versus humanoid robotic range of motion (4327–4332).
69. Morgan, *Lure of the Image*, 12.
70. Ibid.
71. Keating, *The Dynamic Frame*, 97.
72. Ibid., 79, 96, 97.
73. Ibid., 98. See also Keating, "A Homeless Ghost" and "Motifs of Movement and Modernity."
74. Shape Flow.
75. Morgan suggests that "imperfect" follow shots indicate authenticity, in nonfiction work especially, because "the filmmakers could not anticipate the movement of their subjects," yet this technique can be mobilized in fiction cinema as well, creating an effect that the camera "both does and does not exist in the world of the film" (Morgan, *Lure of the Image*, 58).
76. Body Attitude.

NOTES TO PAGES 211–224 259

77. Gabbard discusses the cinematic reference here to Frank Tashlin's *The Girl Can't Help It* (Gabbard, *La La Land*, 93).
78. Damien Chazelle, in conversation with author, July 20, 2018.
79. Panaglide footage, in contrast to Steadicam footage, does emphasize a feeling of reactivated Light Weight Effort in its inherent bobbing motion, visible in Bird's examples (see Bird, "Feeling and Thought as They Take Form").
80. Effort Life.
81. Laban, *Choreutics*, 94.
82. Dillon, "*La La Land*."
83. Damien Chazelle, in conversation with author, July 20, 2018.
84. Email from Damien Chazelle to Mandy Moore, August 4, 2015. Damien Chazelle personal collection.
85. Bird, "Dancing, Flying Camera Jockeys," 55.
86. Bird, "Feeling and Thought."
87. Isola, "Sit Down with Ari Robbins."
88. Bird, "Dancing, Flying Camera Jockeys," 57.
89. Bird, "Feeling and Thought."
90. Ibid.
91. Many recordings of Contact Improvisation jams exist online. See, for example, a Contact Improv jam at Roehampton Dance on May 20, 2011, https://www.youtube.com/watch?v=QdKZlryJ4HY.
92. Bird, "Dancing, Flying Camera Jockeys," 56.
93. Damien Chazelle, in conversation with author, July 20, 2018.
94. Free Flow Effort.
95. Bound Flow Effort.
96. Damien Chazelle, in conversation with the author, February 20, 2020.
97. Ibid.
98. Lattanzio, "Lin-Manuel Miranda."
99. Josh Spiegel (@mousterpiece), "Movie-musical directors, hold a shot for more than two seconds of dancers performing choreography. You can do it. I believe in you." Twitter post, June 27, 2021, https://twitter.com/mousterpiece/status/1409233716900212739.
100. Justin Peck (@justin_peck), "One of the things I'm most proud of about our @ westsidestorymovie is that the entire cast gives a fully authentic and genuine performance in their dancing . . ." Instagram post, December 11, 2021, https://www.instagram.com/p/CXWPcYplFmK/.
101. See appendix 2 for this quantitative data.

Appendix 1

1. Laban, *Mastery of Movement*, 12.
2. Maletic, *Dance Dynamics*, 59

260　NOTES TO PAGES 224–228

3. Ibid., 60.
4. Ibid.,
5. Maletic, *Dance Dynamics*, 59.
6. Laban, *Choreutics*, 10.
7. Ibid., 94.
8. Moore, "Introduction," 95.
9. Ibid., 101.
10. Ibid.

Appendix 2

1. Bordwell, *Way Hollywood Tells It*, 121.
2. This average comes from a quantitative study I have done of 260 numbers from 31 Hollywood musicals, spanning from 1933 to 1961. The chosen numbers come from well-known films from the period like *Dames*, *Top Hat*, *Singin' in the Rain*, *The Band Wagon*, *Seven Brides for Seven Brothers*, and *West Side Story*, as well as from films selected randomly according to the method used in Bordwell, Staiger, and Thompson, *The Classical Hollywood Cinema*, 388–389.

References

Archival Collections

Fonds Jacques Demy, the Cinémathèque française. Paris, France.
Jerome Robbins Papers, Jerome Robbins Dance Division, The New York Public Library for the Performing Arts. New York, USA.
Jacques Demy collection, Ciné-Tamaris. Paris, France.
Fonds Pathé, Jérôme Seydoux-Pathé Foundation. Paris, France.

Bibliography

Abdul-Jabbar, Kareem. "How 'La La Land' Misleads on Race, Romance and Jazz." *Hollywood Reporter,* February 15, 2017. https://www.hollywoodreporter.com/news/general-news/la-la-land-disappoints-bigoted-race-portrayal-childish-romance-975786/.

Abramovitch, Seth. "Steven Spielberg Met with Puerto Ricans About 'West Side Story' Concerns." *Variety,* January 15, 2019. https://www.hollywoodreporter.com/movies/movie-news/steven-spielberg-met-puerto-rican-activists-west-side-story-concerns-1176285/.

Acevedo-Muñoz, Ernesto R. *West Side Story as Cinema: The Making and Impact of an American Masterpiece.* Lawrence: University Press of Kansas, 2013.

Allen, Robert C., and Douglas Gomery. *Film History: Theory and Practice.* New York: McGraw-Hill, 1985.

Altman, Rick. *The American Film Musical.* Bloomington: Indiana University Press, 1989.

Altman, Rick. "From Homosocial to Heterosexual: The Musical's Two Projects." In *The Sound of Musicals,* edited by Steven Cohan, 19–29. London: British Film Institute, 2010.

American Film Institute. "Q&A with Jacques Demy." 1971; Criterion, 2014. DVD.

Amiel, Mireille. "Jacques Demy: Le Joueur de flûte." *Cinema 76,* no. 205 (1976): 102–106.

Angiboust, Sylvain. "Chanter le jour, chanter la nuit: Notes sur la musique dans les films de Jacques Demy." *L'avant-scène cinéma,* no. 602 (2013): 62–69.

Appadurai, Arjun. "Disjuncture and Difference in the Global Cultural Economy." *Theory Culture Society* 7, no. 2–3 (1990): 295–310. DOI: 10.1177/026327690007002017.

Aprahamian, Serouj "Midus." *The Birth of Breaking: Hip-Hop History from the Floor Up.* New York: Bloomsbury, 2023.

Argyle, Michael. *Bodily Communication.* London: Methuen, 1975.

Austin, Guy. *Contemporary French Cinema: An Introduction.* Manchester, UK: Manchester University Press, 2008.

Austin-Smith, Brenda. "Acting Matters: Noting Performance in Three Films." In *Theorizing Film Acting,* edited by Aaron Taylor, 19–32. New York: Routledge, 2012.

262 REFERENCES

Backstein, Karen. "'Stayin' Alive': The Post-Studio Hollywood Musical." In *American Film History: Selected Readings, 1960 to Present*, edited by Cynthia Lucia, Roy Grundmann, and Art Simon, 286–303. Chichester, UK: John Wiley, 2016.

Bales, Melanie, and Karen Eliot, eds. Introduction to *Dance on Its Own Terms: Histories and Methodologies*, 3–8. New York: Oxford University Press, 2013.

Balio, Tino. *MGM*. New York: Routledge, 2018.

Banes, Sally. *Democracy's Body: Judson Dance Theatre, 1962–1964*. Ann Arbor: UMI Research Press, 1993.

Banes, Sally. *Terpsichore in Sneakers: Post-Modern Dance*. Middletown, CT: Wesleyan University Press, 1987.

Baron, Cynthia, and Sharon Marie Carnicke. Introduction to *Reframing Screen Performance*, 1–10. Ann Arbor: University of Michigan Press, 2008.

Bartenieff, Irmgard, and Dori Lewis. *Body Movement: Coping with the Environment*. Abingdon: Routledge, 2002.

Basinger, Jeanine. *The Movie Musical!* New York: Penguin Random House, 2019.

Bazin, André. "The Evolution of Film Language." In *What Is Cinema?*, translated by Timothy Barnard, 87–106. Montreal: Caboose, 2009.

Bazin, André. "*Umberto D*: A Great Work." In *What Is Cinema? Volume 2*, translated by Hugh Gray, 79–82. Berkeley: University of California Press, 2005.

Becker, Svea, and Bruce Williams. "What Ever Happened to *West Side Story*? Gene Kelly, Jazz Dance, and Not So Real Men in Jacques Demy's *The Young Girls of Rochefort*." *New Review of Film and Television Studies* 6, no. 3 (December 2008): 303–321.

Belton, John. "Cinemascope and the Widescreen Revolution." *Cinégrafie* 16 (2003): 244–253.

Beltrán, Mary C. *Latina/o Stars in U.S. Eyes: The Making and Meanings of Film and TV Stardom*. Urbana: University of Illinois Press, 2009.

Bench, Harmony. *Perpetual Motion: Dance, Digital Cultures, and the Common*. Minneapolis: University of Minnesota Press, 2020.

Berson, Misha. *Something's Coming, Something Good: West Side Story and the American Imagination*. Montclair, NJ: Applause, 2011.

Berthomé, Jean-Pierre. *Jacques Demy: les racines du rêve*. Nantes: Atalante, 1982.

Billard, Pierre. *L'âge classique du cinéma français: du cinéma parlant à la Nouvelle Vague*. Paris: Flammarion, 1995.

Bird, Katie. "Dancing, Flying Camera Jockeys: Invisible Labor, Craft Discourse, and Embodied Steadicam and Paraglide Technique from 1972 to 1985." *Velvet Light Trap* 80 (Fall 2017): 48–65.

Bird, Katie. "Feeling and Thought as They Take Form: Early Steadicam, Labor, and Technology (1974–1985)." *[in]Transition: Journal of Videographic Film & Moving Image Studies* 7, no. 1 (2020). https://intransition.openlibhums.org/article/id/11271/.

Birdwhistell, Ray L. *Kinesics and Context: Essays on Body Motion Communication*. Philadelphia: University of Pennsylvania Press, 1970.

Bordwell, David. *Figures Traced in Light: On Cinematic Staging*. Berkeley: University of California Press, 2005.

Bordwell, David. *Making Meaning: Inference and Rhetoric in the Interpretation of Cinema*. Cambridge, MA: Harvard University Press, 1991.

Bordwell, David. *Narration in the Fiction Film*. London: Routledge, 1997.

Bordwell, David. *On the History of Film Style*. Cambridge, MA: Harvard University Press, 1999.

REFERENCES 263

Bordwell, David. *Ozu and the Poetics of Cinema*. Ann Arbor: Michigan University Press, 2004.

Bordwell, David. *Planet Hong Kong: Popular Cinema and the Art of Entertainment*. 2nd ed. Madison, WI: Irvington Way Institute Press, 2011.

Bordwell, David. *Poetics of Cinema*. New York: Routledge, 2008.

Bordwell, David. "The Viewer's Share: Models of Mind in Explaining Film." In *Psychocinematics: Exploring Cognition at the Movies*, edited by Arthur P. Shimamura, 29–52. New York: Oxford University Press, 2013.

Bordwell, David. *The Way Hollywood Tells It: Story and Style in Modern Movies*. Berkeley: University of California Press, 2006.

Bordwell, David, Janet Staiger, and Kristin Thompson. *The Classical Hollywood Cinema: Film Style and Mode of Production to 1960*. New York: Columbia University Press, 1985.

Bouzet, Ange-Dominique, "1997, scénario idéal pour le cinéma. Selon un bilan du CNC, la production française augmente et se diversifie." *Libération*, March 5, 1998. https://www.liberation.fr/culture/1998/03/05/1997-scenario-ideal-pour-le-cinema-selon-un-bilan-du-cnc-la-production-francaise-augmente-et-se-dive_232268/.

"Boy and Girl Dancers." *The Stage and Television Today*, October 6, 1966, 15.

Bradley, Karen K. *Rudolf Laban*. New York: Routledge, 2009.

Brannigan, Erin. *Dancefilm: Choreography and the Moving Image*. New York: Oxford University Press, 2011.

Brooks, Virginia. "From Méliès to Streaming Video: A Century of Moving Dance Images." In *Envisioning Dance on Film and Video*, edited by Judy Mitoma, 54–60. New York: Routledge, 2002.

Brunick, Kaitlin L., James E. Cutting, and Jordan E. DeLong. "Low-Level Features of Film: What They Are and Why We Would Be Lost Without Them." In *Psychocinematics: Exploring Cognition at the Movies*, edited by Arthur P. Shimamura, 133–148. New York: Oxford University Press, 2013.

Burch, Noël, and Geneviève Sellier. *The Battle of the Sexes in French Cinema, 1930–1956*. Durham: Duke University Press, 2014.

Butterworth, Jo, and Liesbeth Wildschut. "Conceptual and Philosophical Concerns: Section Introduction." In *Contemporary Choreography: A Critical Reader*, edited by Jo Butterworth and Liesbeth Wildschut, 5–9. New York: Routledge, 2009.

Butterworth, Jo, and Liesbeth Wildschut. "General Introduction: Studying Contemporary Choreography." In *Contemporary Choreography: A Critical Reader*, edited by Jo Butterworth and Liesbeth Wildschut, 1–5. New York: Routledge, 2009.

Cadalanu, Marie. "Expérimenter le film musical: le musical à l'épreuve du court-métrage." *French Screen Studies* 20, no. 3/4 (2020): 265–284. https://doi.org/10.1080/26438 941.2020.1743949.

Caen, Michel, and Alain Le Bris. "Entretien avec Jacques Demy." *Cahiers du cinéma*, May 1964, 1–14.

"Cancan Again Kicks Up Stir in Paris Revues." *Variety*, July 29, 1953, 11.

Carr, Edward Hallett. *What Is History?* New York: Random House, 1961.

Carroll, Noël, and William P. Seeley. "Cognitivism, Psychology, and Neuroscience: Movies as Attentional Engines." In *Psychocinematics: Exploring Cognition at the Movies*, edited by Arthur P. Shimamura, 53–75. New York: Oxford University Press, 2013.

Carter, Alexandra. "Destabilising the Discipline: Critical Debates about History and their Impact on the Study of Dance." In *Rethinking Dance History: A Reader*, edited by Alexandra Carter, 10–19. Abingdon: Routledge, 2004.

264 REFERENCES

Carter, Alexandra, and Janet O'Shea, eds. Introduction to *The Routledge Dance Studies Reader*, 1–16. New York: Routledge, 2010.

Centre national de la danse. *Danse/Cinéma*. Paris: Capricci, 2012.

Champclaux, Christophe. *La comédie musicale et Fred Astaire*. Paris: Editions Seven Sept, 2008.

Chion, Michel. *Audio-Vision. Sound on Screen*, edited and translated by Claudia Gorbman. New York: Columbia University Press, 1994.

Chion, Michel. *La comédie musicale*. Paris: Cahiers du cinéma, 2002.

"Choreography—using vitality to create mood." *The Stage and Television Today*. August 7, 1980, 18.

Clech, Thierry, Frédéric Strauss, and Serge Toubiana. "D'un port à l'autre: Entretien avec Jacques Demy." *Cahiers du cinéma*, December 1988, 10–11, 57–59, 61–62.

Clover, Carol J. "Dancin' in the Rain." In *Hollywood Musicals, The Film Reader*, edited by Steven Cohan, 157–167. New York: Routledge, 2002.

Cohan, Steven. *Hollywood Musicals*. New York: Routledge, 2019.

Cohan, Steven. *Incongruous Entertainment: Camp, Cultural Value, and the MGM Musical*. Durham, NC: Duke University Press, 2005.

Cohan, Steven. "Introduction: Musicals of the Studio Era." In *Hollywood Musicals, The Film Reader*, edited by Steven Cohan, 1–16. New York: Routledge, 2002.

Cohan, Steven. "Introduction: How Do You Solve a Problem Like the Film Musical?" In *The Sound of Musicals*, edited by Steven Cohan, 1–18. London: British Film Institute, 2010.

Conway, Kelley. *Chanteuse in the City: The Realist Singer in French Film*. Berkeley: University of California Press, 2004.

Conway, Kelley. "France." In *The International Film Musical*, edited by Corey K. Creekmur and Linda Y. Mokdad, 29–44. Edinburgh: Edinburgh University Press, 2012.

Cooper, Betsy. "The Body Censored: Dance, Morality and the Production Code during the Golden Age of the Film Musical." In *Dance on Its Own Terms: Histories and Methodologies*, edited by Melanie Bales and Karen Eliot, 97–125. New York: Oxford University Press, 2013.

Corbett, Saroya. "Katherine Dunham's Mark on Jazz Dance." In *Jazz Dance: A History of the Roots and Branches*, edited by Lindsay Guarino and Wendy Oliver, 89–95. Gainesville: University Press of Florida, 2014.

Cornish, Audie. "Movie Interviews: Showbiz Dreams Collide with Reality in 'La La Land,'" *All Things Considered*, December 9, 2016. https://www.npr.org/2016/12/09/504857 051/showbiz-dreams-collide-with-reality-in-la-la-land.

Creekmur, Corey K., and Linda Y. Mokdad. *The International Film Musical*. Edinburgh: Edinburgh University Press, 2012.

Crisp, Colin G. *The Classic French Cinema, 1930–1960*. Bloomington: Indiana University Press, 1993.

"Damien Chazelle in Person!" *The Cinematheque* website, 2018. https://cinema.wisc.edu/series/2018/spring/damien-chazelle-person.

"Dans les coulisses: le tournage de *Trois places pour le 26*." Directed by Jérôme Wybon. *Trois places pour le 26*. Pathé. Blu-ray.

Dauncey, Hugh, and Steve Cannon, eds. *Popular Music in France from Chanson to Techno: Culture, Identity, and Society*. Aldershot, UK: Ashgate, 2003.

Delamater, Jerome. *Dance in the Hollywood Musical*. Ann Arbor, MI: UMI Research Press, 1988.

REFERENCES 265

Deleuze, Gilles. *Cinema 1: The Movement-Image*. Minneapolis: University of Minnesota Press, 1986.

Deleuze, Gilles. *Cinema 2: The Time-Image*. Minneapolis: University of Minnesota Press, 1989.

Dell, Cecily. *A Primer for Movement Description Using Effort-shape and Supplementary Concepts*. New York: Dance Notation Bureau Press, 1977.

Delorme, Stéphane. "Hollywoodland: *La La Land* de Damien Chazelle." *Cahiers du cinema* 729 (2017): 42–43.

"Demy Succeeds With Filmmusicals By Combining U.S.-French Talents." *Variety*, April 4, 1967, 25.

Dillon, Mark. "*La La Land*: City of Stars." *American Cinematographer*, February 27, 2017. https://ascmag.com/articles/la-la-land-city-of-stars.

Dodds, Sherril. *Dance on Screen: Genres and Media from Hollywood to Experimental Art*. New York: Palgrave, 2001.

Doherty, Thomas. *Teenagers and Teenpics: The Juvenilization of American Movies in the 1950s*. Philadelphia: Temple University Press, 2002.

Doty, Alexander. *Flaming Classics: Queering the Film Canon*. New York: Routledge, 2000.

Duggan, Anne E. *Queer Enchantments: Gender, Sexuality, and Class in the Fairy-Tale Cinema of Jacques Demy*. Detroit: Wayne State University Press, 2013.

Dyer, Richard. "Entertainment and Utopia." In *Hollywood Musicals, The Film Reader*, edited by Steven Cohan, 19–30. New York: Routledge, 2002.

Dyer, Richard. *Only Entertainment*. London: Routledge, 2002.

Dyer, Richard. *White* (Twentieth Anniversary Edition). London: Routledge, 2017.

Farmer, Brett. "The Singing Sixties: Rethinking the Julie Andrews Roadshow Musical." In *The Sound of Musicals*, edited by Steven Cohan, 114–127. London: British Film Institute, 2010.

Faden, Eric. "Visual Disturbances." *[in]Transition: Journal of Videographic Film & Moving Image Studies* 5, no. 4 (2019). https://intransition.openlibhums.org/article/id/11335/.

Feinberg, Scott. "'Awards Chatter' Podcast — Damien Chazelle ('La La Land')." *Hollywood Reporter*, February 20, 2017. https://www.hollywoodreporter.com/movies/movie-news/awards-chatter-podcast-damien-chazelle-la-la-land-977676/.

Ferrara, Serena. *Steadicam: Techniques and Aesthetics*. Oxford: Focal Press, 2001.

Feuer, Jane. *The Hollywood Musical*. Bloomington: Indiana University Press, 1993.

Feuer, Jane. "The Self-Reflexive Musical and the Myth of Entertainment." In *Hollywood Musicals, The Film Reader*, edited by Steven Cohan, 31–40. New York: Routledge, 2002.

Flageul, Elsa. "La trilogie de Jacques Demy: 'Lola,' 'Les Parapluies de Cherbourg,' 'Les Demoiselles de Rochefort.'" PhD diss., Université de la Sorbonne Nouvelle (Paris), 2001.

Fordin, Hugh. *The Movies' Greatest Musicals*. New York: Frederick Ungar, 1984.

Foster, Susan Leigh. *Choreographing Empathy: Kinesthesia in Performance*. London: Routledge, 2011.

Foster, Susan Leigh. *Reading Dancing: Bodies and Subjects in Contemporary American Dance*. Berkeley: University of California Press, 1986.

"France's Oscar Is 'Cesar'; Semi-Smooth Start." *Variety,* April 7, 1976, 7.

Franceschina, John. *Hermes Pan: The Man Who Danced with Fred Astaire*. New York: Oxford University Press, 2012.

Frederick, Robert. "French Film Youths Study English As Part of Wider Course in Dollars; Goldschmidt's Angles & Projects," *Variety*, April 27, 1966, 5, 26.

266 REFERENCES

"French Producer Holds 'Cancan'" (Sez Its French) Title Against 20th-Fox)." *Variety*, November 16, 1955, 5.

Frodon, Jean-Michel. *L'âge moderne du cinéma français: de la Nouvelle Vague à nos jours*. Paris: Flammarion, 1995.

Gabbard, Krin. "*La La Land* Is a Hit, but Is It Good for Jazz?" *Daedalus* 148, no. 2 (2019): 92–103.

Garcia, Desirée J. "*La La Land*'s Debt to Ethnic Musicals of Yore." *Zócalo Public Square*, February 14, 2017. https://www.zocalopublicsquare.org/2017/02/14/la-la-lands-debt-ethnic-musicals-yore/ideas/nexus/.

Garcia, Desirée J. *The Migration of Musical Film: From Ethnic Margins to American Mainstream*. New Brunswick, NJ: Rutgers University Press, 2014.

Garcia, Desirée J. *The Movie Musical*. New Brunswick, NJ: Rutgers University Press, 2021.

Genné, Beth. *Dance Me a Song: Astaire, Balanchine, Kelly, and the American Film Musical*. New York: Oxford University Press, 2018.

Gerstner, David A. "Christophe Honoré's *Les Chansons d'amour* and the Musical's Queer-Abilities." In *The Sound of Musicals*, edited by Steven Cohan, 188–199. London: British Film Institute, 2010.

Goffman, Erving. *The Presentation of Self in Everyday Life*. New York: Doubleday, 1959.

Gombrich, E. H. *The Sense of Order: A Study in the Psychology of Decorative Art*. London: Phaidon Press, 1984.

Grant, Barry Keith. *The Hollywood Film Musical*. Malden, UK: Wiley-Blackwell, 2012.

Grant, Catherine. "The Audiovisual Essay as Performative Research." *NECSUS* 5, no. 2 (2016): 255–265.

Grant, Mark N. *The Rise and Fall of the Broadway Musical*. Hanover, NH: University Press of New England, 2004.

Griffin, Sean. *Free and Easy? A Defining History of the American Film Musical Genre*. Hoboken, NJ: Wiley, 2018.

Griffin, Sean. "The Gang's All Here: Generic versus Racial Integration in the 1940s Musical." *Cinema Journal* 42, no. 1 (2002): 21–45.

Grugeau, Gérard. "Entretien avec Jacques Demy: allume, on ne voit pas ce qu'on dit!" *24 images* 42 (1989): 59–61.

Guarino, Lindsay, and Wendy Oliver. Introduction to *Jazz Dance: A History of the Roots and Branches*, xv–xix. Gainesville: University Press of Florida, 2014.

Guest, Ann Hutchinson. *An Introduction to Motif Notation*. Southwold, UK: Dance Books, 2000.

Halberstadt, Michèle. "Entretien avec Jacques Demy." *Première*, November 1988.

Haraway, Donna J. "A Manifesto for Cyborgs: Science, Technology, and Socialist Feminism in the 1980s." In *The Haraway Reader*, 7–46. London: Routledge, 2004.

Harris, Andrea. *Making Ballet American: Modernism Before and Beyond Balanchine*. New York: Oxford University Press, 2018.

Haseman, Brad. "A Manifesto for Performative Research." *Media International Australia Incorporating Culture and Policy* 118, no. 1 (2006): 98–106.

Haustrade, Gaston. "Entretien (Jacques Demy)." *Cinéma 81*, no. 271–272 (1981): 77–81.

Hawhee, Debra. *Moving Bodies: Kenneth Burke at the Edges of Language*. Columbia: University of South Carolina Press, 2009.

Hawkins, Robert. "Filmmusicals' O'Seas Accent." *Variety*, May 3, 1967, 5, 78.

Heldt, Guido. *Music and Levels of Narration in Film: Steps across the Border*. Chicago: Intellect, 2013.

REFERENCES 267

Henneton, Diane. "Jacques Demy's Musical Comedies: An Homage to the American Show Musical." *French Forum* 37, no. 3 (2012): 221–239.

Herrera, Brian Eugenio. *Latin Numbers: Playing Latino in Twentieth-Century U.S. Popular Performance*. Ann Arbor: University of Michigan Press, 2015.

Herzog, Amy. *Dreams of Difference, Songs of the Same: The Musical Moment in Film*. Minneapolis: University of Minnesota Press, 2010.

Hill, Rodney. "Demy Monde: Jacques Demy and the French New Wave." PhD diss., University of Kansas, 2006.

Hill, Rodney. "Demy Monde: The New-Wave Films of Jacques Demy." *Quarterly Review of Film and Video* 25, no. 5 (2008): 382–394.

Hill, Rodney. "Donkey Skin (Peau D'âne)." *Film Quarterly* 59, no. 2 (2005): 40–44.

Hill, Rodney. "The Films of Jacques Demy: Introduction." *Post Script* 35, no. 2 (2016). 3–13.

Hill, Rodney. "The New Wave Meets the Tradition of Quality: Jacques Demy's *The Umbrellas of Cherbourg*." *Cinema Journal* 48, no. 1 (2008): 27–50.

Hogue, Peter. "Forgotten and Unlucky: 'The Young Girls of Rochefort." *Velvet Light Trap* 14 (1975): 34–35.

Hopper. "Russ Tamblyn Rose Fast the Slow Way" *Los Angeles Times*, October 23, 1955. D1.

Horst, Carole. "'West Side Story's' Iris Menas Brings New Dimension to Old Character." *Variety*, January 8, 2022. https://variety.com/2022/film/spotlight/west-side-storys-iris-menas-brings-new-dimension-to-old-character-1235148646/.

Hoyt, Eric. *Hollywood Vault: Film Libraries Before Home Video*. Berkeley: University of California Press, 2014.

Hunting, Kyra, and Amanda McQueen. "A Musical Marriage: The Mash-up Aesthetic as Governing Logic in *Glee*." *Quarterly Review of Film and Video* 31, no. 4 (2014): 289–308. https://doi.org/10.1080/10509208.2013.855016.

Igartuburu, Elena. "Fugitive Plots: Adaptation, Storytelling, and Choreography in *Cabin in the Sky* and *Stormy Weather*." *European Journal of American Studies* 18, no. 2 (2023). https://doi.org/10.4000/ejas.20211.

Isola, Kaitlyn. "Sit Down with Ari Robbins." *The Tiffen Company blog*, June 6, 2019. https://tiffen.com/blogs/imagemaker/sit-down-with-ari-robbins.

Iyer, Usha. *Dancing Women: Choreographing Corporeal Histories of Hindi Cinema*. New York: Oxford University Press, 2020.

Jacobs, Lea. *Film Rhythm after Sound: Technology, Music, and Performance*. Berkeley: University of California Press, 2014.

"Jacques Demy, ou l'arbre gémeau." Directed by Lauren Billard, Michel Bonne, and Thierry Bourdiec. 2008. *Trois places pour le 26*. ARTE France and Ciné-Tamaris, 2008. DVD.

Johnson, William. "More Demy: In Praise of *The Young Girls of Rochefort*." *Film Comment* 32, no. 5 (1996): 72–76.

Jones, Carlos. "Jazz Dance and Racism." *Jazz Dance: A History of the Roots and Branches*, edited by Lindsay Guarino and Wendy Oliver, 231–239. Gainesville: University Press of Florida, 2014.

Jowitt, Deborah. *Jerome Robbins: His Life, His Theater, His Dance*. New York: Simon & Schuster, 2004.

Kappenberg, Claudia. "Does Screendance Need to Look Like Dance?" *International Journal of Performance Arts and Digital Media* 5, no. 2–3 (December 2009): 89–105. https://www.tandfonline.com/doi/abs/10.1386/padm.5.2-3.89/1.

Kauf. "Shows Abroad: Sir Buccaneer." *Variety*, November 4, 1964, 64.

268 REFERENCES

Kaufman, Sarah L. "Triumphant 'La La Land' Demonstrates the Power of Dance to Tell a Story." *Washington Post*, December 30, 2016. https://www.washingtonpost.com/entertainment/theater_dance/triumphant-la-la-land-demonstrates-the-power-of-dance-to-tell-a-story/2016/12/30/22a28c10-cc85-11e6-a747-d03044780a02_story.html.

Keathley, Christian. "La Caméra-stylo: Notes on Video Criticism and Cinephilia." In *The Language and Style of Film Criticism*, edited by Alex Clayton and Andrew Klevan, 176–191. New York: Routledge, 2011.

Keathley, Christian, Jason Mittell, and Catherine Grant, eds. *The Videographic Essay: Practice and Pedagogy*. n.p., 2019. http://videographicessay.org.

Keating, Patrick. *The Dynamic Frame: Camera Movement in Classical Hollywood*. New York: Columbia University Press, 2019.

Keating, Patrick. "A Homeless Ghost: The Moving Camera and Its Analogies." *[in]Transition: Journal of Videographic Film & Moving Image Studies* 2, no. 4 (2016). https://intransition.openlibhums.org/article/id/11364/.

Keating, Patrick. "Motifs of Movement and Modernity." *MOVIE: A Journal of Film Criticism* 7 (2017): 98. https://vimeo.com/170535380.

Kennedy, Matthew. *Roadshow!: The Fall of Film Musicals in the 1960s*. New York: Oxford University Press, 2014.

Kessler, Kelly. *Destabilizing the Hollywood Musical: Music, Masculinity, and Mayhem*. New York: Palgrave Macmillan, 2010.

Kessler, Kelly. "Gone in a *Flash(dance)*: The Estrangement of Diegetic Performance in the 1980s Teen Dance Film." In *Movies, Moves, and Music: The Sonic World of Dance Films*, edited by Mark Evans and Mary Fogarty, 129–149. Sheffield, UK: Equinox, 2016.

Klein, Amanda Ann. "Genre." In *The Craft of Criticism*, edited by Michael Kackman and Mary Celeste Kearney, 195–206. London: Taylor & Francis, 2018.

Laban, Rudolf von, and Lisa Ullmann. *Choreutics*. Alton: Dance Books, 2011.

Laban, Rudolf von, and Lisa Ullmann. *The Mastery of Movement*. Alton: Dance Books, 2011.

La Bardonnie, Mathilde. "Les Césars d'Antenne 2." *Le Monde*, April 6, 1976, 26.

Lacombe, Alain, and François Porcile. *Les musiques du cinéma français*. Paris: Bordas, 1995.

"La La Land." Box Office Mojo. https://www.boxofficemojo.com/release/rl241141249/.

Lattanzio, Ryan "Lin-Manuel Miranda Says He's 'Truly Sorry' for 'In the Heights' Colorism: 'We Fell Short.'" *Indiewire*, June 14, 2021. https://www.indiewire.com/2021/06/lin-manuel-miranda-in-the-heights-colorism-backlash-1234644482/.

LaViers, Amy, and Magnus Egerstedt. "Style Based Robotic Motion." In *2012 American Control Conference*, 4327–4332. IEEE, 2012.

Layani, Jacques. *Jacques Demy: Un portrait personnel*. Paris: Editions L'Harmattan, 2016.

Layson, June. "Dance History Source Materials." In *Dance History: An Introduction*, edited by Janet Adshead-Lansdale and June Layson, 18–31. Abingdon, UK: Routledge, 1994.

Lazen, Matthew. "'En Perme à Nantes': Jacques Demy and New Wave Place." *Studies in French Cinema* 4, no. 3 (2004): 187–96.

Le Gras, Gwénaëlle. "Soft and Hard: Catherine Deneuve in 1970." *Studies in French Cinema* 5, no. 1 (2005): 27–35.

Len. "Review: Trois places pour le 26." *Variety*, November 16, 1988, 19.

Lerouge, Stéphane. "Michel Legrand, la moité de Demy." In *Le Monde enchanté de Jacques Demy*, edited by Matthieu Orléan, 80–82, 216–21. Paris: Skira-Flammarion, 2013.

Lewis, Hannah. "The Virtuosic Camera: Nostalgia, Technology, and the Contemporary Hollywood Musical." In *The Oxford Handbook of the Hollywood Musical*, edited by Dominic Broomfield-McHugh, 567–586. New York: Oxford University Press, 2022.

REFERENCES 269

Locatelli, Massimo. "Paul Fraisse's Psychology of Rhythm: A Case for Filmology?" *Cinéma & Cie* 22, no. 38 (2022): 83–96. https://doi-org.proxy2.library.illinois.edu/10.54103/2036-461x/17202.

Lovell, Alan, and Peter Krämer. Introduction to *Screen Acting*, 1–9. Edited by Alan Lovell and Peter Krämer. London: Routledge, 1999.

Mac. "Shows Abroad: Carrie." *Variety,* October 30, 1963, 67.

Mackrell, Judith. *Reading Dance*. London: Michael Joseph, 1997.

Madison, Ira III, "La La Land's White Jazz Narrative." *MTV News*, December 19, 2016. https://www.mtv.com/news/5qr32e/la-la-lands-white-jazz-narrative.

Magny, Joël. "Les mi-lieux de Demy." *Cahiers du cinéma* 414 (1988): 6–9.

Maille, Nicolas. "*Les Demoiselles de Rochefort*: un musical 'en-chanté' et 'en-dansé.'" *L'avant scène cinéma*, no. 602 (2013): 6–11.

Maletic, Vera. *Dance Dynamics: Effort and Phrasing*. Columbus: Grade A Notes, 2005.

Mandelbaum, Jacques. "'Sur quel pied danser': un conflit social dissous dans une comédie musicale." *Le Monde*, July 1, 2016. https://www.lemonde.fr/cinema/article/2016/07/05/sur-quel-pied-danser-un-conflit-social-dissous-dans-une-comedie-musicale_4963861_3476.html.

Marie, Michel. "Jacques Demy and the French New Wave." In *Jacques Demy*, edited by Quim Casas and Ana Cristina Iriarte, 13–25. Madrid: Filmoteca Española, 2011.

Martin, Marie-Claude. "Cinéma: La comédie musicale renaît grâce à *Jeanne et le garçon formidable*." *Le Temps,* April 24, 1998. https://www.letemps.ch/culture/cinema-comedie-musicale-renait-grace-jeanne-garcon-formidable.

Marx, René. "Demy par Varda." *L'avant scène cinéma*, no. 602 (2013): 44–48.

McCarren, Felicia. *French Moves: The Cultural Politics of le hip hop*. New York: Oxford University Press, 2013.

McKechnie, Shirley, and Catherine J. Stevens. "Visible Thought: Choreographic Cognition in Creating, Performing, and Watching Contemporary Dance." In *Contemporary Choreography: A Critical Reader*, edited by Jo Butterworth and Liesbeth Wildschut, 38–51. New York: Routledge, 2009.

McLean, Adrienne L. *Being Rita Hayworth: Labor, Identity, and Hollywood Stardom*. New Brunswick, NJ: Rutgers University Press, 2004.

McLean, Adrienne L. *Dying Swans and Madmen: Ballet, the Body, and Narrative Cinema*. New Brunswick, NJ: Rutgers University Press, 2008.

McLean, Adrienne L. "Feeling and the Filmed Body: Judy Garland and the Kinesics of Suffering." *Film Quarterly* 55, no. 3 (2002): 2–15.

McLean, Adrienne L. "Flirting with Terpsichore: Show Dancing in 1930s Hollywood Musicals." In *Perspectives on American Dance: The Twentieth Century (Volume I)*, edited by Jennifer Atkins, Sally Sommer, and Tricia Young, 67–81. Gainesville: University Press of Florida, 2018.

McQueen, Amanda. "After 'The Golden Age': An Industrial History of the Hollywood Musical, 1955–1975." PhD diss., University of Wisconsin–Madison, 2017.

Michael, Charlie. *French Blockbusters: Cultural Politics of a Transnational Cinema*. Edinburgh: Edinburgh University Press, 2019.

Michel, Marcelle, and Isabelle Ginot. *La danse au 20e siècle*. Paris: Larousse, 2008.

Mirisch, Walter. *I Thought We Were Making Movies, Not History*. Madison: University of Wisconsin Press, 2008.

Mittell, Jason. "Deformin' in the Rain: How (and Why) to Break a Classic Film." *Digital Humanities Quarterly* (2021) 15:1. http://www.digitalhumanities.org/dhq/vol/15/1/000521/000521.html.

270 REFERENCES

Mittell, Jason. "Videographic Criticism as a Digital Humanities Method." In *Debates in the Digital Humanities 2019*, edited by Matthew K. Gold and Lauren F. Klein, 224–242. Minneapolis: University of Minnesota Press, 2019.

Moore, Carol-Lynne. *The Harmonic Structure of Movement, Music, and Dance According to Rudolf Laban: An Examination of His Unpublished Writings and Drawings*. Lewiston, ME: Edwin Mellen Press, 2009.

Moore, Carol-Lynne. "Introduction to Laban Movement Analysis and Harmonic Theory (Abridged Version)." Carol-Lynne Moore, 2010.

Moore, Carol-Lynne, and Kaoru Yamamoto. *Beyond Words: Movement Observation and Analysis*. New York: Routledge, 2012.

Morgan, Daniel. *The Lure of the Image: Epistemic Fantasies of the Moving Camera*. Berkeley: University of California Press, 2021.

Moskowitz, Gene. "Les Demoiselles de Rochefort." *Variety*, March 1, 1967, 6.

Moskowitz, Gene. "French Like Cow and Gang Films: Why Not Anglo-American Tuners?" *Variety*, January 8, 1969, 30.

Moskowitz, Gene. "Lido, Paris." *Variety*, December 9, 1964, 59.

Moskowitz, Gene. "Moulin Rouge, Paris." *Variety*, April 19, 1967, 101.

Moskowitz, Gene. "'West Side Story' Breaks Rule That Paris Hates Modern U.S. Musicals." *Variety*, April 5, 1961, 2, 72.

Mueller, John. "Fred Astaire and the Integrated Musical." *Cinema Journal* 24, no. 1 (1984): 28–40.

Mueller, John. *Astaire Dancing: The Musical Films*. Columbus, OH: Educational Publisher, 2010.

Muñoz, José Esteban. *Disidentifications: Queers of Color and the Performance of Politics*. Minneapolis: University of Minnesota Press, 1999.

Murphy, Mekado. "Damien Chazelle Narrates a Scene From 'La La Land.'" *New York Times*, December 8, 2016. https://www.nytimes.com/2016/12/08/movies/damien-chazelle-narrates-a-scene-from-la-la-land.html.

Naremore, James. *Acting in the Cinema*. Berkeley: University of California Press, 1988.

Naze, Alain. *Jacques Demy: L'enfance retrouvée*. Paris: l'Harmattan, 2014.

Neale, Steve. *Genre and Hollywood*. London: Routledge, 2000.

Negrón-Muntaner, Frances. *Boricua Pop: Puerto Ricans and the Latinization of American Culture*. New York: New York University Press, 2004.

Neupert, Richard. *A History of the French New Wave Cinema*. Madison: University of Wisconsin Press, 2007.

Neupert, Richard. "Jacques Demy's *Bay of Angels*: A New Wave Mode of Production." *Post Script* 35, no. 2 (2016): 14–21.

Noisette, Philippe. *Danse contemporaine mode d'emploi*. Paris: Flammarion, 2010.

Nye, Edward. *Mime, Music and Drama on the Eighteenth-Century Stage: The Ballet d'Action*. Cambridge: Cambridge University Press, 2011.

O'Leary, Alan. "Workshop of Potential Scholarship: Manifesto for a Parametric Videographic Criticism." *NECSUS* (Spring 2021). https://necsus-ejms.org/workshop-of-potential-scholarship-manifesto-for-a-parametric-videographic-criticism/.

Orléan, Matthieu, ed. *Le Monde enchanté de Jacques Demy*. Paris: Skira-Flammarion, 2013.

Orléan, Matthieu. "Los Angeles Trip (1967–1979)." In *Le Monde enchanté de Jacques Demy*, edited by Matthieu Orléan, 114. Paris: Skira-Flammarion, 2013.

"O'Seas Chill Reducing U.S. Musicals; Only Handful Current or Planned; Watch 'Porgy' European Playoff." *Variety*, Jan 20, 1960, 3.

REFERENCES 271

Ovalle, Priscilla Peña. *Dance and the Hollywood Latina: Race, Sex, and Stardom*. New Brunswick, NJ: Rutgers University Press, 2011.

Oyallon-Koloski, Jenny. "A Dance in Disguise: Figure Movement and Genre Play in Jacques Demy's *Peau d'âne*." *Post Script* 35, no. 2 (2016): 59–74.

Oyallon-Koloski, Jenny. "Danceploitation, Musical Disruption, and Synergy in *Saturday Night Fever, Flashdance*, and *Breakin'*." In *Musicals at the Margins: Genre, Boundaries, Canons*, edited by Julie Lobalzo Wright and Martha Shearer, 15–27. New York: Bloomsbury Academic, 2021.

Oyallon-Koloski, Jenny. "Genre Experimentation and Contemporary Dance in *Jeanne et le garçon formidable*." *Studies in French Cinema* 14, no. 2 (2014): 91–107.

Oyallon-Koloski, Jenny. "Musical Grid Videographic Deformations." Vimeo, 2017–present. https://vimeo.com/showcase/6525706.

Parker, Andrew, and Eve Kosofsky Sedgwick. Introduction to *Performativity and Performance*, 1–18. Edited by Andrew Parker and Eve Kosofsky Sedgwick. New York: Routledge, 1995.

Pearson, Roberta. *Eloquent Gestures: The Transformation of Performance Style in the Griffith Biograph Films*. Berkeley: University of California Press: 1992.

Père, Olivier, and Marie Colmant. *Jacques Demy*. Paris: Editions de La Martinière, 2010.

Phelan, Peggy. *Unmarked: The Politics of Performance*. London: Routledge, 1993.

Plantinga, Carl. *Alternative Realities*. New Brunswick, NJ: Rutgers University Press, 2020.

Powers, John. "*La La Land* Director Damien Chazelle Used to Really Hate Musicals." *Vogue*, December 8, 2016. https://www.vogue.com/article/la-la-land-director-dam ien-chazelle-interview.

Powrie, Phil, and Marie Cadalanu. *The French Film Musical*. London: Bloomsbury, 2020.

Preston-Dunlop, Valerie. *Looking at Dances: A Choreological Perspective on Choreography*. London: The Noverre Press, 2014.

Prince, Steven. *A New Pot of Gold: Hollywood Under the Electronic Rainbow, 1980–1989*. Berkeley: University of California Press, 2000.

"Radio-Télévision." *Le Monde*, April 3, 1976, 12.

Raja, Norine, "*Jeanne et le garçon formidable*, la comédie musicale qui chantait les années sida." *Vanity Fair* (France), April 21, 2018. https://www.vanityfair.fr/culture/ecrans/ story/jeanne-et-le-garcon-formidable-vingt-ans-apres/1932.

Ramaeker, Paul. "Demy in the New Hollywood: *Model Shop*." *Post Script* 35, no. 2 (2016): 41–58.

Ramaeker, Paul. "New Hollywood: 1981–1999." In *Cinematography*, edited by Patrick Keating, 106–131. New Brunswick. NJ: Rutgers University Press, 2014.

Reeser, Todd W. *Queer Cinema in Contemporary France: Five Directors*. Manchester, UK: Manchester University Press, 2022.

Reynolds, Debbie. *Debbie: My Life*. New York: William Morrow, 1988.

Reynolds, Nancy, and Malcolm McCormick. "Dance in the Movies." In *No Fixed Points: Dance in the Twentieth Century*, 708–743. New Haven, CT: Yale University Press, 2003.

Reynolds, Nancy, and Malcolm McCormick. *No Fixed Points: Dance in the Twentieth Century*. New Haven, CT: Yale University Press, 2003.

"'Rochefort' First Big Scale French Tunepic." *Variety*, July 6, 1966, 20.

Rosenbaum, Jonathan. "Not the Same Old Song and Dance." jonathanrosenbaum.net. Posted June 25, 2022. https://jonathanrosenbaum.net/2022/06/not-the-same-old-song-and-dance/.

272 REFERENCES

Rosenberg, Douglas. *Screendance: Inscribing the Ephemeral Image.* New York: Oxford University Press, 2012.

Rubin, Martin. "Busby Berkeley and the Backstage Musical." In *Hollywood Musicals, The Film Reader*, edited by Steven Cohan, 53–61. New York: Routledge, 2002.

Rubin, Martin. *Showstoppers: Busby Berkeley and the Tradition of Spectacle.* New York: Columbia University Press, 1993.

Ruyter, Nancy. *The Cultivation of Body and Mind in Nineteenth-Century American Delsartism.* Westport, CT: Greenwood Press: 1999.

"Saul Chaplin: 'U.S. Musicals O'Seas Need Ingenuity,'" *Variety*, March 9, 1960, 17.

Schatz, Thomas. *Boom and Bust: American Cinema in the 1940s.* Berkeley: University of California Press, 1997.

Schatz, Thomas. *Hollywood Genres: Formulas, Filmmaking, and the Studio System.* New York: McGraw-Hill, 1981.

Schonig, Jordan. "The Follow Shot." *[in] Transition: Journal of Videographic Film & Moving Image Studies* 5, no. 1 (2018). https://intransition.openlibhums.org/article/id/11369/.

Schonig, Jordan. *The Shape of Motion: Cinema and the Aesthetics of Movement.* New York: Oxford University Press, 2022.

Shakespeare, William. *Romeo and Juliet*, edited by Peter Holland. New York: Penguin Books, 2000.

Shore, Michael. *The Rolling Stone Book of Rock Video.* New York: Rolling Stone Press, 1984.

Sicilien, Jacques. "L'amour toujours. . . 'Trois places pour le 26,' un film de Jacques Demy." *Le Monde*, November 24, 1988, 13.

Simsi, Simon. *Ciné-Passions: Le guide chiffré du cinéma en France.* Paris: Editions Dixit, 2012.

Simsolo, Noël. "Entretien avec Jacques Demy." *Image et son: revue de cinéma*, no. 247 (1971): 70–79.

Smith, Alison. *French Cinema in the 1970s: The Echoes of May.* Manchester, UK: Manchester University Press, 2005.

Smith, Jeff. "Ancillary Markets— Recorded Music: Charting the Rise and Fall of the Soundtrack Album." In *The Contemporary Hollywood Film Industry*, edited by Paul McDonald and Janet Wasko, 143–152. Oxford: Blackwell, 2008.

Smith, Jeff. "Black Faces, White Voices: The Politics of Dubbing in Carmen Jones." *Velvet Light Trap* 51 (2003): 29–42.

Smith, Jeff. "Bridging the Gap: Reconsidering the Border between Diegetic and Nondiegetic Music." *Music and the Moving Image* 2, no. 1 (2009): 1–25.

Smith, Tim J. "Watching You Watch Movies: Using Eye Tracking to Inform Film Theory." In *Psychocinematics: Exploring Cognition at the Movies*, edited by Arthur P. Shimamura, 165–191. New York: Oxford University Press, 2013.

Smith-Autard, Jacqueline M. *Dance Composition.* New York: Routledge, 2004.

St. John, Graham. Introduction to *Victor Turner and Contemporary Cultural Performance*, 1–40. Edited by Graham St. John. New York: Berghahn Books, 2008.

"The Stage: 'Carrie.'" *The Stage and Television Today*, October 10, 1963, 15.

Stewart, Ken. "Music as Written: Dublin." *Billboard*, January 11, 1964, 30, 31.

Stilwell, Robynn J. "Le Demy-monde: The Bewitched, Betwixt and between French Musical." In *Popular Music in France from Chanson to Techno*, edited by Hugh Dauncey and Steve Cannon, 123–138. Burlington, UK: Ashgate Publishing Company, 2003.

Studd, Karen, and Laura Cox. *EveryBody Is a Body.* Indianapolis, IN: Dog Ear Publishing, 2013.

"Subtitle Plot, Lyrics in Italics: And O'Seas Must Run 'West Side' Uncut." *Variety*, August 9, 1961, 4.

Taboulay, Camille. *Le cinéma enchanté de Jacques Demy*. Paris: Cahiers du cinéma, 1996.

Taylor, Aaron. Introduction to *Theorizing Film Acting*, 1–18. Edited by Aaron Taylor. New York: Routledge, 2012.

Thomas, Tony. *That's Dancing!* New York: Abrams, 1984.

Thompson, Kristin. *Breaking the Glass Armor: Neoformalist Film Analysis*. Princeton, NJ: Princeton University Press, 1988.

Tiomkin, Dimitri. "'Filmusicals' 2d 'Golden Age' Per Dimitri Tiomkin." *Variety*, August 15, 1962, 43.

Tremois, Claude-Marie. "Le Film Invisible de Jacques Demy: Anouchka," *Télérama*, July 16, 1986, 14–18.

"Tunepix: High Risk." *Variety,* January 8, 1969, 15.

Virtue, Nancy. "Cubism and the *Carnivalesque* in Jacques Demy's *Les Demoiselles de Rochefort*." *Post Script* 35, no. 2 (2016): 22–40.

Virtue, Nancy. "Jacques Demy's *Les Parapluies de Cherbourg*: A National Allegory of the French-Algerian War." *Studies in French Cinema* 13, no. 2 (2013): 127–140.

Waldron, Darren. *Jacques Demy*. Manchester, UK: Manchester University Press, 2015.

Weis, Elizabeth, and John Belton, eds. *Film Sound: Theory and Practice*. New York: Columbia University Press, 1985.

Wells, Elizabeth A. *West Side Story: Cultural Perspectives on an American Musical*. Lanham, MD: Scarecrow Press, 2011.

Williams, Alan. *Republic of Images: A History of French Filmmaking*. Cambridge, MA: Harvard University Press, 1992.

Yoo, Si-Hyun. "Body Actions Handout." New York: Laban/Bartenieff Institute for Movement Studies, 2013.

Zaumer, Ben. "Oscars: 'La La Land,' Just How Musical Is It Really?" *Hollywood Reporter,* February 26, 2017. https://www.hollywoodreporter.com/movies/movie-news/oscars-la-la-land-just-how-musical-is-980194/.

Filmography

Akerman, Chantal, dir. *Jeanne Dielman, 23 Quai du Commerce, 1080 Bruxelles*. Paradise Films, 1975. Film.

Akil, Salim, dir. *Sparkle*. Stage 6 Films, 2012. Film.

Ardolino, Emile, dir. *Dirty Dancing*. Vestron Pictures, 1987. Film.

Ashby, Hal, dir. *Bound for Glory*. United Artists, 1976. Film.

Badham, John, dir. *Saturday Night Fever*. Paramount Pictures, 1977. Film.

Barratier, Christophe, dir. *Les choristes*. Vega Film, 2004. Film.

Barratier, Christophe, dir. *Faubourg 36*. Pathé, 2008. Film.

Barry, Gérome, dir. *Swing Rendez-vous*. Épicentre Films, 2023. Film.

Berri, Claude, dir. *Jean de Florette*. DD Productions, 1986. Film.

Berri, Claude, dir. *Manon des sources*. DD Productions, 1986. Film.

Besson, Luc, dir. *Le grand bleu*. Gaumont, 1988. Film.

Calbérac, Ivan, dir. *On va s'aimer*. Mandarin Films, 2006. Film.

Calori, Paul, and Kostia Testutand, dirs. *Sur quel pied danser*. Loin Derrière L'Oural. 2016. Film.

274 REFERENCES

Carné, Marcel, dir. *Les Portes de la nuit*. Société Nouvelle Pathé Cinéma, 1946. Film.

Carné, Marcel, dir. *Les Visiteurs du Soir*. Production André Paulvé, 1942. Film.

Carney, John, dir. *Once*. Samson Films, Summit Entertainment, 2007. Film.

Carter, Thomas, dir. *Save the Last Dance*. Cort/Madden Productions, 2001. Film.

Chabrol, Claude, dir. *Le Cri du hibou*. Civite Casa Films, 1987. Film.

Chatiliez, Étienne, dir. *Agathe Cléry*. Produire à Paris, TF1 Films, 2008. Film.

Chazelle, Damien, dir. *Guy and Madeleine on a Park Bench*. 2011. Film.

Chazelle, Damien, dir. *La La Land*. Summit Entertainment, Black Label Media, 2016. Film.

Chazelle, Damien, dir. *Whiplash*. Bold Films, Blumhouse Productions, Right of Way Films, Sierra/Affinity, 2014. Film.

Chu, Jon M., dir. *In the Heights*. Warner Bros, 2021. Film.

Cocteau, Jean, dir. *La Belle et la Bête*. DisCina, 1946. Film.

Collard, Cyril, dir. *Les Nuits fauves*. Banfilm, La Sept Cinéma, 1992. Film.

Coppola, Francis Ford, dir. *One From the Heart*. Zoetrope Studios, 1981. Film.

Cukor, George, dir. *Let's Make Love*. Company of Artists, 1960. Film.

Cukor, George, dir. *My Fair Lady*. Warner Bros., 1964. Film.

Curtiz, Michael, dir. *White Christmas*. Paramount Pictures, 1954. Film.

DaCosta, Morton, dir. *The Music Man*. Warner Bros., 1962. Film.

Demy, Jacques, dir. *Une Chambre en Ville*. Progéfi, 1982. Film.

Demy, Jacques, dir. *Les Demoiselles de Rochefort*. Madeleine Films and Parc Film, 1967. Film.

Demy, Jacques, dir. *L'événement le plus important depuis que l'homme a marché sur la lune*. Lira Films, 1973. Film.

Demy, Jacques, dir. *Lady Oscar*. Kitty Films, 1979. Film.

Demy, Jacques, dir. *Lola*. Rome Paris Films, 1961. Film.

Demy, Jacques, dir. *Model Shop*. Columbia Pictures Corporation, 1969. Film.

Demy, Jacques, dir. *Les Parapluies de Cherbourg*. Madeleine Films and Parc Film, 1964. Film.

Demy, Jacques, dir. *Parking*. France 3 Cinéma, 1985. Film.

Demy, Jacques, dir. *Peau d'âne*. Marianne Productions and Parc Film, 1970. Film.

Demy, Jacques, dir. *The Pied Piper*. Sagittarius Productions Inc., 1972. Film.

Demy, Jacques, dir. *Trois places pour le 26*. Renn Productions, 1988. Film.

Dickson, William K. L., dir. *Annabelle Butterfly Dance*. Edison Studios, 1984.

Dickson, William K. L., dir. *Carmencita*. Edison Studios, 1984.

Dickson, William K. L., dir. *Sandow*. Edison Studios, 1984.

Dieterle, William, dir. *Fashions of 1934*. Warner Bros., 1934. Film.

Dieterle, William, dir. *Salome*. Columbia Pictures, 1953. Film.

Ducastel, Olivier, and Jacques Martineau, dirs. *Crustacés et Coquillages*. Agat Films & Cie, Bac Films, Cofimage, 2005. Film.

Ducastel, Olivier, and Jacques Martineau, dirs. *Drôle de Félix*. Arte France Cinéma, Canal+. 2000. Film.

Ducastel, Olivier, and Jacques Martineau, dirs. *Jeanne et le garçon formidable*. Les Films du Requin, Canal +. 1998. Film.

Donen, Stanley, dir. *Funny Face*. Paramount Pictures, 1957. Film.

Donen, Stanley, dir. *Seven Brides for Seven Brothers*. Metro-Goldwyn-Mayer, 1954. Film.

Donen, Stanley, and Gene Kelly, dirs. *It's Always Fair Weather*. Metro-Goldwyn-Mayer, 1955. Film.

Donen, Stanley, and Gene Kelly, dirs. *On the Town*. Metro-Goldwyn-Mayer, 1949. Film.

REFERENCES 275

Donen, Stanley, and Gene Kelly, dirs. *Singin' in the Rain*. Metro-Goldwyn-Mayer, 1952. Film.

Eastwood, Clint, dir. *Jersey Boys*. Warner Bros., 2014. Film.

Enright, Ray, dir. *On Your Toes*. Warner Bros., 1936. Film.

Firstenberg, Sam, dir. *Breakin' 2: Electric Boogaloo*. Cannon Films, 1984. Film.

Fletcher, Anne, dir. *Step Up*. Touchstone Pictures, Summit Entertainment, 2006. Film.

Fogelman, Dan, showrunner. *Galavant*. ABC, 2015–2016. TV.

Forman, Miloš, dir. *Hair*. United Artists, 1979. Film.

Fosse, Bob, dir. *The Pajama Game*. Warner Bros., 1957. Film.

Fosse, Bob, dir. *Sweet Charity*. Universal Pictures, 1969. Film.

Gadhvi Sanjay, dir. *Dhoom 2*. Utopia Films, Yash Raj Films, 2006. Film.

Giraldi, Bob, dir. "Beat It," Thriller. Epic Records, 1983. TV.

Giraldi, Bob, dir. "Love Is a Battlefield," Live from Earth. Chrysalis Records, 1983. TV.

Gluck, Will, dir. *Annie*. Sony Pictures Entertainment, 2014. Film.

Gracey, Michael, dir. *The Greatest Showman*. 20th Century Fox, 2017. Film.

Greenwald, Robert, dir. *Xanadu*. Universal Pictures, 1980. Film.

Hawks, Howard, dir. *Gentlemen Prefer Blondes*. Twentieth Century Fox Film Corporation, 1953. Film.

Hill, George Roy, dir. *Thoroughly Modern Millie*. Universal Pictures, 1967. Film.

Honoré, Christophe, dir. *Les Bien-aimés*. Why Not Productions, 2011. Film.

Honoré, Christophe, dir. *Les Chansons d'amour*. Alma Films, 2007. Film.

Hooper, Tobe, dir. *Lifeforce*. The Cannon Group, 1985. Film.

Hooper, Tom, dir. *Les Misérables*. Universal Pictures, 2012. Film.

Landis, John, dir. *The Blues Brothers*. Universal Pictures, 1980. Film.

Landis, John, dir. "Thriller" Thriller. Epic Records, 1983. TV.

Lang, Walter, dir. *Can-Can*. Suffolk-Cummings productions, 1960. Film.

Lang, Walter, dir. *The King and I*. 20th Century Fox, 1956. Film.

Lee, Spike, dir. *School Daze*. Columbia Pictures, 1988. Film.

LeRoy, Mervyn, dir. *Gold Diggers of 1933*. Warner Bros., 1933. Film.

Lima, Kevin, dir. *Enchanted*. Walt Disney Pictures, 2007. Film.

Lloyd, Phyllida, dir. *Mamma Mia!* Universal Pictures, 2008. Film.

Luhrmann, Baz, dir. *Moulin Rouge!* 20th Century Fox, 2001. Film.

Lumet, Sidney, dir. *The Wiz*. Universal Pictures, 1978. Film.

Lyne, Adrian, dir. *Flashdance*. Paramount Pictures, 1983. Film.

Mamoulian, Rouben, dir. *Silk Stockings*. Metro-Goldwyn-Mayer, 1957. Film.

Mankiewicz, Joseph, dir. *Guys and Dolls*. Metro- Goldwyn-Mayer, 1955. Film.

Margolin, François, dir. *Mensonge*. Cuel Lavalette Productions, France 3 Cinéma, Les Films Alain Sarde, 1992. Film.

Marshall, Rob, dir. *Chicago*. Miramax, 2002. Film.

Marshall, Rob, dir. *Into the Woods*. Walt Disney Studios, 2014. Film.

Marshall, Rob, dir. *Mary Poppins Returns*. Walt Disney Studios, 2018. Film.

Minnelli, Vincente, dir. *An American in Paris*. Metro-Goldwyn-Mayer, 1951. Film.

Minnelli, Vincente, dir. *The Band Wagon*. Metro-Goldwyn-Mayer, 1953. Film.

Minnelli, Vincente, dir. *Brigadoon*. Metro-Goldwyn-Mayer, 1954. Film.

Minnelli, Vincente, dir. *Meet Me in St. Louis*. Metro-Goldwyn-Mayer, 1944. Film.

Minnelli, Vincente, dir. *On a Clear Day You Can See Forever*. Metro-Goldwyn-Mayer, 1970. Film.

Minnelli, Vincente, dir. *Yolanda and the Thief*. Metro-Goldwyn-Mayer, 1945. Film.

276 REFERENCES

Moore, Jason, dir. *Pitch Perfect*. Universal Pictures, 2012. Film.
Murphy, Dudley, dir. "Black & Tan." RKO Radio Pictures, 1929. Film (short).
Murphy, Ryan, showrunner. *Glee*. Fox, 2009–2015. TV.
Negulesco, Jean, dir. *How to Marry a Millionaire*, 20th Century Fox, 1953. Film.
Ophüls, Max, dir. *Madame de . . .* Gaumont, 1953. Film.
Ortega, Kenny, dir. *High School Musical 2*. Walt Disney Pictures, 2007. TV.
Ortega, Kenny, dir. *High School Musical 3: Senior Year*. Walt Disney Pictures, 2008. Film.
Oz, Frank, dir. *Little Shop of Horrors*. The Geffen Company, 1986. Film.
Ozon, François, dir. *Huit femmes*. Mars Distribution, 2002. Film.
Parker, Ol, dir. *Mamma Mia: Here We Go Again*. Universal Pictures, 2017. Film.
Preminger, Otto, dir. *Porgy and Bess*. Samuel Goldwyn Productions, 1959. Film.
Reisner, Charles, dir. *The Hollywood Revue*. Metro-Goldwyn-Mayer, 1929. Film.
Renoir, Jean, dir. *French Cancan*. Gaumont, 1954. Film.
Resnais, Alain, dir. *On connaît la chanson*. Arena Films, Caméra One, France 2 Cinéma,
    Vega Film, Greenpoint Films, 1997. Film.
Ross, Herbert, dir. *Footloose*. Paramount Pictures, 1984. Film.
Ross, Herbert, dir. *Pennies from Heaven*. Metro-Goldwyn-Mayer, 1981. Film.
Rouch, Jean, and Edgar Morin, dir. *Chronique d'un été*. Argos Films, 1961. Film.
Sack, Alfred N., dir. "St. Louis Blues." RKO Radio Pictures, 1929. Film (short).
Sandrich, Mark, dir. *Shall We Dance*. RKO Radio Pictures, 1937. Film.
Sandrich, Mark, dir. *Top Hat*. RKO Radio Pictures, 1935. Film.
Shankman Adam, dir. *Hairspray*. New Line Cinema, 2007. Film.
Sherman, Vincent, dir. *Affair in Trinidad*. Columbia Pictures, 1952. Film.
Sidney, George, dir. *Bye Bye Birdie*. Columbia Pictures Corporation, 1963. Film.
Sidney, George, dir. *Half a Sixpence*. Paramount British Pictures, 1967. Film.
Sidney, George, dir. *Kiss Me Kate*. Metro-Goldwyn-Mayer, 1953. Film.
Silberg, Joel, dir. *Breakin'*. Cannon Films, 1984. Film.
Spielberg, Steven, dir. *West Side Story*. 20th Century Studios, 2021. Film.
Stevens, George, dir. *Swing Time*. RKO Radio Pictures, 1936. Film.
Stone, Andrew L., dir. *Stormy Weather*. 20th Century Fox, 1943. Film.
Tati, Jacques, dir. *PlayTime*. Spectra Films and Jolly Film, 1967. Film.
Taurog, Norman, dir. *Little Nellie Kelly*. Metro-Goldwyn-Mayer, 1940. Film.
Taymor, Julie, dir. *Across the Universe*. Columbia Pictures, 2007. Film.
Temple, Julien, dir. *Earth Girls Are Easy*. Vestron Pictures, 1988. Film.
Tilton, Robert, dir. "Jazz Dance." Rhapsody Films, 1954. Film (short).
Varda, Agnès, dir. *Cléo de 5 à 7*. Ciné-Tamaris, 1961. Film.
Varda, Agnès, dir. *Les Demoiselles ont eu 25 ans*. Ciné-Tamaris, 1993. Film.
Varda, Agnès, dir. *Jacquot de Nantes*. Ciné-Tamaris, 1991. Film.
Vidor, Charles, dir. *Cover Girl*. Columbia Pictures Corporation, 1944. Film.
Walters, Charles, dir. *Easter Parade*. Metro-Goldwyn-Mayer, 1948. Film.
Walters, Charles, dir. *The Glass Slipper*. Metro-Goldwyn-Mayer, 1955. Film.
Wilder, Billy, dir. *Some Like It Hot*. United Artists, 1959. Film.
Wise, Robert, and Jerome Robbins, dirs. *West Side Story*. The Mirisch Corporation, Seven
    Arts Productions, 1961. Film.
Young, Terence, dir. *Black Tights*. United Artists, 1961. Film.
Zemeckis, Robert, dir. *Who Framed Roger Rabbit*. Warner Bros., 1988.
Zinnemann, Fred, dir. *Oklahoma!* RKO Radio Pictures and Twentieth Century Fox Film
    Corporation, 1955. Film.

Index

For the benefit of digital users, indexed terms that span two pages (e.g., 52–53) may, on occasion, appear on only one of those pages.

Figures are indicated by *f* following the page number.

Academy ratio (1.37:1), 15, 65, 211
Acevedo-Muñoz, Ernesto, 61–62, 63, 240n.68
Across the Universe (2007), 190–91
Action Drive, 224*t*
ACT UP organization, 162–63, 164
aesthetic (decorative) function, 3, 36–37, 38–39, 51, 99–108
Affair in Trinidad (1952), 170–71
agency, 23–24, 209–12. *See also West Side Story*
"aggregate" musicals, 32, 37
Akil, Salim, 190–91
"Alter Ego" dance sequence, 40–41
Altman, Rick, 39, 57, 108–9, 132, 234–35n.15, 236n.35, 258n.56
ambiguous realism, 204–8
American Delsartism, 5
analytical data
    Average Shot Length, 228
    budget data, 227, 227*t*
    classical Hollywood musical number data, 229*t*
    comparative data for *Jeanne et le garçon formidable*, 230*t*
    comparative data for *La La Land*, 230*t*
    comparative data for *Les Demoiselles de Rochefort*, 227*t*
    comparative data for *Trois places pour le 26*, 228*t*
    contemporary Hollywood data, 229*t*
    general Hollywood data, 228
    music video data, 229*t*
    quantitative film data, 228, 228*t*
An American in Paris (1951)
    budget, 95–96

dream ballet, 101, 203
    film locations, 102–3
    percentage of film that musical numbers comprise, 101
anamorphic lenses, 15, 64–66, 239n.44
Annabelle Butterfly Dance (1894), 5
Annie (2014), 190–91
"Apache Dance" number, 60
Ashby, Hal, 209–10
aspect ratio
    Academy ratio, 15, 65, 211
    anamorphic lenses, 15, 64–66, 239n.44
    CinemaScope, 15, 64–65, 211
Astaire, Fred, 30, 35, 37–38, 60, 107, 146, 195–96, 236n.45
Audiovisual Law (1986), 163–64
auditory shifts, 41–42, 44–45
Austin, Guy, 164
Average Shot Length (ASL), 228
Awake State Effort, 224*t*

Bachchan, Abhishek, 192–93
Bachchan, Aishwarya Rai, 192–93
Bacon, Lloyd, 182–83
Badham, John, 161, 190
Bagouet, Dominique, 172
Balanchine, George, 258n.56
Balio, Tino, 31
Ballets des Champs-Élysées, 96–97
Bamba, Amy, 182
Band Wagon, The (1953), 146
    budget, 95–96
    "Dancing in the Dark" number, 35, 37–38, 201–2
    "Triplets" number, 36–37
Banes, Sally, 171, 173

278 INDEX

Barker, Jennifer, 210
"Barn Dance" number, 35–36
Barry, Gérome, 154
Bartenieff, Irmgard, 237n.7
Bartenieff Fundamentals, 211
Basic Body Actions, 54–55, 226, 226t
Basinger, Jeanine, 251n.3
Basu, Bipasha, 192–93
Bausch, Pina, 129, 172
Bazin, André, 22, 169
Beach Party musicals, 161
"Be a Clown" song, 251n.3
"Beat It" music video (1983), 129, 131
Beauregard, Georges de, 93–94
"Beautiful Girl Montage" number, 36–37
Béjart, Maurice, 96–97, 171–72, 178
Benatar, Pat, 131
Bergerson, Wayne, 206–7
Bergson, Henri, 10–11
Berkeley, Busby, 27–28, 36, 41, 65, 146,
    182–83, 202–3
Bernstein, Leonard, 56
Berri, Claude, 21, 127–28, 129–31
Bettis, Valerie, 170–71
Biograph, 5
Bird, Katie, 209–10, 217–19
"Black & Tan" (1929), 195–96
Black Tights (1961), 96–97
Blues Brothers, The (1980), 131–32
Bodard, Mag, 93–94
body attitude, 225
Body category, 54–55, 211, 225–26
    Basic Body Actions, 54–55, 226, 226t
    body attitude, 225
    body part phrasing, 226
    movement, 225
    multiunit movement, 226
    single-unit movement, 225
    stillness, 225
body part phrasing, 226
Bonnaffé, Jacques, 183–84
Bordwell, David, 65–66, 193–94, 235n.27,
    257n.25
    comment on filmmakers, 13–14
    Les Demoiselles de Rochefort, 99–100,
        101, 109–10
    mise-en-scène, 5–6
Bouajila, Sami, 253n.22

Bound Flow Effort, 54–55, 223t, 240n.63
    La La Land, 211–12
    Le Cri du hibou, 133–34
    Les Demoiselles de Rochefort, 113f
Bound for Glory (1976), 209–10
"Boy Next Door, The " number, 110
Bradley, Karen, 11–12
Brannigan, Erin, 6, 133, 159–60
Breakin' (1984), 131, 161, 190
bridges, 22–23, 159–60
Bright, Maureen, 99
"Broadway Melody" number, 36–37, 41
Brown, Garrett, 209–10
Brown, Nacio Herb, 29–30, 47–48
Brown, Trisha, 172
"Brush Up Your Shakespeare" number, 43
budgeting and budget comparisons,
    243n.22
    budget data, 227, 227t
    Les Demoiselles de Rochefort, 94–96
    Trois places pour le 26, 129–32, 248n.30,
        248n.31
"bursting" into song, 1–2, 32–33,
    43, 159–60
Bye Bye Birdie (1963), 36, 161

Calbérac, Ivan, 186–87
Calori, Paul, 154, 186–87
camera movement. *See also* Steadicam
    camera as dancer, 209–12
    French Cancan, 102
    La La Land, 209–19
    Les Demoiselles de Rochefort, 114–
        15, 212–13
    Meet Me in St. Louis, 212–13
    mobility, stability, and aesthetics
        of, 212–17
    overview, 209–19
    Seven Brides for Seven Brothers, 212–13
    Singin' in the Rain, 49–50
Canal + TV station, 163–64
Can-Can (1960), 60, 85–86
Carmencita (1894), 5
Carney, John, 190–91
Caron, Elize, 173
Caron, Leslie, 96–97
Carter, Thomas, 191
carving/shaping, 226

INDEX 279

casting
nonprofessional dancers in lead roles, 30, 197–99
West Side Story, 62–64
"catch-step melt" phrase, 103–7, 105*f*, 106*f*
causal narrative function, 35, 38
center of the frame ("center bias"), 9
Césars, 247–48n.11
Chabrol, Claude, 92, 133–34
Chakiris, George, 20–21, 61–62, 63, 91, 94–95, 98–99, 130, 239n.22, *See also Les Demoiselles de Rochefort*; *West Side Story*
Chaplin, Saul, 86
Charisse, Cyd, 30, 35, 36, 42–43, 146, 201–2
Chazelle, Damien, 3, 15, 16, 154, 188. *See also La La Land*
Guy and Madeleine on a Park Bench, 201
musical realism, 23–24
Chicago (2002), 167–68, 190–91
Chion, Michel, 53*f*
Chirac, Jacques, 164
Chopra, Uday, 192–93
choreographic contrast
Les Demoiselles de Rochefort, 119–20
West Side Story, 71–72
choreography. *See* cinematic choreography
choreographic contrast, 71, 119–20
defined, 5–6
political choreography, 180–86, 182*f*, 183*f*
"Choreography" number, 254n.38
Chronique d'une été (1961), 195–96
Chu, Jon M., 221
CinemaScope, 15, 64–65, 211
cinematic choreography
continuity editing and, 15
diegetic slippage, 200
effect of loss of choreographer-filmmakers and dancer-actors on, 197–98
general discussion, 4–13
implicit meaning created by, 16–17
overactive viewing and performative research, 8–13
reflexive musical clusters, 155–56
skillsets need for, 222
subtle power of, 2–3

cinéma verité , 195–96
"clap step," *West Side Story*, 81–82, 82*f*, 83*f*, 84*f*
classical Hollywood musical number data, 229*t*
Cloquet, Ghislain, 120–21
"clothesline" staging, 65
Cocteau, Jean, 96–97
Cohan, Steven, 22, 29–30, 32, 39, 236n.45
Cole, Jack, 99
Collard, Cyril, 162–63
comparative data
Jeanne et le garçon formidable, 230*t*
La La Land, 230*t*
Les Demoiselles de Rochefort, 227*t*
Trois places pour le 26, 228*t*
complex ("flamboyant") shot techniques, 10
connotative meaning (implicit information), 8–9
Contact Improvisation, 174–75, 219, 255n.61, 259n.91
continuity editing, 15, 66, 73–76, 79–80
contrast, 9
control, 76–86. *See also* Flow Effort
Conway, Kelley, 152–53
"Cool" number, 76–86, 81*f*, 82*f*, 83*f*, 84*f*, 241n.76
Cornish, Audie, 188
corporeal shifts, 44–45
Cover Girl (1944), 40–41
Coyne, Jeanne, 30
Cross, Tom, 219–20
Cukor, George, 44
Cunningham, Merce, 172
Curtiz, Michael, 254n.38

DaCosta, Morton, 36
Dale, Grover, 20–21, 91, 94–95, 98–99, 130, 243n.20, *See also Les Demoiselles de Rochefort*
d'Amboise, Jacques, 213
Damraoui, Mohamed, 182
"Dance at the Gym" sequence, 1, 85–86
dance culture
relationship between film culture and, 16
shifts in, 15–16

280 INDEX

Dance Dynamics (Maletic), 224
"Dancing in the Dark" number, 35, 37–38, 201–2
Dancing with the Stars (TV series), 194
danse contemporaine , 21. *See also Trois places pour le 26*
  choreographed dance phrases, 178*f*
  emergence of, 128
  Jeanne et le garçon formidable, 23, 169–80
  nontraditional performance spaces, 178
  Sur quel pied danser, 186–87
  On va s'aimer, 186–87
Darrieux, Danielle, 91. *See also Les Demoiselles de Rochefort*
Davar, Shiamak, 192
DeBose, Ariana, 87
decorative (aesthetic) function, 3, 36–37, 38–39, 51, 99–108
Delamater, Jerome, 57, 235n.21, 238n.21
Deleray, Jean- François, 182
Delsartre, François, 171–72
del Toro, Guillermo, 1
de Mille, Agnes, 97–98, 202–3, 258n.56
Demy, Jacques, 3, 16, 91–93, 151–54, 162–63, 169, 247n.126, *See also Les Demoiselles de Rochefort; Trois Places pour le 26*
  connection to *Jeanne* film, 253–54nn.25–26
  distaste for monetary aspects of filmmaking, 242n.18
  influence on Damien Chazelle, 23–24, 195–96, 200, 203–4, 207, 212–13, 220
  influence on Olivier Ducastel and Jacques Martineau, 162, 165–69, 178, 181, 186–87
  Lady Oscar, 126–27, 247n.4
  Les Demoiselles de Rochefort, 20–21
  Les Parapluies de Cherbourg, 93–94
  L'évènement le plus important depuis que l'homme a marché sur la lune, 247n.4
  Lola, 93–94
  Model Shop, 123–24
  notes for "Rencontres" number, 104*f*
  Peau d'âne , 123–24, 126–27, 206–7
  The Pied Piper, 247n.4
  preproduction notes for *Les Demoiselles de Rochefort*, 244n.63

staging changes for "Chanson de Simon" number, 117*f*
Trois places pour le 26, 21, 125–54
Une Chambre en Ville , 181
view of music videos, 131–32
work with theater and opera productions, 127–28
Demy, Mathieu, 23, 162–63, 253–54n.25, *See also Jeanne et le garçon formidable*
Deneuve, Catherine, 91, 93–94, 99, 123–24, 153. *See also Les Demoiselles de Rochefort*
denotative information, 8–9, 34–36, 100–1, 143
Dhoom 2 (2006), 192–93
diagonal movement, 225
Dickson, William K. L., 5
diegesis, 4–5, 22–23
"Diegetic Flutters," 159–60, 159*f*
diegetic plurality
  The Band Wagon, 146
  diegetic shifts, 45–47
  diegetic "slippage," 198
  Jeanne et le garçon formidable, 174, 180
  La La Land, 200–2, 208
  Les Demoiselles de Rochefort, 101–2, 107
  overview, 34
  performative shifts, 42–45
  pluralistic paradigms, 39–40
  Singin' in the Rain, 39–50
  spatiotemporal shifts, 40–42
  West Side Story, 76, 79, 85–86, 88
diegetic reassessments, 144–47
diegetic shifts, 45–47
Dieterle, William, 170–71, 202–3
"Dil Laga Na" number, 192–93
dimensional or axial movement, 225
directional movement, 226
Direct Space Effort, 223*t*
  La La Land, 211–12
  Les Demoiselles de Rochefort , 113*f*
  West Side Story, 77–78
Donen, Stanley, 3, 16, 254n.38
  influence on creators of *La La Land*, 195–96, 203, 212–13
  influence on Damien Chazelle, 220
  Seven Brides for Seven Brothers, 35–36, 65, 213

Singin' in the Rain, 27–28, 33–34, 47, 51
On the Town, 40–41
Dorléac, Françoise, 91, 99. See also Les
    Demoiselles de Rochefort
"Douce folie" number, 147–51, 148f, 149f
dream ballet
    An American in Paris, 101, 203
    diegetic "slippage," 199–200
    expanding diegetic space, 41
    La La Land, 23–24, 202–8
    Oklahoma!, 202–3
    Singin' in the Rain, 27–28, 203
    Stormy Weather, 170–71
    temporal shifting, 41–42
    use of symbolic function, 36
Dreamgirls (1981) Broadway
    production, 129
Dream State, 112, 112f, 224t
Drôle de Félix/ The Adventures of Felix
    (2000), 253n.22
dual focus distraction, 116–22, 120f
dubbing, 236n.47, 239n.32
Ducastel, Olivier, 3, 16, 23, 143,
    154, 162, 253–54n.25, See also
    Jeanne et le garçon formidable
Dunham, Katherine, 170–71, 202–3
Dyer, Richard, 64, 234–35n.15
Dynamosphere, 54

Earth Girls Are Easy (1988), 131–32,
    236n.44
Easter Parade (1948), 249n.43
Eastwood, Clint, 190–91
eclecticism, 155–56. See also Les
    Demoiselles de Rochefort; Trois places
    pour le 26
École technique, 242n.6
editing and staging
    continuity editing, 15, 66, 73–76, 79–80
    diegetic slippage, 199–202
    editing rates for musical
        numbers, 191–94
    Franco-American style, 194–96
    Jeanne et le garçon formidable, 168–69
    La La Land, 199–202, 219–20, 221
    Le Cri du hibou, 133–34
    Trois places pour le 26, 131–32
Effort category, 54–55, 224t

camera movement, 211–12
impactive phrasing, 246n.99
Impulsive phrasing, 118–19, 246n.99,
    249n.57
Vibratory phrasing, 250n.69
Effort Movement Factors. See also Flow
    Effort; Space Effort; Time Effort;
    Weight Effort
    defined, 223
    Flow Effort, 112f, 211–12, 223t
    Space Effort, 77–78, 223t
    Time Effort, 223t
    Weight Effort, 112, 223t
Effort States
    Awake State, 224t
    Dream State, 112, 112f, 224t
    Mobile State, 55, 134, 150–51, 185–
        86, 224t
    Remote State, 224t
    Rhythm or Near State, 224t
    Stable State, 55, 224t
Enchanted (2007), 190–91
ensemble numbers, 16
    overview, 65–66
    Porgy and Bess, 60
    West Side Story, 57–58, 63, 66–76, 86–87
"Epilogue" dream ballet, La La
    Land, 202–8
escapism, 63, 200–1
Evein, Bernard, 91–92
Exertion/Recuperation, 11–12, 55, 79–
    81, 223
expressive function, 20–21, 36, 47–48,
    107–8, 110
external conflict, 66–76

Fabian, Françoise, 4, 21
Fapp, Daniel L., 61–62
Fashions of 1934 (1934), 202–3
Faden, Eric, 103
Ferrara, Serena, 209–10
Feuer, Jane, 156, 234–35n.15, 258n.56
figure movement, 161, 222. See also Laban
    Movement Analysis
    defining, 5–6
    Demy's staging of, 93, 111, 116, 124
    describing and analyzing, 13
    historical context of, 7–8

282   INDEX

figure movement (*cont.*)
  Jeanne et le garçon formidable, 163,
    178–79, 181
  La La Land, 188, 194–95, 221
  language- based descriptors of, 11
  mobile framing, 10
  overview, 1–4
  performative shifts, 44–45
  storytelling power of, 24
  as tool for guiding viewer attention, 8–9
  Trois places pour le 26, 132–33, 135, 152
  videographic approaches, 10–11
film musical. *See also* genre
  actor-dancers, 97–98
  artists of color and, 188–89
  cost of, 17–18, 94
  demands made on viewers of, 24
  dual- focus narrative, 108–9
  editing rates for musical numbers, 191
  genre-specificity, 16–17
  overview, 7, 13–18
  role of *West Side Story* in
    reinventing, 57, 88
  shifting dance cultures and, 15–16
  technological mobility and, 14–15
film structure, 9
"flamboyant" (complex) shot
  techniques, 10
Flashdance (1983), 131, 161, 190
Flatt, Ernie, 30
Fletcher, Anne, 191
Flow Effort, 112*f*, 211–12, 223*t*. *See also*
  Bound Flow Effort; Free Flow Effort
Folies Bergères, 97–98
Folsey, George, 213
Footloose (1984), 161
"forced marriage," 53*f*
Forman, Miloš, 170–71
Forti, Simone, 171
42nd Street (1933), 182–83, 184*f*
Fosse, Bob, 161, 191, 213–15
Foster, Susan, 5–6
Freed, Arthur, 29–31, 47–48, 51
Free Flow Effort, 54–55, 223*t*
  "Cool" number, 76–77
  La La Land, 211–12
  Trois places pour le 26, 134, 135*f*
  West Side Story, 76–78

French Cancan (1954), 243n.22
French dance culture, 128–29
French New Wave, 92
Function/Expression, 55, 223
Funny Face (1957), 102–3

Gabin, Jean, 247–48n.11
Gadhvi, Sanjay, 192
Gajjar, Reshma, 201
Galavant (TV series), 45
Garcia, Desirée, 63, 189, 197, 201
"Garden of Eden" number, 60
Garland, Judy, 110, 236n.45, 249n.43
Genné, Beth, 29–30, 237n.50
genre. *See also* film musical
  changes in industrial conditions and
    expectations, 16–17
  creating meaning, 22
  Demy's experimentation with genre
    conventions, 102, 108–9
  diegetic instability, 200–2
  escapism and, 63
  genre cinema, 17
  genre codification, 29–33
  genre emphasis, 165–69
  genre experimentation, 162
  genre studies, 155
  genre theory frameworks, 51–52
  "mongrel genre," 234–35n.15
  musical labor, 144–47
  narrative continuity and, 100–1
  show musical subgenre, 141–47
Gentlemen Prefer Blondes (1953), 102–
  3, 116–18
Gershwin, Ira, 37–38
"ghost singers," 239n.32
Ginot, Isabelle, 96–97, 171–72
Giron, Sylvie, 23, 164–65, 172, 173–77,
  253n.22
Glee (TV series), 191, 193–94
glide reflection, 138
Gluck, Will, 190–91
Godard, Jean-Luc, 92
Goldschmidt, Gilbert de, 93–94, 123
"Good Morning" number, 36
Gorbman, Claudia, 45–46
Gosling, Ryan, 7, 23–24, 188–89
Graham, Martha, 258n.56

INDEX 283

Grant, Catherine, 156
Greatest Showman, The (2017), 220
Griffin, Sean, 29–31, 194, 252n.3
Grustein, Pierre, 142
Guy and Madeleine on a Park Bench (2011), 201
Guys and Dolls (1955), 65

Hagen, Jean, 42–43
Hair (1979), 170–71
Hairspray (2007), 190–91
Half a Sixpence (1967), 95–96
handheld cinematography, 211
Haney, Carol, 30
Harper, Kenneth, 94
Hart, Pamela, 99
Haseman, Brad, 10–11
Hawks, Howard, 116–18
Hayworth, Rita, 170–71
Hernandez, Callie, 214*f*
Herrera, Brian Eugenio, 62–63, 65–66, 69–70
Herzog, Amy, 254n.33
High School Musical 2 (2007), 190–91
Hill, George Roy, 95–96
hip hop dance, 128, 129, 248n.27
HIV/AIDS, depiction in film, 162–63. *See also Jeanne et le garçon formidable*
Hollywood data
contemporary, 229*t*
general, 228
Hollywood Reporter, 1–2
Hollywood Revue, The (1929), 47–48
Honoré, Christophe, 154, 162
hoofers, 97–98
Hooper, Les, 190–91
Hooper, Tobe, 133
"How Lovely to Be a Woman" number, 36
How to Marry a Millionaire (1953), 65
Huit femmes / 8 Women (2002), 162, 168
Hurwitz, Justin, 201, 221
Hyman, Eliot, 123, 242n.14

IDHEC (Institut Des Hautes Études Cinématographiques), 92
Impactful/increasing-intensity, 224*t*
impactive phrasing, 246n.99

imperfect bodies. *See also Jeanne et le garçon formidable*
Jeanne et le garçon formidable, 180–86
La La Land, 189–90
implicit information (connotative meaning), 8–9
Impulsive/decreasing-intensity, 224*t*
Impulsive phrasing, 118–19, 246n.99, 249n.57
Indirect Space Effort, 223*t*
"Cool" number, 78–79
Les Demoiselles de Rochefort , 112*f*
individualism, 71, 218–19
industrial resources, 29–31
information overload, 9
informative narrative function, 35
Inner/Outer, 55, 223, 224*t*. *See also* Laban Movement Analysis
Institut Des Hautes Études Cinématographiques (IDHEC), 92
integrated musical numbers, 235n.29
integration, 234–35nn.15–16, 235nn.21–22, 236n.33, *See also* musical integration; narrative integration
internal conflict, 73–86
In the Heights (2021), 220, 221
Into the Woods (2014), 190–91
intuitive knowledge of movement, 10–11
"invisible" (minimalist) shot techniques, 10
"Isn't This a Lovely Day" number, 201
"It Ain't Necessarily So" number, 60
Iyer, Usha, 6

Jackson, Michael, 129, 131
Jacquot de Nantes (1991), 92
"Java du séropo" number, 167*f*, 169*f*, 175–77
"Jazz Dance" (1954), 195–96
Jean de Florette (1986), 129–30
Jeanne et le garçon formidable (1998), 161–87
budget, 163–64
choreographed dance phrases, 178–80, 178*f*
comparative data for, 230*t*
dance contemporaine, 169–80
genre emphasis, 165–69

284 INDEX

Jeanne et le garçon formidable (1998) (*cont.*)
"Java du séropo" number, 166*f*, 167*f*,
169*f*, 175–77
"La vie à credit" number, 166–67
overview, 161–63
physical emphasis, 164–65
political choreography, 180–86,
182*f*, 183*f*
politics of illness, 3
Production History, 163–69
tango scene, 177*f*, 177
Jersey Boys (2014), 190–91
Jooss, Kurt, 171–72
Judson Dance Theater, 171

Katz, Norman, 94
Keating, Patrick, 10, 210–11
Kelly, Gene, 3, 15, 16, 20–21
"Alter Ego" dance sequence, 40–41
appearance on *The Muppet Show*,
244n.43
"Broadway Melody" number, 41
dream ballets, 27–28, 30, 36, 101, 203
industrial resources, 29–31, 51
lamp post pose, 28*f*
Les Demoiselles de Rochefort (1967), 94–
95, 98–99, 130
"New York, New York" montage, 40–41
Singin' in the Rain dance number, 27–
28, 45, 47–50
"You Were Meant for Me"
number, 40–41
Kessler, Kelly, 17
Kidd, Michael, 65, 213, 254n.38
Kinesphere, 54, 78–79, 211, 224–25. *See
also* Space
kinesthetic narrative integration, 76–86
Kiss Me Kate (1953), 43, 146
knowledge structures (schemata), 8–9,
38, 42–43
Kushner, Tony, 87

Laban, Rudolf, 11–13, 54, 171–72, 233n.46
Axial movement, 225
Spell Drive, 133
symmetry operations, 138

Laban/Bartenieff Movement Studies
(LBMS), 6–7, 10, 11–12, 53–54
LMA vs., 233n.42
movement taxonomy, 54–55
Laban Movement Analysis (LMA), 11–13
Body category, 54–55, 211, 225–26
camera movement, 210–12
Dynamosphere, 54
Effort category, 54–55
Effort Drives, 224*t*
Effort Movement Factors, 223, 223*t*
Effort States, 224*t*
impactful/ increasing-intensity, 224*t*
impulsive/ decreasing-intensity, 224*t*
Kinesphere, 54, 78–79, 211, 224
LBMS vs., 233n.42
Mobile State, 55, 134, 150–51, 185–86
mobility/stability, 55
overview, 53–55
resilient, 224*t*
"Seeing Movement in Cinema" title
screen, 53*f*
semantic fields, 223
Shape category, 54–55, 226
Space category, 54, 224–25
Space Harmony, 54–55
vibratory, 224*t*
Labanotation, 233n.46
Lady Oscar (1979), 126–27, 247n.4
La La Land (2016), 3, 188–222
"A Lovely Night" number, 198–
99, 201–2
ambiguous realities, 204–8
"Another Day of Sun" number, 201–2
aspect ratio, 15
camera movement, 209–19
comparative data for, 230*t*
diegetic instability, 200–2
dream ballet, 202–8
editing and staging, 219–20
"Epilogue" number, 202–8, 205*f*, 206*f*, 208*f*
Franco-American style, 194–96
imperfect bodies, 189–90
Moore's role in, 7
nonprofessional dancers in lead
roles, 197–99

ordinary dancing, 197–99
overview, 23–24, 188–90
Production History, 190–99
production parallels to *Les Demoiselles
de Rochefort*, 196
"Someone in the Crowd" number, 198–
99, 213–17, 217*f*
"Start a Fire" number, 195
Landis, John, 131–32
Lang, Jack, 163–64
Lang, Walter, 60, 238n.2
"La parfumerie" number, 139
Laurents, Arthur, 56
"Laurie Makes Up Her Mind"
number, 202–3
"La vie à credit" number, 166–67
LBMS. *See* Laban/Bartenieff Movement
Studies
learned frameworks (schemata), 8–9,
38, 42–43
Le Cri du hibou (1987), 133
Ledoyen, Virginie, 23, 162–63. *See also
Jeanne et le garçon formidable*
Legrand, Michel, 91–92, 93–94, 125,
247–48n.11
Lehman, Ernest, 61–62
Les Demoiselles de Rochefort (1967)
aesthetic play, 3, 38–39
budget comparison, 94–96
camera movement, 212–13
"catch- step melt" phrase, 103–7,
105*f*, 106*f*
comparative data for, 227*t*
dancers, 96–98
decorative excess, 99–108
"De Hambourg à Rochefort"
number, 121–22
denotative narrative, 38–39
dual focus distraction, 116–22, 120*f*
"Les Rencontres" number, 166–67, 166*f*
"Love Numbers," 109–16, 112*f*,
113*f*, 114*f*
musical excess, 100–3
overview, 20–21, 91–93
parallels to *La La Land*'s
production, 196

Production History, 93–99
"Rencontres" number, 103–7, 104*f*
replete framing, 103–8
romantic play, 108–22
"Toujours, jamais" number, 122
transnational musical solutions, 98–99
Les Misérables (2012), 190–91
Les Nuits fauves (1992), 162–63
Les Parapluies de Cherbourg (1964), 93–94,
95–96, 153
"Les Rencontres" number, 166–67, 166*f*
"Let's Call the Whole Thing Off"
number, 37–38
*L'événement le plus important depuis
que l'homme a marché sur la lune*
(1973), 247n.4
Lido night club, 97–98, 243n.33, 243n.34
Lifeforce (1985), 133
Light Weight Effort, 223*t*, 259n.79
Jeanne et le garçon formidable, 174–75
La La Land, 211–12
Les Demoiselles de Rochefort, 113*f*
Panaglide footage, 259n.79
West Side Story, 77–78
Lima, Kevin, 190–91
liminal space, 45–46
Lindy Hop, 63, 81–82, 84*f*, 241n.92
Little Nellie Kelly (1940), 47–48
Little Shop of Horrors (1986), 131–32
LMA. *See* Laban Movement Analysis
location shooting, 102–3, 139, 178, 213,
244n.60
Lola (1961), 93–94
"Lonesome Polecat" number, 213, 214*f*,
254n.38
Loring, Eugene, 65, 258n.56
"Love Is a Battlefield" music video (1983),
129, 131
"Love Numbers," 109–16, 112*f*-14*f*
Luhrmann, Baz, 167–68, 190–91
Lumet, Sidney, 254n.38
Lyne, Adrian, 131, 161, 190

Maddox, Matt, 128
Maen, Norman, 20–21, 91–92, 93, 99,
244n.43

286 INDEX

"Make 'Em Laugh" number, 41–42, 251n.3
Maletic, Vera, 224
Mamou, Sabine, 253–54n.25
Mamoulian, Rouben, 65, 239n.43
Mankiewicz, Joseph, 65
Manon des sources (1986), 129–30
Margolin, François, 162–63
"Maria" number, 60
Marin, Maguy, 129
Marshall, Rob, 167–68, 190–91
Martineau, Jacques, 3, 16, 23, 154, 162,
    180–81. *See also Jeanne et le garçon*
    formidable
Mary Poppins Returns (2018), 191
Massine, Léonide, 258n.56
May, Mathilda, 21, 132, 151–52. *See also*
    Trois places pour le 26
    Le Cri du hibou, 133–34
    Lifeforce, 133
McCarren, Felicia, 128
McLean, Adrienne, 6, 13, 17, 258n.56
meaning-making mechanisms, 24
Meet Me in St. Louis (1944), 244n.59
    budget, 95–96
    camera movement, 212–13
    "The Boy Next Door," 110
menas, iris, 87
Mensonge (1992), 162–63
metadiegetic music, 45–46
Metro-Goldwyn-Mayer (MGM)
    industrial resources, 29–31
    working conditions, 30–31
Meyers, Jillian, 196
Michel, Marcelle, 96–97, 171–72
Mille, Agnes de, 97–98
Miller, Ann, 249n.43
Miller, Valarie Rae, 198–99
minimalism and excess
    decorative excess, 99–108
    dual focus distraction, 118–19
    love numbers, 109–16
    musical excess, 100–3
minimalist ("invisible") shot
    techniques, 10
Minnelli, Vincente, 41–42, 101–2, 110
Miranda, Lin-Manuel, 221

Mirisch, Harold, 58, 59, 238n.3
Mirisch, Walter, 239n.26
Mirisch Corporation, 58, 61–62, 64–65
mise-en-scène in film, 5–6, 15, 40–41, 127,
    184–86, 206*f*
Mittell, Jason, 10–11
Mizuno, Sonoya, 214*f*
mobile framing, 10
Mobile State, 55, 134, 150–51, 185–
    86, 224*t*
mobility/stability, 11–12, 55. *See also*
    Laban Movement Analysis
Model Shop (1969), 123–24
modern dance, 254n.38
Molloy, Molly, 128
Montand, Yves, 4, 21, 125, 126–27. *See also*
    Trois places pour le 26
Moore, Annabelle, 5
Moore, Carol-Lynne, 11–12, 138, 232n.35
Moore, Jason, 190–91
Moore, Mandy, 2, 7, 22–24, 159–60, 194,
    196, 198. *See also La La Land*
Moreno, Carmen Dauset, 5
Moreno, Rita, 61–62, 87, 239n.22,
    239n.32
Morgan, Daniel, 199–200, 210–11,
    258n.75
Morin, Edgar, 195–96
"Moses Supposes" number, 32–33, 44
Moskowitz, Gene, 97
Moulin Rouge! (2001), 167–68, 190–92
Moulin Rouge night club, 97–98, 243n.33,
    243n.34
movement, defined, 225
movement baselines, 133–35, 135*f*, 136*f*,
    137*f*, 138*f*, 140*f*
movement evolution, 136–41
Mueller, John, 37–38, 234–35n.15,
    235n.27, 235n.29, 236n.31, 236n.33
multiunit movement, 226
Murphy, Dudley, 195–96
Murphy, Ryan, 193–94
musical eclecticism, 155–56. *See also Les*
    Demoiselles de Rochefort; Trois places
    pour le 26
musical excess, 100–3

musical foundations. *See* Laban Movement Analysis; *Singin' in the Rain*; *West Side Story*
musical integration, 31–32, 33, 57, 234–35n.15
musical labor, 144–47
musical norms, 31–33. *See also* genre
musical realism, 23. *See also* "Diegetic Flutters"; *Jeanne et le garçon formidable*; rhythmic realism
Music Man, The (1962)
  "Pick- a- Little, Talk- a- Little" number, 36
  "Ya Got Trouble" number, 44
music video data, 229*t*
My Fair Lady (1964), 44

narrative and stylistic categories
  decorative function, 36–37, 38–39, 51
  denotative function, 35–36
  diegetic shifts, 45–47
  expressive function, 36
  organizational paradigms, 34–39
  overview, 33–47
  performance distinctions, 42–45
  pluralistic paradigms, 39–47
  Singin' in the Rain, 33–47
  spatiotemporal distinctions, 40–42
  symbolic function, 36
narrative integration, 37–38, 51, 57, 76–86, 173
  Disney, 256n.11
  West Side Story, 76–86
natural movement, 173
Neale, Steve, 17, 234–35n.15, 235n.17
Ned Wayburn Institute of Dancing, 97–98
Negulesco, Jean, 65
neoclassicism in French ballet, 96–97
Neupert, Richard, 92
"New York, New York" montage, 40–41
Nicholas Brothers, 40–41
Nikolaïs, Alwin, 172
Nixon, Marni, 239n.32
nonhuman movement, 6–7
nonprofessional dancers in lead roles, 30, 197–99

Noyes, Betty, 42–43

O'Connell, John, 192
Odums, Rick, 128
Oklahoma! (1943) stage musical, 202–3
Oklahoma! (1955), 36
Once (2007), 190–91
On connaît la chanson / Same Old Song (1997), 162, 168
On the Town (1949)
  budget, 95–96
  film locations, 102–3
  "New York, New York" montage, 40–41
  percentage of film that musical numbers comprise, 101
On va s'aimer (2006), 186–87
On Your Toes (1936), 258n.56
Ophüls, Max, 102
Ortega, Kenny, 161, 190–91
Oz, Frank, 131–32
Ozon, François, 162

Pan, Hermes, 30, 60, 65
Panavision, 64–66, 239n.44
Parker, Andrew, 7–8
Parking (1985), 153
Pasek, Benj, 220–21
Passion Drive, 77, 224*t*
Pasternak, Joe, 31
Paul, Justin, 220–21
Paxton, Steve, 171, 174–75
Peau d'âne (1970), 123–24, 206–7
Peck, Justin, 1, 87–88, 221–22, 259n.100
Pennies from Heaven (1981), 162
Penzer, Jean, 135
performative shifts
  auditory, 44–45
  corporeal, 44–45
  Kiss Me Kate, 43
  The Music Man, 44
  My Fair Lady, 44
  overview, 42–43
  Singin' in the Rain, 42–45
Perrin, Jacques, 91. *See also Les Demoiselles de Rochefort*
"personality dissolve," 108–9

288 INDEX

Peters, Michael, 125, 127–28, 129, 131, 151–52
Petit, Roland, 96–97
phrasing of movements, 246n.99
physical emphasis, 164–65
Piccoli, Michel, 91. *See also Les Demoiselles de Rochefort*
"Pick-a-Little, Talk-a-Little" number, 36
Pied Piper, The (1972), 247n.4
Pitch Perfect (Moore), 190–91
planar movement, 225
Plantinga, Carl, 22
Platt, Marc, 213
Play Time (1967), 103
pluralistic paradigms, 39–47. *See also* diegetic plurality
Poirot-Delpech, Matthieu, 167–68*f*
political choreography, 182*f*, 183*f*
    choreographic objections, 180–81
    expressing sociopolitical discontent, 182–86
    Jeanne et le garçon formidable, 180–86
Porgy and Bess (1959), 60
Porter, Cole, 251n.3
postmodern dance, 171–72
Preminger, Otto, 60
Production History
    Jeanne et le garçon formidable, 163–69
    La La Land, 190–99
    Les Demoiselles de Rochefort, 93–99
    Singin' in the Rain, 29–33
    Trois places pour le 26, 126–32
    West Side Story, 58–66
prologue sequence, *West Side Story* (1961), 61*f*, 66–76, 67*f*, 72*f*, 73*f*, 75*f*
    continuity editing, 73–76
    narrative exposition, 67–70
    parallels, 70–73
    Sharks' *développé*, 66
Prunenec, Sylvain, 175

quantitative film data, 228, 228*t*
Quick Time Effort, 211–12, 237n.54, 255n.66

racial/cultural considerations, 62–64, 221, 235n.24

racial integration, 235n.24
Rainer, Yvonne, 171
Rall, Tommy, 213
Ramalingom, Fabrice, 175
Raskine, Michel, 182–83
realism, 23, 234–35n.15, *See also* rhythmic realism
    ambiguous realism, 204–8
    Demy's films, 153
    reality vs. fiction, 142–43
    stylistic realism, 220
    West Side Story, 63–64
referential information, 8–9
reflection, symmetry, 138
reflexive musical content, 45
reflexivity, 155–56
Reisner, Charles, 47–48
Remote State Effort, 224*t*
"Rencontres" number, 103–7, 104*f*
Renoir, Jean, 102, 169, 243n.22
replete framing, 103–8
Resilient Effort, 224*t*
Resnais, Alain, 162, 254n.33
Reynolds, Debbie, 30, 42–43
rhythmic realism. *See also La La Land*
    In the Heights , 220, 221
    West Side Story, 221–22
rhythmic shifts, 41–42
Rhythm or Near State Effort, 224*t*
Riccio, Michael, 196
Richards, Jeff, 213
Rivette, Jacques, 92
Robbins, Ari, 23–24, 196, 209, 213–17, 218, 220
Robbins, Jerome, 1–3, 16, 20, 238nn.2–3, *See also West Side Story*
    end of Hollywood career, 241n.76
    letter from Harold Mirisch to, 238n.3
    preproduction notes of *West Side Story*, 240n.58
    restaging choreography for *The King and I*, 238n.2
Rogers, Ginger, 37–38, 201–2
Rohmer, Eric, 92
romantic play, 108–22
Roshan, Hrithik, 192–93
Ross, Herbert, 161, 162

INDEX 289

Rosson, Harold, 14, 48–49
rotation, 138
Rothe, Jessica, 214*f*
Rouch, Jean, 195–96
Rubin, Martin, 39, 41, 42–43, 100–1, 234–35n.15, 236n.36
Ryall, Tom, 17

Sack, Alfred N., 195–96
"Saint-Germain-des-Prés" number, 139–40, 140*f*
Salome (1953), 170–71
Sanders, Dirk, 98–99
Sandgren, Linus, 15, 23–24, 196, 199–202
Sandow (1894), 5
Sandow, Eugene, 5
Sandrich, Mark, 37–38, 201–2
Saturday Night Fever (1977), 161, 190
Save the Last Dance (2001), 191
schemata (knowledge structures; learned frameworks), 8–9, 38, 42–43
Schneider, Stanley, 247n.126
Schonig, Jordan, 13
Scott, Tom Everett, 204
Sedgwick, Eve Kosofsky, 7–8
"Seeing Movement in Cinema" title screen, 53*f*
Seven Arts Productions, 20–21, 58, 64–65, 94, 123
Seven Brides for Seven Brothers (1954)
  "Barn Dance" number, 35–36
  camera movement, 212–13
  "Lonesome Polecat" number, 213, 214*f*, 254n.38
Shall We Dance (1937), 37–38
Shape category, 54–55, 226
  carving/shaping, 226
  directional movement, 226
Shape Flow, 113*f*, 114*f*, 226
Shawn, Ted, 5
Sherman, Vincent, 170–71
show musical subgenre, 141–47
Sidney, George, 95–96, 161
  Bye Bye Birdie, 36, 161
  Half a Sixpence , 95–96
  Kiss Me Kate , 43, 146

Silberg, Joel, 131, 161, 190
Silk Stockings (1957), 65, 239n.43
Simmons, J. K., 204
Singin' in the Rain (1952), 3
  Academy ratio, 15
  "Beautiful Girl Montage" number, 36–37
  "Broadway Melody" number, 36–37, 41
  budget, 95–96
  camera stabilization, 14
  decorative function, 36–37
  denotative function, 35–36
  diegetic plurality, 47–50
  diegetic shifts, 45–47
  The Dueling Cavalier scene, 41–42
  expressive function, 36
  "Good Morning" number, 36
  "Make 'Em Laugh" number, 41–42, 251n.3
  "Moses Supposes" number, 32–33, 44
  narrative and stylistic categories, 33–47
  organizational paradigms, 34–39
  overview, 19, 27–29
  performance distinctions, 42–45
  pluralistic paradigms, 39–47
  Production History, 29–33
  spatiotemporal distinctions, 40–42
  symbolic function, 36
  titular dance number, 27, 28*f*
  "Would You?" number, 35–36
  "You Are My Lucky Star" number, 43–44
  "You Were Meant for Me" number, 36, 40–41
single-unit movement, 225
Sitson, Gino, 182
"Slaughter on Tenth Avenue" number, 258n.56
Smith, Jeff, 45–46
Smith, Tim, 9
Sobchack, Vivian, 210
"Someone in the Crowd" number, 213–17, 217*f*
Sondheim, Stephen, 56
So You Think You Can Dance (TV series), 194

290   INDEX

Space category, 224–25
  Kinesphere, 224–25
  spatial subdivisions, 225
  stability/mobility, 225
Space Effort, 77–78, 211, 223t. *See also*
    Direct Space Effort; Indirect Space
    Effort; *West Side Story*
Space Harmony, 54–55
Sparkle (2012), 190–91
spatial subdivisions, 225
spatiotemporal shifts, 40–42
  "Alter Ego" dance sequence, 40–41
  "Broadway Melody" number, 41
  "Make 'Em Laugh" number, 41–42
  "New York, New York" montage, 40–41
  overview, 40
  Singin' in the Rain, 40–42
  Yolanda and the Thief, 41–42
  "You Were Meant for Me"
    number, 40–41
Spell Drive, 133, 224t
Spiegel, Josh, 221, 259n.99
Spielberg, Steven, 1, 87–88, 191, 221–22
Spiero, Jean-Pierre, 247–48n.11
stability/mobility, 225
Stable State, 55, 224t
Standford, Thomas, 61–62, 73–74
"Start a Fire" number, 195
Steadicam, 14
  Bound for Glory, 209–10
  Jeanne et le garçon formidable, 167–68
  La La Land, 209–10, 217–19
Step Up (2006), 191
stillness, defined, 225
Stilwell, Robynn, 45–46
"St. Louis Blues" (1929), 195–96
Stone, Andrew L., 40–41, 170–71, 202–3
Stone, Emma, 7, 23–24, 188–89
Stormy Weather (1943), 40–41, 170–
    71, 202–3
Streisand, Barbra, 236n.45
Strong Weight Effort, 223t
  Jeanne et le garçon formidable, 174–75
  La La Land, 211–12
stylistic realism, 220
Sudden Time Effort, 211–12, 223t. *See also*
    Quick Time Effort

"Summertime" number, 60
supradiegetic space, 39–40
Sur quel pied danser (2016), 186–87
Sustained Time Effort, 223t
  La La Land, 211–12
  West Side Story, 77–78
symbolic function, 36
symmetry operations, 138, 138f
synchronized sound technology, 14

Tamblyn, Russ, 61–62, 213, 239n.22
tango scene, *Jeanne et le garçon formidable*
    (1998), 177, 177f
tap dancing, 97–98
Tati, Jacques, 103
Taurog, Norman, 47–48
Taymor, Julie, 190–91
technological mobility, 14–15
  audio recording, 15
  camera stabilization, 14
  editing and staging, 15
Temple, Julien, 236n.44
temporal shifts, 41–42. *See also*
    spatiotemporal shifts
Terto, Francisco Miranda, 177
Testut, Kostia, 186–87
Testutand, Kostia, 154
Tharp, Twyla, 170–71
Thompson, Kristin, 8–9, 99–100, 101, 103
Thoroughly Modern Millie (1967), 95–96
"Thriller" (1983) music video, 129, 131
Tilton, Robert, 195–96
Time Effort, 223t
  Quick Time Effort, 237n.54, 255n.66
  Sudden Time Effort, 211–12
  Sustained Time Effort, 77–78, 211–12
Tiomkin, Dimitri, 88
Todd-AO technology, 60
Top Hat (1935), 201–2
Toro, Guillermo del, 1, 231n.1
translation, 138
"Triplets" number, 36–37
Trois places pour le 26 (1988)
  "Au concert" number, 134–35, 137–38
  budget, 129–32
  choreographing character
    development, 132–41

"Ciné qui chante" number, 145
comparative data for, 228t
diegesis, 4–5
diegetic reassessments, 144–47
"Douce Folie" number, 4–5, 147–51,
    148f–49f
filming locations, 139
final ending, 144f
financial failure of, 151–52
flipping duality of reality and
    fiction, 142–43
French dance culture, 128–29
generic discomfort, 3
"La parfumerie" number, 137–38, 139
movement baselines, 135f
musical labor, 144–47
original ending, 142–43, 144f
overview, 21–22, 125–26
Production History, 126–32
"Saint-Germain-des-Prés" number,
    139–40, 140f, 145–46
as show musical genre, 141–47
white-collar aspects of, 141–42,
    144–45
Truffaut, François, 92
Tudor, Andrew, 17

Umbrellas of Cherbourg, The (1979), 127
Une Chambre en Ville (1982), 181

Varda, Agnès, 92, 123–24, 162–63,
    253–54n.25
Vera- Ellen, 42–43
Vibratory phrasing, 224t, 250n.69
videographic criticism, 2–3, 10, 13
videographic works
    "Diegetic Flutters," 159–60, 159f
    "Endless Conversations," 155f, 155–56
    Laban Movement Analysis, 53–55
    reflexivity, 155–56
    "Seeing Movement in Cinema,"
        53f, 53–55
Vidor, Charles, 40–41
Vision Drive, 224t
vocal dubbing, 236n.47, 239n.32

Wand, Betty, 239n.32

Warners–Seven Arts, 122–23, 242n.14
"Web of Dreams" number, 202–3
Weight Effort, 112, 223t
    Jeanne et le garçon formidable, 174–78,
        175f, 176f
    Light Weight Effort, 77–78, 113f, 174–
        75, 211–12, 223t, 259n.79
    Strong Weight Effort, 174–75, 211–
        12, 223t
weight sensing and shifting, 174–77
West Side Story (1961)
    adapting stage version for film, 56–58
    budget, 95–96
    "clap step," 81–82, 82f, 83f, 84f
    continuity editing, 73–76
    "Cool" number, 76–86, 81f, 82f, 83f, 84f,
        241n.76
    film locations, 102–3
    kinesthetic narrative integration,
        76–86
    lack of inclusive casting, 62–64
    "Maria" number, 60
    narrative exposition, 67–70
    overview, 20
    Panavision, 64–66
    parallels, 70–73
    percentage of film that musical numbers
        comprise, 101
    prejudiced conflict, 3
    Production History, 58–66
    prologue sequence, 1–2, 61f, 66–76, 67f,
        72f, 73f, 75f
    Sharks' *développé*, 66
    stylistic solutions, 59–62
West Side Story (2021)
    choreographic realism and shot
        lengths, 221–22
    "Dance at the Gym" sequence, 1, 85–86
    editing rates for musical numbers, 191
    rhythmic realism, 221–22
Whiplash (2014), 194–95
White Christmas (1954), 254n.38
Wigman, Mary, 171–72
Wise, Robert, 1–2, 3, 16, 20, 238n.3,
        See also West Side Story
Wiz, The (1978), 254n.38
Wood, Natalie, 63, 235n.26, 239n.32

292 INDEX

Woodlee, Zach, 193–94

Xanadu (1980), 131–32

"Ya Got Trouble" number, 44
Yolanda and the Thief (1945), 41–42
"You Did It" number, 44
Young, Terence, 96–97

"Young and Healthy" number, 182–83, 184*f*
"You Were Meant for Me" number, 36, 40–41
Yves, Mathilda, 4

Zegler, Rachel, 87
Zinnemann, Fred, 36